Beyond
Multicultural Education:

International Perspectives

Kogila A. Moodley
Editor

Detselig Enterprises Ltd.
Calgary, Alberta

©1992 Kogila A. Moodley

Canadian Cataloguing in Publication Data

Main entry under title:

Beyond multicultural education

Consists of edited papers from a conference held in Vancouver, Dec. 14–17, 1989.
Includes bibliographical references.
ISBN 1-55059-029-4

1. Intercultural education. 2. Education and state. 3. Multiculturalism—Canada. 4. Minorities —Education. I. Moodley, Kogila.

LC1099.B49 1992   371.97   C92-091139-0

Detselig Enterprises Ltd
Suite 210 1220 Kensington Rd. N.W.
Calgary, Alberta
T2N 3P5

Printed in Canada   SAN 115-0324   ISBN 1-55059 029-4

Contents

Section III: Educational Transformation for Empowerment

Section IV: Alternative Models

Contributors

Frances E. Aboud, Professor of Psychology, McGill University

Heribert Adam, Professor of Sociology, Simon Fraser University

Mary Ashworth, Professor Emerita, Language Education, University of British Columbia

James A. Banks, Professor of Education and Director, Center for Multicultural Education, University of Washington, Seattle

Christine Bennett, Professor of Social Studies and Multicultural Education, Indiana University, Bloomington

Carole Pigler Christensen, Professor, School of Social Work, University of British Columbia

Elizabeth G. Cohen, Professor of Education and Sociology, Stanford University

Geneva Gay, Professor, Curriculum and Instruction, University of Washington, Seattle

Carl A. Grant, Professor, Curriculum and Instruction, University of Wisconsin-Madison

Jagdish Gundara, Head, Centre for Multicultural Education, Institute of Education, University of London

Gerd R. Hoff, Professor, Primary School Education and Intercultural Education, Free University of Berlin

Crispin Jones, Centre for Multicultural Education, Institute of Education, University of London

Verna J. Kirkness, Associate Professor, Administrative Adult and Higher Education, University of British Columbia

John Lewis, Assistant Professor, Educational Psychology and Counselling, McGill University

Keith A. McLeod, Professor of Education, University of Toronto

Susan Millar, Research Associate, Pennsylvania State University

Kogila A. Moodley, Associate Professor, Social and Educational Studies, University of British Columbia

Fernand Ouellet, Professor, Collectif der'recherches Interculturelles, University of Sherbrooke, Québec

Micheline Rey-von Allmen, Faculty of Psychology and Education, University of Geneva and Department of Public Education

Ronald J. Samuda, Professor Emeritus, Educational Psychology, Queen's University

Acknowledgments

The chapters contained in this book were presented at an international conference of the International Association of Intercultural Education, entitled "Education in Plural Societies: A Review of International Research and Practices in Intergroup Relations," at the University of British Columbia during December 14–17, 1989.

I should like to thank the Secretary of State, Ministry of Multiculturalism, for a grant that made this conference possible, and the Office of the President, University of British Columbia, for generous support. My appreciation goes to Dr. Ronald Samuda, who was the co-organizer of the conference; to all participants; to Carla Spinola, who assisted with the smooth-running of the conference and with editorial assistance of the manuscript. Finally, but not least, to Wong Poh Peng, who stoically stood by at many levels beyond administrative and secretarial assistance. Needless to say, none of these individuals are responsible for opinions articulated in this volume. All shared in the successful outcome of three days of stimulating discussions among theorists and committed practitioners of multicultural and anti-racist education in Canada and abroad.

Detselig Enterprises Ltd. appreciates the financial support for this project from the Secretary of State and the continued support for its publishing program from Canada Council and Alberta Foundation for the Arts.

Introduction

Kogila A. Moodley

The debate about the increasing salience of ethnicity and "race" as bases of differential life chances, likelihood of success or failure and of intergroup conflict, raises the question of what role the institution of education can be expected to play.

Conventional wisdom refers to education as the pervasive cure for prejudice and intolerance. However, noble attempts by dedicated teachers notwithstanding, ethnocentrism and racism reflect individual predispositions and social forces beyond the reach of conventional pedagogy. Particularly, if ethnic antagonisms reflect structural inequality or competition for power, it would be naive to assume that such attitudes could be wiped out in the classroom. Such sober conclusions do not diminish the importance of anti-racist and anti-parochial education, but protect it from the romanticization of the well-intended. Ethnic entrepreneurs or the self-styled community leaders who claim to speak in the name of fragmented subordinates often do as much harm to multicultural education in multi-ethnic societies as those who insist on conformity to the historical tradition of the majority. They share an anti-intellectualism that denigrates scholarship which first of all asks pertinent questions before it prescribes solutions.

Ethnicity usually refers to the sense of belonging which a group shares mobilized on the basis of descent, language, religion, common cultural values, political unity or territory. While the literature on ethnicity is vast, four major emphases and their accompanying educational options are distinguishable: cultural, psychological, economic and political.

Firstly, the cultural focus considers ethnicity as a given. Characteristics such as shared kinship, place of origin, physical signifiers, and common customs which may become the basis for groups to strengthen boundaries *vis-à-vis* non members, are seen as having a vitality of their own. Clifford Geertz (1963) for instance, points to the primordial nature of these ties. Their durability and flexibility is seen by Daniel Bell (1975) as providing both intrinsic and instrumental rewards.

State policies endorsing multiculturalism, as in the Canadian case, are based on a view that ethnic differences are worth perpetuating to enhance the character of Canadian society. If education is to gear itself to this view of ethnicity, then various ethnic cultures must be nurtured in educational institutions. Perpetuation of ethnic cultures, if carried to its ultimate, requires at the very least, knowledge of, and immersion in, the languages of these cultures. Successful implementation of cultural perpetuation, is of course hardly possible in a society where teaching and learning take place predominantly through the medium of the English language, and where success is strongly dependent on how well dominant mainstream norms, lifestyles and accents can be emulated. Since the aim of education in most societies is to integrate its members, such a policy could be seen to raise tolerance for difference or undermine national unity by institutionalizing diversity at the expense of necessary cohesion. Yet until societies reach the point where ethnic differences are actually considered virtues in the marketplace, lip-service celebration of cultural difference is likely to exclude minorities from competing equally. Inflation of cultural difference often ghettoizes minorities. Furthermore, such a focus on cultural variety and uniqueness seldom addresses the prevalence of cultural hierarchies. The crucial difference between racial and ethnic groups and their differential incorporation in Canadian society is noticeably neglected. While perceived racial differences have no intrinsic merit and are invidious distinctions for discrimination, ethnicity in the form of cultural heritage maintenance may indeed be worthy of preservation. But all too often the celebration of the exotic results in exclusion from real competition, by neglecting the skills necessary in the marketplace in favor of pseudo recognition of marginality. Minorities have to guard against these traps.

Secondly, from an economic focus, as best depicted through a Marxist perspective, ethnicity is a response to structured inequality and economic forces such as regional uneven development. From this viewpoint, ethnicity is seen as epiphenomenal to class interests. Ethnic consciousness is considered as a substitute for class consciousness and, it is hoped, in time will inevitably wither away. Proponents of this perspective therefore tend to consider education for ethnic awareness as somewhat irrelevant and counterproductive to the development of basic class identification. Indeed, ethnic and racial cleavages in colonial and post-colonial situations closely correspond to class cleavages. Yet, as van den Berghe (1967) argues, this does not permit the reduction of ethnic and racial differences to class differences, for ethnic and racial cleavages persist in the absence of significant class differences between ethnic groups. Conversely, class cleavages can and do exist within the same ethnic or racial group. With visible minorities entering Canada as wellheeled entrepreneurs — outside the point system or family sponsorship — the social stratification within outgroups has increased. Gone are the times when all immigrants were poor and part of the European surplus of unemployed peasants. There is a prevalent image of new migrants who sport ostentatious status symbols and degrees of consumerism which the mainstream resents in the name of undeserved affluence. Affirmative action programs for all visible minorities therefore become questionable when, for example, Asian-Canadians are overrepresented at post-secondary institutions or in upper income brackets. The increasingly color-blind alliance between local and off-shore capital highlights, in the Marxist perspective, the salience of class over race. All of this of course says little about the racism such individuals experience, regardless of education or financial success.

Thirdly, the psychological perspective looks at the way in which ethnic differences are utilized by the propagandist. According to Adorno (1950), among others, the authoritarian personality is based on weak ego development through harsh early socialization. The result is a basically insecure individual, who represses impulses, views life as threatening and perceives social relationships in terms of power. Consequently rigidity, a tendency toward stereotyped thinking, avoidance of introspection and excessive moralism are typical. Attributes such as "toughness" are glorified as opposed to "weakness". The world is sharply defined in categories of black and white, right or wrong, good or bad. In short, there is little "grey" or in the middle for the authoritarian and dogmatic character. Closure rather than openness characterizes such individuals. What makes individuals susceptible to embracing such worldviews? Why are some immune to the messages of the agitator while others feel the need to identify with strong leaders and groups? The revival of nationalism and chauvinism in the "socialist" East European societies points to the limitations of Marxist indoctrinations in internationalism. It reinforces Rokeach's hypothesis that right-wing and left-wing authoritarianism share a common dogmatism.

The structure of schools frequently reinforces authoritarianism. If prejudice formation is to be reduced or eliminated, educational institutions could focus on changing socialization patterns within the school to strengthen ego development. Education toward critical thinking and democratic political socialization would be important. Stressing similarities between various groups and increased opportunities for contact with members of other groups over shared goals have also shown some success in breaking stereotypes. However, the serious limitations that are posed in working at this level ought not to be denied. People discriminate despite increased information. In short, character deficiency is very difficult to counteract with better information. Nor is this facilitated by economic insecurities, when out-groups are seen as competitors.

Fourthly, there is the political focus. The mobilization of real or imagined characteristics distinguishing one group from another to articulate claims on political institutions is another dimension. Glazer and Moynihan (1975), for instance, assert that ethnic allegiances are cemented by mutual interests. Ethnicity is also seen as having a certain fluidity which allows it to be politically activated and deactivated, depending on circumstances.

The rise of Quebec nationalism after the failure of Meech Lake is a case in point. Non-French speaking immigrants in Quebec rightly feel more uncomfortable and threatened than in equally hostile English Canada. The Quebec nationalists who seek sovereignty advocate a much harsher line toward First Nations People who long for the same. Nationalism — in other words, politicized ethnicity — always carries with it exclusion of those who do not belong. The Quebec school texts that instill pride and love for the unique history of a people, at the same time lead to social distance toward those who are also rightful inhabitants of the land.

From this perspective, there is the potential for politicization through education. Awareness about political processes, access to institutions, degrees of legal equality, could all be related to the life chances of different groups. Indeed, this will not leave the dominant group unchallenged in its position and will likely upset its monopoly. Recognition of the political power that ethnic groups have, in terms of voting strengths and their potential to manipulate and extract spoils in the political game, could make the crucial difference between alienated stigmatized status and involved participants with self-esteem.

However, neither of these four foci alone can fully come to grips with the Canadian situation, since the openness of the public school system in English Canada atomizes ethnic group members and militates against ethnic cohesion, giving them the illusion that if they want to, they can make it on their own. This belief in individual success erodes the formation of ethnic cohesiveness.

Some assumptions regarding the homogeneity of cultural identifications of minorities in Canada underlying most studies in the area of multiculturalism and education need to be questioned. Characteristics such as shared kinship, common place of origin, physical features, common customs and values are falsely seen as having a vitality of their own. In contrast to a primordialist emphasis, ethnicity is considered situational and instrumental. Major structural changes such as the rise of the welfare state, the improved legal status of immigrants, their prevailing secularization and geographic dispersal, have led to a decline of ethnic cohesion except in Quebec. Multiculturalism as a policy has, in line with the assumption of cultural intactness, focused on a reified, depoliticized and privatized conception of ethnicity: one which overemphasizes lifestyles and neglects ethnic inequalities. The educational implications of this decline of instrumental ethnicity in favor of symbolic ethnicity are drawn.

These issues are addressed in various ways in this book. The chapters focus on four major dimensions pertaining to education in multicultural societies. The first section deals with macro-sociological comparative, critical perspectives about the relationship between ethnicity, race, nationalism and a range of state policy responses. The cases of Britain, Canada, South Africa, the United States and Western Europe provide a valuable spectrum of policy constellations and priorities. Conservative and progressive forces grapple with each other about the entrenchment or elimination of structures perpetuating race and ethnicity as evident in the ongoing debate about affirmative action policies.

The second section offers linguistic, psychological and counselling perspectives on the need for multicultural education. Greater recognition of home languages, other than English, is proposed as a way to valorize students' heritages. Multicultural education is proposed for the better education of counsellors and as a way to reduce prejudice.

In the third section, the theme of multicultural education for empowerment through a transformationist curriculum is highlighted. Contributions point to the need to go beyond multicultural education from a local context to establish broader global linkages, to address issues of human rights and the tenets of common core values, and to enhance cross-cultural understanding. A theoretical overview looks at the present locus of multicultural education research and where we need to move in the future.

In the fourth section an interesting alternative cultural revitalization model is proposed for indigenous minorities who have largely been given short shrift in multicultural education with its predominant focus on immigrant minorities. Similarly a Quebecois experience-based model of intercultural teacher education sheds light on the invaluable process of teacher immersion in the situation of "the other." Finally, transcending the emphasis on cultural diversity, one perspective highlights the broader heterogeneity present in most classrooms, proposes differential status evaluation and ways of altering these.

All these dimensions point to the need for constant redefinition of priorities in education for a multicultural society. Papers elaborate, caution, clarify and call for reflection on approaches to be used. Practitioners are offered points of orientation for shaping their own special needs.

References

Adorno, T.W., Frenkel-Brunswik, E., Levinson, D.E. & Nevitt Sanford, R. (1950). *The Authoritarian Personality*. New York: Harper & Row.

Bell, D. (1975). "Ethnicity and social change." In N. Glazer & P. Moynihan (eds.), *Ethnicity: Theory and Experience*. Cambridge, Mass.: Harvard University Press.

Geertz, C. (1963). "The integrative revolution: primordial sentiments and civil politics in the New States." In C. Geertz, *Old Societies and New States*. New York: The Free Press.

Glazer, N. & Moynihan, P. (eds.) (1975). *Ethnicity: Theory and Experience*. Cambridge, Mass.: Harvard University Press.

van den Berghe, P.L. (1967). *Race and Racism*. New York: John Wiley.

Section I

Critical International Perspectives

Ethnicity, Nationalism and the State

Heribert Adam

Education in plural societies differs from ethnically homogeneous contexts in that it assumes the additional task of socializing for national cohesion or, alternatively, separatism. In plural societies, education is likely to be more politically charged. Unless educators want to be the blind servants of the powers that be, a critical understanding of the interplay between ethnic identity and state policies is required.

Since our understanding cannot derive from the local context alone, it must include the comparative and historical experience of nationalism, racism and genocide elsewhere in order to derive appropriate local policies. Only if we acquire a thorough grasp of the nature of ethnicity can we adequately deal with the specific situation at hand. Unfortunately, much of well-intended race relations education, for example, often amounts to "do gooding" ad hoc measures. In Canada, official multiculturalism is embraced and offered for export as if it were the solution to intergroup antagonism everywhere.

My central thesis — that there can be no general theory of ethnicity and nationalism — highlights the predicament of comparative research on education in polyethnic societies. Nor can there be universally valid educational prescriptions. Whether ethnic revival fulfils a reactionary or a progressive role depends on the historical situation. Even in the same society cultural identity fulfils different functions for different groups. For native Indians heightened cultural awareness is an asset in Canada, for German-Canadians ethnic origin is better buried forever. For Jewish people, delving into their painful history strengthens solidarity and group cohesion — for the descendents of their tormentors the same weakens ethnic bonds out of shame for the atrocities committed in the name of kinship. In South Africa for example, culture and ethnicity have become terms of ill repute for all progressive people because of their manipulative use by the apartheid regime. In the Soviet Union, on the other hand, the Stalinist repression of regional autonomy has made collective cultural revival a vehicle for freedom and emancipation. Being a Lithuanian nationalist now amounts to a legitimate act of resistance.

This then is an invitation to reflect on such broad comparative snippets of the differing role of ethnicity in divided societies. Only when we achieve some clarity about the relationship between ethnicity and state policies worldwide can we lose the naivete about our own educational projects.

Explaining the origin of nationalism is a useful beginning. Benedict Anderson's perceptive book, *Imagined Communities* (1983) explains the paradox that without physical contact people of a vast land, nevertheless, feel strong bonds of kinship. Historically, this imaginary vision of a national family became possible with the invention of the print media. Reading the morning paper substituted the morning prayer. The feeling that there are others who hold similar opinions and beliefs created a national consciousness, mobilized by the intelligentsia and reinforced by their common language. "Through that language, encountered at Mother's knee and parted with only at the grave, pasts are restored, fellowships are imagined and futures dreamed" (Anderson, 1983:140). A distinct language and or religion marks the group as unique and gives it a common destiny.

While a distinct language and religion facilitates imagined bonds, it is no guarantee for inclusion of all who belong to such a group. In fact, some of the worst atrocities in history were committed against in-group members. You do not have to belong to an out-group to become a target of state violence, as is frequently assumed. The best examples are the Stalinist purges of the 1930s. Loyal, dedicated communists were murdered in the thousands after the infamous show-trials. While these state massacres frequently had anti-semitic overtures — and thereby designated an untrustworthy out-group within the party in-group — the physical elimination of a high proportion of the Russian officer corps constituted an even more obvious attack on fellow ethnics by the same kin-group. It made possible the Nazi military advance into the Soviet Union because it had fatally weakened the Russian defense capacities. A similar phenomenon occurred in Cambodia: the majority of Khmer Rouge victims in the "killing fields" were fellow ethnic Khmers.

These examples call into question the fashionable sociobiological explanation of ethnic antagonism as inclusive fitness maximization. The assumed preference for kin over non-kin is no iron law of evolutionary conditioning. Rather, specific political-historical circumstances explain far more effectively, why genetically related family members are also set up as strangers.

This can be demonstrated with another example of rejection of kin in favor of inclusion of non-kin. In South Africa, the ruling Afrikaner National Party — although itself only representative of about six percent of the population — has recently been engaged in a bitter conflict with fellow ultra-right Afrikaners. Moreover, the ruling minority historically insisted on the exclusion of culturally identical so-called coloreds, their own genetic relatives. Imagined racial bonds with distant Europeans prove far stronger for apartheid supremacists than the real kinship ties with their brown offspring.[1] Ruling groups, however, enlarge their boundaries only if they are sufficiently threatened or too weak to do it alone. Then the imagined community can also include former outsiders, even people with a different skin color. Nationalism changes to patriotism (Shaw & Wong, 1989). Everyone who lives in the land can claim equal citizenship, regardless of origin.

Fortunate, indeed, are the immigrant societies that historically skipped the nationalists phase and started off with a policy of patriotic multiculturalism. They saved themselves the traumatic phases of redefining a collective identity, and the policies of reluctant co-optation. Moulding a new formation out of national entities proves far more difficult and fragile than starting with individual newcomers.

The painfully slow attempts to create a European community in the face of antiquated nationalisms testifies to this resilience of ethnicity. The difficulties are mainly due to inevitable sacrifices, both materially and symbolically that equalization policies demand from differentially developed regions. Why should we pay for a dilapidated Britain, ask the wealthy Germans in reply to British reluctance to depart with an antiquated sovereignty. Fragile as the new visions must be, a post-national mentality nevertheless gains ground. Economies of scale provide new opportunities and individual mobility. Instead of reading only national papers, the European elite now also reads the *International Herald Tribune*. New pan-European institutions emerge, from a parliament to a university and a common currency. Above all, television frequently broadcasts the same programs, particularly soccer games simultaneously in different countries. An infantile soap opera like "Dallas" undermines traditional morality, and the "Cosby Show" constantly sanitizes stigmatized ethnicity through embourgeoisement. Soon former iron-curtain countries will also be cultural victims of Hollywood seduction as they have already been invaded by the world food of hamburgers, Coke and fries. At the end only an isolationist Islam or the autocrats of Tianamen Square will hold out for a while against a world culture that treats historical ethnicity as a commercial tool, to be exported, marketed or manufactured as the trends dictate. At that stage it may well become progressive again to be an unashamed nationalist; a quaint ethnic, proud of an historical heritage, that reminds the atomized consumers of a lost community; a nostalgic advocate of belonging who resists cost-benefit calculations with a spirituality that differs from religious sectarianism.

Like Marxists, liberal development theorists view ethnicity as an impediment to modernization. The undesirable primordial affinities, so the developmentalist and Marxists believe, will crumble under the pressure of class interests and national unity. In the wishful thinking of modernization theory, quoted in Cynthia Enloe (1973:261) at the beginning of the 70s: "Like a midwife, an ethnic group may assist at birth but should be ready to depart soon afterward. Groups founded on ethnic allegiance compete with the nation-state. Such competition is intolerable because the nation-state is the vehicle for development."

Historically, however, nation-states are frequently unable to overcome the resilience of ethnicity, as events in Eastern Europe and Africa so clearly demonstrate.[2] The survival of ethnicity is not due to a magical quality of primordialism. Neither does evolutionary conditioning for kinship preference guarantee the resilience of ethnicity, as the sociobiologists maintain. Ethnicity may boil down to nepotism, as van den Berghe (1983) stresses, but it does so for a political not a genetic reason. Where the ruling elites of nation states force their version of centralized development on peripheral regions they actually strengthen ethnicity. Far from the midwife departing when the nation is born, the state coercion against its constituent entities guarantees their resentful life, regardless of their pronounced death in doctrinaire Leninism and liberal modernization edicts for developing countries alike.

At present, the Soviet Union is the clearest case in point. The Soviet Republics feel like conquered entities. The former sovereign Baltic States in particular consider themselves exploited, neglected and deprived rather than being modernized by the Russian centre. As the crumbling of the Soviet empire proves, enforced patriotism is not a prerequisite to development but an impediment. Resistance against conquest in all its manifestations explodes in collective emotions with the symbols of a glorified past uniting the victims joyously in newly found freedoms. Ironically, the disciplined spontaneity that Rosa Luxemburg expected to overthrow capitalism is now practised by the oppressed against Stalinist communism.

The revival of ethnonationalism in Eastern Europe moreover manifests itself within the very party leadership that was supposed to eliminate it. In the conflict between the patriotic doctrine of a greater Soviet Union and regional loyalties in Lithuania or Azerbaijan, it is not the masses versus the party but the regional party leadership versus the Central Committee. Local elites easily mobilize a frustrated constituency in the name of separatist identities. Progressive demands for autonomy and democracy resurface together with age-old racism and anti-Semitism. Decades of communist rule merely suppressed traditional hatreds instead of eradicating them. The xenophobic Russian Pamyat now threatens Gorbachev's liberalization most.

Democratic polyethnic states have little reason to feel smug, although their state cohesion rests mostly on voluntary association. In Canada, the United States and Australia, historical conquest has destroyed First Nation People more lastingly than Stalinism in the Soviet Union or apartheid in South Africa. Western settler-states could afford democracy and now an official ideology of multiculturalism, because numbers and technology were on their side. In moral terms, the subtle welfare colonialism and paternalistic tutelage of native "wards of the state" is as pernicious as the open coercion of totalitarian and authoritarian regimes.

It is therefore not surprising that cultural revival is advocated by Western natives as well. Indigenous groups are aggressively asserting their separate identities and unique qualities in political, social and legal spheres. However, this affirmation of traditional bonds, customary law or separate native education co-exists with acculturation. Native ethnicity does not have the power or religious intent to retreat into orthodox isolation, like Hutterite colonies or Hassidic communities. However, indigenous people want to control the pace and the manner of their incorporation. There is no blind rejection of modernity among native political activists, but an attempt to regulate and select on their own terms. For example, the desire to acquire scientific competence goes together with a rewrite of a biased social studies curriculum. Values of communalism often reject individual consumerism. A people that, above all, have been made to suffer from loss of collective pride and individual self-worth can indeed benefit from cultural revival, as long as it sheds the illusion that the lost hunting and fishing economy can be recreated in the suburbs of Vancouver. Where the logging and mining multinationals continue to make inroads into the preserves of a natural habitat, aboriginal people serve the environmental interests of all humankind by insisting on their land claims. Dialectically, parochial native ethnicity contributes to global survival.

It is helpful to start from the premise that the world has to become a more integrated place because of the increased global interdependence — from refugee streams into developed countries to environmental impacts worldwide. These imperatives will increasingly constrain national sovereignty and lead to larger political units despite ethnically mobilized resistance by those who are short-changed in the process. How will this inevitable global integration take place? Which historical experiences can guide future policies?

Integration can take place in three ways:

1. In **submissive integration**, a minority immigrant or group is incorporated into the culture of the host society on its terms. The newcomers give up their way of life. They become part of a pre-existing dominant culture. They assimilate and loose their identity by redefining themselves as a fully integrated part of the new order. This is the state policy of France toward migrants from Algeria or of West Germany toward Turkish workers and their children. The Turks are pressured either to become Germans or to return to Turkey. The option of remaining Turkish in Germany is not available because Germany does not define itself as an immigrant society. No allowance is made for multiculturalism that would permit

an Islamic German identity. The expectations for the newcomers are to acculturate in every respect.

2. In **interactionist integration** both minority and majority work out a new *modus vivendi*. Ideally, they both abandon a previous identity and merge into a new one. The romanticized notion of the United States melting pot symbolizes this amalgamation of different heritages into a new whole. Recognition of permanent interdependence forges new relationships in which past exclusivist identities wane into a broader definition of belonging to a new formation. Divisive religious identities are relegated to the private sphere. The creation of a European Common Market not only reduces the economic sovereignty of nation-states by mutual contractual agreement but also attempts to gradually substitute historical national consciousness with a new European political identity.

3. **Multicultural integration** denotes a pluralist conception. Ethnic groups retain their differences and co-exist side by side. In extreme cases, they merely tolerate each other. Politically, they share power as mobilized entities in an institutionalized truce called consociationalism (Lijphart, 1977). To all intents and purposes, pluralist arrangements hide inequality and mystify a cultural hierarchy. Blacks, living in the ghettos of the United States, for example, co-exist involuntarily in sub-economies of poverty. Even the Canadian or Australian state policy of multiculturalism obfuscates the continued dominance by members of charter cultures under the pretences of cultural equality of all immigrants. The immigrant's retention of home culture in fact impedes their competitiveness in the new marketplace. South African Bantu education sought to restrict blacks to traditional occupations by lowering expectations of new skills and wider visions in favor of pride in a tribal heritage.

Yet official pluralism seems far more conducive to relative intergroup harmony than submissive or interactionist integration, particularly in immigrant societies. In comparative perspective, Canadian society ranks remarkably high on this score. Despite simmering racism just under the complacent facade, compared with Britain or the United States, Canadian race relations so far can be held up as a model. In a society with widespread resentment, scapegoating and a vast potential for ethnic strife (in addition to the separate Quebec issue not discussed here) there has yet to emerge a Le Pen, an Enoch Powell, an indigenous Ku Klux Klan or a neo-fascist Republican Party. The Doug Collins and Keegstras of Canada notwithstanding, open racist platforms find little public respectability and support among opinion makers.

Again the reasons for the Canadian difference to Western Europe or the United States do not lie in a collective virtuousness or better education for tolerance, but in a specific political constellation. Most likely individual Canadians are as susceptible to being mobilized by racist agitators as Germans, British or South African whites. There does not exist anywhere a collective immunity against the authoritarian temptation under the appropriate circumstances. What distinguishes Canada above all, is a weak national identity that does not encourage a self-confident "host" group to impose its cultural definitions on the rest. With two charter cultures officially recognized, and all Canadians, except the First Nations People, being immigrants, pluralism is — so to speak — built into the national consciousness. Out of 25 million in the 1986 census, only 69 000 identified themselves as Canadians when asked about their ethnic origin. But more significant than such subjective currents are objective conditions that resulted in state policies on ethnicity that crucially differ from European countries.

Unlike Western European countries, the Canadian state needs continued immigration to fill an underpopulated land and offset a declining birthrate. Vastly increased immigration is advocated by Canadian business. The upper limits to the number of immigrants are not determined by their availability, but by what the landed population considers reasonable without open opposition. The three federal parties rely heavily on the ethnic vote, reinforced by a voting system which militates against right wing extremist parties. All three established parties must look to the centre of the political spectrum to gain increased support. Therefore, none can afford to adopt a racist anti-immigration stance.

Furthermore, the Canadian establishment, including conservative provincial politicians in British Columbia, has now entered into an alliance with offshore capital, particularly from Hong Kong. Increased capital inflow from abroad is seen as having various economic benefits. Many immigrants enter Canada now as established members of a foreign bourgeoisie or professional strata rather than as unskilled workers from an underdeveloped periphery, as was the case with post-war immigration into Britain from its colonies or into Central Europe from the South. The diversification of Canadian immigration in terms of origin and class position makes it more difficult to "ghettoize" and stigmatize the newcomers. The state itself has no interest in encouraging what British Marxists (Miles, 1982:153-67) have called "the process of racialization" or "racial categorization."

On the contrary, official multiculturalism popularizes tolerance and open-mindedness. Various state agencies and party functionaries court the ethnic entrepreneurs. Large sums are spent on an ethnic lobby that falsely promises it can deliver the vote of communities which no longer exist. Yet for the sake of images and public relations purposes state bureaucrats pretend that the self-appointed lobbyists represent ethnic communities "out there" with whom they are in intimate touch. The ethnic entrepreneurs, on the other hand, including many well intentioned academics, are readily co-opted through research grants, subsidies and lucrative appointments to advisory boards. "Multiculturalism which in the 1960s had been a brave, creative idea and in the 1970s pretended to be a tool of social planning, had, by the 1980s become a multi-million dollar government-sponsored business," comments a writer in *Saturday Night* (December, 1989).

Social scientists must ask themselves which role they play in this context. Are they the grateful recipients of state patronage with their critical sting bought off and pacified by ever larger grants for pedestrian research? Or can they use, as Kogila Moodley argues (in this volume), official policy creatively to multiculturalize the mainstream, empower the minorities and transform a cultural hierarchy toward a democracy of equals? After all, only 3 out of 295 members of the Canadian parliament come from so-called visible minorities!

Not least, academics in the field of multicultural education must examine their own biased conceptualizations rather than allow their definitions of the problem to be dictated by the official discourse. For example, we should stop talking about "host" societies. It highlights the status of guests. The sooner immigrants become part of the "host" and are accepted as equals, the better for inter-ethnic harmony. Why do we still speak of "visible minorities"? Is the mainstream invisible? Does the power-elite want to be invisible in the normal exercise of control, compared with the "different" intruders? In Canadian reality, the minorities are the non-visible groups and the mainstream imposes its power visibly on the rest.

Finally, it is **not** time to heed the warning of a British colleague (Phizacklea, 1984:200): "If social scientists continue to use the term 'race' . . . because people act as though 'race' exists, then they are guilty of conferring analytical status on what is nothing more than an ideological construction." We should study racism as an ideology and discriminatory praxis, but the object of our inquiry ought not to be "race in itself." Since the notion of race has no "descriptive or explanatory importance" (Miles, 1984:218), we should also avoid using it in our surveys or everyday discourse.

The ultimate aim of education in a plural society such as Canada should not be a consciousness of **multiracialism** or harmonious co-existence between groups of a different phenotype but **nonracialism**: that is genuine color-blindness where the markers of difference have become as irrelevant for life-chances and social status as the color of the hair or shape of the ears.

Notes

1. In reality, however, a closer analysis shows that political reasons led to the exclusion of coloreds. The formerly enfranchised group would have overwhelmingly voted for the opposition and thereby jeopardized the dominance of the ruling party. In a broader non-racial Afrikaner nation the power-holders would have had to share the spoils of office (Adam & Moodley, 1986).

2. Many of the Third World inter-ethnic wars would have long simmered down had it not been for the continued arms supply by outside powers. Thus the United States has continued to ship arms to the UNITA forces in Angola or the Mujahedin in Afghanistan. Equally, the Soviet Union has continued to back the Ethiopian regime. Its intransigence in refusing to allow an effective autonomy or self-determination to major groups within the former empire of Halle Selassie has been the chief cause of a devastating civil war. The respected British Afrikanist Basil Davidson (*The Independent*, Letter to the Editor, 20 October 1989) has commented: "This is a policy of war, stubbornly followed now as before that stands in absolute contrast to Moscow's claim to support policies of peace. Moscow has the power to curb these wars and even help to end them. Moscow does precisely the reverse." Indeed, as long as the so-called ethnic regional conflicts around the world do not seriously enter the East-West summits and both willingly dump obsolete weapons on their adopted clients the death and misery of millions is unlikely to end.

References

Adam, H. & Moodley, K. (1986). *South Africa Without Apartheid*. Berkeley: University of California Press.

Anderson, B. (1983). *Imagined Communities*. London: Verso.

Enloe, C. (1973). *Ethnic Conflict and Political Development*. Boston: Little Brown.

Lijphart, A. (1977). *Democracy in Plural Societies*. New Haven: Yale University Press.

Miles, R. (1982). *Racism and Migrant Labour*. London: Routledge & Keagan Paul.

Miles, R. (1984). "Marxism versus the sociology of 'race relations'?" *Ethnic and Racial Studies*, 7(2): 217-37.

Phizacklea, A. (1984). "A sociology of migration or 'race relations'? A view from Britain.", *Current Sociology*, 32(3): 199-218.

Shaw, R.P. & Wong, Y. (1989). *Genetic Seeds of Warfare. Evolution, Nationalism and Patriotism*. Boston: Unwin.

Solomos, J. (1986). "Varieties of Marxist conceptions of 'race, class and the state': A critical analysis." In J. Rex & D. Mason, *Theories of Race and Ethnic Relations*. Cambridge: Cambridge University Press.

van den Berghe, P.L. (1981). *The Ethnic Phenomenon*. New York: Elsevier Press.

Nation States, Diversity and Interculturalism: Issues for British Education

Jagdish Gundara and Crispin Jones

This chapter is an attempt to develop some of the major issues in intercultural education as they are manifested within the British context.[1] Although reference will be made to current English[2] educational policy and practice in relation to national diversity, the principal purpose of this paper is to examine some of the issues that underpin such policy and practice but which in themselves are seldom analyzed. The consequences of this, in England at least, are profound. Much of the work in relation to education in and for a multicultural society in Britain contains internal contradictions, and, more importantly, is ineffective in both reducing the discriminatory and prejudiced behavior of many white pupils, teachers and students and in improving the educational attainments of many groups of minority students.

Thus this chapter examines firstly, the debate about definitional terms in relation to concepts of the nation state and pluralism,[3] in order to clarify the context within which the educational debate takes place. This contextual continues with an analysis of the ways in which the concept of multiculturalism may be best examined. The model chosen is based on an investigation of social group discrimination within nation state contexts, initially using a model derived from the comparative education work of Nicholas Hans (1949). In turn this leads to a taxonomic arrangement by which state responses to diversity might be analyzed. The analytical and conceptual structures derived from this analysis are then used to examine current educational policy and practice in Britain, including a critique of the "new right" radicalism and its influence on such educational policies.

The very first point to be made is the confusion that often arises over the use of the terms Briton, Britain and British. The confusion is at its most disturbing when used by the English. To many English people, English/British, England/Britain are synonyms. Clarification of this, a task that the Scots, the

* An earlier version of this chapter has appeared in I. Alldin & K. Bacchus (eds.). (1990). *Education in Multicultural Societies.* Boston: Ginn Press.

Welsh and the other British minorities find non-problematic, is both a starting point for analysis and leads in itself to a re-examination of concepts of the nation, nationality(ies), nationalism and the nation state.

The above is a more helpful starting point compared to the more usual examination and discussion of terms such as multicultural, multiracial and multiethnic in relation to education, although those terms do need scrutiny. However, it is only through an earlier discussion of the concept of the nation that these terms achieve their full resonance.

Thus, we would argue that most, if not all nation states, are stratified polyethnic states using a variety of mechanisms to maintain their social and economic stratification, usually presented with an accompanying rhetoric emphasizing societal cohesion. Such stratification has operationalizing criteria attached to it in addition to those of class/status and gender, **because** of the way in which the modern nation state is structurally and ideologically constructed. In other words, it is not surprising that the modern nation state is based on a fallacious ideal-typical model of a small scale society. This is because the modern unitary nation state disguises its predatory[4] origins by attempting to demonstrate a hegemonic unity in terms of its citizens' allegiances and affiliations.

Such a unity is, in fact, a codification of the dominant group(s) social and economic arrangements, a legitimation of an unequal set of socio-economic arrangements. Thus, the model that has emerged through this process is one that asserts that access to membership of that nation requires:

- the capacity to operate within certain linguistic and economic parameters; and

- acceptance of notions of a common history, religion and other socio-cultural factors.

Failing to operate within these parameters or unwillingness to accept them makes the individuals liable to being construed by that nation state as outsiders, or more pejoratively, as "alien." Within this model, members of a nation state should share one or, most likely, more of the following characteristics:

- the same language and economic arrangements

- a common history

- if religion is present, it should be one accepted, if not believed in, by all

- a common set of cultural practices, which include aesthetic preferences.

And so on. Groups that fail to meet these and similar criteria are seen as "the other" or as "alien" to the nation and can be seen as potentially divisive. The "aliens" and the "other" lack cohesive capacity by definition and are seen as a divisive element within the nation. Consequently, there is a tendency to locate such groups at the periphery of the nation, not accepted but tolerated to a degree that is dependent on the economic and socio-political needs of the dominant group or groups within that nation; such group(s) often see themselves as the legitimately constituted nation, and use the "others" as a means of maintaining such a ideological fiction. Such a perspective helps to position many minority ethnic and racial groups at the periphery of the nation, in cultural, political, economic as well as spatial terms.

This is currently well illustrated in France, where recent electoral successes by an extreme right wing party were built upon such excluding and exclusive concepts of the nation (Marnham, 1989). Sadly, such success has led the Socialist government to indicate that it is thinking of tightening up immigration controls and increasing the rate of expulsion of illegal immigrants (Marnham, 1989). It is worth noting that this last point, on illegal immigration, although seemingly unexceptionable, is very likely to be seen and experienced by many in the French Muslim community as tacit approval for their greater harassment by various national agencies, particularly the police.[5]

This marginalization process, of which the above is a contemporary example, is not a new thing and has a long history in the British context. The process has been well illustrated by the work of Hechter (1975). As his analysis suggests, the denial of a capacity to belong to the nation leads to marginalization of the groups who are so positioned, some because they can be "racially" defined (as is the case with black people in the British context), and others as "different" (the case of the Irish). Developing from this analysis, it can be seen that this has clear implications for both British cities, within which live the great majority of Britain's black population, and for the education that is provided in them. This is because of the spatial consequences that can arise from the increase in intra-collective communication and associated greater status solidarity that results from rejection by, and/or hostility from dominant and/or majority groups within British society. In other words, ghetto formation, in both its physical and spiritual manifestations, remains an active element in British urban society.

At one level, it is not surprising that immigrant groups (using the term in its correct sense) in Britain, as elsewhere, are often placed into this marginal position by the dominant groups within the nation state.[6] Their socio-spatial marginalization is reinforced by legislation concerning their status in British society. Thus, linking up with the earlier idea of "Britishness," successive British governments have tied themselves up in the knots of ever more complex immigration and nationality laws, the purpose of which is to preserve the nation from being "swamped" by alien — that is, black — cultures. That this legislative framework is as it is a serious issue, and one which few other nation states either wish or are able to resolve in a satisfactory manner. Indeed, if the subordinated groups are defined out of the concept of the nation, and can only belong through a process of self-denial and rejection of their own identity, it is difficult to see how such exclusive states can do otherwise. What is perhaps surprising, and is most certainly a cause of equally serious concern, is the marginalization of certain groups within the British nation state who are **not** immigrant. In other words, many black British citizens remain as marginalized as their immigrant ancestors, unlike white British citizens with similar origins.

Thus, the consequent racist stratification in Britain, as in many other nation states, sustains and creates national divisions that result in advantaged and disadvantaged groups having unequal access to power and resources. And it is the reproduction of this through the education system that helps to ensure its inter-generational continuation.[7] An example of this process can be seen in the history and contemporary position of the long established black community in Liverpool. Still often regarded as in some way not British, primarily because they are black, they are economically and socially marginalized within a city that is itself in a similar position *vis-à-vis* the southeast dominated British nation state. Furthermore, as a recent government report indicated, their educational attainment continue to remain at a very low level, despite community efforts to make the education system more responsive to their educational needs (Department of Education and Science [DES], 1985).

Furthermore, the failure in both imagination and policy by government that has led to an increasing ethnic and racial socio-spatial differentiation in the cities of Britain, has serious implications for inner city school populations. For example, in Tower Hamlets, an inner city borough in London, where 46 percent of the primary pupils speak a language other than English as their first language, there are 29 schools (out of a total of 95) where the majority of pupils have a home language other than English and at least two where none of the children have English as their home language (London Boroughs of Tower Hamlets, 1988). This is a trend which the open admissions policies introduced by the recent 1988 Education Act is likely to intensify for the Act enables white parents to avoid sending their children, if they wish, to schools with a high percentage of black pupils.[8] And, like the similar argument that took place some decades ago in the United States, separate schools for black and white children are, in the vast majority of cases, as inherently unequal here as they were (are) there.[9]

Such examples demonstrate that within metropolitan democratic societies like Britain, peripheral groups, however defined, seldom have access to significant institutions in a manner sufficient to bring about a reallocation of power and resources. Such groups consequently remain unrepresented, under represented or tokenistically represented in the dominant social institutions. A survey by the Inner London Education Authority (ILEA)of its school governors in 1985 well demonstrates this point. It found that although Afro-Caribbean pupils constituted 15.6 percent of the school population, only 2.7 percent of school governors were from that group. A similar picture (11.7 percent:1.7 percent) was apparent in relation to the Asian community (ILEA, 1985). This lack of adequate representation usually implies an equal lack of power, although the exceptions to this are important areas for study.[10]

This state of affairs raises a further perplexing issue, namely, the nature of the epistemological stance that is taken in relation to the concept of an individual's, or more problematically, a group's perception of objective interests (Habermas, 1976; Lukes, 1974). More simply, what does group silence in the face of such denial of access and resources imply? For example, if a minority group makes no comment about an educational policy that effects its members, does this mean acquiescence, approval or realistic resignation, the "it makes no difference what we say anyway" stance?

Only detailed empirical case by case studies have given any pointers, of which, perhaps, the most useful British example is Peter Saunders' examination of urban politics in Croydon, a Conservative party dominated local authority in outer London, which indicated that all such responses were possible (Saunders, 1980). And he states:

> Put another way, it seems that grievances are often subjectively recognized, but that they fail to surface in the political system because of fatalism (it would not do any good to protest), fear (what would happen to us if we did protest?) and exclusion (how can we protest?) (Saunders, 1980:295).

Such a seeming unhelpful finding is in fact most helpful, as it emphasizes the complexity of the issues involved, particularly those when groups and/or individuals seek to speak for "their" community.

That difficulty notwithstanding, the issue for minority groups attempting to make their voice heard in education, as elsewhere, seems to be one of constructing an anti-hegemonic ideology that offers the possibility of successful intervention and/or protest. Unfortunately, much of what passes for multiculturalism, in education, as elsewhere, does not attempt this. Walzer's note in relation to the United States has equal validity in the British context when he comments:

> But ethnic pluralism as it developed in the United States, cannot plausibly be characterized as an antistate ideology. Its advocates did not challenge the authority of the federal government. (Walzer, 1982:11)

The consequences of the analysis put forward in this chapter are clear. The multicultural, plural nature of the modern state has to be acknowledged as a major problematic for those states whose cohesion is defined in terms of the core values of an exclusivist dominant group. Current events in the Soviet Union are not to be regarded as some sort of exotic ethnic and national flowering of little concern to Western nation states, save in terms of political and economic advantage. Within Britain, the Welsh and the Scots look at events in Lithuania, Latvia and Estonia with more than a passing interest. Similarly, in Spain, elected members of the national parliament belonging to Herri Batasuna, the political wing of ETA, are currently challenging the very legal authority of the Spanish national constitution in relation to Basque national aspirations. (Llewellyn, 1989)

These, and other examples, bring to the fore fundamental questions, albeit phrased in a pragmatic fashion, namely, can the modern polyethnic and culturally plural nation state survive in its current guise, and how should a national education system deal with this issue? In order to address these questions more systematically, the concept of diversity has to be clarified.

With the nature of the modern nation state being more problematic than is often maintained in educational discourse, those elements that traditionally have been seen as its constituents are in a similar position. Their problematic position is, however, seen as such, although from differing perspectives, by both the left and the right. For Professor Roger Scruton, a well-known British right wing radical critic of progressive views of multiculturalism, the criteria for multiculturalism are also the criteria for the unitary nation state:

> language, religion, custom, associations and traditions of political order —
> in short, all those forces that generate nations. (Scruton, 1982:14)

The use of the singular rather than the plural for language, religion and custom is significant. Used, however, as a plurality, the terms that Scruton uses may be developed in such a manner as opens up the reality, rather than the mythology of the modern nation state. And, of course, such terms used in an attempt to understand the pressures that weigh upon national education systems are not new. Over 40 years ago, Nicholas Hans identified religious, linguistic, geographical, racial and political "factors" as ones of significance in understanding the range of issues that face national educational systems (Hans, 1949).

Such a framework has often been the implicit basis for much analysis of multiculturalism by British writers. However, we would develop it to include a wider range of significant categories. This has two purposes. It enables a more sophisticated analysis of societal diversity to be made than is customary and it can be used to critique the simple polarities that are frequently used by the various institutions of the nation state to define and divide their population.

Using this framework, national diversity would be defined in terms of **axes** of social and national division rather than simple polarities, themselves often based on a simple "them" and "us" division. More, the axes intersect among themselves, bringing about a greater range of potential diversities within a given society. Thus, social categories such as class, status, gender, sexual orientation, race, language, religion, disability and spatial location or territoriality can be used in very different ways, reflecting the individual or institutional attitude toward the unitary nation state.

Such a mode of analysis helps in our understanding of the genesis of stereotypes in the wider society and the educational stereotypes that they foster and engender. Of particular significance here would be the way in which concepts of intelligence and educability are differentially ascribed to groups within the nation on the basis of these stereotypes. For example, in many British schools, Afro-Caribbean boys are seen as non-academic students although supposedly good at certain types of games. (Even the games are supported by stereotypes, however; it took many years before British Afro-Caribbean professional football players could ever be seen as anything but fast offensive players, devoid of the temperament and skills that make a good defensive player.) Green's work on classroom interactions, reported on in the Swann Report, (DES, 1985) clearly revealed how the stereotypes that teachers had of minority students were a significant factor in their interactions with such students, usually, but not always, to the student's detriment.

The consequences of all of this can lead to a seeming confirmation of the stereotype, a sort of self-fulfilling prophecy. Certainly, such practice is likely to be a significant contributor to the poor educational attainments of many minority group children in British schools.

This links in with a further factor, namely that the educational attainment of minority group children is based on notions of success and excellence that are defined in majority cultural terms. This is clearly a complex area that needs considerably more attention than will be given here. However, given the massive increase in assessment in British schools that is being brought about through the implementation of the 1988 Education Act, it is likely to be an issue of increasing significance over the next few years.

National diversity is ignored and/or parodied through such educational arrangements and stereotypes. But as was just suggested, such factors are not the sole contributors to poor educational attainment. School organization, the curriculum, teaching styles, indeed the whole pedagogic economy of the school seldom challenges the dominant assertions about the diversity within British society. If the dominant assertions go unchallenged, working class children may be regarded as stupid, with their parents perceived as uncaring about their children's education. Stereotypical gender roles for both boys and girls may be reinforced and seldom challenged, while religions other than Christianity may be still regarded as having only peripheral importance in relation to school based education.

Such a list could go on and on. What even these few examples reveal however, is the potential value of such a taxonomic framework for the effective analysis of the racism, xenophobia, prejudice and discrimination that too often mark the British education system's response to societal diversity. It also demonstrates that struggles over gender and class/status oppression within (and between) nation states are interlinked with those over, say, race, religion and language. Furthermore, at the level of practical intervention in the educational process, such taxonomic frameworks enable a more effective analysis of the issues to be made, with the ensuing potential for more successful intervention and reform.

It was asserted earlier in this chapter that much thinking about multiculturalism in Britain has been over simplified and often atheoretical.[11] It is consequently not surprising that effective social, and educational policy and practice in relation to societal diversity has been equally oversimplified and often ineffective. And this ineffectiveness is visible whatever the political stance that has been taken.

Furthermore, taxonomic frameworks for analysis such as those initially put forward by Street-Porter (Street-Porter, 1976) although invaluable in their time, need reworking in terms of current knowledge. Also, her taxonomic framework came to be used in a rather ill-thought out and mechanistic manner, as for example, by the Inner London Education Authority, (ILEA, 1983) rather in the way Piaget's developmental theories were mistaught and misrepresented in initial teacher training in Britain in the 1960s and 1970s.

Reworking is also needed for two further reasons:

- The taxonomies too often ignore the fact that Britain, like other European nation states, has always been a multicultural society and has not just recently become one.

- They equally often ignore debates within education about educational disadvantage and poor attainment that help bind the debate about multiculturalism in education to a broader, and more useful, set of educational issues. (Other issues that ought to be covered here are those of equality of educational opportunity and outcomes, educational entitlements and issues relating to more general democratic and human rights.)

However, the taxonomies are worth revisiting, as they do contain valuable elements, most noticeably the recognition of the power of the minority communities themselves in the alteration of educational policy and practice.

Much of the debate about anti-racist education within the British context during the 1980s ignored, or was unaware of, the significance of the black minorities' interventions in policy debates throughout the 1970s and early 1980s.

Such a re-evaluation also points, not so much to a framework of societal and educational response to diversity on a continuum from assimilation, through integration, cultural pluralism and anti-racism, but to an **oscillating polarity**, between separation/segregation and assimilation, or put another way, between pluralism and "unitarianism." Such a model is one on which British practice can be better located, as it allows for the backwards and forwards nature of British educational policy and practice in this area.

Such a taxonomy can be used to explore briefly the way in which the various interested parties in British education changed and renegotiated their roles in the light of changing educational policies and practices. Although the motive for such changes may have laid outside of the educational debate, an attempt will be made to interweave the two themes.

Up until the 1980s, educational policy in relation to societal diversity followed the Street-Porter model. There appeared to be a slow move in both general social policy, and in educational policy in particular, toward an acceptance of cultural pluralism and an acknowledgment of the racism and xenophobia in the wider society that schooling was doing all too little to prevent. The apogee of this movement in education was the publication in 1985 of the official governmental enquiry into the educational performance of minority groups within the British educational system. The Swann Report is a valuable source, summarizing much of what had and had not been achieved over the previous two decades (DES, 1985).

However, many of its main recommendations were disregarded by government. With hindsight, this can be seen as inevitable, given the ideological shifts that were taking place in political thinking at that time. For the move to the right, as it is still too often crudely referred to as, was in fact a more complex set of realignments and repositionings on the part of the Conservative Government, and the Conservative Party and its supporters.

There are at least three elements in this ideological restructuring. The first was market libertarianism. Often associated with the monetarist economic writings of Hayek, it placed an unusual reliance on the power of the market to regulate not just inefficiency but to benefit and assist wealth creation, from which all ultimately will benefit, although to differing degrees. In other words, certain forms of inequality, particularly economic inequality, were seen as a necessary part of the market's regulatory power. As Sir Keith Joseph, at one time Minister of Education in the Conservative administration, said:

> The blind, unplanned, uncoordinated wisdom of the market ... is overwhelmingly superior to the well researched, rational, systematic, well meaning, co-operative, science based, forward looking, statistically respectable plans of governments ... (Lawton, 1989:35)

The opposition to most aspects of the social consensus that had prevailed in Britain since 1944 is clear. From this perspective, if there were problems with educational attainment, untrammelled market forces, as in say a voucher policy where parents could pick and choose an education to their liking, would quickly restore efficiency into the system.

The second element in this conservative restructuring was not new. Indeed, it was the old style Conservatism often associated with even more extreme forces of reaction. Its supporters wanted to interfere with the market. This was seen as sometimes essential in order to maintain the greater values of social order and national sovereignty. In respect of diversity, where the workings of a free market might encourage temporary in-migration in order to keep wages down, this strand of conservatism wished for ever stronger immigration controls to keep "visible" minorities from entering the country. Many went even further, encouraging the "repatriation" of those already here, whether British black or immigrant; indeed, they made little or no distinction between the two groups. If this group within the Conservative party had an educational policy, it was one that centred around the defence of white English culture and the need for an educational policy that promoted its ascendency and reinforced assimilation into this culture.

For much of the 1960s and 1970s, the educational views of this element were seldom considered outside of the narrow confines of the group concerned. However, they gained wider support within the Conservative administration, and the mass media, as the right wing counter to what was increasingly being seen as the "loony left."

In education, their particular ire was directed at anti-racist education, particularly as espoused by Labour controlled Local Education Authorities such as the ILEA and the London Boroughs of Brent and Haringey. Interestingly, these Authorities policies on gender were seen as equally threatening to all those values which the English held dear, or so they thought. Policies relating to gays and lesbians were seen by this group, with the enthusiastic and prurient support of a significant proportion of the national press, as being intended to turn all children into gays and lesbians. As the Hillgate Group asserted, in a document that clearly influenced the 1988 Education Act, there was a real worry that "traditional" values were being destroyed with schools, "preaching on behalf of homosexuality, sexual license and social indiscipline . . ." (Hillgate, 1986:4).

On religious matters, they were slightly more tolerant, perhaps because they recognized similar reactionary tendencies in certain elements within the range of religious faiths which were now such a feature of British inner city schools. However, religious tolerance went against the spirit of assimilation, and their tolerance was seldom more than provisional, as the 1988 Education Act showed.

The third strand is, in many ways, in conflict with this traditional right wing element of conservative thinking. This final strand is also interesting in that its proponents are not just in the Conservative party. This strand is meritocratic, and is based on the assumption that if the race is fair, the losers deserve to lose and the winners deserve all the prizes. To this group, tradition is worthless unless it supports efficiency, modernization and the development of a meritocracy. Such a meritocracy is not egalitarian but within it, people, and by implication, school children, get their just desserts.

Clearly, there is much in common with the market-led strand of thinking, although the two groups differ markedly on the question of the degree to which government should intervene in the process. In education, it means that nothing is to be left unquestioned if it cannot demonstrate its contribution to the economic growth of the society. Given the innate conservatism that most education systems embody, this perspective is enthusiastic about root and branch reform. In the early 1980s, this strand of thought had begun to remove huge areas of educational activity away from the Department of Education and Science and also away from schools, as the huge expansion of vocational education and training (partly induced by political worries about the high levels of youth unemployment, was initiated and run from a rival ministry, the Department of Trade and Industry.)

Opposition to these dynamic new elements in Conservative educational thinking was belated and often equally disastrous. There was a demand to return to, or perhaps more accurately, stick with the educational consensual policies of the 1960s and 1970s, with their stress on relevance, mixed ability teaching and the value of the non-selective comprehensive secondary school. As this system had not worked for many minority school students, it was not a strategy likely to gain a high level of their support. However, it must be borne in mind that earlier, alternative strategies had even less to offer, with nostalgia for grammar schools disguising the fact that they had never really been a significant instrument for working class social mobility and would most likely have offered very little to minority communities, both in terms of access and outcome. And when the electorate returned a Conservative government with an even bigger majority in 1987 which quickly moved to attack this consensus, there was little specific minority protest. Subsequent opposition policy was to move away from the consensus as well, toward what might be thought of as a more social democratic educational model, in the hope of capturing the middle ground of educational politics, still seen as one of the keystones of electoral victory. Whether this policy works will be decided in the General Election, likely to be held in 1992. In the meantime, the schooling system grapples with the details of the new Education Act, and has little time to assess alternative strategies, even if they existed.

This has consequently meant that the movement back to social policies based on assimilation has largely gone unchallenged, given the electoral unpopularity of pluralism within England. It has also meant that when the Government introduced the Education Reform Bill in 1987, incorporating much of the educational thinking that had emerged within the Conservative party over nearly a decade in office, the opposition to the Bill was often ill organized and inefficient.

The consequence is an Education Act which is likely to do little to enhance the educational aspirations of minority parents and pupils. The introduction of inherently unfair market forces into education will very likely parallel and ultimately strengthen those forces outside which maintain many minority group adults in unemployment or poorly paid work. The return to "traditional" (that is, English white male middle-class) values within the curriculum will further alienate many children from their schooling. Worse, if successful, it will alienate them from their own communities as they attempt to assimilate into a society which does not want them and into an epistemological system in which they have no place or voice. And if the changes in the education system are seen as making it more meritocratic, failure within it will bring about even greater stigmatization than there is at present. Finally, it could be argued that these changes contain within them an implicit espousal of assimilation, which, if accurate, is likely to continue and deepen current educational inequalities.

The details of the Act are too great an area for explication here. However, there is an evolving literature (Jones, 1989; Bash & Coulby, 1989) which details the consequences for education of this shift in political and educational thinking that has taken place over the last decade. It is, of course, not unique to Britain, and as elsewhere, the initiatives that have resulted from it, although currently engaging the concern of all who work in education in Britain, are just as likely to appear in a further decade's time as marking the ending of a process of change rather than a beginning. If the concept of an oscillating polarity has value, the need is therefore to identify those factors that might lead to this change, that is, that pluralism returning to the British educational agenda. To do this, there is a need to examine Britain's developing relations with its European partners, for they suggest one possible route for such a change.

To do this, one must relook at some recent European history. In January, 1848, in Palermo in Italy, the people came onto the streets to protest against the incompetence of their ruler, Ferdinand II of Naples. In the months that followed, the demonstrations spread across Italy and by the end of the year, few parts of Europe had not been shaken by rebellion, revolution or protest. In France, the Second Republic had been established, in Austria-Hungary, Metternich was forced out of office, while in Britain, the activities of the Chartists made fear of revolution a major concern of government. (1848 also saw the publication of the *Communist Manifesto*.) A primary focus of this continental revolution was national aspirations faced with inflexible and conservative authoritarianism. Yet by 1849, counter-revolutions had regained for the authoritarians much of the power lost in 1848. The very speed of the changes had been too great for permanence.

Nineteen eighty-nine will go down in the history books in a very similar way to 1848. Hopefully, there has as yet been no equivalent to 1849. What perhaps links 1848 with 1989, however, is the extraordinary power of nationalism within the European context, the powerful emotions that such nationalism can engender and the dramatic speed with which its message travels.

Thus, as England moves toward a narrow exclusivist definition of the British nation, events within the Soviet Union, Eastern Europe and the European Community appear to be moving in an opposite direction, pulling Britain, willy-nilly, in their footsteps. The moves within Britain and other European Community states toward greater economic and even political unity, for example, pose further questions to add to those raised in the previous sections and indeed act as a counter to those aspects of current British educational policy that appear to encourage a flattening assimilationist perspective and practice. This is because issues of nationality and nationalism which pose very real questions for all shades of political and educational opinion within the Community are increasingly seen by national governments as being best resolved by a much greater plurality within, as well as between, the nation states that make it up.

Britain has always hoped that certain **between** nation state issues could be resolved through the mechanisms of the Community, for example those relating to Spain and Gibraltar and Northern Ireland and the Republic of Ireland. What Britain, or at least its current Government is loath to accept, is a plurality **within** the nation state, whether that be meeting the aspirations of the Scots in Scotland or the British Afro-Caribbeans in England. Indeed, they take some comfort for this view as the events in Eastern Europe unfold themselves, seeing them as a reaffirmation of nation state singularity.

In educational terms, however, dramatic recent events do little to change the assimilationist tendencies enshrined in the 1988 Education Act, although the long term consequences of such events will very likely be profound. Indeed, much current argument within the European Community over education still centres on the legality of Community involvement in educational work in the first place, as it is a power reserved to the nation states by the original Treaty of Rome. However, it has been a concern with the educational fate of migrants and other minorities across Europe that has frequently kept the educational debate within the Community alive and flourishing, even when the debate has to be conducted without too much overt reference to formal schooling.

As an example of the value of such a debate, concern about language within the Community has meant a series of legally binding European Community Directives about language and the language rights (including educational entitlements) of minorities that move in a counter direction to that which the British Government would wish to go. Market forces and the neutrality of the meritocracy are not seen as being enough to match the linguistic and associated educational aspirations of migrants and other national minorities.

Indeed, much of the blame for current educational inadequacies in relation to these groups is seen as being caused by inadequate national governmental responses. These national inadequacies have been documented over a long period, (Gundara, Jones & Kimberley, 1982) and this has helped to ensure that a counterbalancing debate is held in opposition to that espoused with the British nation state. Most recently, a vast initiative for language teaching, the Lingua Project, was bitterly opposed by Britain on the grounds that it dealt with education.[12] Although the British view was very likely technically correct, the project had the enthusiastic backing of other states and has been adopted. Its implementation will hopefully help to support those in Britain who seek to ensure that the issue of linguistic plurality and the educational needs of bilingual learners will remain alive within mainstream educational debate in Britain.

Perhaps most importantly of all however, is not an educational debate at all but one about the nature of the new European society that is emerging as the Community moves toward greater economic and political union. The assimilationist ideology of the British nation state, seemingly gaining power within British education as the new Education Act is implemented, is widely decried by our Community partners as being outmoded and unrealistic. And that debate is no longer one that remains unheard by the British electorate as their world view increasingly becomes one that is shaped within a Community context.

Some consequences of this change are already apparent. The "Eurospeak" phrase for pluralistic initiatives in relation to education, "intercultural education" (Batelaan, 1983; Jones & Kimberley, 1986; Jones & Kimberley, 1990) has enabled educationists across the community and within the wider European context that is supported by the Council of Europe, to exchange concepts, contexts and practice within an agreed and accepted common frame of reference. This potential for development and change extends beyond educationists. Minorities, for example the Romany, have made new groupings that transcend national boundaries, giving them the potential to make more effective interventions both at the national and the European levels. It also has the potential to enable minorities to gain a platform in their own right, avoiding, if they wish, the device of using the nation state of origin as their sponsor.

Thus, a new world is called into being, as it were, to counter the old. As educational policy in Britain moves in the direction of assimilation, Europe helps support those forces within British education who desire a more pluralistic perspective. To predict the outcome of this debate is beyond the scope of this chapter. Its prospect does, however, provide us with an opportunity to end on a modestly optimistic note.

Notes

1. This chapter is a development of work currently being undertaken by the Centre for Multicultural Education, University of London. We are grateful to Keith Kimberley and Paul Whelan for their helpful comments.

2. The words Britain, England and the United Kingdom refer to different national entities. As discussed later in the chapter, the problem is that the English conflate the terms, ignoring the existence of not just the Welsh, Scottish and Irish nationalities within the United Kingdom, but also other non-territorial British groups such as Afro-Caribbeans.

3. This is done to clarify the subsequent educational analysis, rather than to constrain it through pre-specification.

4. By the term "predatory," we imply the manner in which the modern nation state has developed through time by the incorporation of other territorial groups. Examples of this would be the French nation state and the Bretons, and the English nation state and the Welsh. However, these modern examples are based on earlier often forgotten annexations, for example, the Friesians in the Netherlands.

5. This problem is of course not confined to France. Currently, for example, there is a fierce debate within Italy about the need to strengthen immigration controls and to police them more effectively.

6. The plural used is deliberate, as the marginalization is not solely the province of one dominant elite.

7. This is not to argue for this form of stratification as being the sole factor in inequalities within society. Class/status and gender are clearly equally important areas for analysis.

8. Recent cases in Britain where parents have wished to move their children from multiracial to monoracial (white) schools are not breaking Britain's Race Relations Act, according to the Department of Education and Science. This however, may have to be tested in the courts before the issue is finally clarified.

9. It is important to note here that if the minority community itself sets up a separate school, as is beginning to happen in Britain, a different set of outcomes may occur.

10. See, for example, the case studies in Castells, M. (1983), *The City and the Grassroots*. London: Arnold.

11. Of course, it could be argued that some of the writing in the area has been excessively and unhelpfully theoretical.

12. The recent key debate about this ambitious and expensive (200 million ECU) program, was approved by the EC Education Council in May 1988 only after prolonged and acrimonious debate about the right of the EC to be involved in schools. For details of the actual LINGUA program, c.f. *Eurydice Info*, No. 8, December 1989.

References

Bash, L. & Coulby, D. (1989). *The Education Reform Act: Competition and Control*. London: Cassell.

Batelaan, P. (1983). *The Practice of Intercultural Education*. London: Commission for Racial Equality.

Castells, M. (1983). *The City and the Grassroots*. London: Arnold.

Department of Education and Science (DES). (1985). *Education For All (The Swann Report)*. London: HMSO.

Gundara, J., Jones, C. & Kimberley, K. (1982). *The Marginalization and Pauperization of the Second Generation of Migrants in France, the Federal Republic of Germany and Great Britain, Relating to the Education of the Children of Migrants*. (Final Report and three National Case Studies). Brussels: Commission of the European Communities.

Hans, N. (1949). *Comparative Education*. London: Routledge.

Habermas, J. (1976). *The Legitimation Crisis*. London: Heinemann.

Hechter, M. (1975). *Internal Colonialism: The Celtic Fringe in British National Development*. Berkeley: University of California Press.

Hillgate Group. (1986). *Whose School? A Radical Manifesto*. London: The Hillgate Group.

Inner London Education Authority (ILEA). (1983). *Race, Sex and Class*. London: ILEA.

Jones C. & Kimberley, K. (1990). *Intercultural Perspectives on the National Curriculum for England and Wales*. London: Centre for Multicultural Education, Institute for Education.

Jones, C. & Kimberley, K. (eds.). (1986). *Intercultural Education: Concept, Context, Curriculum*. Strasbourg: Council of Europe.

Jones, K. (1989). *Right Turn: The Conservative Revolution in Education*. London: Hutchinson.

Lawton, D. (ed.). (1989). *The Education Reform Act: Choice and Control*. London: Hodder & Stoughton.

Llewellyn, H. (1989). "Speaker expels Basque deputies." *The Independent*, 5 December, 1989.

Lukes, S. (1974). *Power: A Radical View*. London: Macmillan.

Marnham, P. (1989). "French extremists gain from hostility towards Muslims." *The Independent*, 5 December, 1989.

Saunders, P. (1980). *Urban Politics*. Harmondsworth: Penguin.

Scruton, R. (1982). "Thinkers of the Left: E.P. Thompson." *Salisbury Review* 1, Autumn, 1982.

Street-Porter, R. (1976). *Race, Children and Cities*. Milton Keynes: Open University Press.

Tower Hamlets, London Borough of. (1988). *Tower Hamlets Education: Getting it Right. Draft Development Plan*. London: London Borough of Tower Hamlets.

Walzer, M. (1982). "Pluralism in political perspective." In Walzer et al. *The Politics of Ethnicity*. Cambridge Mass.: Belknap Press/Harvard University Press.

Walzer, M. et al. (1982). *The Politics of Ethnicity*. Cambridge, Mass.: Belknap Press/Harvard University Press.

The State of Multicultural Education in the United States

Geneva Gay

Multicultural education is surviving but not flourishing in the United States. The 1980s did not create an environment or climate highly conducive to its ideals and goals. Public policy concerns concentrated on economic and political constraints; social conservatism marked the ideological tenor of the times; educational excellence was equated with achieving higher levels of cognitive knowledge as measured by standardized test scores; and electronic technology enthralled virtually everyone. Issues fundamental to multicultural education were conspicuously absent from the mainstream proposals of this so-called era of educational excellence. It emphasized content mastery in academic subjects, quantitative criteria of achievement, and the homogenization of standards of educational performance. Affective skills, such as values analysis, awareness of and respect for cultural pluralism, the celebration of human diversity, and educational equity were largely ignored. Even when concerns for globalism and internationalizing the curriculum began to appear late in the decade their potential linkages with multicultural education were not made.

Despite an appealing rhetoric of progress and substantive reform the programmatic and ideological emphases of educational developments in the United States in the 1980s were, in actuality, a de facto policy of containment and regimentation. The most telling symbol of this focus was the rallying cry for "back to the basics." It meant perpetuating a status quo orientation that was highly selective with respect to advocating academically able students, less freedom for students in academic choices, and training for the job market. Conversely, the basic premises and purposes of multicultural education are designed to maximize individual choice and flexibility, academic freedom, human diversity, and personal liberation and empowerment. Thus, most of the 1980s remedies for educational problems in the United States fit "the regressive [societal] tenor of the times — more traditional courses, more mechanical testing, a lust for 'excellence,' and a token glance at equality" (Shor, 1983:407).

Many of these conditions continue in full force as the 1990s begin, and are joined by a new challenge. This is the recent attack launched against multicultural education by some conservative scholars, who are getting a lot of play in the national media. They falsely accuse multicultural education of replacing scholarship with interest group propagandizing, balkanizing the country, ignoring the existence of a mainstream culture, attempting to replace national culture with ethnic minority cultures, politicizing the curriculum, and trying to impose particularistic ethnic viewpoints on all education. Illustrative of this opposition is the scathing criticism of "A Curriculum of Inclusion," a 1989 report produced by a New York State Task Force on Minorities. One critic, Gerald Sirkin (a retired professor of economics), published a statement in the *Wall Street Journal* on January 18, 1990. He distorted the report's recommendation for school curricula to stop equating United States heritage with Eurocentric origins only and include more information about people of color, as a call for Western culture to be supplanted by the cultures of African Americans, Hispanics, Asian Americans and American Indians.

Together these forces make the prospect of incorporating multicultural issues easily into all educational programs, policies and practices rather dubious. Yet, there are some developments underway in the United States which reaffirm the need for, and offer a new lease on life for multicultural education. These include major changes in societal and school demographics, the shifting balance of economic and political alliances in the nation and world, and changing directions in school reform priorities and proposals. A thorough understanding of the state of multicultural education in the United States requires an assessment of it within the context of these sociopolitical developments.

Analytical Framework

A dialectic or interactive relationship exists between schools, society and politics; between the time, place and circumstance of society and the educational process. Because "schooling and its consequences cannot be separated from other aspects of society" (Kimball, 1974:272) they must be examined and understood within the cultural and political context of a given social system. Theodore Brameld (1957) argues that education derives its meaning and energy from the environment of people and things. It is able to affect that environment only to the extent that the conditions and resources necessary for influence are readily available to it. Natural, social and human environments are the prime conditioners of education's reason for being, creative potentials, tools and materials, and practical limitations. Therefore, "if we are ever to come to grips with . . . the most persistent problems that confront education in our 'time of trouble' we shall first have to come to grips with pervasive problems . . . of the [cultural] environment" (Brameld, 1957:5-6).

Brameld also describes education as being always normative, which is the source of some of the most perplexing tasks confronting school reform. That is, schools must face their problems in the "marketplace of values where . . . the traffic of education and of culture meet and intermingle" (Brameld, 1957:13). Shinn's (1972) point of view is similar to Kimball and Brameld. He contends that because schools do not exist in isolation from the larger society there is a constant and engaging interplay between the sociopolitical climate and culture of the community and what goes on in schools. Shor (1983:407) is even more graphic in his declaration that "economics, community life and literacy, commercial mass culture and political action outside the classroom grossly influence the fate of education."

These perceptions tell us that the structure and content of any system of education, and all of its component parts, are influenced directly by what is happening in the broader society at any given point in time. This means that developments in multicultural education need to be examined within the context of different environmental settings, political climates and social/cultural systems. Thus, the movement in the United States has some structural contours, substantive aspects and "personality traits" that are quite different from similar developments in Canada, various European nations, England and Australia. As a result, discussions about multicultural education are more meaningful when they are informed by socio-ecological or contextual analyses. Consistent with this orientation, the current state of multicultural education in the United States will be discussed here within the context of the social, political and economic developments which occurred or crystallized in the 1980s.

Another common characteristic of educational innovations that has major implications for understanding the state of multicultural education in the United States is the tension between theory and practice. Ideally, these two forces should complement each other, but they are often disparate, even contradictory in actuality, if not in intent. One frequently outpaces the other. This is the case with multicultural education. As a result, it is virtually impossible to generalize developments across both theory and practice. To compensate for this chasm, the state of multicultural education theory and practice are discussed separately.

Societal Traits and Trends

Cultural pluralism, the sociological concept upon which multicultural education is grounded, is still not accepted unequivocally as a real, desirable and enriching reality in mainstream United States society and schools. Many policy makers, school leaders and funding agencies continue to ascribe to the mistaken notion that the United States is a melting pot in fact or desire. They believe that the only way for schools to deal with cultural diversity is to expedite assimilation into mainstream society by teaching the same things in the same ways to all students. Racial, ethnic, economic, social and linguistic backgrounds are of no consequence in the educational process. To these skeptics the study of cultural diversity overshadows human commonalities, ideals of democracy, and the presence of a national culture, and jeopardizes national unity. Any ideas or actions which challenge these premises (as multicultural education does) are suspect, and do not fare very well in ideological endorsements or funding allocations.

Because of these beliefs held by significant power brokers and percentages of the population the struggle over the legitimacy, appropriateness, and functions of multicultural education in the United States persists. A tendency prevails among many educators and lay citizens to equate cultural differences with racial inferiorities, and to assume that multicultural education is in conflict with high quality general education. These misconceptions lead them to resist multicultural education for fear that it will cause racial tensions and compromise educational standards.

Even some individuals who claim to be proponents of multicultural education misunderstand some of its most fundamental tenets. They think of it as a "racial minority thing," designed to serve the needs of only a select group of students. As such it is treated as a peripheral issue, an afterthought, an appendage, worthy of consideration only when there are large numbers of minimally-performing racial minorities present, or in school environments where there are racial tensions. Thus, attention to cultural pluralism in the United States is too often reserved for crisis interventions, instead of being a routine occurrence in the daily educational experiences of all students.

The culture of the United States is strongly crisis-oriented, and is driven by a "quick fix" mentality. The education system mirrors these orientations in its tendency to be voguish, to respond to those issues that have the loudest, most strident advocacy voices and political clout; and to jump quickly from one fashionable bandwagon to another. Multicultural education and ethnic pluralism were neither in vogue nor the centre of major political crisis in the 1980s. The strident political protests and demands from oppressed ethnic groups which initiated its inception in the late 1960s and early 1970s were largely silent, and replaced in the political spotlight by other issues. Among these were Japan's challenge to the United States dominance of the world's marketplace; the glamour and mystique of computers and other electronic technology; declining test scores of academic achievement; the AIDS crisis and drug abuse; concerns for restructuring schools; and a strong resurgence of neo-isolationist nationalism. The desire for quick and quantifiable, guaranteed solutions to complex social problems have led Americans to demand short-term educational investments, and easily recognizable proof of progress. The intrinsic nature of multicultural education is the diametric opposite of these. It is affective, qualitative, requires long-term investments, and its effects are not easily translated into standardized test scores.

Shifting demographic trends in the society and schools of the United States indicate that the actual numbers and ratios of people of color are growing exponentially to whites. This growth is due to a number of factors, including birth rates, the overall youth of racial minorities and increased immigration from non-white, non-Western, non-European countries. In its April 9, 1990 cover story "Beyond the melting pot," *Time* dubbed this trend "the browning of America." The author of the article explains that:

> Already 1 American in 4 defines himself or herself as Hispanic or nonwhite. If the current trends in immigration and birth rates persist, the Hispanic population will have further increased an estimated 21 percent, the Asian presence about 22 percent, blacks almost 12 percent and whites a little less than 2 percent when the 20th century ends. By 2020 . . . the number of U.S. residents who are Hispanic or nonwhite will have more than doubled, to nearly 115 million, while the white population will not be increasing at all. By 2056 . . . the 'average' U.S. resident . . . will trace his or her descent to Africa, Asia, the Hispanic world, the Pacific Islands, Arabia — almost anywhere but white Europe (Henry, 1990:28).

An America beyond the melting pot among school-age populations already exists in many parts of the United States. This is particularly notable in coastal states and major metropolitan areas. For example,

> In New York state some 40 percent of elementary and secondary children belong to an ethnic minority. Within a decade, the proportion is expected to approach 50 percent. In California . . . Hispanics . . . account for 31.4 percent of public school enrollment, blacks add 8.9 percent, and Asians and others amount to 11 percent — for a nonwhite total of 41.5 percent . . . Some 12 000 Hmong refugees from Laos have settled in St. Paul. At some Atlanta low-rent apartment complexes that used to be virtually all black, social workers today need to speak Spanish . . . The Detroit area has 200 000 people of Middle Eastern descent (Henry, 1990:28-29).

These population trends have many implications for multicultural education. Two of these are especially noteworthy. One is nested in the shifting numerical ratios and distributions of ethnics in the population. The other is grounded in attitudes about cultural diversity, and the principles of democratic policy making and problem solving. Members of the currently dominant racial and ethnic group in the United States may be threatened by the impending loss of their numerical advantage, power and influence. Added to these concerns are suspicions of and prejudices toward the "unknown," which are bred by ethnic and cultural ignorance and isolation. As James Banks has asserted on numerous occasions, most people in the United States live in ethnic enclaves, and they tend to fear, devalue, or suspect others who reside outside their own isolated geographic, experiential, valuative, cultural and/or ideological communities.

In his article, "Beyond the Melting Pot," William Henry (1990) proposes that changing ethnic demographics will have major impacts on politics, education and economics in the United States. A truly multicultural and multiracial society will be harder to govern because of difficulties in forming and maintaining functional political coalitions. Tensions among groups may accelerate because of competition for jobs, housing and other limited resources. The debate over what the outcomes, content and processes of education should be, and the place of ethnic and cultural pluralism in these, will become even more complex than it is now. However important and challenging these issues are, Henry feels an even greater one has to do with the effects of becoming a majority non-white country will have on the nation's psyche, individuals' personal sense of self and new definitions of what it means to be American. He projects that,

> . . . citizens will feel an even greater need to debate where the nation's successes sprang from and what its unalterable beliefs are . . . which myths and icons to evoke in education, in popular culture, in ceremonial speech-making . . . which is the more desirable heroism . . . (Henry, 1990:31).

A second significant implication of the browning of the United States is how the democratic principles on which the country itself is founded will be interpreted. If the dominate group sets the cultural standards of the country, then what is "normative" in the society with respect to majority rule, negotiated conflict resolution and representative democracy, will need to change radically. It most certainly could not continue to be Eurocentric, necessarily grounded in a Western ideology, or even determined by a single group. Instead, the normative model American may be more Eastern in outlook, and culturally eclectic — encompassing a confluence of cultural inputs. There are preliminary indications that some educators are beginning to recognize and respond to the political, philosophical and pedagogical ramifications of changing ethnic demographics.

Developments around the world are causing some Americans to reconsider their country's traditional role of dominance and unquestionable leadership in international affairs, a position that they have long thought to be infinitely invincible. They also are implanting in America's consciousness peoples and parts of the world that it hardly knew existed, or thought inconsequential. Many of these have cultures, values and worldviews that are quite different from what the United States is accustomed to. Some of these changes include Japan's economic and technological might which is challenging the dominance of the United States in the world marketplace; the increasing rate and magnitude of foreign investments in the country; the crumbling of the communistic bloc throughout Eastern Europe; unprecedented dialogues with the USSR on critical global concerns; the relative ease with which strident political rivalries are set aside, albeit temporarily, in the face of catastrophes, such as the nuclear plant explosion at Chernobyl and recent earthquakes in Armenia and Iran; the reunification of Germany; overtures of the de Klerk administration in South Africa toward relaxing its apartheid policy; and the escalation of tensions in the Middle East. The intimate involvement of the United States in these world affairs extend the contextual parameters of multicultural education to global dimensions.

The resurgence of blatant acts of racism, sexism and classism which took place throughout the United States during the 1980s also attest to the need for multicultural education in schools. The fact that these were particularly graphic at some of the most prestigious colleges and universities mean they cannot be easily dismissed as isolated acts of ignorance by individuals living on the fringes of society. Other evidence of persistent racial discrimination and social injustices are apparent in employment patterns; disparities in educational opportunities and outcomes; the retreat of state and national governments from support of social programs and civil rights legislation; the growth of racial purist groups such as the skinheads, neo-Nazis and White Aryan Resistance; and the return to gender exploitation and ethnic stereotyping in popular culture. Mass media advertising, television programs and commercial cinema are especially illuminating on the latter trend.

Simultaneously, American society witnessed several culturally different, but ironic, "firsts." African Americans, Asian Americans and handicapped individuals were finalists and winners in the "coveted" Miss America and Miss USA beauty pageants. A major African American actor who was once ostracized by the entertainment industry for his "militant" politics and campaigns against racism in Hollywood was nominated to receive an Academy Award for portraying a traditional subservient role. A person who was known to have once been an active member of the Ku Klux Klan was elected to a major state government office.

The ease with which these ironies occurred without any public outcry of either celebration or opposition suggest a society of contradictions and transitions with respect to cultural pluralism. The relative silence of the majority toward them may be indicative of political apathy and a lack of social consciousness. In the midst of this environment, multicultural education struggled to prevail. In many ways its theoretical dimensions went counter to social trends, while its practice was congruent with and reflective of the political times and sociocultural context.

Developments in Theory

Both qualitative and quantitative growth occurred in multicultural education theory during the 1980s. The qualitative features are most apparent in the ideological grounding that scholars use to explain the meanings, messages, missions and effects of multicultural education. They can be gleaned from the writings of a relatively small group of academicians who have been active in the movement most of the time since its inception about 20 years ago. The quantitative growth is due largely to the expanding range of referent groups and substantive concepts that have been added to the parameters of the field. What began initially as an endeavor to include the cultural heritages, life experiences and contributions of and combat discrimination against ethnic groups of color in school curricula, has been expanded by many educators to several other categories of diversity. These are gender, national origin, social class, first language, handicapping conditions and intellectual ability. Significant increases in the actual numbers of consumers, funding levels and programmatic implementations are not attributes of this quantitative growth. In fact, on these dimensions, the 1980s was a decade of major decline for multicultural education in the United States.

Another indicator of advancements in theoretical developments is the conceptual maturity which has emerged in scholarly discourse about the educational implications of cultural diversity. The way proponents talk about the definitional components, substantive content, intrinsic and instrumental value, operational strategies, relationship with general principles of learning and even politicizing the pedagogy of multicultural education convey greater depth of analysis, clarity of meaning and power of persuasion. Advocates are devoting more attention to establishing conceptual, philosophical and logical connections between multicultural education and other educational values and priorities. This is a significant departure from prior efforts which tended to argue the need for and legitimacy of studying cultural diversity solely on their own inherent merits. Theoretical linkages are now being made to current prominent concerns in the United States such as academic excellence, at-riskness, effective schooling, restructuring schools and equity in educational opportunities.

Over time there has also been a gradual shift in the scholarship of the field from "what is multicultural education" and "why it is important," to "how multicultural education can and should be implemented." This emphasis encompasses both substantive and methodological issues, has more of a process than product orientation, and applies more metacognitive and analytical skills than mechanical and technical ones. Increasingly, attention to isolated sample lessons or units on cultural diversity is being replaced with efforts to place multiculturalism into the broader structural contexts and ideational canons of American education. Rather than telling teachers exactly what to do in the classroom, multicultural education scholars are providing conceptual paradigms for determining how to make better decisions that are more responsive to cultural pluralism at all levels of the educational enterprise. Thus, compendia of instructional strategies, learning activities, materials and resources are supplanted by analyses of the structural, environmental and procedural routines of habitual schooling operations to determine how they are discriminatory to culturally different students. The results constitute the bases for deciding what reform interventions are appropriate for multi-culturalizing the educational process. They represent a paradigmatic shift in understanding the implications of cultural pluralism for schooling which leads to the personal empowerment of teachers with respect to multicultural decision making. The new paradigms question the validity of the "environmental deficiency" and "individual responsibility" explanations of the school failure of mass numbers of culturally different students and proposes "situational competency" and "incompatibilities between home and school culture" models. These analyses use social science concepts, content and techniques to explain, on a deeper level, the meaning of some commonly accepted principles of multicultural education such as it must be systemic, interdisciplinary, comprehensive and integrative. That is why when Young Pai (1984:7) contends that "to reject or demean a person's cultural heritage is to do psychological and moral violence to the dignity and worth of that individual," George Spindler (1987) proposes the resolution of cultural incompatibilities as the means to school success for culturally different students, and Solon Kimball (1974) declares that learning is as much a function of cultural conditioning and expectations as innate intellectual capabilities, their arguments are so powerful and enticing. The content and style of these analyses and explanations represent a significant growth in the conceptual maturity of multicultural education theory.

Another indication of this paradigmatic shift is the frequency with which questions about how to implement multicultural education are answered with conceptual suggestions for curriculum **inclusion, incorporation** and **mainstreaming**, and employing culturally diverse perspectives in common educational experiences. Evidence of it can be gleaned from comparing the content and tone of handbooks and activity guides such as Tiedt & Tiedt (1990) *Multicultural Teaching* with the more conceptual issue analyses found in Banks & Banks (1989) *Multicultural Education: Issues and Perspectives* and Sleeter & Grant (1988) *Making Choices for Multicultural Education*. A third sign is the increasing importance given to contextualism in theoretical discourse about multicultural education. That is, tying its fundamental ideals, concepts and premises to pedagogical principles derived from social and developmental psychology, cultural and educational anthropology, learning theory, sociolinguistics, cross-cultural communications and interpersonal relations. Of particular importance are ideas about educational decision making within the context of sociocultural realities; the confluence of cultures in American society and schools; and the dialectical interaction between cognition and culture, ethnicity and education, and schooling and society. In a 1989 speech at Purdue University, Henry Cisneros, former mayor of San Antonio, Texas, made some well-crafted and powerfully astute arguments for multicultural education as an imperative to the economic survival of the United States. Invariably, the intent of making these connections is to demonstrate, through conceptual analysis and logical deduction, the reconstructive and transformative potential of multicultural education for both schooling and society. The reasoning technique may be called "pedagogical bonding" in that it explicates the common ties between issues and principles of cultural pluralism, multicultural education, general pedagogy and learning theory.

These developments suggest the emergence of a true theory of multicultural education. An educational theory is the integration of ideas from many different disciplines into a coherent system of thought to explain relationships among various phenomena. They illustrate the fundamentally interdisciplinary nature of multicultural education. It is dependent upon a confluence — a synergy — of concepts, principles and procedures, from many different disciplines for its ideological, organizational, substantive and operational guidance.

Broadening definitional parameters of multicultural education by expanding the referent groups to be included is also part of its theoretical development. Whereas social, political, economic and educational disadvantages attributable to **racial identity** and **related oppression** were the driving forces of the initial conceptions of multicultural education, more varied bases of oppression are evoked in contemporary dialogues about diversity. They include gender, age, handicapping conditions, social class, religion, national origin, global location and regionality. Reasons given for these inclusions are strongly influenced by sociological analyses, and appeals to shared bonds of social and educational exclusion of discrimination; interdependence of their social destiny; and the potential strength embedded in a confluence of concerns and coalitions of actions across all oppressed groups. Some scholars contend that culture and ethnicity are overemphasized, and that the focus should be structural inequalities in society affecting all oppressed people, such as powerlessness, unequal distribution of resources, poverty and undereducation. They argue that sexism, racism, classism and ethnicity cannot be fully understood or resolved by treating them as separate phenomena, affecting each of the victimized groups in isolation. In fact, they are closely interrelated with each other, and the structure and culture of mainstream society in the United States (Suzuki, 1984; Sleeter & Grant, 1988).

Gollnick & Chinn (1983) believe cultural identity is based as much on socioeconomic level, religion and gender as ethnic group membership and identification. Therefore, their conception of multicultural education includes understanding such key concepts as racism, sexism, prejudice, discrimination, oppression, power and equality. Among its critical components are ethnic studies, minority studies, bilingual education, women's studies, cultural awareness, human relations, values clarification and urban education. In a recently edited publication, Banks & Banks (1989) also endorse a comprehensive approach to multicultural education. However, while incorporating many of the same content issues, they define and justify it somewhat differently. They view responsiveness to national origins, religion, gender, social class and ability group characteristics within the purview of multicultural education as a complement, not a replacement, to more specialized studies of ethnic and cultural groups. All are essential to understanding the complexity of cultural diversity in the United States and the world.

The all-inclusive conceptions of multicultural education appear to be consistent with three of its major underlying principles. These are greater personal liberation and social justice for all groups; the celebration of human diversity in the educational process; and the centrality of multifaceted cultural pluralism in the historical, social and cultural development of the United States. It may even be politically expedient and timely, but it is also pedagogically problematic. How can school practitioners manage all of these constituent groups and issues under one conceptual framework with the depth and integrity that each deserves? This is not to suggest that social and educational disparities associated with gender, class, handicappism and language are not unconscionable and should not be remediated. The question is how much can be included under the rubric of multicultural education without the concept losing its focus. An all-inclusive approach may inadvertently cause attention to be distracted from those deep-seated, troublesome issues and effects of the racist legacy in the United States. A second danger is that it may give skeptics too many convenient excuses and opportunities to perpetuate the status quo. Conceivably, local education agencies could claim that their programs for physically disabled students or the gifted and talented simultaneously meet the obligation to do multicultural education. A third caveat is that the substantive focus may emphasize oppression to the exclusion of other elements of **cultural** diversity. Throughout multicultural education theory there is consensus that the "culture" of different groups should be included in educational programs. Although there is not universal agreement on what culture is, some common characteristics do exist. It is difficult to concede that some of the groups embraced in the all-inclusive approach to multicultural education constitute a culture according to the conventions accepted by even the most liberal scholars of culture.

Where in the educational process should multicultural education be included? This question has also generated quite a lot of thought. The various responses and related reasons given indicate developmental growth in the theory of education for and about cultural diversity. Invariably, in recent discourse, the suggestion is that multicultural education should be systematically integrated, incorporated, infused and/or mainstreamed into the entire educational enterprise. The appeal is multicultural education for all students in all subjects at all grade levels. This idea has been a part of the dialogue among a few theorists for some time now, but has only recently become the popular password of virtually all proponents, including even the most noviatiate.

The theoretical notion of multicultural education infusion is a powerful idea and worthy goal, as are the explanations attesting to its desirability. However, they lack sufficient guidance in how to translate the idea of infusion into actual practice. As a result, this powerful conceptual principle may be merely appealing rhetoric that becomes a facade for doing nothing, or doing something entirely different. It sounds politically conciliatory, pedagogically desirable, and even easy to do. The former may be true but the latter certainly is not. In fact, multicultural education integration or infusion is a sophisticated theoretical construct that can be rather challenging to operationalize in practice. As Hilda Hernandez (1989:v) suggests, "incorporating multicultural education in the classroom is in some ways analogous to putting together an elaborate jigsaw puzzle. Although the vision of what the final outcome should be is clear, fitting the pieces together is not always an easy task." It requires a level of knowledge, conceptual and application skill mastery that most educators simply do not have at this point in time.

Many proponents of multicultural education infusion do not challenge the fundamental organization, values and ethos of the education system in the United States. Either by oversight or intention they implicitly endorse the validity of its basic underlying premises and structures, albeit with some much needed improvements. Some other advocates are aggressively challenging the basic value assumptions as well as practice of the United States education system. These challenges are generating some new critical constructs and proposals for educational reform to achieve more genuine multiculturalism. Some of the new ideas are the social construction of knowledge; the dialectic relationship between cognition and culture, and educational quality and equality; alternative means and pathways to achieving common performance outcomes; cultural context teaching; situational competences and multiple intelligences; and educational transformation and social reconstruction. Symbolic of these shifts in focus are writings by educationists such as Bob Suzuki (1984) calling for curriculum transformation; James Banks (1989) suggesting the systemic restructuring of schooling to embrace multiculturalism; Christine Sleeter and Carl Grant (1988) proposing multicultural education for social reconstruction; and Christine Bennett (1990) and Geneva Gay (1990) declaring that multicultural education is a conduit of equity and excellence for culturally different students. Their proposals depend heavily upon the substantive content and ideological principles derived from the research by educational anthropologists (Boggs, Watson-Gegeo & McMillen, 1985; Hsu, 1969; Kimball, 1974; Spindler, 1987), sociolinguists (Cazden, John & Hymes, 1985; Hall, 1976; Kochman, 1981; Trueba, Guthie & Au, 1981) and social psychologists (Neisser, 1986; Spencer, Brookins & Allen, 1985) which document the sociocultural contextualism of teaching, learning and schooling in the United States.

All of these indicators of growth in multicultural education theory suggest that its development is due more to the quality of the ideas and arguments being presented than to the appearance of entirely new ones per se. Many of the conceptual ideas emphasized in current scholarship have been themes in multicultural discourse for some time. Whereas earlier they were largely embryonic and offered rather tentatively, they are now increasingly characterized by ideological depth, greater logical clarity and coherency and pedagogical prowess, as well as being more carefully grounded in social science constructs, and accepted principles of effective teaching and learning. Together they create a theoretical portrayal of multicultural education as a phenomenon that is, by nature, intent and content, interdisciplinary, integrative, inclusive, comprehensive, transformative, liberative, celebratory and permeative. Its goals of improving the relevance, accuracy and effectiveness of education for all students within the context of the culturally pluralistic realities of American society and the world require systemic reform of the deep structures, values and ethos of schooling. Therefore, a central theme of most current theoretical perceptions of multicultural education is its potential for revolutionizing education and, ultimately, revitalizing society.

Multicultural Education in Practice

The state of multicultural education practice is almost the inverse of theory. While there has been a strong element of sustenance and continuity in its theoretical developments, multicultural practice has tended to remain rather sporadic, fragmentary, superficial and haphazard. There are many "starts and stops," a lot of attrition and turn-overs in program priorities and leadership, to the extent that every school year seems like a new beginning in multicultural education. Many school practitioners still engage primarily in definitional, awareness and justification activities. That is, they tend to concentrate on "what is multicultural education" and "why is it important." Their instructional programming leans too much toward special events and celebrations, exotic ethnic artifacts, isolated activities or units and selected reference to heroic cultural contributions in a few subjects, especially social studies and language arts. Questions are frequently raised and skepticism expressed about whether multicultural education distracts attention away from the mastery of general basic skills and high standards of academic excellence for all students.

These attitudes and behaviors persist despite the fact that virtually every professional organization, state and local educational agency in the United States include items in their policy mandates and goal statements which have direct implications for multicultural education. The following are illustrative of these:

- One of the Indiana State Department of Education Curriculum Goals states, "Subject matter taught in public schools should prepare children for productive lives in a pluralistic and changing global society."

- The fifth item in Connecticut's Statewide Educational Goals for Students is "Understanding society's values." Part of what students are expected to do to accomplish this goal include understanding, respecting and appreciating the inherent strengths in a pluralistic society; the humanity they share with other people; the values and achievements of their own and other cultures; international issues and skills needed to participate in a global society; and learning to live and work in harmony with others.

- Michigan's goal of democratic citizenship includes developing awareness and concern for the rights and well-being of others, positive self-concepts and knowledge of and respect for one's own values, ethnic background and culture.

- The American Association for the Advancement of Science (AAAS) includes in its recommendations on the scientific literacy needed by all students seven key aspects of human society. These are cultural effects on human behavior; organization and behavior of groups; processes of social change; social trade-offs; forms of political and economic organizations; mechanisms for resolving conflict; and national and international social systems.

Little of significance happens in public education in the United States without a dependable source of financial support. This has been consistently lacking in multicultural education since the mid-1970s. The 1980s witnessed severe cutbacks in federal funding for education in general, and particularly for programs designed to expand the social justice and educational opportunities of historically oppressed groups. These fiscal casualties included ethnic heritage studies grants, bilingual education, gender equity, minority student rights initiatives and staff development for cultural diversity. What little funding that was available was placed in the category of non-differentiated "block grants" for special needs populations, such as Chapter 1 (economic disadvantage), at-risk and LEP (Limited English Proficiency) initiatives. These reductions and changes in funding formulas have produced a plethora of administrative structures and bureaucratic procedures to improve proficiency in basic skills for students who are highly prone to fail in school, without simultaneously attending to the content goals and objectives of multicultural education.

Many school practitioners continue to operate on the mistaken assumption that multicultural education is only about and for recent immigrants and people of color. Or they take the position that "we've already done that" (meaning it is not in vogue), "we don't have a need for it" (meaning there are no children of color in their schools, or there are no expressed racial hostilities among the students), and/or "they are in the United States now so they need to learn the language and adjust to the common culture." These attitudes become effective excuses for not doing anything to implement multicultural education in schools.

There were major declines across the 1980s in the visibility of multicultural education in professional communication channels most accessible to school practitioners — journals, conference presentations, textbooks and other instructional materials. A case in point are publications and programs provided by the Association for Supervision and Curriculum Development (ASCD), an organization whose membership is primarily middle level, public school administrators, who are responsible for program planning and instructional supervision. Each year ASCD produces an annual conference with more than 200 program features, approximately 100 regional curriculum study institutes, two journals (*Educational Leadership* and the *Journal of Curriculum and Supervision*), a yearbook and several monographs. It also has a growing portfolio of audio and video media products. Issues related to multicultural education have been disproportionately underrepresented and sporadic in all of ASCD's programmatic activities for the last several years. For example, in the five-year period between 1985 and 1989 *Educational Leadership* published more than 700 articles, an average of 145 across eight issues per year. Less than 30 (about four percent) of these articles were devoted to multiculturalism with people of color as the primary unit of analysis.

Another prestigious professional organization with one of the largest readerships and highest ranking status as a leader in the field of general educational thought and practice is Phi Delta Kappa. Its journal, the *Phi Delta Kappan*, is published 10 times per year. Between 1985 and 1989 the *Kappan* published approximately 570 featured articles, with a yearly average of 114. Only 38 (less than seven percent) of the total dealt with multicultural issues, such as equity, urbanity, disadvantage, tracking, gender and globalism. Again, people of color were not the focus in most of these discussions.

A significant number of the few articles on multicultural education were restricted to "special sections or editions" in the journals of both ASCD and Phi Delta Kappa, rather than being distributed across all of the thematic topics covered. Special sections in separate editions of the *Kappan* on the disadvantaged (five articles), women in school administration (five), gender in education (six) and immigrants (six) accounted for 22 of the 38 articles in the five-year period. *Educational Leadership* followed a similar pattern. For instance, 6 of the 24 articles in one 1989 issue dealt with racism.

The record of specific subject matter journals during the same period was no better than the *Kappan* and *Educational Leadership*. Between 1985-1989 *Science Teacher*, the official journal of the National Science Teachers Association (NSTA), published more than 360 articles, an average of eight per issue. Only four of these dealt with multicultural concerns — two on gender in 1985, one on minorities in 1986 and one on learning disabilities in 1988. The *English Journal* of the National Council of Teachers of English (NCTE), published approximately 545 articles during the same period. This averaged out to 14 per year. Sixty-two (a little less than 12 percent) discussed various elements of cultural pluralism. However, these were neither evenly distributed nor integrated throughout the different topics discussed within any given edition, year, or across the five-year period. Seven articles (all in one journal) in 1985, two in 1986 and five in a single issue in 1989 dealt with women and gender. One entire edition of the journal in 1988 was devoted to minority learners. *Social Education* of the National Council for the Social Studies (NCSS) gave a special section (six articles) of one issue in 1987 to gender and two articles on sex equity in 1988. Its entire March 1989 issue focused on minorities and the news, and one in 1988 had nine articles on prejudice.

The paucity of writings about multicultural education in practitioner journals represents a qualitative as well as quantitative decline. Most of the few articles in the journals cited above were not written by recognized leaders in the field who have established records of scholarship and continuity of involvement. While the ideas proposed by these new voices may be profound, they lack the power of persuasion which derives from "proven expertise," and an established "track record" that is so revered in the community of educators.

They tended to be "one-time contributors." The most nationally known and prolific writers in multicultural education were absent from the practitioners' forums in the 1980s. They channelled their writings to books and monographs. Thus, the sustained dialogue which characterizes developments in multicultural education theory is absent in recent literature of school practice.

The pattern of how professional organizations and their journals addressed culturally pluralistic issues are telling indications of the state of multicultural education practice in general. The *English Journal* and *Social Education* are especially disheartening since the subject areas they represent are frequently considered most naturally compatible with and conducive to multicultural teaching. Classroom teachers and school leaders look to their professional organizations for guidance in content selections and procedures for designing and implementing instructional programs. The fact that these organizations tend to ignore multiculturalism or relegate it to special sections and editions of their journal models a message that their members are quick to emulate. That is, despite rhetoric to the contrary (infusion and incorporation), multicultural eduction is reserved for selected times and occasions, while the regular routines of curriculum and instruction continue largely untouched by cultural pluralism.

A trend similar to that in professional journals occurred in textbooks. Their language, content and tonality also showed a subtle, but consistent retreat from commitment to multiculturalism during the 1980s. This retreat is manifested in several ways. First, the treatment of culturally different groups and issues became less direct, assertive and frequent. Yet the body of information available from which to choose content for study was much better because of an overall increase in the quality of scholarship on ethnic and cultural diversity. Second, the treatment given to cultural diversity in textbooks continued to be limited to introductory factual information, awareness and superficial analysis. Issues like racism, powerlessness, equity, justice, cultural imperialism, hegemony, social transformation and cultural essence, which require higher order intellectual challenges like critical thinking, values analysis, social action and conflict resolution were largely evaded. Third, despite rhetoric about infusion and integration, textbooks persisted in relegating most multicultural concerns to the periphery of their content and context, under such headings as "special events," "contemporary issues," and "social problems." Fourth, there was a rapid return to using restrictive perspectives and constructs in dealing with the human and American experience that had previously been targets of criticism and presumed reform. Probably the most symbolically significant examples of this retreat are the return to the convention of using masculine (such as he, mankind and man) words to refer to the holistic human experience, the raging debate over the liberal arts canon in colleges and universities, and the recent scathing attacks on New York state's proposed "Curriculum of Inclusion." All of them suggest how recalcitrant what Barbara Tye (1987) calls the "deep structures" of schooling are to multicultural changes. By deep structures she means beliefs about the desirable organization, procedures, substance and purposes of education that are deeply rooted in the value assumptions and ethos of mainstream culture.

Several textbook analyses (Davis, et al., 1986; Sewall, 1987) conducted in the 1980s confirm these trends. Generally, they agree that significant progress has been made in eliminating blatant racial and gender biases. But subtle distortions and underrepresentation of race, ethnic, class and gender diversity prevail. These are apparent in the perspectives given (which are almost exclusively Eurocentric, Anglo, suburban and middle-class), assumptions made, questions asked and the prolific use of male-dominated language.

The preparation of teachers with respect to multicultural education follows a pattern very much like the other dimensions of school practice. Policy regulations for including cultural diversity do exist, such as the National Council for the Accreditation of Teacher Education (NCATE) standards and various states' departments of education licensure requirements. Five of NCATE's 94 standards stipulate requirements specific to multicultural education. These are: providing teacher education students with knowledge and skills about cultural influences on learning; meeting the individual learning needs of culturally diverse and exceptional populations; multicultural and global perspectives; recruiting students from diverse economic, racial and cultural backgrounds; and faculty compositions that represent cultural diversity. The Indiana Standards for Accreditation of Teacher Education Programs stipulate that elementary teacher preparation should develop understanding of the social, emotional, physical and health characteristics of children and the relation of children to their environment. They also will license a bilingual and bicultural endorsement, and an ethnic and cultural studies minor.

Most colleges of education have not responded to these regulations with carefully planned, comprehensive programs about cultural diversity. Multicultural education initiatives tend to be relegated to a few separate courses, whose availability depends upon the presence of minority faculty members. Many of these courses are not required for graduation and licensure. Neither NCATE nor state departments of education require mandatory courses on cultural diversity to meet their multicultural accreditation standards. Thus, courses and experiences which constitute the common core of learning in teacher education, give only incidental, unsystematic and ad hoc treatment to cultural diversity. Although claims are frequently made that since multicultural education is infused in foundational courses, separate ones are not necessary.

Examinations of course syllabi and related textbooks do not validate this contention.

Future Outlook

A renewed interest in multicultural education emerged during the last two or three years of the 1980s. There are some developments underway in the United States and the world that are likely to further fuel a resurgence in the quantity and quality, level and magnitude, depth and breadth of both multicultural education theory and practice. The catalytic forces are political, pedagogical, social and economic in nature.

The changing demographics of schools and society in the United States are already prompting discourse about and activities in multicultural education. Children of color and poverty constitute overwhelming majorities in all large urban city school systems, and these percentages are growing. Yet, the percentage of teachers and school administrators of color is declining. Thus, the referential orientation of teachers and students, which is fundamental to effective learning, may be widening, due to differences in race, education, economics, background experiences, ethnicity and culture. Professional preparation programs need to be reformed radically to develop competencies to bridge these existential gaps. Throughout the nation local education agencies have begun to increase efforts to provide their teachers and administrators with knowledge of cultural diversity and methods for implementing multicultural education.

The real and potential dramatic impact of changing ethnic demographics on academic performance has significant implications for generating new interest in multicultural education. Many of the ethnics of concern in United States schools are indigenous groups and immigrants with racial identities, cultural values, languages, learning routines and educational aspirations that are quite different from the Western, Eurocentric-based traditions of which teachers are accustomed. These differences can have debilitating effects on school performance. The much bemoaned decline in standardized achievement test scores may be a function of who (ethnically and culturally) takes the tests. For example, youth whose families are relatively recent arrivals to the United States or have long histories of being discriminated against in the country may not have the vested allegiance, value orientations and personal desire to internalize the subtleties of its historical, cultural and ideological traditions. These dispositions can affect how students perform on social studies, writing and literature tests.

Another potential connection between ethnic demographics and school performance as measured by test results is the continuing and widening gap between mathematics and verbal scores. There may be something about the structure, procedures and content used to test mathematics achievement that are more compatible with the way some immigrant and indigenous culturally different students are accustomed to learning. Or, it may be a function of sociolinguistic communication characteristics since the academic areas (like science, writing, reading and social studies) which rely heavily upon language arts skills are the most problematic for culturally different students. These contentions need to be carefully analyzed, expedited and remediated with multicultural education perspectives and interventions. Indicative of the growing recognition of these possibilities is the frequency with which culturally-based learning style analyses are entering dialogues about improving the academic achievement and performance appraisal of culturally different studonto.

The dubious success of school reform efforts of the 1980s means that the challenge will prevail in the 1990s, as well as generate some alternative proposals. Some are already beginning to emerge that are related ideologically to the principles and purposes of multicultural education. Whereas the 1980s focused on educational improvement for a select few students who were academically able and college bound, the rallying cry of the 1990s is quality education for all and the inseparability of educational equity and excellence. This vision is articulated in recent publications by almost all professional organizations, journals and monographs. Statements from three of these capture the essence of the ideological shift and illustrate the directions of the trend. *Science for All Americans*, produced by AAAS, declares that the United States is failing to adequately educate too many of its students. To reverse this pattern, reform must focus on the learning needs of all children, all grades, all subjects and all components of the educational system. It states explicitly that the 12 common core learnings it proposes for science education are equally applicable to all students regardless of their social circumstances and career aspirations. The National Research Council's publication, *Everybody Counts*, takes a similar position in its reform proposals for mathematics education. The title itself symbolically represents the overarching message that equality for all students requires educational excellence for all. *Access to Knowledge* grew out of a 1989 invitational conference sponsored by the College Entrance Examination Board. It offers a set of compelling arguments linking the absence of educational equity and excellence for all students to a nation at risk economically, morally and politically. It reconceptualizes the problem of school failure by shifting the primary burden of it from the responsibilities of individual students to institutional insufficiencies. The report also proposes that equal access to schools is not the answer to the problem. Rather, since knowledge is power, and ultimately school reform should bring about a redistribution of power, there must be equal access to high social status, high capital-value knowledge for all students.

Both the tone and content of these and other educational arguments now being advanced appeal to principles of educational quality and equality within the context of cultural realities and the verities of teaching and learning as sociocultural process. As such they are identical to the ideological grounding of multicultural education. Proponents of cultural diversity have been discussing the linkages among content, process and context in teaching and learning for some time. Now the dialogue is becoming reciprocal between subject matter specialists and multicultural education advocates. Therefore, functional, conceptual and programmatic partnerships between them, which will mean improved performance for both, are now more probable and plausible. This is an area of tremendous growth for multicultural education in the near future.

Political and economic changes occurring throughout the world are other catalysts for renewing interest in multicultural education. Democratization in Eastern Europe, the reunification of Germany, the threat of war in the Middle East, the growing economic might of Japan and Korea, the emerging receptivity of the USSR and China toward competitive market economies, unstable balance of powers and the catastrophic level of social problems in Africa, and the growing level of foreign investments in the United States are changing the dynamics of international diplomacy. The United States is becoming less of the dominant voice of influence in world affairs. The most crucial human rights and social concerns (war, peace, power, food production and distribution, health, national debts, self-determination, human dignity) are transcendent of national geopolitical boundaries, making global interdependence a force in the everyday lives of average American citizens in unprecedented ways. The major actors and arenas that are intimately involved in trying to solve these problems are increasingly ethnically, culturally, racially and regionally diverse.

The challenges these issues pose to United States citizenry and leadership as they try to understand and negotiate various international perspectives and priorities on common human concerns may cause them to be more self-reflective as a nation. One part of the challenge requires developments in global literacy while the other necessitates learning how to deal with cultural pluralism within a national context. Initiatives are already underway (especially in colleges and universities) to internationalize the curriculum. Their causes and intents are similar to the principles undergirding the study of cultural pluralism. Thus, global literacy and multicultural education are pedagogically, ethically and ideologically compatible. They can be natural extensions, as well as conduits of each other. That is, the techniques, processes and effects of studying one can serve as guidelines and prototypes for studying the other.

Forging conceptual and operational partnerships with globalism and internationalism should stimulate significant growth in multicultural education.

Business and industry have begun to actively explore cause and effect linkages between their productivity and profit margins and cultural pluralism. Three examples illustrate this trend. One is a videotape and accompanying training modules entitled, "Making the Right Moves" (1986). It was produced by Southwestern Bell Telephone Company and aired on the Public Broadcasting Service television network. It is designed to examine the dilemmas of minority management in corporate America. The second is a multi-media series, including three videotapes and related written materials, on "Valuing Diversity" (1987). The series is intended to sensitize business and industry management to how culture affects interpersonal relations and job performance in the workplace. Third, more and more human services professions like nursing and health care, the restaurant and hospitality industry, social work and psychological counseling are including multiculturalism as a major strand in their training programs.

These activities and trends are very influential signals for American education. They provide a kind of legitimacy and mandate for studying cultural pluralism that cannot be dismissed easily. U.S. schools have a long history of taking guidance, in the form of mandates, models and validation of significance, from business and industry on what should be priorities in education. As the corporate world becomes more actively engaged with issues of cultural diversity, schools are likely to follow suit by increasing their efforts in multicultural education. Corporate endorsements can do more in a very short time to move cultural pluralism to a central focus in educational reform than multicultural advocates have been able to do in more than 20 years.

Conclusion

The decade of the 1990s should be an exciting and challenging time for multicultural education in the United States. Whereas the 1980s was an era marked by survivalism and selective growth, the 1990s may witness widescale renewal and development. New arenas of support and endorsement are surfacing. These include business and industry, world developments, the changing demographics of schools and society, and new paradigms for educational analysis and reform. Together they make the case for cultural pluralism and multicultural education more persuasive. However, the most compelling motivators for growth in multicultural education are the connections being made between economics and ethnicity, and the expressed interest of business and industry in valuing and managing diversity in the workplace.

Developments in multicultural education theory will probably continue in directions which are already underway, but with additional vigor and rigor.

The aims will be to achieve more conceptual depth and clarity; more pedagogical bonding with general principles of effective teaching, foundational values and prevailing educational priorities; and more use of social and behavioral science concepts, content and techniques to inform multicultural pedagogy. Undoubtedly, this growth will not produce total unanimity or consensus. Multicultural education has never been without more than its fair share of criticism. Just as proponents will be invigorated by the developments discussed earlier, so will its critics. Some of this is already evident. However, criticism can be seen as an indication of healthy development. Do serious critics spend time and efforts on insignificant issues that have no social consequence? Probably not. Although the proverbial gap between multicultural theory and practice will probably continue in the sense of them not forming a perfect union, they may converge more. We may see a movement toward greater consistent and concerted efforts to ensure that school reform programs are carefully aligned with ideological principles, and that theoretical ideas and constructs are employed to assess the verities and effects of multicultural education practices. Irrespective of the specific forms it may take, multicultural education in the United States during the 1990s will experience new vitality in both magnitude and quality, theory and practice.

References

Banks, J.A. (1987). *Teaching Strategies for Ethnic Studies*, Fourth Edition. Boston: Allyn & Bacon.

Banks, J.A. (1989). "Integrating the curriculum with ethnic content: Approaches and guidelines." In J.A. Banks & C.A.M. Banks (eds.), *Multicultural Education: Issues and Perspectives*. Boston: Allyn & Bacon.

Banks, J.A. & Banks, C.A.M. (eds.). (1989). *Multicultural Education: Issues and Perspectives*. Boston: Allyn and Bacon.

Bennett, C.I. (1990). *Comprehensive Multicultural Education: Theory and Practice*, Second Edition. Boston: Allyn & Bacon.

Boggs, S.T., Watson-Gegeo, K. & McMillen, G. (1985). *Speaking, Relating, and Learning: A Study of Hawaiian Children at Home and at School*. Norwood, NJ: Ablex Publishing Corporation.

Brameld, T. (1957). *Cultural Foundations of Education: An Interdisciplinary Exploration*. New York: Harper & Row.

Cazden, C.B., John, V.P. & Hymes, D. (1985). *Functions of Language in the Classroom*. Prospect Heights, IL: Waveland Press.

Davis, Jr., O.L., Ponder, G., Burlbaw, L.M., Garza-Lubeck, M. & Moss, J. (1986). *Looking at History: A Review of Major U.S. History Textbooks*. Washington, DC: People for the American Way.

Gay, G. (1990). "Teacher preparation for equity." In H.P. Baptiste, Jr., H.C. Waxman, J. Walker de Felix & J.E. Anderson (eds.), *Leadership, Equity and School Effectiveness*. Newbury Park, CA: Sage Publications.

Gollnick, D.M. & Chinn, P.C. (1983). *Multicultural Education in a Pluralistic Society*. St. Louis: C.V. Mosby Company.

Goodlad, J.I. & Keating, P. (eds.). (1990). *Access to Knowledge: An Agenda for our Nation's Schools*. New York: College Entrance Examination Board.

Hall, E.T. (1976). *Beyond Culture*. New York: Doubleday.

Henry, III, W.A. (April 9, 1990). "Beyond the melting pot." *Time*, 135:28-31.

Hsu, F.L.K. (1969). *The Study of Literate Civilizations*. New York: Holt, Rinehart & Winston.

Indiana Standards for Accreditation of Teacher Education Programs. (n.d.). Indianapolis: Indiana Department of Education.

Kimball, S.T. (1974). *Culture and the Educative Process: An Anthropological Perspective*. New York: Teachers College Press.

Kochman, T. (1981). *Black and White Styles in Conflict*. Chicago: University of Chicago Press.

"Making the right moves." (1986). St Louis: Southwestern Bell Telephone Company.

National Research Council. (1989). *Everybody Counts: A Report to the Nation on the Future of Mathematics Education*. Washington, D.C.: National Academy Press.

Neisser, E. (1986). *The School Achievement of Minority Children: New Perspectives*. Hillsdale, NJ: Lawrence Erbaum Associates.

Pai, Y. (1984). "Cultural diversity and multicultural education." *Lifelong Learning*, 7: 7-9, and 27.

Science for all Americans. (1989). Washington, D.C.: American Association for the Advancement of Science.

Sewall, G.T. (1987). *American History Textbooks: An Assessment of Quality*. New York: Educational Excellence Network, Teachers College, Columbia University.

Shinn, R. (1972). *Culture and School: Socio-cultural Significances*. Scranton: Intext Educational Publishers.

Shor, I. (1983). "Equality is excellence: Transforming teacher education and the learning process." *Harvard Educational Review*, 56:406-426.

Sirkin, G. (January 18, 1990). "The multiculturalists strike again." *The Wall Street Journal*, 215:A14.

Sleeter, C.E. & Grant, C.A. (1988). *Making Choices for Multicultural Eduction: Five Approaches to Race, Class and Gender*. Columbus, OH: Merrill Publishing Company.

Spencer, M.B., Brookins, G.K. & Allen, W.R. (eds.). (1985). *Beginnings: The Social and Affective Development of Black Children*. Hillsdale, NJ: Lawrence Erbaum Associates.

Spindler, G. (ed.). (1987). *Education and Cultural Process: Anthropological Approaches*, Second Edition. Prospect Heights, IL: Waveland Press.

Standards, Procedures and Policies for the Accreditation of Professional Education Units. (1990). Washington, D.C.: National Council for the Accreditation of Teacher Education.

Suzuki, B.H. (1984). "Curriculum transformation for multicultural education." *Education and Urban Society,* 16:294-322.

Tiedt, P.L. & Tiedt, I.M. (1990). *Multicultural Teaching: A Handbook of Activities, Information and Resources,* Third Edition. Boston: Allyn & Bacon.

Trueba, H.T., Guthrie, G.P. & Au, K.H.P. (eds.), (1981). *Culture and the Bilingual Classroom: Studies in Classroom Ethnography.* Rowley, MA: Newbury House Publishers.

Tye, B.B. (1987). "The deep structure of schooling." *Phi Delta Kappan,* 69:281-283.

"Valuing Diversity." (1987). San Francisco: Copeland Griggs Productions.

Culture in Transition: A View from West Berlin

Gerd R. Hoff

In December 1989, during a conference in Vancouver, I referred to the then most recent political event, the fall of the Berlin wall, as the first major crack in the iron curtain and a symbol of the upcoming victory of democracy and freedom. I pointed out that some people may not be happy about the influx of East German thinking in the West. Meanwhile, the unification of Germany has taken place. The euphoria about this event has vanished and the people in East and West have become aware of some unpleasant and unwelcome realities. There are severe cuts in spending in the official sector in the former Federal Republic States (West) of Germany as well as surplus taxes on petrol and income. There are no jobs[1] and drastically increased prices in the former Democratic States (East). In addition to non-acceptance of formerly gained qualifications, employees from the East may earn only 60 percent of the income of their Western counterpart. In the field of education, people must deal with a totally different school system adopted from the West including new decentralized responsibilities.

As early as 1989, I asked, will people understand this to mean that there is only room left for "Germans" in Germany? Before we can examine this question, it is necessary to look at the history of migration into this city and the current situation of migrants in West Berlin.

Berlin, and Germany as a whole, is geographically located in a central position in Europe. It has, therefore, experienced numerous waves of migration throughout its history. Berlin has gained both culturally and linguistically from these migrations. Originally a Slavic settlement, Berlin became the capital of one of the seven German electors in the 15th century, a dynasty (of the Hohenzollern) emigrating from Suebia in Southwest Germany. Very sparsely populated, the town welcomed farmers, craftsmen and merchants from all German speaking countries as well as from Holland, Sweden, Italy and Bohemia (today Czechoslovakia). Later many people came from Poland and other East European countries, being Slavics, Jews, Sinti or Roma. With the beginning of industrialization in the 19th century, Turks came to work in the tobacco industry and people from literally all European countries added to the cultural diversity of Berlin.

There is a French cathedral next to a German one in the centre of East Berlin (the old city). Both are similar in style and importance, highlighting the fact that in the 18th century one out of four inhabitants spoke French. The only Russian-Orthodox Bishop outside of Russia resides in his own cathedral in West Berlin. A Sunnite mosque and a Muslim cemetery survive from the times of the German Kaiser. Up until the beginning of this century one of the most populated boroughs in West Berlin (Neukölln) was called Böhmisch-Rixdorf (meaning Bohemian/Czech village). In the other major working class borough, Wedding, the Roman Catholic church held services in the Polish language until the beginning of World War I. Only two synagogues survived the fierce burning and destruction of Nazi power and war, but one of the largest Jewish cemeteries in Europe, in East Berlin, still remains. It is not possible to begin an adequate discussion here concerning the devastating consequences for millions of Berliners that were a result of the two world wars which originated from this city, forced emigration, and the holocaust against the Jews during the "Third Reich."

In Berlin until 1964, most of the non-German residents were members of the allied forces. In October 1964, when officials in the Federal Republic of Germany rewarded the millionth *Gastarbeiter* coming from Portugal with a moped, there were still less than 300 Turks working in Berlin. Their numbers grew by more than 150 people a week from November, 1964. This was due to the extreme need for an unskilled labor force on the part of German industry. In the early 60s, shortly after the wall went up and Berlin lost its "natural" source of labor, workers were desperately needed to make an economic "boom" possible.

In October 1964 there were only 9 000 people registered as unemployed in Berlin but more than 20 000 jobs were on offer. Thus, the German government entered into contracts with Italy, Spain, Portugal, Yugoslavia, Greece and Turkey. Subsequently, German employment agencies opened in all of these countries, and German contractors started their recruiting work in the capitals and main cities. Most of those hired were single, without their families or partners, and many reported traumatic experiences. For young Turkish women and girls, for example, it was often the first time that they had to present themselves to a man who inspected their teeth and tested their muscles in order to determine whether they were fit for hard labor. These women also found it "humiliating and frightening to give blood and urine for testing in order to find out if they were ill or pregnant" (*Der Tagesspiegel*, November 12, 1989).[2]

The situation changed completely after the oil crisis in 1973. From this year on, migration was limited to spouses and children of *gastarbeiters* who were already there. It was at this time that the restrictions became even greater in Berlin where *Ausländer* were forbidden to rent a flat or a room in three out of the twelve boroughs which the authorities thought were too densely populated with "foreigners." (This legislation still exists in 1991.)

The Berlin population has changed rapidly since the 1960s. In 1968 there were about 54 000 migrant workers; in 1978 - 196 000 and in 1987 - 223 000 according to the official statistics. Today 45 percent of the "non-German" population are Turkish, by far the largest minority group. The Yugoslavs with only 12 percent follow. There are no precise figures about the Poles who are also largely represented because most of them have either German passports or are short term visitors.

It is important to point out here that the overwhelming majority of the *Ausländer* I have been describing, now fulfil all the criteria that would be required in a country like Canada to become passport holders. They are residing permanently in Berlin and have been for more than five years; they are working, paying taxes and have a fair command of the German language. However, the Federal Republic sees herself as a "non-immigration" country:

> ... like most of the European countries [the FRG] wanted [only] labour to come and work and not to settle in the countries of immigration ... (Gundara, 1991)

German citizenship is extremely difficult to achieve. You must be born to German parents, or you have to be a legitimate child of a German father or an illegitimate child of a German mother. There is no right to vote for "non-Germans" neither for parliament nor for the local councils. To become a German, you need to be resident for eight years, speak the language, disclaim your former citizenship and be prepared to serve in the *Bundeswehr* (army). There are exceptions for people married to a German and Jews with German relations.

On the other hand you will get a German passport within days after your arrival in the country, without speaking a word of German, and you will have the right to vote if you come from Poland, Russia or Romania and you can claim at least one German grandparent. In this case, you need only to assure the authorities that you and your family want to be German. Until recently there were only very limited numbers of people from Eastern Europe who have entered the Federal Republic under these conditions. But *glasnost* and *perestroika* have allowed the numbers to grow rapidly. In the past few years, two new groups began playing their part in the process of culture in transition: the *Aussiedler* (ex-settlers from Eastern Europe) and the *Übersiedler* (trans-settlers) those from the German Democratic Republic whose numbers increased greatly since the escape movement through other Warsaw pact countries in the summer of 1989. By the end of September 1989, 13 percent of all unemployed people in West Berlin came from these groups (*Der Tagesspiegel*, November

5, 1989). In December 1989 there were 130 000 of each group without a job in the Federal Republic (*Der Spiegel*, 4/90:41).

By the middle of 1991, the situation changed out of necessity, but not for the better for minorities inside Germany. There are no more trans-settlers because there is only one Germany and everyone is free to move. The younger and better-trained people are moving to the Western states where there are more employment possibilities, leaving the so-called "New States of Germany" (former GDR) with the more problematic people such as the aged, one parent families with many children and poorly-trained, unmotivated young people.

Xenophobic reactions and neo fascist activities focus especially on the groups of ex-settlers and asylum-seekers (the official German name for "refugees"). The figures for both groups have been increasing since the Federal Office of Statistics reported that:

Refugees:	1989:	120 000	1990:	193 000
Ex-settlers:	1989:	370 000	1990:	400 000 (est.)

In the same year (1990) only 6 500 people managed to obtain an official acknowledgment as political refugees. Most of the other "asylum-seekers" were sent back, unless their countries of origin were in a state of war (for example, Ethiopia, Iran and Lebanon among others). On July 1st, 1991, an important change of law was made entitling refugees to accept employment. Hopefully this will put an end to the prejudiced thinking that refugees are too lazy to work and are just living off taxpayers' money.

To stay with my Berlin example, as everywhere else in FRG, the "guestworkers" were once engaged to fill the gaps in the Berlin labor market after the wall was erected. It seems that there is no longer a need for them following unification, especially since so many East-Berlin workers have been made redundant. It is important to note that most of the minority people have lived in Berlin for more than 15 years, are skilled workers, would not be easy to replace and have the right to stay legally as well as morally.

In Berlin society today, there is a hierarchy of minority groups. It ranges from ex-settlers, guestworkers from Southwest European countries and Greece, following those from Yugoslavia and Turkey, Poles, asylum holders and seekers.

So far, I have tried to describe the background of the different communities that made up the Berlin *Ausländer* population. On October 3rd, 1990, the day of the German unification, they were located as follows: 3 429 318 people were living in Berlin (62.8 percent in the Western boroughs, 37.2 percent in the Eastern) among whom were 310 581 *Ausländer* (foreigners), 9.1 percent of the population. Of these only 22 858 foreigners (as little as 1.8 percent) lived in former East Berlin. But this small community was already forming about one eighth of the whole former GDR — *Ausländer* — population. Anyhow, what emerges is a city that is extremely rich and vigorous in cultural diversity. It is now time to ask then, how the education system within the city has responded to this diversity and what policies have been formulated in the area of intercultural education in Berlin schools. I can be very brief here — there is no policy. As Moodley states in her comparison of the developments of intercultural education in different countries when she speaks of the Federal Republic:

> The Federal state does not recognize the permanency of the (guestworkers) de facto immigration. By treating the migrants as sojourners, it adopted an educational laissez-faire policy (Moodley, 1986:82).

For a short interlude of less than two years (1989/90), while Berlin was ruled by a so called "red-green coalition," there was a possibility to implement some measurements in accordance with school policy based on a principle of intercultural education. As unification brought back a conservative government for the city, the promising changes (for example, bilingual alphabetization) will again be dropped. Up until now, according to the legal code for schooling (*Berliner Schulgesetz und Rahmenplan*), the Berlin school is a German School bound to develop equal chances for every child in the German society. The consequence of this principle is that all *Ausländerkinder* are viewed as underprivileged in terms of their command of German language and culture. Therefore, their only special provision has been German as a second language class, the employment of Turkish teacher assistants — mainly with interpretation tasks — and smaller learning groups (one *Ausländerkind* counting for two German pupils.)

In spite of a hostile response to the practice of intercultural education by West Berlin politicians, by the early 1980s initiatives were started by teachers, parents, and other professional workers to provide the children of migrant workers with more equal opportunities. During this time, alternative schools, neighborhood centres, meeting places for migrant women, adult education courses, language classes in German as a foreign language and in various mother tongues were all created. Counselling programs and partnership apprenticeships between young Germans and young immigrants in on-the-job training schemes were also started. The founding of our Institute for Intercultural Education at the Free University of Berlin is another example of an individual initiative set up by three colleagues and myself without financial or organizational backing from the Berlin Senate. It was only possible because in 1980 the conservative government had not yet come to power.

By the late 1980s, only after massive pressure by teachers unions and university scholars, in-service training in the field of intercultural education was established. This was done on a voluntary basis for practising teachers and was only obligatory as a two hour a week course (lasting one semester) in basic teacher training at the University.

The most recent statistics show that by the school year starting in 1988, 21.9 percent of all pupils in West-Berlin schools and nearly one out of four of school beginners in the first class of primary schools were "non-Germans" (Statistisches Landesamt, Berlin, 1991). These official statistics do not count the number of Polish-speaking Germans, some who need special schooling. In spite of these high figures, there has only been a single government initiative in the field of intercultural education when in the late 1970s Turkish pupils were allowed to opt for Turkish instead of a First Foreign Language. This, in fact, prevented many Turkish pupils from passing the German Abitur which does not accept Turkish, but requires at least five years of study of a recognized foreign language such as Latin, English, French and so on.

Opinion polls organized by the Berlin "Ombudsman for Foreigners' *(Ausländerbeauftragte),* as early as 1980, showed that German people living in a predominantly white middle-class borough (Zehlendorf) rejected a greater interaction with "foreigners" by only 23 percent in comparison to people already living in a mixed working class borough (such as Kreuzberg, Wedding) who rejected such interaction by 40 percent. Forty-eight percent would not think of inviting "foreigners" into their homes or apartments in the mixed boroughs as opposed to 33 percent in Zehlendorf (Infodata Berlin, 1979).

We have to believe that this situation hasn't altered very much during the last decade, where right-wing mass-media and conservative government never tire of uttering concern about "the invasion," "the floods" of "alien" elements or alert us to the "sly way" in which foreigners have taken possession of the country, as a former Senator of the Interior had chosen to call it. There is every reason to believe that public opinion has not changed very much if you read the results of the January 1989 General Elections when the ultra-right wing party "The Republicans" stood for the first time.

The Republicans gained a totally unexpected 7.5 percent of all the votes in Berlin. They gained 4.3 percent in Zehlendorf, 7.1 percent in Kreuzberg, 9.9 percent in Wedding and 9.6 percent in the most densely populated borough of Neukolln. This party has been very successful with voters with low school grades, low incomes, among the young male unemployed and with a substantial number of voters in the 18 to 30 age range (*Stat. Jahrbuch des Landes Berlin*, 1989). Slogans created by the Republicans have included: "Jobs only for Germans" and "Germany must stay German." The leaders of the party favor apartheid and provoke fear of the idea of the "green flag of Islam waving over Germany." As a result of unification, the conservative party regained votes in the Berlin election of the reunited city in December 1990. The overall percentage of the Republicans was reduced to 3.1 percent, which kept them out of Parliament. This percentage can be taken as quite a reliable indicator of the number of ultra-right wing orientated people in Berlin. Although this figure is not a threat to democracy, it is quite frightening for the racial minorities in this city.

What are the implications of all this for the present political situation in Berlin?[3] A new national feeling is growing, while at the same time, due to the recent inner-German migration, there are severe shortages in housing, jobs and social facilities like schools and kindergartens. There is already considerable evidence available to suggest that the second generation children of immigrants in Germany "seem destined for the same position of marginalization and pauperization as their parents" (Gundara, Jones & Kimberley, 1982:30). One can only hope that the new ideas put forward by the Berlin senate will have some power to counteract the harsh economic and educational realities faced by most children of migrant workers. If things have been difficult up until now for minority groups in Berlin, one can only imagine that the situation will worsen with the competition arriving from East Germany.

It is within this climate that the subject of unification has been turned into reality by the West German government. There is no room here to give an adequate analysis of the political implications of the crumbling of the wall and whether the collapse of a corrupt regime (a very familiar event among the nations of the Western hemisphere; for example, Watergate in the United States and the Flick Affair in the Federal Republic) is proof that communism does not work, that socialism has falsified itself. I can only state briefly that socialism never had a chance in the Democratic Republic or in the other "second world" countries of the Eastern bloc. The events that are taking place now in Eastern Europe show us once again what we know from classical studies, from hoary antiquity, that oligarchies don't last forever, that people cannot be cheated indefinitely, that a nation cannot prosper if it uses a major part of its gross national product to build weapons and to pay an army. The Democratic Republic has been run as a capitalist enterprise with a socialist label. Therefore it is impossible to presume as Ronald Reagan does "that communism has had its chance, it does not work!" (*BILD*, November 11, 1989).

But it would be completely irresponsible for us not to see the danger of growing nationalism. Unfortunately, there is no tradition in the history of German thinking that democracy and nation can exist at the same time. According to the Austrian socialist writer Günther Nenning, a feeling for one automatically excludes you from the other:

"It is fortunate that the renewed German question is amalgamated into the European one. Germany shouldn't be an impossible unified nationstate, but a

Geisterreich, a realm of spirits, focusing on shared culture, history, language" (*Der Spiegel*, 47/89:83).

This idea of the *Geisterreich* is, for me, as frightening as the "nation state" itself. Once again it denies the existing cultural diversity within German society.

My worst fears about the new situation in Berlin were affirmed when I read a letter to the editor of the *Tagespiegel*, the largest, liberal newspaper in Berlin. It was written by one of my former students, a Turkish woman and a qualified teacher. She refers to an article by a contributor who gave his impressions of meeting people from East Berlin in his street and describing how he felt so much closer to them than to the many "foreigners" who have been actually living in the same road for a long time. She writes:

> Being an immigrant, I would love to share the happy feelings of the other Berliners while the borders to the GDR are opening. But this article shows me that I was right to be afraid that these new arising national feelings would develop at the cost of the minorities living here . . . You must realize that you are depriving us of this special type of 'nestwarmth' that you create while meeting your compatriots in your 'euphoria.' At the same time you are alienating us from our home town (*Der Tagespiegel*, December 3, 1989).

My former student, Muazzez Rekkali, was in fact born in Berlin. She reports that she has seen a Turkish greengrocer giving away his grapes for free to the people from East Berlin, celebrating the special occasion of the fallen wall like most other Berliners. She writes that she would have liked to have read about examples like this one, when the hospitality of the West Berlin people is described. For, "otherwise it is to be feared that the minorities will be crushed by the German-German embracement."

Up until very recently, the authorities in West Berlin have done little to promote the idea of cultural diversity and education for a multicultural society. Politicians have clearly failed to use the chances they had during the last 25 years to create an educational policy that was capable of recognizing the cultural pluralism and linguistic diversity of its people. The German understanding of "integration" is still embedded in the word "assimilation." This can be best explained by examining the following quote by the current President of the Federal Republic, Baron Dr. von Weizsäcker, who declared when he became Governing Mayor of Berlin in 1981:

> The Senate of Berlin understands that our 'foreign fellow citizens' in the long run will have to make a decision between two possibilities: Either to return to their old native country — the senate will grant any incentive and material to support this — or to stay in Berlin, the latter to include the decision to become a German permanently. We don't accept a third way, to stay and to refuse to become a Berliner (quoted in Essinger & Kula, 1987:64).

This statement implies that Turks will not be integrated into Berlin society as Turks, but if as single individuals they wish to become a citizen they must put an end to their being Turkish. As Essinger & Kula point out: "Instead of aiming to live together with equal rights, we develop a new way of colonizing a Turkish minority." Thus, the German understanding of "integration" into West European society must be seen as expressively racist. According to Leiris: "the idea of an inborn superiority is rooted among an overwhelming majority of the white people, even amongst those who would not define themselves as racists" (Leiris, 1985:72). Following this definition it becomes clear that our present hostility against "foreigners" is a problem of racism.

Unfortunately, the same ideals, the same prejudices, the same xenophobia can be observed in the former German Democratic Republic, even if we had little notice about it. There were reports about segregation of "guestworkers" from Vietnam, Cuba and Angola in the Democratic Republic. They were kept in camps and did not meet Germans outside the plants, factories or fields in which they were working. There have been hostile actions against Poles, who were allowed to travel more freely much earlier. There were reports about neo-Nazi activities in connection with demonstrations in East Germany. Violent skinheads were observed, swastikas were painted at the Soviet war memorial in East Berlin and at a war cemetery in Gera, Thuringia. There were rumors about the foundation of DA (Deutsche Alternative), an East German branch of an ultra-right wing group in the Federal Republic. Their catch phrase: *"Das vierte Reich kommt "* (The fourth "reich" is coming) (*Der Spiegel* 3/90:76). So there is little hope of an improvement to the distressing situation faced by minority groups as a result of German unification.

During the summer of 1991, politicians of all parties were discussing the question as to how to keep the asylum-seekers out of the country. They do it mainly because they are influenced by the incidents caused by the neo fascist and racist groups in too many cities of the new states of Germany. In Hoyerswerda, in Saxony for example, the only way some of the refugees could be protected against the nationalist attacks by youth-gangs and skinheads, supported by some of the local residents was to shelter the approximately 150 people (most of them Romanian or Vietnamese) inside army barracks, thus granting direct protection.

Instead of looking for political and educational solutions to the problem, politicians continue to intensify and reinforce fears of "alienation" among the German people and possibly contribute to the increasing numbers of neo-nationalist thinking. The wall is gone. But there is good reason for my former Turkish student to be afraid, if in its place emerges a new spirit of nationalism between German and German at the expense and exclusion of the different migrant communities who have also begun to view Berlin as their "hometown."

Let me conclude by quoting Vaclav Havel, one of the most prominent figures to emerge during these dramatic changes in Europe which we are witnessing each day, a playwright who has become the first President of a free Czechoslovakia for more than 40 years. I quote from his speech of acceptance for the Peace Prize of German Publishers, awarded to him in Frankfurt/Main in 1989. A speech he was prevented from delivering in person — but that was as long ago as October 1989! He says:

> ... we are now better equipped than ever before to see the human world as it really is: a complex community of thousands of millions of unique, individual human beings, in whom hundreds of beautiful characteristics are matched by hundreds of faults and negative tendencies. They must never be lumped together into homogeneous masses beneath a welter of hollow cliches and sterile words, and then en block — as "classes," "nations," or "political forces" — extolled or denounced, loved or hated, maligned or glorified (Havel, *The Independent*, December 9, 1989).

This clearly indicates that the time has come for Germans to rid ourselves of the notion that we are a monocultural society. The policy and practice for intercultural education has the potential to teach us how to live together and to develop a multicultural society. This is something which we haven't achieved yet — anywhere in Europe.

Notes

1. Following an independent opinion of McKinsey & Co., Heidelberg University Professor Dieter Feddersen gives a prognosis saying: about 4 million out of 9.25 million gainfully employed persons will have to lose their jobs by 1992/93 (*Der Tagesspiegel*, 26 July 1991).

2. All German quotations have been translated by Gerd Hoff.

3. The transitional process in Germany as well as in Central and Eastern Europe is continuing all the time. This article was written in December 1989 and revised in September 1991. It is unavoidable that the situation will have developed further by the time this paper is in print.

References

Essinger, H. & Kula, O. (1987). *Padagogik als Inter-kultureller Prozess*. Felsberg: Migro-Verlag.

Gundara, J. (1991). In H. Barkowski & G. Hoff, (eds.) *Berlin Interkulturell*. Berlin: Colloquium Verlag.

Gundara, J., Jones, C. & Kimberley, K. (1982). *Research Into Factors of Marginalization and Pauperization of the Second Generation of Migrants in France, FRG and*

GB relating to the Education of the Children of Migrants, Commission of the European Communities.

Havel, V. *The Independent,* December 9, London.

Infodata. (1979). In H. Essinger, A. Hellmich, & G. Hoff, (eds.), *Auslaenderkinder im Konflikt.* Königstein/Ts: Athenaeum Verlag.

Leiris, M. (1985). *Die Eigene und die Fremde Kultur; in: Ethnologische Schriften Bd. 1,* Frankfurt.

Moodley, K. (1985). "Reflections on some comparative developments in intercultural education." UHA, *Intercultural Training of Teachers,* Stockholm: National Board of Universities and Colleges.

Nenning, G. (1989). "Deutsches Glück and Unglück." *Der Spiegel* 47/89, Hamburg.

Statistisches Landesamt (1989). *Statistisches Jahrbuch,* Berlin.

Statistisches Landesamt (1990). *Die Kleine Berlin-Statistik,* Berlin.

Ethnicity, Power, Politics and Minority Education

Kogila A. Moodley

Priorities for effective minority education are always embedded in the socio-political context. Some minorities in the United States have demanded ethnic studies, black studies, Chicano studies and Native Indian education as ways of redressing discrimination and psychological deprivation. Other politically excluded groups, such as South African blacks, denigrate multiculturalism as a tool. In their view, ethnic curricula exploit cultural differences for subjugation and fragment the disenfranchised. Instead South African progressives prefer a common curriculum which is essentially the same as that offered their rulers, but with a more accurate depiction of the history of contact and resistance. In West Germany, on the other hand, cultural ghettoization of migrant-workers in some provinces, is motivated by the hope that they will eventually return to their country of origin. In Canada, multicultural education has been hailed as a way of integrating different groups within common institutions, by fostering a common respect for each other's heritage cultures. The underlying assumption of most educators is that if minority youth learn about their own cultures they will develop ethnic pride, improve their self-images and ultimately improve their school performance.

This chapter looks at the interaction between ethnicity, power, politics and the state of minority education in comparative perspective. Firstly, the analysis draws upon the experiences of different groups in Canada, West Germany and South Africa to reflect on commonalities and differences. Secondly, in a focus on Canada, ways in which different minorities fare under well-intended programs of multicultural education, will be explored. For this purpose, Ogbu's (1978) important distinction between "immigrant minorities" and "caste-like minorities" will be utilized.

---

*An earlier version of this chapter was published in R. Samuda (ed.). (1986). *Teaching Methods for a Multicultural Society. Toronto: Intercultural Social Science Publications, 1-14.*

Commonalities and Differences

While the three settings, Canada, South Africa and West Germany, obviously differ considerably in their histories, political values, human rights records and educational policies, there are some commonalities. All three societies consider themselves Western style liberal democracies, although in South Africa, this applies to the dominant minority only. They have all had the experience of waves of immigration, from culturally divergent societies. In South Africa, the long standing conflict is not with newer immigrants but with the majority population, classified "non-white." Both Canada and South Africa share a multilingual population within an official bilingual order. Germany, on the other hand, is basically unilingual and denies that it is an immigrant society. Its 12 percent "guest workers" in the labor force remain as aliens in a caste-like position. In all three societies similar economic needs have led to quite different educational policies, based on different political cultures and perceptions of identity by the dominant section. Nevertheless, both Canada and South Africa officially employ notions of multiculturalism while Germany remains ambivalent on the concept.

State policies with regard to the education of minorities are firmly linked with political hegemony. It was in Canada that multiculturalism has first been entrenched as official policy. In 1971, the policy became the Liberal Government's response to the *impasse* between French-speakers in Quebec and the English provinces, the constant tensions involving Native rights, as well as the pressure to recognize immigrant minorities. While admitting the special claims of the French, and to a lesser extent Native people, the policy neutralized them all to the status of "equal groups." By formally acknowledging the varieties of cultural adherence in the Canadian mosaic, the existing cultural hierarchy was in no way threatened but stabilized by diffusion of claims of inferiority and superiority with pluralism. Conservative as well as social democratic administrations have subsequently embraced the policy with equal enthusiasm. The Canadian mosaic was elevated to a national consensus and official ideology while de facto membership in the charter cultures continued to determine life chances.

In Germany, the school system was totally unprepared for the influx of 4.5 million foreign immigrants and their children since the late 1960s. The federal state does not recognize the permanency of this de facto immigration. By treating the migrants as sojourners, it adopted an educational laissez-faire policy. This vacuum became filled by regional responses to minority integration in an obvious educational crisis in a staunchly monocultural society. The constitutionally entrenched educational autonomy of the "Lander" prevented a central response and allowed for experiments according to regional prejudices toward the despised but economically useful aliens.

In South Africa, educational policy in the 1950s and 1960s developed as an explicit tool in the implementation of political apartheid. The four racial groups were expected to be proud of their imposed identity. Black education beyond a minimal level was considered dangerous for white dominance. However, with the breakdown of apartheid ideology under economic imperatives, the curriculum could no longer be racialized. The debate subsequently shifted focus not only on educational content but by the differential allocation of expenditure and the most appropriate organization of the segregated system for an integrated economy.

West Germany relies heavily on the labor of foreign workers. Most prominent among these are Turks. So-called guest workers, two-thirds of them from Southern European countries, comprise 12 percent of the entire German labor force. In some cities such as Berlin and Frankfurt the percentage of permanent foreign citizens approaches 25 percent. Although further recruitment was banned in 1973, the numbers swelled due to the entry of family members who were permissible immigrants. While their labor continues to fill a need, their presence as foreigners is at best ambivalently received. Stringent criteria preclude most from qualifying for citizenship, though it is theoretically possible after ten years of uninterrupted residence. Most foreign migrants neither wish to give up their original citizenship nor do they want to return to their impoverished country of origin. This applies particularly to migrants from Turkey who comprise more than one third of all foreign workers.

The German anxiety about not legalizing a de facto immigration society is based on two tenets: (1) The commitment to a monocultural state requiring the assimilability of the foreigner, and (2) avoidance of importing religious and ethnic turmoil from the periphery to the centre (Wilpert, 1983). For the most part, Turkish guest workers, reluctant to shed an Islamic culture of origin, continue to live as rightless, stigmatized foreigners, even though they have acquired permanent residence rights and real welfare benefits.

In contrast to foreigners in the Scandinavian countries or The Netherlands, German guest workers have not been granted municipal voting rights. In those European countries where these rights are granted after three or five years of residence they have not led to the feared "alien parties" contesting elections but generally see the foreigners voting for a variety of established parties.

Canada, in contrast to the German situation, considers itself a country of immigration. Immigrants may acquire citizenship after three years of residence. Official policy values the retention of cultural heritages, and dual citizenship is permissible. At the same time political integration and adaptation into a multi-nation state is stressed.

South Africa combines the exclusionist nature of the German policy with lip service to the official multiculturalism of Canada. In the name of continued "sound" race relations, it has excluded from political participation in the central parliament the indigenous majority and gave symbolic recognition to long standing minorities of color such as Indians and so-called coloreds in separate chambers. Together this numerical majority is reduced to the status of immigrants, eternally awaiting limited participation in the polity. The state, in its official rhetoric, values cultural diversity and cultural self-determination along the lines it specifies and controls as long as it fragments the numerically stronger majority. Politically excluded blacks in South Africa consequently dismiss any emphasis on cultural retention as part of the state's divisive ideology. Instead, they see access to political power as the central issue. Concerns about cultural differences are firmly and emphatically rejected in favor of a general, non-racial inclusiveness, transcending different ethnicities. The South African opposition strives to transform an undemocratic, authoritarian indoctrination into a participatory and politically relevant education. Their vision for a post-apartheid society embraces a common society rather than an explicitly plural one. Since 1990, the state has also shifted in its public articulation of the same goals.

Whereas at the beginning of the century, Canada received mainly the rural surplus population of Europe, new Canadian immigrants now emanate from both rural and urban backgrounds around the world. The newcomers, unlike their predecessors, are dispersed throughout the occupational strata, are economically upwardly mobile, and strongly achievement-oriented. The table on the following page indicates the distribution of educational achievement of males from major ethnic groups.

While European minorities still succeed more in access to positions of status and power, visible minorities too, despite their increasing battle with subtle racism, strive successfully for white collar, professional and entrepreneurial occupations. Consequently, minority ethnics are found throughout the social structure, save in the top echelons of the power elite.

In contrast, immigrants in Germany, for the most part, come solely from working class and peasant backgrounds. Their educational level is accordingly low. In the new society they continue almost exclusively in menial jobs or low status positions in the service sector.

The South African situation of employment of subordinates is more complex. Africans are largely in the same position as guest workers in Germany. Caste barriers have been slow to shift. Indians, and, to a lesser extent, coloreds, the other subordinate group, tend to continue the "middle minority person" role as small traders, middle-management bureaucrats in the public and private sector, as well as workers. As is to be expected they have sizeable bourgeois middle-classes in contrast to the African majority where most belong to a ghettoized urban proletariat.

Distribution of Educational Achievement of Males 15 Years and Over, 1981

	Less than Gr. 9	Gr. 9-13 but no Certificate or Diploma	High Certificate or Diploma	Trade Certificate or other Diploma Community College or Some University	University Degree
British Isles	15.6%	34.4%	17.0%	22.7%	10.3%
French	25.9	23.6	20.1	23.0	7.4
Other European	23.7	27.6	14.9	24.0	9.8
Indo-Pakistani	8.9	21.3	16.2	24.0	29.7
Indo-Chinese	16.0	28.9	20.3	17.2	17.6
Japanese	10.8	24.6	20.5	23.8	20.4
Korean	4.0	22.5	21.8	16.8	34.8
Chinese	16.7	26.5	18.6	17.1	21.1
Pacific	13.4	31.9	17.2	27.6	9.9
Islands	6.9	28.7	16.5	31.4	13.7
Native People	42.2	35.8	7.7	12.7	1.6
Central South American	12.7	27.5	20.1	25.0	14.7

Note: Data are for people reporting single ethnic origin only. Because of rounding, totals
          may not equal 100%.
Source: Statistics Canada, 1981 Census.

In all three societies, the economic roles fulfilled by these minorities reflect a crucial overall division of labor. The productivity of the minorities depends on their educational level, literacy and skill. A more detailed description of educational policies in the three cases can highlight the various definitions of multiculturalism in the context of these different economic and political exigencies.

West Germany

Given the decentralization of education in Germany and the autonomy of the different states or "Lander," there is no one policy which applies to all states. What consensus does exist is: (1) that compulsory education be extended to include all children including those of foreign workers, and (2) that their pre-school and preparatory education be accelerated to provide assistance with the transition into German society. It is considered appropriate to continue with mother-tongue instruction and subsequently move to Germany. There is widespread recognition of the right of foreign children to be educated through the medium of their mother-tongue. Whether this should be done by teachers from the home country or by German teachers trained in those languages is still contended. The preference seems to lie heavily in favor of the former. Yet the danger of increased influence of conservative or repressive regimes over their émigré citizens, as in the case of Turkey, causes some consternation among both democratic Turks and Germans alike. Since the teachers are selected by the authorities in Turkey and often work closely with their Intelligence Services, the West German democracy effectively tolerates undemocratic practices and repressive indoctrination on its soil. So far the West German educational authorities have conveniently neither claimed a decisive say in the selection of foreign teachers nor in the content of the curriculum which is considered an extension of home education.

Little consensus prevails on the issue of whether guest workers' children should be integrated into the regular school system or educated in separate schools. Those provinces usually ruled by Social Democrats, in favor of incorporating the minorities into German society are supportive of integrated education as well. The aim is to officially accept the presence of migrants and pursue a policy which is meant to neither assimilate nor segregate them into impenetrable ethnic ghettos (Rist, 1979:350).

The success of the educational integration effort is substantial. In the most populous German province, Nordrhein-Westfalen, 95 percent of all foreign children are now taught in the same classes as Germans, while in 1980 almost two-thirds were instructed separately. The failure rate of foreign children sank from 60 percent in 1980 to 30 percent in 1985. In this relatively progressive province with 220 000 foreign children (of whom 140 000 are of Turkish origin), the percentage of foreign students in the various types of German high schools has also doubled since 1980, so that at the most demanding and prestigious gymnasiums three percent are non-Germans.

Conservative strongholds, such as Bavaria on the other hand, have pursued separate educational arrangements on the grounds that this facilitates identity maintenance and the return to the homeland. Beyond this, very little is spelled out as to how guest worker children are to be integrated into the school situation. It is perhaps reflective of the ambivalence surrounding their presence. They are expected to work and function in the economy as competent Germans. Yet, they ought never to lose sight of their roots in the country of origin, to which they are supposed to eventually return. The dilemma goes even further, in that for many, those "roots" entail Islamic foundations. Given the Islamic cultural revival there is also a dread that the Koran schools involved in the extolled cultural maintenance may well be counter-productive to the German ethos of sexual emancipation and civil secularization.

According to Turkish-German agreements, Turkish migrants had to be recruited from the most remote rural areas rather than from the Turkish cities. Wedded to semi-feudal conditions in their homeland the sudden transfer into an industrial urban German environment constituted a double predicament. Given the traditional Islamic rules of conduct, the role of women became a particularly contentious issue. In their desire to protect the traditional way of life, the ghetto provided a shield against potential individualization as well as discrimination. Once huge ethnic conglomerates had emerged — such as the suburb Kreuzberg in West Berlin — no educational policies toward integration could succeed. In order to avoid similar situations elsewhere several cities have imposed quotas of foreign pupils in each school.

Under conditions of increased unemployment guest workers are prime targets of hostility. As in Canada and elsewhere, newcomers are seen as the cause of unemployment for locals and as a drain on limited resources. This insecurity spills over into a competitive educational system.

Immigrant children in Germany face some of the problems of working-class children everywhere. They lack the material resources and the cultural capital to succeed in the way their German counterparts do. Due to the limited education of their parents and their lack of recognized fluency in German, they are unable to draw upon the parental resources that other children do. This is especially evident in the completion of homework which is heavily emphasized in German schools (Rist, 1979:366-367). In addition to those structural handicaps, migrant children are raised in a marginal situation knowing neither the land of their so-called roots, nor accepted in the only society they really know. The hidden curriculum emphasizes that they do not and will not count. This situation of structural segregation is especially poignant for second generation immigrant children.

South Africa

As is well known, South Africa uses segregated educational institutions at all levels for its four racial groups, regardless of linguistic and cultural commonalities between them. This reflects the historical forced separation of segments in residential areas and political rights. The intellectual underpinnings of apartheid in the curriculum, particularly history textbooks has been amply documented (Adam & Moodley, 1986). Black poverty is assumed to be a natural state. With little emphasis on pre-colonial Africa, the texts are mainly devoted to events in Afrikaner history. Blacks are portrayed as posing problems to the whites. This colonial and Eurocentric bias, views world history mainly in terms of competing nationalisms. The apartheid indoctrination, however, is not based on the teachings of crude racism, but on the more insidious myth that whites occupied an empty land, that black underdevelopment is self-inflicted and the conquerors amply deserve their spoils.

The gross inequality in education merely reflects the larger inequality in life chances. The black students, coming from materially impoverished backgrounds, are severely handicapped in the competition with their white counterparts in addition to the many legal barriers. The vastly higher drop-out rates are merely one indicator. Above all, the educational system does little to compensate for the societal inequality but reinforces it by a differential allocation of resources along racial lines. The expenditure per capita for a black student is one tenth of that for its pampered white counterpart. As a consequence, teacher-student ratios are much higher in the poorly equipped black schools compared with the vastly better facilities in the other groups.

However, the racial groups are no longer taught according to different curriculum norms and standards. At the end of the secondary school phase black school-leaving students write an examination similar to that in white schools. They have to meet the same requirements for matriculation exemption as any other candidates. They also write these tests in their second language. The medium of instruction in the first four years is in one of the black languages, after which, almost without exception, English is adopted as the medium. This is done at the behest of blacks themselves, who view English as the medium for occupational equality.

However, both the inferior resource allocation and the second language instruction combine to ensure a much higher failure rate for blacks than whites despite similar syllabi.

Levels of Education in South Africa by Racial Group (1980)

	Whites	Blacks
None	15.6%	48.2%
-Std 6	15.1	37.5
Std 6	9.0	6.2
Std 7	6.1	3.0
Std 8	16.9	3.0
Std 9	5.1	0.9
Std 10	19.5	0.8
Diploma & Std 9, 10	8.4	0.35
University Degree	4.20	.05

Source: Central Statistical Services, *Financial Mail*, February 1, 1985, 53.

At the same time, better education ranks on top of all black aspirations. Educational credentials are seen as the only feasible route for a better life, and minimal status in a society in which most other normal routes for advancement are blocked. The state had to respond both to the political frustrations as expressed in the black educational institutions as well as to the shifting economic imperatives for a more skilled workforce.

From the early 1970s and then accelerated by the Soweto uprising in 1976 and the rise of the Botha administration, a new ideological discourse was adopted by the South African state. "Separate development" was no longer a goal in itself, worthy of pursuing because of its intrinsic value. Instead, it became an ad hoc policy to be applied, modified or even discarded according to other imperatives. This instrumental legitimation allowed state planners to be pragmatic. No longer bound by a sacred ideology or principle, they could show flexibility to compromise according to changing pressures and exigencies. In short, the dominant group increasingly embraced a technocratic perception of its political environment.

The new alliance between government and big business together with the split in the ruling party has also helped to push economic needs on the agenda and ideological concern in the background. The labor needs of the economy now dominate the educational debate. It is no longer possible to restrict blacks to be hewers of wood and drawers of water, as the old "Bantu education" policy had envisaged. Changing demands for a skilled workforce, trained in vocational and technical skills that the white sector alone could no longer fill, have altered educational priorities. In addition, the new strategy of co-opting the relatively privileged urban sector into the system implied higher education for a future black middleclass. It is envisaged as a bulwark against the rural underdogs and stabilizers of free enterprise against socialist visions.

Both expectations have thus far failed to materialize. The expected depoliticized defense of the status quo by the relatively privileged black students turned into the most politicized and longlasting school unrest the society has ever experienced. Petty grievances about learning conditions were combined with the much deeper resentment of being second-class citizens and having no future at all in the new constitutional designs and stagnating economy. The prime objects of co-optation, the urban educated black sections with the much sought-after residence and work rights, have turned out to be the most militant rejectionists, given the imposed racial order and status grievances. Material promises so far have not been successful in diffusing the feelings of symbolic deprivation in a racial order.

This trend continues despite increased expenditures on black education. Although overall unit costs (excluding capital expenditure) in 1984/85 of R156 per black student, R498 per colored, R711 per Indian and R1211 per white student, still reflect vast discrepancies, the educational budget for the first time supersedes military expenditures. Much of this, of course, is spent on needless duplication of segregated facilities. Salaries of teachers with the same qualifications, however, were equalized although only 24 percent of the total black teachers corps of 120 650 in 1982 had the minimum platform of senior certificates plus professional training. Most black teachers were severely underqualified or had no professional training at all.

The dialectic of education lies in the economic need to train people, which simultaneously undermines the restrictive intentions and purposes for which the education was provided. While the number of white students has basically remained the same, in line with the declining white population, the numbers of black students at the various educational institutions between 1978 and 1983 increased from 467 000 to 678 500 and at tertiary level from 19 900 to 44 300. The appearance of black university graduates in such sizeable numbers on the job market is a new phenomenon and distinguishes the South African economy from its African counterparts elsewhere.

An educated class of this size can no longer content itself with political rightlessness even if substantial payoffs accompany the expected accommodation. It is precisely the fulfilment of material equality which enables people to tackle the political and social inequality. The South African educational system has yet to find an answer to this predicament.

The establishment has diagnosed a crisis of education in South Africa. Various Commission reports (notably the de Lange Commission) have addressed the crisis, no longer in terms of ideological content or curriculum, but mainly in organizational terms. What now dominates the debate is how scarce resources should be allocated among the racial groups and educational administration effectively organized.

There is a tendency to ignore the political underpinnings of the conflict in education as well as the conflict at large in favor of treating the antagonisms as a management problem. Unlike the social engineering approach from above, the political perspective of most black spokespersons focuses on conflicting interests. It probes how the competing claims can be reconciled through institutionalized bargaining. It explores how the parties can be empowered to participate meaningfully in the bargaining process according to mutually acceptable procedures that bestow legitimacy to the policy.

The management approach of the government, on the other hand, adopts manipulation as its principle technique. It is one-sided by imposing solutions on the weaker party in the hope that it will succumb to the stronger opponent. The management perspective basically denies that there are conflicting interests. It assumes that the interest of the dominant party also benefits its adversary. From this assumption, it becomes a question of removing obstacles ("agitators") to an unquestioned goal of maintaining consensus. At the same time, this educational policy aims at fragmenting resistance and co-opting useful allies. However, the slightest provocation triggers coercion. While manipulative management of conflict may succeed for a while on the basis of superior resources, it lacks legitimacy and carries increased costs of domination compared with the political incorporation of universal franchise and equal citizenship.

Canada

Multicultural education in Canada reflects much of the ambiguousness that the policy itself embodies. It has had a mixed reception ranging from ignorance as to what it is, to fear of its role in Balkanization of the nation. Essentially, however, multicultural education takes place as something superimposed on an Anglo-mainstream curriculum. Arguments in favor of this approach are varied. Multicultural education emphasizes the equal value of all cultures, and as such, it attempts to redress the devalued image of non-Anglo backgrounds (Wilson 1984). It has been seen as a way in which the self-concepts of minority children are raised by including their heritages and presence in the curriculum (Verma & Bagley, 1982). Yet others see multicultural education as a superficial palliative, which does little to recognize the real needs of language education, inequality of access, and of the racism which differentiates between physically assimilable minorities and visible ones. Hence the praxis of multicultural education is very varied (Moodley, 1986). This is heightened by the fact there is no national policy on multicultural education. Each province assigns its own priority to different agendas. Some provinces such as Ontario, Alberta and Saskatchewan have firmly committed themselves toward the goal of multicultural education. Others pursue very focused attempts at local levels, such as the Toronto and Vancouver School Boards, which have directly addressed the issue of race relations in conjunction with representatives of local communities. Despite the latter's commitment, a 1989 evaluation of the Vancouver School Board's Race Relations Policy showed implementation to be very uneven. Few schools displayed evidence of carefully conceived action plans. Whole school initiatives were lacking. There was teacher resentment toward required plan preparation, as well as very limited collaboration between schools and communities (Echols & Fisher, 1989).

Underlying the ambivalence about multicultural education is the fact that the pluralistic view of Canadian society is only nominally accepted. More rhetoric than praxis is evident when it comes to the power and status distribution resulting from genuine pluralism. The celebration of difference at the educational and ideological level is not carried through to the higher echelons of the Canadian political hierarchy that are largely closed to ethnics, especially visible minorities (Moodley, 1983).

Nor is the focus on visible minorities as a blanket category meaningful, when it comes to addressing vastly disparate needs. The significant difference between certain "immigrant minorities" and "subordinate or caste-like minorities" (Ogbu, 1970) lies in their performance and chances of mobility. The "immigrant minorities" tend to be newer immigrants, usually of South Asian, and Southeast Asian origin who are often over represented in the post-secondary educational sector. By contrast, groups such as Native Indian and West Indian students are underrepresented at the post-secondary level and constitute a caste-like minority. Their "caste-like" status is often related to the channelling which begins with the groups' entrenched position in certain sectors of the labor market. It is reinforced by streaming which takes place at the secondary school level, where black students, especially West Indian, and Native Indian students are automatically assumed to be intellectually inferior (North York Board of Education, 1985).

As long as education continues in this vein, de-emphasizing access, multicultural education will continue to arouse an interminable debate. To be meaningful, the practice of multiculturalism must focus on the special needs of specific minorities, as opposed to overall cultural programming which often only reproduces the cultural hierarchy. Such programs would assume a critical self-analysis on the part of school personnel and educators about the ways in which they may unwittingly aid and abet the process of minority failure. We need also to take seriously the argument of Stone (1981), a British social psychologist of West Indian origin, who rejects multicultural education as "a distraction from the primary function of schooling." She argues that it is poor schooling which has to be blamed for the underachievement of black pupils and that multicultural education merely compounds the oppression of black children. In this regard, the increasing literature on effective teaching of minorities warrants more careful attention.

Conclusion

The German and South African case studies indicate that neither education of subordinate groups can succeed in any meaningful sense unless the political question of "education for what" is solved satisfactorily first. Curriculum experiments, administration reorganization of instruction as well as educational expenditures do not substitute for unresolved political contradictions. Successful education of minorities hinges on a political consensus between dominant and subordinate groups. Canada's multicultural policy, despite its ideological overtones and obvious political intentions, so far comes closest to satisfying the educational aspirations of both majority and minority in an ethnically divided society, as long as it can avoid the political consequences of its logic. In the Canadian situation, state policy has accepted the different roots and origins. Rejection of the melting pot approach has also served to distinguish Canadian identity from its American neighbor. However, the mere acknowledgment of varieties of cultural adherence in the Canadian mosaic has in fact stabilized an existing cultural hierarchy. Whether the ideological promise of Canadian multiculturalism can be fulfilled will largely depend upon ways in which the prospect of cultural equality is translated into equal access to positions of power and status for the newcomers.

In the South African situation, on the other hand, the state rationalizes its fragmentation of the population by imposing and exaggerating "cultural differences." In this context, the label multiculturalism has been imported from the Canadian and American contexts to gain acceptability for older forms of control. Government opponents unequivocally reject multiculturalism as state ideology which they see as undermining their access to political participation on equal terms. In this situation, the politically excluded "culturally-different" groups reject multiculturalism in favor of a common society approach. They see an overemphasis on "cultural difference" as a divide and rule policy and a hindrance to equal participation in government. Contrary to the trend elsewhere, South African political activists emphasize the need for educationally sound teaching through the medium of universal languages such as English. Likewise, progressive Germans distrust mother-tongue instruction. Instead, they view mastery of German language as a precondition for success in mainstream society. At the same time they defend the vision of a multicultural Germany in a united Europe against the conservative insistence on German identity as an educational priority.

Identity maintenance may be important for the self-confidence of minorities, but the acquisition of marketable skills can challenge an occupational hierarchy. The motherhood plea for tolerance of diversity often overlooks the vital precondition for equal incorporation of marginalized outsiders: the demand for their skills will ultimately prove stronger than their cultural acceptance which is frequently retarded by well-intentioned programs of cultural maintenance.

References

Adam, H. & Moodley, K. (1986). *South Africa Without Apartheid*. Berkeley, CA: University of California Press.

Boos-Nunning, U. (1981). "Müttersprachlische klassen fur auslandlische kinder: Eine kritische diskussion des bayerischen offenen modells." *Deutsch Lerner*, Zeitschrift für den Sprach unterricht mit auslandischen Arbeitnehmer, 21:40-70.

Echols, F. & Fisher, D. (1989). *An Evaluation of the Vancouver School Board's Race Relations Policy*. Vancouver.

Enloe, C.H. (1973). *Ethnic Conflict and Political Developments*. Boston, MA: Little Brown.

Grant, N. (1977). "Educational policy and cultural pluralism." *Comparative Education*, 13:2.

Hans, N. (1949). *Comparative Education*. London: Routledge & Kegan Paul.

Hans, N. & Lauwerys, J.A. (1949). "The problems of independence." *Yearbook of Education*.

Holmes, B. (ed.). (1980). *Diversity and Unity in Education*. London: Allen & Unwin.

Horowitz, D. (1971). "Multiracial policies in the New States: Toward a theory of conflict." In R.T. Jackson & M.B. Stein (eds.), *Issues in Comparative Politics*, New York: St. Martin's Press.

Jackson, R. (1977). *Plural Societies and New States*. Berkeley, CA: University of California Press.

Kallaway, P. (ed.). (1984). *Apartheid and Education*. Johannesburg: Ravan Press.

Kirp, D. (1979). *Doing Good by Doing Little*. Berkeley, CA: University of California Press.

La Belle, T.J. & White, P.S. (1980). "Education and multi-ethnic integration." *Comparative Education Review*, 24(2).

McLean, M. (1981). "Comparative approaches to multi-culturalism and education in Britain." Occasional Paper No. 3. London: University of London Institute of Education.

Marcum, J.A. (1982). *Education, Race and Social Change in South Africa*. Berkeley,CA: University of California Press.

Moodley, K. (1983). "Canadian multiculturalism as ideology." *Ethnic and Racial Studies*, 6(3):360-331.

Moodley, K. (1986). "Canadian multicultural education: Promises and practices." In J. Banks & J. Lynch, (eds.), *Multicultural Education in Western Societies*, London: Holt, Rinehart & Winston Ltd.

Mumford, W.B. & Orde-Brown, G.S. (1937). *Africans Learn to be French*. Evans.

North York Board of Education. (1985). *How to Deal With Racial Incidents*. Scarborough.

Ogbu, J. (1979). *Minority Education and Caste*. New York: Academic Press.

Rist, R. (1979). "On guest worker children in Germany." *Comparative Education Review*, 23(3):355-369.

Rist, R. (1980). "Die ungewisse zukunft der gastarbeiter, eingewanderte Bevolkerungsgruppen verandern wirtschaft und gesellschaft." Stuttgart.

Samuda, R., Berry, J.W. & Laferriere, M. (eds.). (1984). *Multiculturalism in Canada*. Toronto: Allyn & Bacon.

Singleton, J. (1977). "Education and ethnicity." *Comparative Education Review*, 2(1), 2/3.

Stone, M. (1981). *The Education of the Black Child in Britain*. Glasgow: Fontana.

Verma G. & Bagley, C. (eds.) (1982). *Self Concept, Achievement and Multi-cultural Education*. London: Macmillan Press.

Watson, K. (1979). "Educational policies in multicultural societies." *Comparative Education*, 15(1).

Wilpert, C. (1983). "From guest-workers to immigrants: Migrant workers and their families in the FRG." *New Community*, 11, 1/2:137-142.

Wilson, J.D. (1984). "Multicultural programs in Canadian education." In R. Samuda et al. (eds.) *Multiculturalism in Canada*. Toronto: Allyn & Bacon.

Wirt, F.M. (1979). "The stranger within my gate: Ethnic minorities and school policy in Europe." *Comparative Education Review*, 23(1).

Young, C. (1976). *The Politics of Cultural Pluralism*, Madison, WI: University of Wisconsin Press.

From Words To Action

Micheline Rey-von Allmen

In preparation for the conference held in Vancouver on "Education in Plural Societies," I set out to describe the work done in Geneva through an intercultural perspective. I intended to describe some of the positive results we have obtained here, but more particularly, the difficulties we have run into, to draw attention to the many pitfalls that await all of us who work in this area and which we must do our best to avoid. I chose to speak on the difficulties that we have run into here in Geneva, because this is the context that I know best. These difficulties, however, correspond to phenomena and to processes common to all contexts.

As I prepared for the conference, I found that it was not so easy to generalize from my experience, since we do not share knowledge of specific contexts. I realized that every word that I used and every example that I provided would require explanation if my audience were to understand my presentation and its pertinence to their own situation (for example, on Switzerland's language policies and immigration policy, on our public school system, on the ways that we use terms in Geneva). The limits of a conference presentation being what they are, I chose instead to limit my discussion.

In this chapter, I would first like to articulate the relationships between terminology and social relations and to explain what it means to me. This is necessary since I always try to give an intercultural perspective to the actions which I have the opportunity to instigate or to develop, both at the international and local (Geneva or Switzerland) level. I also use this perspective to question and evaluate practice[1]. Then in conclusion, I will provide a brief description of the educational context in Geneva.

Terminology and the Representation of Migratory Movement, Social Relations and Intercultural Relations

The terms we use to express ourselves are less universal than we might first think. Much like the tip of an iceberg, the visible and explicit meaning of

---

*Translated from French by Patricia Lamarre

a word is much smaller than its hidden and implicit meanings. In the first part of my paper, I will argue that words:

- reflect our perception of the world;

- have an historical and contextual weight;

- serve both to "witness" and to "bring about" action.

Words: Reflections of How We Perceive the World

Language is a "reflection of a reflection" (Marcellesi & Gardin, 1974). Language reflects our perception of the world, perceptions that are in themselves representations of reality sieved through cultural and social values. Words, therefore, acquire certain orientations. These orientations need to be revealed and their implications questioned.

Words distort reality, partly because they reflect power relations; but words do more than mirror, they give form to our representation of the social structure and serve to consolidate that structure. In this sense, words cannot be considered innocent. For example, terminology is often manacheist. By this I mean that terminology reflects social convictions which are built on a logic of binary opposites. By creating terms that reflect social convictions, we have, in a sense, validated the convictions themselves (for to have a name is to exist).

As examples of how terms exist in a binary relationship within our own field of study, I offer the following: migrant/autochthon,[2] minority/majority, normal/abnormal. Since the terms exist in opposition to each other, it is possible to think of the individuals defined by these terms as also existing in opposition. It is easy to move from the juxtaposition of terms to the juxtaposition of relationships within a community. The ways of the majority group are "normal," which leaves all other groups and that which is "abnormal."

But who will we define as migrant and who as autochthon when the population of a country is itself the result of successive and different migratory movements? How long does a person remain a migrant or an immigrant or an emigrant? What characteristics will be used to distinguish migrants from autochthons? One's country of origin? One's passport or one's parents' passport (and if so, which parent, the mother or the father?) One's professional status? Or bank account? Or stability? Having done military service? The language one speaks or doesn't speak? Where are migrants? In the (so-called) host countries or in the (so-called) countries of origin? How will we distinguish between host countries and countries of origin? In reality, society can no longer define itself using terms like migrant and autochthon. Identity is multidimensional, one's sense of belonging pluralized and the ways in which we differ diverse. Migration, social change and the questioning of identity are concerns in all countries and societies. Typical migrant/autochthon, host country/country of origin terms — defined through the opposition of their respective and exclusive characteristics — do not exist.

Manacheist logic cannot be used to define the contemporary world. Its simplistic, binary logic is the logic of the frontier, of black and white, of true and false, of categories that are juxtaposed and rigid. Real life is a much more complex system of interaction and power relations, of flexibility and movement across time and space, a relational dynamic that can only be grasped through dialectics and in which action, always a precarious enterprise, must remain vigilant and critical. Social life, and in particular the school environment, is part of this complex reality which is so difficult to apprehend. How difficult then to manage?

Words are not tied to fixed and unchanging meanings but represent through conventions, but also through lack of any better way to express the complexity and diversity of real life, only segments of an entire network of relations. We must be aware of these limitations and yet choose our words carefully, selecting the most appropriate and the most efficient, bearing in mind how they will be understood in a particular context and by a specific group of people.

Furthermore, **society generates categorization** which obscures the universality of phenomena and the complexity of problems, fragmenting understanding and awareness (which is perhaps the hidden intent of categorization). The habit of differentiating is so ingrained that it is difficult for us to grasp that differences and similarities actually overlap in daily life.

In a conversation, speakers use words which refer to representations of reality and which are also their own interpretation of reality. While some criticize "terminological blurring" which results from the refusal to accept the limitations of terms, it is my opinion that words, since they carry context-bound meanings, must always be examined and questioned since words have the power to influence and orient action.

The Historic and Contextual Weight of Words

My second point is that words have contextual and historic weight. There is no guarantee that the nuances of a word in one context and to one group of people will be the same in another context with another group of people — even if one relies on the best dictionaries or translators. This is often the cause of misunderstandings at the level of international discussion. When one changes country, region or language, one runs into problems with terminology since local use of terms is affected by regional traditions, the conventions of language and the political and legal structures in place.

A case in point is the use of terms such as **migrant, emigrant** and **immigrant**. The use of these terms is delicate in any country. In the former

Federal Republic of Germany, the terms immigrant and immigration were avoided. They implied political commitment. Authorities, acting within a national policy which discouraged the permanent establishment of migrant workers in the country, therefore, avoided using these terms.

In my own case, I have deliberately chosen to use the term migrant generically, encompassing not only the people that are arriving or have arrived in the host country, but also those that are leaving or have left the country of origin. I also use the word migration to describe the movement of people from one region to another. I adopted these terms in the late sixties and have found it useful. During the sixties, there was a call for action against the overpopulation of Switzerland by foreigners. As the subject became touchier, the term "foreigner" virtually became taboo. In international organizations, the term "migrant" was then coming into vogue and had positive connotations (in the public mind, migrants were educated and professional and their departure from the country often deplored). I adopted the term "migrant" because it put immigrants in a more positive light, reversing taboos both in substance and action.

I have continued to use the term, but it is important to note that in Francophone countries some definitions of migrant are quite far from my own definition. That is the subject of discussions. For some, the term migrant has become synonymous with migrant worker and has negative connotations. Other migrants refuse to be put in this category and as a consequence new terms have flourished which more visibly reflect status (for example, internationals, "coopérants,"[3] refugees, asylum seekers, and so on). There is also discussion of how appropriate it is to use terms like "migrant," "emigrant" or "immigrant" to describe people living in a country or region for more than one generation (a pertinent question). Second and third generations of migrants do not always wish to be stigmatized by such terms, preferring recognition as full citizens. These terms, with their underlying binary logic (which I have already criticized), sanction differentiation and rejection, a process that the children of migrants can justly refuse.

Even though discrimination and rejection exist no matter what the latitude, in Anglo-Saxon countries it is not usual to approach the problem as one related to migration. During the sixties, the United States was more concerned with integration than migration. While migratory movements had some historical bearing on the problems of the existing social structure, the struggle against discrimination was seen as one to eradicate social class disadvantage, slums and inner cities, by equalizing the educational opportunities of ethnic minorities and recognizing the rights of black Americans (civil rights movement). Nor did Great Britain feel concerned with migratory movement. In the seventies, Great Britain chose not to participate in the work undertaken by the

Council of Europe to improve the education of migrants, the reason being that minorities generally held a British passport.

In other European countries, such as Switzerland, foreign workers with no fixed address were the most vulnerable to, and often the victims of discrimination based on xenophobia (the fear of foreigners) rather than racial prejudice. Action against local forms of discrimination, therefore, could not be fought under the banner of anti-racism. Discrimination, however, eventually became racist as political refugees arrived in Switzerland from other countries. This is evident in the following statement: *"L'appartheid ne sera pas notre passé, il est notre avenir"* — "Apartheid is not our past. It is our future." (Monnier, 1988). In various countries, new immigrant communities have formed that are not always well received either for historical reasons (as is the case with North African communities in France), for reasons of religious difference or racial prejudice. As our situation begins to resemble that of Anglo-Saxon countries, the terms we have borrowed from Anglo-Saxon countries take on their Anglo-Saxon meaning.

The term **"minority"** is another example of how a term has different meanings in Anglo-Saxon and Francophone countries. In Francophone countries, "minority" traditionally referred to linguistic groups that were historically included in the national community (for example, Romands in Switzerland, and Bretons in France.) The term "minorities," however, increasingly replaces the term "migrants" (a growing tendency since Anglophone countries have shown interest in the work of the Council of Europe[4] on that matter). This has in some contexts reinforced protectionist tendencies and provided arguments for those who would promote intercultural work between national cultural groups (one, but only one modality of intercultural relations) at the expense of relations with immigrant communities of foreign origin, the latter being more problematic and therefore preferably ignored. On the other hand, use of the term has led to new thinking and studies of the different forms of individual and group integration, prompting French anthropologists to turn their attention to communities within their own country. Furthermore, since the Council of Europe has adopted an intercultural perspective, which includes not only migrants but all kinds of minorities, discrimination against groups such as Gypsies and other travelling people has been re-examined — a form of discrimination that needs to be addressed in many countries.

The discussion of the adequacy of terms (migrant, minority, community) must take into account the specific contexts in which terms are used. It is important that we make a distinction between superficial phenomena on the one hand which vary from place to place (the marginalization of different populations, the different forms of discrimination, the specific consequences of discrimination); and on the other hand, the causes, processes and functions of interactions, strategies and perspectives which are more general and global and which will allow for transversal analysis and action. Recognizing the differences of each context should not lead to closed relations. While the context may change, interactions are always present. The analysis of terminology is part of our effort to improve our comprehension of phenomena and our ability to describe them. To carefully choose terms is to undertake a worthwhile interrogation which contributes to our awareness and our ability to bring about social change.

Like the term minority, **"intercultural"** has been the subject of misunderstanding when it has been translated from one language to another, or used in different cultural contexts.

I offer here my definition of an intercultural perspective.

It is important that we recognize the dynamic that is part of contemporary reality, brought about by the diversity of migratory movement and the many levels of cultural exchange. The resulting interaction, which shapes and eventually transforms society, needs first to be described objectively and scientifically. Secondly, it is important that action and social projects promote interaction which contributes to mutual respect and the construction of a society founded on solidarity rather than inequality. If an intercultural perspective is based on the recognition of diversity and the acceptance of a plurality of norms, it is essentially a dialogue, an interaction and an exchange. Indeed it is then a dynamic process which leads to the creation of new meanings derived from the diversity to the construction of a history and social community. Intercultural education grows out of this definition of an intercultural perspective. While it is grounded in the real needs of migrants who must be welcomed and integrated into a new community, an intercultural education has a broader goal: education towards solidarity and human rights.

The plurality and the proximity of terms in use today has led to a tendency to either juxtapose or refuse terms. In my opinion, they should not be thought of in opposition, nor should they be thought of as synonymous.

International contact has increased collaboration between, for example, English and French being the two languages used within the Council of Europe and the IAIE. As a result, words have spread beyond their original (cultural, linguistic, geographic, institutional) areas of use, sometimes being translated approximately or used for "trendiness." While words might sometimes lose a part of their original meaning within a context, they might also be enriched as they evolve through other contexts and through theoretical discussions. This has been the case with terms such as multicultural, pluricultural, intercultural and transcultural. I offer here my own understanding of these terms.

I give the prefixes of these terms their full etymological value. Multicultural (multi = many) and pluricultural (pluri = several) can be used for static description. All societies are multicultural or pluricultural. They bring together groups and individuals of many or several different cultures. Intercultural, on the contrary, refers to a dynamic process. The term itself explicitly affirms interaction and interdependence. An intercultural perspective calls for positive interaction between the different components of society. It represents not only a reference, but a methodology and a perspective for action.

"Intercultural," by giving full value to the prefix "inter," implies interaction, exchange and interdependance. In addition, the root word "culture" is given its full meaning: recognition of values, of life styles, and the symbolic representations that individuals and social groups refer to in their relationships with each other and in their understanding of the world. The term "intercultural" recognizes the range of interaction possible within a culture as well as between cultures and this within the changing dimensions of time and space.

I proposed this distinction between multicultural and intercultural to the Council of Europe during a discussion that marked the end of an intercultural teacher training program in Aquila, during which participants requested a clarification of definitions (Rey, 1982). This distinction is now generally accepted by people who refer to the work of the Council of Europe.

As for the term "transcultural," it defines a movement, crossing-over of frontiers. Like the terms pluricultural and multicultural, it does not imply dialectic movement or reciprocity. Interaction is not specifically excluded by the term, but neither is it formulated explicitly, or, as in intercultural, considered part of the underlying concept.

"Multiculturalism" is essentially an Anglo-Saxon movement. It is tied to the recognition of ethnic minorities. But these minorities have been perceived as marginal to the majority group. As a term, "multicultural" has been criticized for its tendency to juxtapose, to marginalize and to isolate communities by freezing them into ethnocentric identities.

When the intercultural perspective adopted by the Council of Europe was presented in Anglo-Saxon countries, and notably Britain, it inherited the debate around culturalism and multiculturalism. Interculturalism, however, calls for the re-evaluation of existing models since it adds the dimension of integration and the awareness of existing power relations, and proposes the development of interaction.

The current use of the term "multicultural" in Francophone countries is quite different from its use in Anglo-Saxon countries. As a term, it is relatively neutral and not the subject of a polemic debate of the type surrounding the term "intercultural." It should be noted that an intercultural perspective, as I have defined it in this article, does not reflect consensus and is not universally accepted.

Following the impact of the new "intercultural" perspective, another term has come into use which further blurs distinctions. The American term "cross-cultural" had until this time been translated into French as "transculturel." It is now more frequently translated by the trendier term "interculturel." "Interculturel," is now used in the social sciences and has lost its original reference to interaction. It may refer to a comparative approach and be limited methodologically to the study of cultures through juxtaposition. This is evidently the case for the term *"psychologie interculturelle"* translating the English "cross-cultural psychology." It is also used in this way by the ARIC (*Association pour la recherche interculturelle*, a Francophone association for intercultural research). The tendency to use intercultural in this way is evident in the following definition in Brill & Lehalle (1988):[5]

> In the terminology we have adopted, purely comparative aspects will be called 'intercultural,' the identification of local variables (in particular between individuals) will be referred to as 'intracultural,' and the term 'transcultural' will be used to describe the pursuit of more general processes rather than any particular cultural effort.

The authors add as a footnote:[6]

> This terminology is in keeping with that used in international publications, however, it does not correspond to that found in certain French language publications (where 'intercultural' signifies the interaction or contact between cultures and 'transcultural' translates incorrectly the English term 'cross-cultural.'

It is certainly tempting to deplore the multiplicity of terms and definitions that are currently in use. These, however, reflect reality and call for tolerance, even towards terminology. Furthermore, the diversity of uses stands as witness to the diversity of traditions. It is important, however, to see beyond the words themselves and critically examine their use.

To conclude this discussion, we can say that words serve to witness as well as to bring about action. Their adequacy and their efficiency should not be considered outside of their context of use. While researchers might aspire to a scientific esperanto of terms, an etic approach that is objective and neutral, there is no way to avoid the pluri-emic (the plural and emic nature of the) negotiation of terms. Perhaps this discussion of terms between researchers is in itself a worthwhile form of intercultural communication.

Words as Witness and as Acts

An intercultural approach, and in particular intercultural education, has been the subject of many criticisms. I will address two of these criticisms which attack on opposite fronts.

On the one hand, an intercultural perspective has been accused of being unscientific and utopian. It is, however, the dynamic nature of the term "intercultural" which is its greatest force: it is productive at the scientific level and effective at the level of social and educational action. To refuse the dynamics of interculturalism at the scientific level is to admit that it is methodologically difficult for the social sciences and the humanities to deal methodologically with the complexity of interaction and dialectic movement. An intercultural perspective thus reveals the urgency with which researchers must work if they wish to make a contribution to our knowledge and understanding of social structures which are constantly being renegotiated and transformed. At the educational level, we can simply state that there is no such thing as education without a perspective. If we refuse one perspective or social project, implicitly we are choosing another. By refusing an intercultural project, are we not choosing the established order (status quo) and power relations which privilege our own social group?

On the other hand, an intercultural perspective has been attacked for its neglect of the power relations which exist in and between social communities. Specifically, an intercultural perspective has been charged with ignoring the role of racism in today's society. This criticism is related to the one levelled at the culturalist movement to which the intercultural perspective has been quickly assimilated. In other instances, criticism has been fostered in reaction to reductionist practices within the school system.

This criticism is ill-founded if we refer to the historical and geographical context in which the intercultural approach has been developed: recognizing the inequality of educational opportunity and of linguistic and cultural exchange (Bourdieu 1977), efforts were made to democratize studies and equalize educational opportunity; the so-called social or linguistic "deficit" were questioned and efforts were made to go beyond compensatory education and to emancipate groups which had been most deprived. In an unequal world, an intercultural perspective provides strategies:

- to question our convictions, whether they are egocentric, sociocentric, or ethnocentric;

- to transform the representations through which we make judgments and take action;

- to modify the value given to different abilities, norms and cultures (which may or may not be present in the local community);

- to transform and diversify the existing power structure and give equal rights to groups that have been depreciated as to their cultural referents, their skills and their means of expression;

- to break down isolation and acknowledge the complexity of the relationships existing between cultures, social classes, institutions, education, school subjects and scientific subjects, as well as between human beings of all races; and

- to develop communication and negotiation between individuals, groups and communities that are positive and enriching for all parties involved.

I hope that the term "intercultural" will keep its underlying meaning of interaction and thus, remain a driving force, a reference and the subject of discussion, at the level of research as well as in education and social life. It is of course a long road from project to fulfilment and it remains to be seen how well strategies work.

Words have a life span and their vitality can diminish. Other words and other approaches may feed and revitalize them and perhaps eventually replace them. There is no cause for alarm, however, only the need to remain alert to what lies beneath words.

Integration of Immigrants and Intercultural Relations in Geneva

The Department of Public Education for the canton of Geneva has recently defined the guidelines for its educational policy. Within them, the field of "Education for an Open and Plural Society" is mentioned *(Départment de l'instruction publique, 1989)* . According to this, various responsibilities may be defined which require increased efforts to welcome newly arrived migrants, encourage social and educational integration (including adult education programs), as well as the development of a relationship based on reciprocity between all members of the community, promote education for solidarity and the development of human rights within an intercultural perspective, open not only to Europe but to the whole world.

It is important to emphasize that Geneva is a cosmopolitan canton and that students come from all over the world.

Many migratory trends exist concurrently. Distinctions can be made between migration from Mediterranean countries, essentially bluecollar workers and their families; migration from countries neighboring Switzerland which have similar social structures; migration from other industrialized countries (primarily upper management and white-collar); and other immigrants coming from all over the world and who can be divided into all echelons of society but primarily the higher echelons. Migratory movement is not limited to international immigration, there is considerable internal migration within Switzerland, as well as emigration to other countries. The social fabric is woven out of successive migratory waves, each with its own characteristics, needs and conditions, which are not only different at the outset, but over time. The successful integration of second and third generations of migrants is an important task in the educational system. Simultaneously, the school system must be ready for the arrival of new populations (seasonal workers, manual laborers and their families, refugees) with geographical, cultural and linguistic backgrounds very different from the Swiss ones. They come from Portugal, Yugoslavia and Turkey, but also Latin America, Africa, the Middle East and Asia. This immigration modifies our social and educational responsibilities as well as the attitude of people towards foreigners.

Here are some statistics to illustrate the diversity within the Geneva school system. (These statistics should be considered approximations since the actual numbers vary slightly from year to year.) Foreign students represent close to 40 percent of the total school population. At the elementary and secondary level in the canton of Geneva, 140 nationalities are represented. About a quarter of the total student population is originally from Southern Europe. Of the Swiss student body (60 percent of the total student population), many come from other cantons (internal migration). More than one third of all students (foreign and Swiss) speak a language other than French as a first language (French is the language of schooling). In classrooms for non-Francophone students, over 40 different first languages were identified.

Clearly, cultural differences need to be considered as well as their potential for enriching education.

A consequence of this diversity is that schools (regardless of the nature of their programs) have many needs and responsibilities. They need:

- infrastructures to welcome and integrate recently arrived non-Francophone migrants;

- to take into account the plurality of cultures within the student body and the range of their abilities, notably social and linguistic ones; and

- to develop education for human rights as well as promote human rights within the local community, and in all regions of the world.

The school has many roles, welcoming and encouraging social integration, teaching, evaluating, helping students to choose orientations, making selections, teaching social behavior, and helping build tomorrow's society. Consequently, this places new requirements on teacher training programs and on the training of all other educational personnel, teachers, principals and other staff who play a role in the daily life of the school: administrators, social workers, school psychologists, technical staff, and so on.

I will mention only some of the efforts which have been made and some of the areas for future action.

As Switzerland has chosen a national linguistic policy based on a territorial principle,[7] immigrants need to learn the local language. French-as-a-second-language (FSL) classes are therefore a necessity and there has been a considerable increase in the number of reception classes.[8]

Geneva set up its first reception classes in 1968, at the *"Cycle d'orientation"* (= junior high level).[9] (I was responsible for them from 1969 to 1989). These classes were for non-Francophone students arriving in Geneva who were between the age of 12 and 15. A second service was created in 1981 for students between 15 and 20 years old at the level of post-obligatory or *"secondaire supérieur"* (= senior high) education. At the primary school, a different solution was chosen: primary students are integrated immediately into the regular primary program, but receive extra support to improve their FSL skills (and other skills if needed).

These reception classes were created within a school system which had undertaken an educational reform project in 1961 and was striving to democratize school and equalize educational opportunities. The goal of reception classes is to help children and adolescents (who have recently immigrated and are facing a way of life which is foreign to them) to learn French and to adapt to the way of life in Geneva, as well as to the school system in which they will be learning. Marginalization is a constant danger, one that particularly threatens the structure of reception classes. However a number of measures have been taken to counter the process or marginalization (Rey, 1979; 1989; in press). Notably:

- Reception classes exist only at the secondary school level, which is divided into different streams. Reception classes allow students a period of social adaptation, of language skills improvement, and, if needed, a chance to catch up in other subject areas **before** choosing an orientation. In principle, all orientations are possible, all streams available, after being in the reception classes, depending on the students' capabilities and aptitudes.

- Only recent migrants (Swiss or foreign) are admitted into reception classes. These classes are not for foreigners or for students with problems. They are for non-Francophone students whether they are Swiss or foreign (though students in reception classes are, for the most part, foreign and some do have severe learning difficulties).

• In the *"Cycle d'orientation,"* reception classes are organized without distinctions being made as to the nationality, language or academic level of students. Age is the only criteria used to organize these classes. The structure of immigration in Geneva being what it is, to differentiate between FSL students as to their academic level or aptitude (which would also leave room for the influence of prejudice) would be the equivalent of dividing groups according to their nationality and their social class. In *"secondaire supérieur"* — the level of senior high education, there is a certain homogeneity of academic level, though, in principle, all orientations remain open after the reception classes, depending on the academic level reached.

• Generally, students spend only one year in the reception class so as to avoid creating a parallel secondary program for foreigners.

• After transfer to the regular program, students continue to receive support if it is needed.

• To allow for more teacher attention, the number of students in the reception classes is limited (maximum of 10 students at the *"Cycle d'orientation"* and 11 at *"secondaire superieur"*).

• Reception class teachers have the same qualifications as teachers in the regular program and can transfer from the reception class program to the regular program and vice versa. It is important that reception class teachers themselves be well-integrated and participate fully within the teaching body.

• Students participate in all aspects of school life as well as in extra-curricular activities (shows, races, outdoor classes, and so on).

But beyond the integration of recent immigrants, there remains the question of interaction between all members of the community and intercultural communication. Research is needed on the process of learning, on the transfer of linguistic and cultural skills from one language to another, on the two-way socialization of students, on relationships between the home and school and on the collaboration between migrants and autochthons.

Furthermore, some students arrive in the Geneva school system with a lag in their academic development or with gaps or deficiencies in their previous schooling; perhaps the school system in their country of origin was inadequate, or the family might only recently have been reunited after a period of separation, or they might have experienced particularly difficult conditions of emigration or integration into the new community. The response of the school system to these problems usually is to offer compensatory programs. In an intercultural perspective, there are other elements to consider which mobilize the interaction between the different partners involved, such as the socio-professional goals of students and their families, their perception of the school and the new society, the establishment of a social network in and out of the school, and so on. Many groups are currently working on these aspects.

Schools are also faced with the problem of **educational rights** (Perregaux & Togni, 1989). The Department of Public Education in Geneva, in collaboration with other agencies, is examining the possibility of regularizing the situation and the schooling of children living in Geneva without government authorization (often the case for the families of seasonal laborers and other workers who have not yet obtained permission to bring their families into the country for lack of suitable accommodation). Recently all these children have been accepted into school. By reducing the dangers of clandestinity and, therefore, the length of time that children of immigrants are outside the school system, we could reduce not only some of the social adaptation problems of these children, but also some of the educational problems faced by the schools and perhaps some of the xenophobic tension provoked by jealousy and inequality.

The educational system is moving towards a **greater awareness of the diversity of languages and cultures** found within schools and towards education for a plural society. Work has been done to develop contacts between the official school and language and culture studies offered to migrant children by the consulates or embassies of their countries of origin. (See the magazine *"Inter-Dialogos."*)

The usefulness of making links between the teaching of various languages does not stop here. Bilingualism was long considered a handicap to a child's development or as something that should only be undertaken by gifted children from socially privileged backgrounds. Lambert (1981), however, has shown that knowing or learning more than one language can have beneficial consequences on the global development of individuals, at the cognitive and the communicative level. (If there are difficulties, these are not at the linguistic level but at the social level, related to the unequal social standings of languages and linguistic groups; it is more important to act on the social level than to try to limit linguistic competence or the teaching of languages). Our concern, both for the teaching of French and of second languages, is to draw on the richness of linguistic skills so that it profits both monolingual and multilingual students (Rey, 1985).

The pluricultural nature of our community (as well as interactions developing on a larger scale which force us to recognize the interdependence of all peoples, not only of Europe but of the world) poses questions of the egocentricity, sociocentricity and ethnocentricity of educational programs. **An education for pluralism should be taught through subject areas across the curriculum and through a wide range of teaching strategies.** Geography, history, art education, environmental studies, language education, literature, etc., all provide opportunities to broaden experience and draw on the wealth of experience and culture present in the classroom and in the surrounding community, and to move, within an intercultural perspective, towards international comprehension and human rights. Within this perspective, teaching materials are being developed and contacts made with resource people from different cultural backgrounds.

A greater openness to diverse cultural experiences and skills has other implications: the school must question existing norms and strive to make them more comprehensive on the level of behavior, social relations, selection factors and even the purposes of selection. Teachers face new questions, as do school psychologists, who work with students and their families whose cultural referents and social experience and aspirations are different. A taskforce of psychologists is presently addressing this new educational challenge with the support of the Council of Europe (Rey (ed.), forthcoming).

The pluralism of society, like the explosion of scientific "progress," has caused **questions of values, of identity and of loyalty** to resurface. Young immigrants are in perhaps the most difficult position, living the tension of many cultural worlds, many citizenships, many philosophies of life and of education, and having to negotiate with all of these. It is young immigrants, however, who incite discussion, who open the road to negotiation and who foreshadow the "métis" world of tomorrow. Questions of identity cut across all of society. The school, as it moves toward its goals of democratization and pluralism, faces these questions as well.

Intercultural education opened the way for a **re-examination of human rights and education for human rights.** These offer reference points for individual and collective rights which can provide explicit guidelines for social behavior. As well, these are social projects which are marked by the era in which they were formulated and which will require the critical spirit and contribution of today's citizens, and tomorrow's, if they are to be achieved and further developed. From this perspective, the school is responsible for not only teaching about human rights, but for living human rights.

In Geneva, many groups are actively working at this large task. But let there be no mistake, "experts" cannot solve this problem. The educational challenge that we face today will require an ever-growing network of initiative, covering in a coherent and articulated manner all of the dimensions that open on to pluralism, supported and relayed by the whole teaching body and the educational and social community (to which both immigrants and autochthons fully belong).

Notes

1. I was able to undertake this task in preparation for an IAIE conference held at Oostkapelle, Netherlands on "Multilingual Initiatives" in February 1990. This work has recently been translated and published in German in Gogolin and al. (1991).

2. In Canada, this refers specifically to First Nations or Native Indian people, while in Switzerland, autochthons or indigenous people refer to the non-immigrant "Swiss."

3. People working for international aid organizations.

4. The Council of Europe was founded in 1949 by 10 countries (current membership is 26) as an intergovernmental organization with three main aims: to protect and strengthen pluralist democracy and human rights; to seek solutions to the problems facing society; to promote the emergence of a genuine European cultural identity. The Council of Europe covers all major issues facing European society with the exception of defense. Its work programme includes the following fields of activity: human rights, media, legal cooperation, social and economic questions, health, education, culture, heritage and sport, youth, local and regional government, and environment.

5. *"Dans la terminologie que nous utiliserons, l'aspect purement comparatif sera dit 'interculturel', l'identification de variables locales (en particulier inter-individuelles) recevra le qualificatif d'intraculturel' et le terme 'transculturel' correspondra à la recherche de processus plus généraux que telle ou telle réalisation culturelle particulière."* (Brille & Lehall, 1988).

6. *"Cette terminologie est en accord avec celle utilisée dans les publications internationales, mais elle ne peut pas correspondre à celle employée dans certains ourvrages publiés en langue française (où 'interculturel' qualifie les interactions ou contacts entre cultures et 'transculturel' traduit à tort le terme anglais 'cross-cultural'"* (Brille & Lehall, 1988).

7. Translator's note: Under a territorial principle, the language of schooling and of local administration is conducted in the language of that territory, or in the case of Switzerland, canton. At the national level, the three official languages — German, French and Italian — are used. In Geneva, the local language, and therefore the language of the school, is French.

8. Translator's note: In French, the term for these classes is *"classes d'accueil"* literally "welcoming classes" or "reception classes." In English, these classes are usually referred to as ESL (English-as-a-second-language) classes, essentially second language classes. Since not only ESL but many subjects are taught in the *"classes d'accueil,"* we shall keep the literal translation: reception classes.

9. The *"Cycle d'orientation de l'enseignement secondaire"* or simply *"Cycle d'orientation"* is, in Geneva, the first level of secondary education. It is attended by all pupils, coming from the 6th grade of primary school, for the last three years of compulsory education (grades 7, 8 and 9, for ages 13 to 15); the higher level of secondary education, which is not compulsory (ages 16 to 19) may be more or less compared with senior high school.

References

Bourdieu, P. (1977). "L'économie des échanges linguistiques." *Langue Française,* 34:17-34.

Bril, B. & Lehalle, H. (1988). *Le développement psychologique est-il universel?* Paris: Presses universitaires de France.

Department de L'Instruction Publique. (1989). *L'an 2000 c'est demain. Où va l'école genevoise?* Genève: Département de l'instruction publique.

Inter-Dialogos. Idées, Expériences, Nouvelles pour L'Education Interculturelle en Suisse, revue bisannuelle. Neuchêtel: Association InterDialogos.

Gogolin, I., Kroon, S., Krüger-Potratz, M., Newmann, V. & Vallen, T. (1991). *Kultur and Sprachenvielfalt in Europa.* Münster/New York: Waxmann.

Lambert, W.E. (1981). "Bilingualism and Language Acquisition." In H. Winitz (ed.) *Native Language and Foreign Language Acquistion.* New York: Annals of the New York Academy of Sciences, 379, Dec. 30:9-22.

Marcellesi, J. B. & Gardin B. (1974). *Introduction à la sociolinguistique.* Paris: Larousse.

Monnier, L. (1988). *L'appartheid ne sera pas notre passé. Il est notre avenir.* Leçon d'adieu présentée le 21 juin 1988 au BFSH 2 de l'Université de Lausanne (polycopié).

Perregaux, C. & Togni, F. (1989). *Enfant cherche école.* Genève: Zoé.

Rey, M. (1979). "L'éducation des enfants (de) migrants dans le canton de Genève." Vers une éducation interculturelle, *Etudes Pedagogiques.* Lausanne, Payot, 127-138.

Rey, M. (1982). *Symposium sur la formation interculturelle des enseignants.* L'Aquila 10-14 mai 1982, Strasbourg: Conseil de l'Europe.

Rey, M. (1985). "Des cribles phonologiques aux cribles culturels: vers une communication interculturelle." *Bulletin.* 41:44-84.

Rey, M. (1989, 2e éd.). "De la classe d'accueil à une éducation interculturelle." In A. Gretler et al., *Etre migrant.* Berne, Francfort/M, New York, Paris, Lang, 279-302.

Rey, M. (in press). "Immigration, ghettoization and educational opportunity." In J. Lynch et al. (eds.), *Cultural Diversity and the Schools,* vol. 3, Basingstoke: Falmer.

Rey, M. (forthcoming). *Psychologie clinique et interrogations culturelles.* Paris: CIEMI/L'Harmattan.

Section II

The Case for Multicultural Education

Projecting the Past into the Future:
A Look at ESL for Children in Canada

Mary Ashworth

The history of Canada is more than the history of its explorers and settlers, its traders and missionaries, its lawmakers and its rebels; it is also the history of its children who were shaped by the times they lived in and who grew up to shape the future of the next generation. The notion of empowerment of children, defined by Longman's *Dictionary of Contemporary English* (1978) as "giving someone the power or lawful right to do something" is relatively new, yet, particularly during the last two centuries, Canadians have empowered and disempowered non-English speaking children of minority groups through their attitudes toward and actions surrounding language, culture, economics and religion. This chapter will look first at the education of the children of six minority groups during the nineteenth and early twentieth centuries: the children of the fur traders; black children; native Indian children; Chinese children; Doukhobor children; and Ukrainian children. In each case a brief examination will be made of the actions of a group or groups of adults — usually, parents, teachers, citizens, clergy, government officials — who empowered or disempowered children. Particular attention will be paid to language. Next, the chapter will look at the present state of ESL (English as a Second Language) across Canada using research both recently completed (Ashworth, 1988) and still in progress and will consider whether present policies and practices empower or disempower children. Lastly, the chapter will project into the future.

In his article "Empowering Minority Students: A Framework for Intervention," Jim Cummins (1986:23) writes: "Students who are empowered by their school experiences develop the ability, confidence, and motivation to succeed academically. They participate competently in instruction as a result of having developed a confident cultural identity as well as appropriate school-based knowledge and interactional structures. Students who are disempowered or 'disabled' by their school experiences do not develop this type of cognitive/academic and social/emotional foundation." Although school days may not be, as the old saying goes, "the happiest days of your life," they are, without question, among the most influential, affecting not only the children's individual futures, but the future of their group and of those who will follow. There are lessons to be learned from the past and present which may affect the future.

The Past

Children of the Fur Traders

The founding of the Hudson's Bay Company in 1670 brought young Englishmen and Scots to northern and western Canada in search of furs. By the early 18th century, the company had established a policy that no wives were to be taken to the posts on the Bay as colonization was not envisaged, neither were the men to have any contact with Indian women. However, the latter order was defied and by 1730 Indian wives were taken *à la façon du pays* — according to the custom of the country. After a ceremony combining some Indian and European customs, excluding the Christian marriage service, the couple set up house. With the coming of children cultural conflicts occurred. In Indian society, control of the children's upbringing was the responsibility of the mother, but European society was based on a patriarchal authority with the father making the decisions.

Initially, the education of these "mixed-blood" children was left to the fathers; those who could, taught the rudiments of literacy to their children along with Christian beliefs. But the future of these children was questionable so long as they had close contact with their Indian relatives — a good future, in the eyes of their fathers, lay in their breaking with their Indian heritage and becoming, as far as possible, white English-speaking young people. This would enable the boys to be employed by the Hudson's Bay Company and the girls to marry Hudson's Bay Company employees. The men of one post in 1807 requested a residential school some distance from the fort to be run by a "female from England of suitable abilities and good moral character and a schoolmaster." It was felt that "The Residence of the Children and their Instructors would be most convenient at a short distance from the Factory . . . such retired Situations would not only estrange the Children from their Indian Acquaintance but present other advantages friendly to the progress of Education, Morality, and Good Order" (Brown, 1977:41). The request was turned down, but in time schools for mixed-blood children were established in the Red River Colony. More and more fathers sent their sons back to England to be educated. Empowering their children meant helping them to rise on the social and economic ladder by suppressing their Indian heritage and taking on all the cultural trappings of their British or Scottish fathers.

As the years passed, the Hudson's Bay Company was forced to lift the ban which prevented its employees from bringing their English wives to the posts, and once this happened the mixed-blood girls were no longer seen as desirable partners. The coming of white settlers threatened both the economic and social status of mixed-blood children and eventually the problems which emerged erupted in the Riel Rebellion. Not even an English-style education could empower children disempowered by race.

Black Children

A little Madagascan slave boy, six or seven years old, is believed to be the first black to have lived in Canada, the forerunner of five waves of blacks to enter Canada during the next 350 years. He was brought to New France in 1628 by David Kirke and sold for fifty half-crowns to a French clerk who resold him to Champlain's master-builder who taught him his catechism.

Slavery in Canada existed on a much smaller scale than in the United States as there were no large plantations. Most slaves were either domestics or manual workers. In the mid-18th century slaves were sold in auctions in large centres such as Montreal and Halifax or advertised in local papers:

JAMES HAYT HAS FOR SALE

A Black boy, fourteen years of age, in full vigour of health, very active, has a pleasing countenance and every ability to render himself useful and agreeable in a family. The title for him is indisputable (*The Royal Gazette*, Saint John, New Brunswick, September 19, 1786).

Society accepted slavery, which could be easily rationalized by regarding people of darker skin as being either backward or less evolved. Even prominent churchmen, Roman Catholic, Presbyterian and Anglican, were slave owners, but by the late 18th century public opinion in both Upper and Lower Canada (Ontario and Quebec) was turning against the practice of slavery, and in 1833 the British Government's Emancipation Act proclaimed slavery illegal throughout the British Empire.

In 1784 a school for black children was opened in Digby, Nova Scotia, with funds from a philanthropic organization called The Associates of the Late Dr. Bray. During the next three years the organization opened three more schools for black children in other communities. The purpose of the schools was to ensure that black children were "properly instructed in the principles of Christianity and that the great and necessary duties of obedience and fidelity to their masters and humility and contentedness with their condition would be impressed on their minds" (Public Archives of Nova Scotia, 1839). There was, of course, an unfortunate paradox that while the associates of the late Dr. Bray may have seen themselves as doing good Christian work, the result was, in fact, to disempower black children by helping to keep them in the place they felt God had set aside for them.

In 1849 William King, an Irishman married to the daughter of a wealthy Louisiana planter and slave-owner, founded the Elgin Settlement for Blacks in Ontario. Three years earlier King had become a minister and missionary of the Presbyterian Church of Scotland. A confirmed abolitionist, he was embarrassed when his father-in-law died and left him 15 slaves. These he freed and took with him to the Elgin Settlement. The first mission school opened in 1850 with 14 black children and two white children. The education of the children was of such high quality — both Greek and Latin were part of the curriculum — that it attracted the attention of other white parents so that by 1854 half the children in the school were white. Two more schools were opened in the ensuing years. These mission schools produced graduates who not only became teachers but who were qualified to enter college. For Mr. King and the members of the settlement empowering children meant giving all children, black and white, the knowledge needed to succeed both in school and in adult life. But the times were not ripe for such views. By 1850 legislation authorizing segregated schooling for black children was in place in both Ontario and Nova Scotia and would not be removed from the books until the mid-1960s.

Native Indian Children

The policy of the Federal Government, with the cooperation of the churches, was to "civilize" the Indians, which, in 1875, according to the Minister of the Interior, meant giving them time "to understand the motives and acquire the habits of the White man, who labors to accumulate wealth in order that he may have the means of support in sickness or old age, or of giving his offspring a start in life" (Department of Indian Affairs, 1875:6). Two years later the Deputy Superintendent General of Indian Affairs wrote, "Education is the primary principle in the civilization and advancement of the Indian Race" (DIA, 1877:6). Clearly the Indian was to be taught to desire money and what it could purchase and to do this he or she must be separated from friends and family. Sir John A. MacDonald, while Superintendent General of Indian Affairs, said in his 1881 report: "The Indian youth, to enable him to cope successfully with his brother of white origin, must be dissociated from the prejudicial influence by which he is surrounded on the reserve of his band. And the necessity for the establishment more generally of institutions, whereat Indian children, besides being instructed in the usual branches of education, will be lodged, fed, clothed, kept separate from home influences, taught trades and instructed in agriculture, is becoming every year more apparent" (DIA, 1881:8).

Ten years later, the Superintendent of Indian Affairs wrote as follows to the Governor General of Canada: "It would be highly desirable, if it were practicable, to obtain entire possession of all Indian children after they attain to the age of seven or eight years, and keep them at schools of the industrial type until they have had a thorough course of instruction, not only in the ordinary subjects taught at public schools, but in some useful and profitable trade, or in agriculture, as the aptitude of the pupil might indicate he was best fitted for. Were such a course adopted the solution of that problem, designated 'the Indian question' would probably be effected sooner than it is likely to be under the present system" (DIA, 1891:xii). Native Indian children were to be empowered to seek manual jobs as domestics or agricultural workers.

Within the residential schools, which were run by the churches, Indian Affairs settled on a policy of "English only." The Superintendent in 1895 described Indian children as being "permanently disabled" if they did not speak English (DIA, 1895:xxiii). Reports from the schools spoke with some pride that the children were giving up their native tongues and speaking English only. Various punishments were meted out to those who opposed the rule and attempted to maintain their first language with siblings and friends. The results of the "English only" policy — seen by the authorities as empowering the children — were disastrous for many children. To begin with, English was often badly taught. The missionaries generally had little knowledge of how to assist second language learning, and in one school the children, who between them spoke a number of different Indian languages, were taught in English by French-speaking nuns. As children were given neither the right nor the opportunity to develop their first language, serious harm was done to generations of children who lost fluency in one language without gaining it in another. Cognitive development depends on ideas and concepts being taken into the mind, stored, retrieved, modified and expanded — and this process uses language. A child who is fluently bilingual can use both languages as channels for the reception of ideas and concepts and for the expression, modification and expansion of these concepts. Where a child is denied fluency in language — any language — the mind stagnates from the paucity of ideas reaching it; it suffers from linguistic malnutrition. By separating them from their linguistic and cultural heritage and by failing to ensure fluency in at least one language, government and churches disempowered native Indian children.

Chinese Children

The Chinese came to British Columbia in substantial numbers during the gold rush of the 1850s. Some settled and a few brought their families over. A trickle of Canadian-born and overseas Chinese children entered the public schools. Anti-Chinese feeling was running high at the turn of the century culminating in the riot of 1907 when an unruly white mob ran through Vancouver's Chinatown smashing windows and terrorizing the inhabitants.

Attempts were made by various groups, but particularly by the Trades and Labour Council, during the first two decades of the 20th century to keep Chinese children, whether born abroad or in Canada, out of the public schools in the province's capital, Victoria. In 1922 the Victoria School Board capitulated to the demands and set aside three schools for the exclusive use of Chinese children. While nominally this was supposed to take care of the problem created by the admission of newly arrived immigrant children who did not speak English, in fact, all Chinese children were required to attend the segregated schools. An additional reason for the segregation was an allegation that, as one trustee had put it, "We know there is not only a tendency with the Chinese to live in insanitary quarters, but a practice" (*Victoria Colonist*, 1922). The Chinese challenged the authorities on that score and the charge was dropped. The Chinese also pointed out that far from being illiterate and lacking fluency in English, some of their children had been at the head of their class and had been promoted to the next grade. The Chinese parents' response to the Board's policy was to boycott the schools. Gradually they wore the Board down with the sense and truth of their statements, and, as the incident took on national and international proportions, the Board was condemned by the press and left unsupported by government.

What lay behind the fiasco was, of course, economics. Members of the Victoria Trades and Labour Council feared for their jobs as young Chinese moved into the labor market where, because of their race, they would be paid less than a white man. Disempowerment rather than empowerment of Chinese youngsters was therefore the aim of many in the white community. But the Chinese knew that fluency in English and Chinese would empower their children. They were opposed to total segregation of non-English speaking children because they felt it delayed their acquisition of English by removing role models. Instead they asked for a program combining integration in regular classrooms with extra help through withdrawal or after school programs. During the boycott, which lasted for the school year, they set up their own schools where children were taught in Chinese, thus enabling them to acquire the skills necessary to secure work in the Chinese community or to return to China if access to jobs in the white community was denied them. Eventually the matter was resolved and the Chinese children returned to the Victoria public schools. But the attempted disempowerment of the children had been clearly linked to the economic hopes and fears of the dominant white community, and its effects well understood by the Chinese community.

Doukhobor Children

In the latter part of the 19th century over 7 000 Doukhobors, "Spirit Wrestlers," settled on the Canadian prairies, refugees from Russian oppression. While many adapted to the new life and became independent farmers, a small sect, the Sons of Freedom, refused to acknowledge the authority of the Canadian and provincial governments in such matters as registering births and deaths and sending their children to school. In 1908 a group of Doukhobors settled in western British Columbia where they owned their land in common, thus removing the need to take the oath of allegiance to the king, a requirement of individuals taking up crown lands, and opposed by the Doukhobors whose allegiance lay only with God.

For three years no attempt was made by the British Columbia government to force the parents in the Kootenay community to send their children to school. For one year some children attended the public school at Grand Forks, but then they were withdrawn. A school built by the Doukhobors at Brilliant closed after one term. Why? asked William Blakemore in 1911 as he conducted an enquiry into the problems surrounding this sect of Doukhobors. Answer: the Doukhobors did not see the schools as empowering their children but as disempowering them. The community gave Blakemore a statement outlining their position and although the English is poor, the substance of their argument is clear:

> The School teaching Doukhobors same did not accepted while being in Russia, and very seldom the children were thought to read and write, and if it had happened it was at home-school. We educate our children by means orally, so as not to have expense for the paper and printing matter. The School education we turned aside by many reasons and the most important of them are:
>
> 1. The school education teaches and prepares the people, that is children, to military service, where shed harmless blood of the people altogether uselessly. The most well educated people consider this dreadfully sinful such business as war, lawful. We consider this is great sin.
>
> 2. The school teaching at the present time had reached only to expedience for easy profit, thieves, cheaters and to large exploitation working-class laborious on the earth. And we ourselves belong to working-class people and we try by the path of honest labor, so we may reap the necessary maintenance, and to this we adopt our children to learn at wide school of Eternal Nature.
>
> 3. The school teaching separates all the people on earth. Just as soon as the person reached read and write education, then, within a short time leaves his parents and relations and undertakes unreturnable journey on all kinds of speculation, depravity and murder life. And never think of his duty, respecting his parents and elder ones, but he looks opposite, turning themselves,

enslaving of the people for their own licentious and insatiableness gluttony (British Columbia, 1913:52).

This position was reiterated in 1913 by Alex Evalenko in his book *The Message of the Doukhobors* when he rejected military drill as being opposed to the teachings of Christ "who brought peace, love and equality to this earth." He accused schools of producing "officials, lawyers, doctors and all manner and species of commercial buy-and-sell men, who have a great need of arithmetic and rapid reckoning, in their insatiable greed for easy money and luxury . . ." He continued: "Being of Russian birth, we yet dwell in our own community and consider ourselves citizens of the entire earthly globe and therefore we cannot regard our residence in British Columbia as fixed for all times. Today we happen to be here, after some time we may find ourselves in another country altogether . . ." (Evalenko, 1913:55).

The Doukhobors saw no need to educate their children in the English-speaking public schools which they believed would destroy the beliefs and the way of life they felt would empower their children. Their own language and way of teaching would suffice. But the British Columbia government thought otherwise and on two occasions in the ensuing years removed Doukhobor children from their homes and put them in institutions where, like it or not, they would get an English-medium education. The first mandated custodial care of Doukhobor children occurred in 1932 when over 600 adults were arrested for staging a series of nude protest marches and were sentenced to three years in prison. The 365 children who were either arrested with their parents or left without someone to care for them were sent to various institutions in the province to await the release of their parents. Twenty years later when these children were grown up trouble broke out in the Kootenays again as the Sons of Freedom resorted to arson and nude marches as their parents had before them and defied the authorities' demand that they send their children to school. Over the next six years approximately 170 children spent some time in an institution in New Denver set aside specifically for the care of truant Doukhobor children. Eventually the Doukhobor parents agreed to send their children to school, a promise which has largely been kept. But 20 years after the New Denver institution closed, fires were blazing in the Kootenays once more.

This brief history shows that what some see as empowerment — the right of children to live in a closed community according to the group's conscience using their own language — is seen by others as disempowerment — the confinement of children within a narrow religious and philosophical framework with no opportunity to examine, much less enter, the larger world outside. The clash between the Sons of Freedom and the British Columbia government demonstrates that religious beliefs can be seen to empower or disempower children depending on the world view of the opposing factions.

Ukrainian Children

At the end of the 19th century when the Ukraine was becoming over populated, the Canadian prairies were underpopulated. A booklet published in 1895 in the Ukraine extolled the virtues of Canada resulting in the first large group of Ukrainians arriving in Quebec City in 1896 on their way to the virgin lands. As the Canadian government was searching for the right kind of settlers for the prairies — agriculturalists — Clifford Sifton, Minister of the Interior, made an arrangement in 1899 with the North Atlantic Trading Company to recruit emigrants: the government was prepared to pay five dollars for each family head and two dollars for each family member. The word spread in the Ukraine and "the stalwart peasants in sheepskin coats," as Sifton described them, came in their thousands. They settled, built homes and raised families.

Most parents were eager for their children to become literate in English but not at the expense of fluency in Ukrainian, the language of the home and of their religious practices, the link between the generations, and a source of pride. If school was the place where children learned English, then home was the place where they would learn and maintain Ukrainian — unless, of course, the school was prepared to let them live and learn in both languages. It seemed at first that schools might accommodate the wishes of the Ukrainian parents. In Manitoba an amendment to the school act in 1890 had made it possible for a group of 10 or more pupils speaking French or any language other than English as their native language to be educated "upon the bilingual system." The first public school district set up by Ukrainians seems to have been started in 1898. But bilingual education, if it was to be effective, required good bilingual teachers and that was where the trouble lay. There were some young Ukrainian men who had received a good education before emigrating to Canada but whose English was too poor for them to be teachers of and in English. On the other hand, there were English-speaking teachers, some with a missionary zeal to work in the new settlements, who lacked any skill in Ukrainian. To cope with this dilemma, the Manitoba Department of Education opened the Ruthenian Training School in Winnipeg with the objective of training Ukrainian-English and Polish-English teachers for the public school system. Saskatchewan and Alberta followed suit, each, in time, establishing a training school for bilingual teachers.

But whereas the Ukrainian parents saw bilingualism as empowering their children, the authorities in the three provinces did not, and their fears that bilingual education meant substandard education were bolstered by the words of respected educators. Norman F. Black, who had published a methodology text entitled *English for the Non-English*, wrote in 1914, "It became evident that in hundreds of Canadian schools, both east and west, in Saskatchewan and Manitoba, as elsewhere, children of non-English speaking parents are wasting precious months and years; that ignorance is blossoming into stupidity and will bear fruit in social incompetence and perhaps in crime . . ." (Black, 1914:93). J.T.M. Anderson, an educator and later premier of Saskatchewan, referred to Manitoba's experiment in bilingual education in retrospect as "unwise legislation" which had resulted in thousands of children growing up in the province in comparative ignorance of the English language. "Fortunately," he wrote, "for the future of Manitoba and the Dominion of Canada this discredited system of bi-lingual teaching has virtually been abolished" (Anderson, 1917:215). C.B. Sissons was equally condemnatory of bilingual education that used a language other than French in conjunction with English. The most usual arguments given for the abolition of bilingual education were, first, that the quality of teaching in bilingual schools was poor, and second, that national unity required that minority group children adopt English, or, as Sissons put it, "English must be the common solvent for all" (Sissons, 1917:215). An "English only" policy would not only empower the individual, it would empower the nation.

But the tenacious Ukrainians, who by 1919 were denied bilingual education in prairie schools because of legislation passed in the provinces of Manitoba, Saskatchewan and Alberta, continued to maintain their Ukrainian language and traditions through classes held after school or on Saturday mornings. Today it is not uncommon to find fourth and fifth generation Ukrainian-Canadians fluent in the language of their forebears. Research has confirmed the wisdom of their action in empowering their children academically as well as culturally through bilingualism.

Discussion

Among the factors which disempowered the children of the six minority groups whose histories have been briefly told above were the following:

1. Due to poor teaching many children did not master English with the fluency necessary to succeed in school or the workplace.

2. Loss and denigration of the children's home language and culture resulted not only in a poor self-concept but further reduced the possibility of success in school by denying them fluency in the home language.

3. Some parents were deliberately denied access to economic rewards accorded those in the dominant group and were kept in low-status,

low-paying jobs which resulted in their children living at or below the poverty line.

4. Laws were enacted which adversely affected both minority parents and children; the public's fear of minority groups far exceeded its love of humankind and its concern for justice.

Of the six groups considered, three of them, the children of the fur traders or mixed-blood children, native Indian children and black children, remain to some degree disempowered. Their less than satisfactory results in school achievement suggest that failure to master the language of abstract thought in English as used in the school system, and the denigration of their home language and culture are still factors that schools have not fully addressed. The parents of many of these children still live in poverty on hand-outs from the government, and while the Charter of Rights forbids discrimination on the grounds of race, enacting a law does not automatically change attitudes or practices.

Two groups have prospered: Chinese children and Ukrainian children. Members of these groups can be found in all the professions as well as in commerce. While the influx of Hong Kong Chinese immigrants and the Asian gang problem have reawakened some of the prejudice that was so prevalent in the early decades of this century, it is unlikely that Chinese children will be disempowered as in the past.

Whether the Sons of Freedom Doukhobor children are today empowered or disempowered depends on one's point of view. Public school education has opened doors for them to a much wider world, but in so doing it has perhaps closed some doors on the heritage their parents hoped to hand on to them.

People then, as now, were faced with choices when it came to empowering or disempowering children. They could, for example, help children:

- to succeed or fail in school;

- to enter the workforce as equals or inferiors;

- to live in a closed community or in the wider world;

- to retain or lose their heritage language and culture;

- to dominate or be dominated.

The term "empowerment" has become the latest catchword, much as "multiculturalism" became some years ago. Today, almost 20 years after Prime Minister Trudeau referred to Canada as a bilingual country in a multicultural framework, the process of defining precisely what is meant by "multiculturalism" continues as the practice of multiculturalism is worked out in the public arena. The term "empowerment" will likely go through the same process as each of the following groups defines the concept from its own standpoint and seeks policies and programs in sympathy with its definition: the majority group, minority groups, students, parents, educators, businesspeople, church leaders, government officials and elected representatives. It is time now to see whether present policies and practices are empowering or disempowering children of minority groups who speak English as their second language.

The Present

In 1973-1974 and again in 1984-1986, with the assistance of government grants, I conducted two surveys of ESL in public schools across Canada. The following represents my findings in the four areas identified in the preceding section: English language training, heritage language maintenance, parents' access to economic rewards, and the law.

English Language Training

It was in Ontario in the 1950s that efforts were made to improve the quality of English teaching to non-English speaking immigrants. ESL teacher training courses were set up by the provincial government and materials were developed, the most notable of these being Carson Martin's *An Introduction to Canadian English*. Slowly, other provinces followed Ontario's lead. Today every province, through its college and university systems, offers training in ESL and most school districts, when hiring ESL teachers, look for proof of some specialized training. This is a far cry from the days when administrators believed anyone who spoke English could teach English as a second language, but particularly if they were considered too old, too sick or too incompetent to teach "normal" children.

Methods of teaching ESL have undergone enormous changes since the days of the audio-lingual method of the 1950s. Curriculum has also changed so that the emphasis is no longer on teaching just English, forcing the children to mark time until they are considered to have enough English to cope with content. Language teaching and content teaching can be carried on simultaneously, reinforcing each other, so that both language learning and content learning are enhanced. Research into second language acquisition has made it clear that while social language may be learned in about two years, it will take a child five to seven years to master the language of abstract thought in the second language. Good teaching is essential if this already long period is not to be extended even further, and here lies one major problem, for while ESL teachers are far better trained than they were 30 years ago, classroom teachers, on the whole, still lack the knowledge they need to help the many ESL children they are likely to meet in their classrooms during a lifetime of teaching. The past has clearly demonstrated through the faulty handling of native Indian children the importance of mastery of the language of instruction if children are to be empowered in terms of the dominant group.

Whereas in the 1950s there were virtually two programs for ESL children, the reception class and the withdrawal program, there are now at least 13 identifiable programs which can be grouped under four headings: (1) self-contained programs, (2) withdrawal programs, (3) transitional programs, and (4) mainstreaming. This variety makes it possible for schools to run programs that cater to the needs of their children within the unique setting of each school. Provincial governments have, over the years, increased the level of funding for ESL classes.

These changes, which are significant, have come about through the cooperation and determination of educators, parents, social workers, concerned citizens and politicians. In some instances people have worked as individuals, but ethnic societies, teachers' organizations and women's groups have played a large part in sustaining pressure on governments, universities and school districts to take actions that would empower ESL children by helping them master English.

Heritage Language Maintenance

As schools were forbidden for many years to teach in any language other than English — or, if not actually forbidden, strongly discouraged from doing so — third language schools, as they were known, sprang up in large and small centres across Canada teaching the languages of minority groups. Largely excluded from this phenomenon were the native Indians, many of whom, having grown up in residential schools, were afraid to teach their children their Indian language knowing that if they spoke it in school they would be punished.

The publication in 1969 of Book IV of the Royal Commission on Bilingualism and Biculturalism entitled *The Cultural Contribution of the Other Ethnic Groups* stirred an interest in the languages of Canada other than French and English. The federal government agreed to fund curriculum and materials development. Organizations of teachers teaching ethnic languages helped to legitimize work which had not previously been highly regarded. National conferences on heritage language maintenance coupled with the establishment at the Ontario Institute for Studies in Education of a centre concerned with research into heritage language learning gave the movement further momentum. Today thousands of children attend classes after school or on Saturday mornings often using materials prepared especially for them. In Ontario, in some schools, heritage language classes are offered during the school day, while in other provinces bilingual classes allow children to live and learn in two languages — English and the language of their home. While the benefits of bilingualism have been established by research, schools are still faced with the problem of finding competent bilingual teachers, particularly of languages not widely spoken.

Indian languages are being resuscitated in many regions of Canada, but due to the English-only policy of years gone by, some languages are spoken by only a few elders and may soon die out. Languages are, however, remarkably tenacious and the efforts of Indian people across Canada to revive their languages and cultures may well be successful.

The momentum begun by the report of the Royal Commission on Bilingualism and Biculturalism has been sustained by the various ethnic societies and some educators. Two other factors have helped: (1) the growing interest in human rights, including language rights, and (2) the size of the ethnic vote.

Access to Economic Rewards

Immigration has always been linked to the workforce. Indeed, once immigration became a serious concern of the federal government it was placed in the same cabinet portfolio as labor. After World War II the booming economy needed more workers and increased immigration was seen as the solution. 282 164 newcomers entered Canada in 1957 and from then until now the yearly number has fluctuated between a low of 71 689 (1961) and a high of 222 876 (1967). The projected figure for 1990 was 200 000 with further increases for the next five years. To be efficient and effective members of the workforce, newcomers need English; otherwise they are condemned to low-status, low-paying jobs, never utilizing the high level skills that many bring with them.

The federal government has funded programs to teach immigrants English and, in some cases, to train or retrain them for jobs. Despite constant complaints that there are not enough classes and that the waiting period to get in is too long, it is nonetheless a considerable improvement from the days when immigrants picked up English as best they could and learned to be content with whatever job they got in the hope that their children would fare better. In addition, the federal Charter of Rights and various provincial Bills of Rights have made it increasingly difficult for employers to engage in overt discrimination against visible minorities as they can now be called to account for racist actions.

Although government programs have improved access to economic rewards for the parents of minority children, many parents, through hard work and determination, have been the authors of their own good fortune — and these qualities they have passed on to their children, but not without criticism. One English-speaking parent was heard to remark that an ESL child in her daughter's class worked very hard and won all the prizes and this, she felt, was not fair to her daughter! Hard work is seen as empowering people — adults and children — by many of those who enter Canada.

But while many children have benefited by the improved and improving economic condition of their parents, for others the future remains bleak. Thousands of children live at or below the poverty line; some of these are immigrant children, many of them are native Indian children. That the vicious poverty cycle they are subjected to disempowers them can be clearly seen by the number of adults on welfare rolls and in prison. The failure of governments (both federal and provincial) to work diligently and compassionately with native people to solve the land claims issue is responsible for some of the economic hardship endured by native children.

The Law

A change in attitude by both the government and many citizens has made it impossible for legislators to enact discriminatory laws of the kind enacted in the latter part of the last century and the first half of this century. The federal Charter of Rights has resulted in various challenges to actions that seem to limit an individual in any way based on race, color or creed. But the law will always have trouble when it must decide between the right of the individual and the right of the group, or when the issue is one in which the morals or principles of one group are in direct opposition to those of another group. Nonetheless, the law has, by reducing discrimination, helped to empower minority group children. A hallmark case in the United States was that of Lau vs. Nichols (1974) when the Supreme Court ruled that the failure of the San Francisco Unified School District to provide English language instruction to non-English speaking children denied them the opportunity to participate in the educational program and hence violated their right to equal educational opportunity as guaranteed by the Constitution of the United States. The message was not lost on Canada.

Law is now seen as upholding rights — the rights of women, of minority groups and of children — and while some discrimination remains in our imperfect society, the changes that have occurred over the last 30 years have been impressive.

The Future

The momentum begun in the 1950s to empower the children of minority groups must continue. Recently a large western school district, recognizing that things were better than they were but not as good as they might be, commissioned three educators to review its current programs for non-English speaking minority children and to make recommendations for the 1990s. In its report the review team laid out five principles it felt should govern the Board's policies and practices in the future:

1. The educational and personal experiences ESL students bring to Canadian schools constitute the foundation for all their future learning; schools should therefore attempt to amplify rather than replace these experiences.

   [The home language and culture are not to be denigrated but appreciated and used to empower the children.]

2. Although English conversational skills may be acquired quite rapidly by ESL students, upwards of five years may be required for ESL students to reach a level of academic proficiency in English comparable to their native English-speaking peers; schools must therefore be prepared to make a long-term commitment to support the academic development of ESL students.

   [Mastery of English by ESL students empowers them.]

3. Interaction with users of English is a major causal variable underlying both the acquisition of English and the ESL students' sense of belonging to Canadian society; the entire school is therefore responsible for supporting the learning and interactional needs of ESL students and ESL provision should integrate students into the social and academic mainstream to the extent possible.

   [Discrimination disempowers — acceptance and integration empower.]

4. If ESL students are to catch up academically with their native English-speaking peers, their cognitive growth and mastery of academic content must continue while English is being learned. Thus, the teaching of English as a second language should be integrated with the teaching of other academic content that is appropriate to students' cognitive level. By the same token, all content teachers are also teachers of language.

   [It is generally true that the higher the level of schooling, the greater the economic rewards. Academic success in school empowers children with regard to later economic rewards.]

5. The academic and linguistic growth of ESL students is significantly increased when parents see themselves, and are seen by school staff, as co-educators of their children along with the school. Schools should therefore actively seek to establish a collaborative relationship with minority parents that encourages them to partici-

pate with the school in promoting their children's academic progress.

This last principle leads into Cummins' comments regarding the importance of "three inclusive sets of interaction or power relations" which he lists as follows:

• the classroom interaction between teachers and students

• relationships between schools and minority communities

• the intergroup power relations within the society as a whole (Cummins, 1986:23).

In my book *Beyond Methodology: Second Language Teaching and the Community* (Ashworth, 1985), I tried to delineate what some of the relationships are between second language teachers and various communities which they serve and which serve them, and to suggest ways in which teachers and communities, local, national, and international, can work more closely for the benefit of both individual students and society as a whole. I suggested then, as I do now, the great need for educators to keep the past and the present in their minds as they plan the future. We have come a long way in 30 years, but the journey is far from over.

Skutnabb-Kangas & Cummins (1988) in their book *Minority Education: From Shame to Struggle* make some telling remarks in their final chapter on language for empowerment. They point out that the education of minorities (and here they are talking worldwide) is organized the way it is, by others, because minorities lack the power to decide themselves. They claim that minorities do not want "power over others" but "power over oneself;" that is, the power to decide their own destinies without encroaching on the rights of others to do likewise. Those in power are unlikely to give it away voluntarily, hence power has to be won in every field, including that of education. They continue, "But the struggle has to be well informed. It has to be based on an adequate description of the past and present . . . It has to be based on a thorough analysis of what happens and why, at both a local and global level . . . It has to be based on a deep and profound intellectual and emotional understanding of what happens . . . We also need accurate accounts and analyses of ongoing struggles, with shortcomings and successes, to learn from each other . . ." (Skutnabb-Kangas & Cummins, 1988:390-391).

While this chapter has looked specifically at empowering the children of non-English speaking minority groups, they are but a part of the total school population, within which are other children disempowered for a variety of reasons. The part must therefore be seen in terms of the whole. Alexander Israel Wittenberg wrote: "In a free society, the very best education must be accessible to every child. This means two things. It means that the very best education this society has to offer must be available to every child, but, in addition, that this education must measure up to the best education that is or has been available anywhere" (Wittenberg, 1968:5-6).

References

Anderson, J.T.M. (1917). *Education of the New-Canadian.* Toronto: Dent.

Ashworth, M. (1988). *Blessed with Bilingual Brains.* Vancouver: Pacific Educational Press.

Ashworth, M. (1985). *Beyond Methodology: Second Language Teaching and the Community.* Cambridge: Cambridge University Press.

Black, N.F., (1914). "Western Canada's greatest problem: The transformation of aliens into citizens," *The Western School Journal,* 9(5).

British Columbia. (1912). *Report of the Royal Commission on Matters Relating to the Sect of Doukhobors in the Province of British Columbia,* Victoria, 1913:T. 52.

Brown, Jennifer S.H. (1977). "A colony of very useful hands," *Beaver,* 307(4).

Cummins, J. (1986). "Empowering minority students: A framework for intervention," *Harvard Educational Review,* 56(1).

Department of Indian Affairs. (1975). *Annual Report.* Ottawa.

Department of Indian Affairs. (1977). *Annual Report.* Ottawa.

Department of Indian Affairs. (1881). *Annual Report.* Ottawa.

Department of Indian Affairs.(1891). *Annual Report.* Ottawa.

Department of Indian Affairs. (1895). *Annual Report.* Ottawa.

Evalenko, A.M. (1913). *The Message of the Doukhobors.* New York: International Library Pub. Co.

Public Archives of Nova Scotia. (1839). *Account of the Institution Established by the Late Dr. Bray and His Associates,* abstract of their proceedings.

Sissons, C.B. (1917). *Bilingual Schools in Canada. Toronto: Dent.*

Victoria Colonist, January 12, 1922:9.

Skutnabb-Kangas, T. and Cummins, J., (eds.). (1988). *Minority Education: From Shame to Struggle.* Clevedon: Multilingual Matters.

Wittenberg, A.J. (1968). *The Prime Imperatives.* Toronto: Clarke Irwin.

Children and Prejudice: Conceptual Issues

Frances E. Aboud

There are three goals that we aim for when trying to create a multicultural society in Canada. One is to create equal opportunity for all members of the society regardless of their ethnic membership. A second goal is to have mutual respect among members of different ethnic groups. And a third is to have pride in one's own heritage. In my own research, I have concentrated on the second and third goals by studying children's respect for members of other groups and pride in their own group. Basically, there are two problems in reaching these goals. One is that because of cognitive immaturity, most young children arrive at school already prejudiced. The second problem is that because of the ethnic status hierarchy of most plural societies, many minority group children arrive at school with little pride in their group. Consequently, kindergarteners are a long way from reaching these two goals. Over the course of the following eight years, some but not all children approach the two goals. They approach the goals of mutual respect and pride in one's heritage as a result of both cognitive maturity and social influences.

I would like to review with you some of the research conducted by myself and others on these two problems. It was only after reviewing this and other published literature that I arrived at the previously mentioned conclusions. To reiterate, the conclusions were: that five-year-olds are highly prejudiced; that most young minority children do not feel proud of their ethnic group; that early prejudice and the later decline of prejudice are largely due to cognitive functioning; and that school and parent influences can either facilitate the decline of prejudice or help maintain prejudice. As it happened, these conclusions went against the prevailing theory of prejudice, namely that children of four years are unprejudiced and actually curious about people from different ethnic groups, but that with age prejudice increases as a result of learning from one's parents or from society (Allport, 1954). Unfortunately most research was not guided by theory; rather it was designed to assess whether prejudice exists but not why it exists. Consequently the old theory remained unchallenged.

Mutual Respect Among Groups

The first goal is that members of different ethnic groups respect each other. This is particularly problematic among majority white children. Their attitudes have been measured using indices of social distance ("put closer to you the people you like and farther away the people you dislike") or assignment of attributes such as kind, smart, mean and selfish. Regardless of the measure used, there is consistent evidence that most white children between the ages of three and five choose a black person as looking bad, as having negative qualities or as being least preferred as a playmate. When the sample includes children from five to seven years, the results are quite clear, with two-thirds and generally more claiming that the Asian, black or Native Indian is bad or disliked. When the responses of children from different age groups are compared, they show an increase in prejudice between four and seven years.

To illustrate these findings, I will describe how children express their prejudice on attitude tests. Williams and Morland developed a test that we have used in our research. The child is presented with 24 items such as: some children are selfish; they like to keep things to themselves and they don't share with their friends. Some items describe a negative attribute and others a positive attribute. The child is asked to point to the person whom the story is about. Two people are drawn on the opposite page, one from the child's in-group and one from the out-group. Most white children have experienced more selfishness from in-group playmates than from out-group children such as blacks. However, the majority of them say that negative stories, such as the selfish one, are about black people and positive stories are about white people. Williams & Morland (1976) consider that a child is biased if over 70 percent of the items are answered that way. Typically, they find that three-quarters of their white children between three and six years show this degree of prejudice. In our own research, Anna-Beth Doyle and I have found 85 percent of white kindergarteners to be biased against blacks and 68 percent against Amerindians. By third grade, only half of the white children were biased. They were more likely to say that blacks and Amerindians had positive attributes and that whites sometimes had negative attributes (Doyle, Aboud & Sufrategui, 1989).

Approximately half of the studies I reviewed from the literature published in the past 20 years found such a decline in prejudice after seven years of age. The others found that prejudice remained at the same high level between seven and twelve years of age. No studies found that prejudice increased. Thus, the old theory that prejudice does not exist in four-year-olds and that it becomes stronger during middle childhood is wrong. Prejudice is strong in four-year-olds and it either remains stable or declines during middle childhood.

The old theory also claimed that children acquire prejudice from their parents, not through direct teaching but simply because children seek the approval of their parents and so imitate them. I found little evidence in the literature for this hypothesis in children under seven years, but some evidence in children over seven years. In other words, the attitudes of children between four and seven do not correlate with their parents' attitudes. Typically these children are much more prejudiced than their parents. Only after seven years is there a slight correlation between child and parent attitudes.

Why then are young children so prejudiced? And what is responsible for the decline of prejudice in some children and the maintenance of prejudice in other children? My judgment is that young children are so prejudiced largely on account of their cognitive immaturity, and that cognitive maturity is responsible for the later decline in prejudice. The cognitive immaturity of four- to seven-year-olds can be characterized in a number of ways which lead to prejudice. Firstly, they are self-centred and in-group-centred because they are not capable of taking the point of view of someone who is different from themselves. We call them egocentric and sociocentric. This is seen in their excessive use of the words ME and I, and in their later obsession with the GOOD GUYS and the BAD GUYS. Secondly, they are dominated by their emotions, motivations and perceptions. The twin emotions of attachment to parents and fear of strangers dominate social interactions for the first two years of life. The need for rewards and for approval dominate early judgments of what is good and what is bad. And perceptions of a person's skin color, hair texture, and language determine a whole host of evaluations about that person. Basically, these four- to seven-year-olds assume that if a person **looks** different, he or she must be bad, wrong and frightening.

The shift for most children comes after seven years of age when they become concrete operational thinkers. This way of thinking allows the child to consider two different dimensions or points of view and to think beyond what they are able to see or perceive. Furthermore, these cognitions become so practised and credible that they can generally override emotions and perceptions. Anna-Beth Doyle and I have studied a number of these concrete operational ways of thinking to see if children use them when thinking about ethnic members. And they do. For example, preschoolers describe themselves and others in terms of concrete observable features only; whereas by eight years of age they begin to think about internal psychological qualities. The same holds true for their spontaneous descriptions of people from different ethnic groups. Another example is their increasing ability to take the role of other people and to understand that different perspectives can be valid. White children can predict at a very young age that, say, a black child will prefer another black child, or a Chinese child will prefer another Chinese child over a white one. However, they think he or she is wrong and that his or her preferences must change. This demonstrates their centred way of thinking. Decentration is expected after seven years of age, and Doyle and I have found that some but not all third graders believe that different preferences exist and that they legitimately arise from different ethnic affiliations. A final example is the concrete operational child's increasing ability to distinguish between people and groups — we refer to this as flexible thinking. It shows up in two ways. One is that children increasingly attribute the same qualities to both their own and other groups. While younger children assign all the positive qualities to their own group and all the negative qualities to out-groups, third graders say that both groups can be kind, smart and friendly, and similarly that both groups can be mean, selfish, and dirty. In other words, we both have some good and some bad. Katz, Sohn & Zalk (1975) have demonstrated another form of flexible thinking beginning in grades four to six. This is the ability to attend to individual differences in out-group members. These are just three examples of cognitive processes which become established, but by no means perfected, during middle childhood, and which are related to a reduction in prejudice.

This decline in prejudice is still a controversial issue. Some researchers believe that it is an artifact of the tests we use. On the one hand, lay people claim that we are forcing the young children to be or to appear prejudiced because of the attributes we ask them to assign and because they are forced to assign an attribute to only one group. Although I agree with some criticisms of these tests, I do not agree with these arguments. Firstly, the attributes we use are ones that have been spontaneously offered by children when describing themselves and their peers. To an adult they sound simplistic and concrete, but to a child they sound appropriate. Secondly, the requirement that children choose one and only one group as kind or mean does force them to make a judgment; however this does not force the child to appear prejudiced and in fact many children have unprejudiced scores. Moreover, when we allow the children to choose more than one group that is kind or mean, the young ones generally stick with one group while the older ones choose more than one group. This is one side of the controversy. The other side comes from researchers who claim that the tests are transparent and that older children are simply faking answers in order to appear unprejudiced. They point to a similar phenomenon in which white children give less prejudiced answers to a black examiner than to a white examiner. I agree that older children understand the desirability of being unprejudiced and that this understanding might be particularly salient to them when tested by an out-group examiner. However, I feel that this is not a problem with the tests, but is a manifestation of the new concrete operational thought that develops after seven years. These children are able to take different points of view and judge that their own tendency to be prejudiced is not socially desirable or acceptable, and will certainly not be acceptable to an out-group examiner. It is exactly these new cognitions that we feel contribute to the reduction of prejudice.

Why do some children maintain high levels of prejudice right on up through adulthood? Within this cognitive developmental framework, there are at least two possible reasons. One is that the ethnic context arouses emotions such as fear or threat. Under conditions of high emotional arousal, we know that people regress to a less mature cognitive level. Without the ability to think flexibly or take different points of view, immature forms of prejudice might once again dominate. A second reason is that although the person has the cognitive skills to be more tolerant, he or she is not applying these skills to the ethnic domain because it is socially acceptable to one's educators, peers and parents to think sociocentrically and inflexibly about out-group members. Very often the new cognitive skills have been applied to some ethnic groups but not to others, and so there exists selective prejudice. This points out the most important way in which schools can be involved in reducing prejudice; namely by facilitating the transfer of these new cognitive skills to the ethnic domain and by communicating by word and deed that prejudice is socially and morally unacceptable. To most children over seven years, these teachings will be new but nonetheless understood to be correct. This is because comprehension generally precedes production. In addition to introducing curriculum materials, some schools have promoted equal status contact among ethnic members through cooperative learning schemes. Once again it is only after seven years of age that such equal status and in-depth contact appears to reduce prejudice.

Pride in One's Heritage

The second goal is for members of different ethnic groups to have pride in their heritage. This is particularly problematic for children from minority groups in Canada. Although they too have their prejudices, in milder form than white children, their problem is an early preference for whites over their own group and a weak identification with their own group. This gradually changes with age so that by nine years of age there is a preference for their own group and a level of prejudice that is comparable to the whites of their own age. Many researchers have interpreted this as a rejection of themselves. This is not necessarily so, particularly among black children who often have high self-esteem despite a preference for whites.

I will review with you some of the research on which these conclusions are based. The self-identification literature uses a number of different tests to determine which ethnic group the child feels most closely associated with and how strong the association is. Some tests simply ask, Are you black? Are you

French Canadian? Are you Jewish? Minority children have no trouble identifying themselves with the correct label at five years. However, when the question is, which of these two dolls or children looks most like you? there is less in-group association. Generally, less than 70 percent of the black children and a lower percentage of Amerindian children say they look most like someone from their group. So although five-year-olds know their ethnic label, they think their appearance is different. When asked about overall similarity to various ethnic groups, minority children rate their in-group closer and more similar than other groups but still not as closely as white children do. Between five and eight years of age, their ethnic identification coalesces on all these measures.

By eight years of age a number of other processes come together. Ethnic constancy is one of these. Ethnic constancy refers to the understanding that one's ethnicity remains unchanged despite superficial changes in appearance, language or clothing, and it remains unchanged because ethnicity is based on one's ancestry. We have found that only concrete operational thinkers understand ethnic constancy, and that ethnic constancy solidifies self-identification.

The second process converging on ethnic identification is in-group preference. Once again, minority children under seven years of age do not typically show strong in-group preference. However, by eight and nine years, most of these children express a preference for their own group. To illustrate, Anna-Beth Doyle and I found that 49 percent of our black kindergarteners were pro-white, and only 7 percent were pro-black (the remainder were unbiased); 38 percent of them were pro-Amerindian. Similar percentages have been reported by researchers in the United States and Britain. Also, similar percentages have been reported with other minority samples such as Hispanics, Native Indians and Asians. This means that almost half the children were saying that positive attributes described white people and negative attributes described minority people. Even when children are allowed to assign positive attributes to as many people as they want rather than to only one, they assign fewer positive ones to their in-group than to whites. By eight years of age, 22 percent or more of the children were pro-in-group.

Pride in one's heritage involves more than merely identifying oneself as a member of a group, thinking of oneself as being similar to other members, and preferring one's group. Researchers such as Jean Phinney (1990) have begun to examine the ethnic identity of minority adolescents using the identity scheme of Jim Marcia which is based on Erikson. The idea is that the development of a mature identity involves an exploration of one's ethnicity and an eventual commitment to an identity that best fits one's needs, an identity in which ethnicity may or may not be important.

To return to the problems of young minority children, we realized that their concrete operational skills were being used to help them solidify their ethnic identification and preference for their own group. Constancy, role taking and flexibility were useful in helping them to see the positive side of their own group in addition to the positive side of other groups. The critical question at this point is why they are so pro-white before seven years of age. It is clear that the ethnic status hierarchy of our society is being internalized by them. But why are they so sensitive to this at an age when they are quite oblivious to other social information, and how do they interpret this information given that they are cognitively unable to think about social status the way an adult does? The answer may lie in the high need for social approval of young children. The need for approval is measured by a scale that determines whether respondents describe themselves excessively in terms of socially desirable qualities. People expect to win others' approval if they appear in socially desirable ways, such as always being good and never telling lies. Crandall, Crandall & Katkovsky (1965) developed a Social Desirability Scale for children and found that the need for approval is high in young children and declines with age. Thus, because of their high need for social approval, young minority children are overly sensitive to information about who wins approval. The information they extract from the media or from their community is not about the economic and political status of ethnic groups, but about who has and who receives the goodies. As it turns out, the items on most tests of prejudice refer to attributes which are highly associated with social approval and disapproval. When you use items tapping personal attachments such as liking or friendship, minority children give higher scores to their own group. Thus there seem to be two parallel evaluation systems functioning in minority children: one concerns a system of social approval which favors whites because of our social hierarchy, and another concerns personal attachments which favor in-group members, particularly family, because of early experiences with parents and siblings.

Schools tend to promote the system of social approval which interferes with the development of pride in one's heritage. Teachers place heavy emphasis on social approval and disapproval as a means of reward and punishment. They also promote values such as cleanliness, neatness, politeness and obedience, values which are culture-specific and classroom-specific (in that many adults would not consider these to be the really important values of life). Because most teachers are white and most book and TV characters are white, these values become associated with whiteness. Society has already become aware of these problems, and has taken steps to change such bias. However, we need to quadruple the number of minority people represented in this type of media and in textbooks — not till it reaches the proportion of the population found in our society but to at least 40 percent if it is to have an impact. We also need to train and hire more minority teachers and principals. These two types of educational intervention help to both reduce prejudice in whites and increase pride in minority children. They are: more in-depth contact/exposure to minority individuals of equal and higher status, and practice in applying specific concrete operational cognitive skills to ethnic persons. These changes come slowly, and some of us are impatient with the pace as we see new generations pass through the school system. I console myself with the view that at least in Canada there is a willingness to change, where 15 years ago there was not.

References

Aboud, F.E. (1988). *Children and Prejudice*. New York: Basil Blackwell.

Allport, G.W. (1954). *The Nature of Prejudice*. Cambridge, Mass.: Addison-Wesley.

Crandall, V.C., Crandall, V.J. & Katkovsky, W. (1965). "A social desirability questionnaire." *Journal of Consulting Psychology*, 29:27-36.

Doyle, A.B., Aboud, F.E. & Sufrategui, M. (1989). "Developmental patterns in positive and negative ethnic attitudes." Paper presented at SRCD meetings.

Katz, P.A., Sohn, M. & Zalk, S.R. (1975). "Perceptual concomitants of racial attitudes in urban grade-school children." *Developmental Psychology*, 11:135-144.

Phinney, J.S. (1990). "Ethnic identity in adolescents and adults: Review of research." *Psychological Bulletin*, 108:499-514.

Williams, H.E. & Morland, J.K. (1976). *Race, Color and the Young Child*. Chapel Hill: University of North Carolina Press.

The Educational and Vocational Aspirations of Students in Relation to Ethnic Group Membership

*Ronald J. Samuda and John Lewis

This chapter fulfils two purposes: it represents our attempt to identify certain aspects of institutional racism linked to the counselling programs in Canadian schools; second, it pinpoints data concerning the aspirations of ethnic minority students and their perceptions of the degree to which guidance counsellors are meeting their special needs.

The project was initiated in response to the widespread perception that ethnic minorities are seriously disadvantaged in the attainment of their career aspirations. Therefore, it was our determination to establish whether or not significant differences exist in the occupational and educational aspirations of ethnic group students when compared with those of the dominant majority culture. Our secondary goal was to examine the policies and practices of guidance counsellors within two school boards with regard to their provisions for educational and vocational counselling especially as those policies and practices affect the ethnic minority school populations. More precisely, the fundamental issue was to identify the extent to which schools are meeting the career and vocational development needs of students who are culturally diverse and different from the mainstream culture by virtue of race, color, and cultural background. In this presentation, we will summarize the methodology, research findings, implications and recommendations emanating from the data.

Methodology

Review of the Literature

At the inception of the enterprise, we carried out an exhaustive survey of the literature in order to establish previous findings relating to our goals. While we recognize the value of those research reports conducted in selected areas

---

*Portions of this chapter appeared in a pilot project report, submitted by R. Samuda, R. Chodzinski, J. Berry, & J. Lewis to the Secretary of State, Canada, 1989.

of the country (Anisef, 1975; Boyd, Goyder, Jones, McRoberts, Pineo & Porter, 1985; Ornstein, 1981; Clifton, 1982 and 1984; Li, 1978; Darroch, 1979; Breton & Rosenborough, 1968), we failed to unearth any definitive study dealing with the problems and the issues of racial and/or ethnic discrimination in career orientation and aspirations.

Some recent studies (Boyd, et al., 1985; Ornstein, 1981) have demonstrated the lesser importance of ethnicity and occupational attainment. However, they were mainly concerned with ethnic groups with relatively high acceptance in Canada, namely, the British, French, German, Dutch and Ukranian. Little attention has been paid to the educational and occupational characteristics of groups on the lower end of the prestige hierarchy, for example, Italian, Portuguese, West Indian and Native People (Berry, Kalin & Taylor, 1977; Pineo, 1977). It should be noted that some observers have recently considered there to be a collapse of the "vertical mosaic" (Pineo & Porter, 1985). That is, the status hierarchy in Canada may have changed considerably in the past 20 years.

Specific Objectives

Since this was really a pilot study, it was limited to the schools of one city only. The objectives of the pilot study were:

- to conduct a trial run of the national study;

- to develop a valid instrument;

- to establish a representative sub-sample of the defined ethnic groups;

- to collect data from the schools of Hamilton to serve as a model for a more expansive project.

Development of the Instrument

No prototype could be found to match the needs of our study. Consequently, we resorted to our own devices in creating a questionnaire. After several revisions, the final product emerged. It was then field tested with a sample of grade 10 and 12 volunteers from two Niagara Region schools to establish time constraints and to ensure that instructions were clearly defined. The final draft was then printed and submitted to the research officers of the Hamilton Boards of Education.

The Sample

Two school boards in the Hamilton area were used. Hamilton was chosen because of its industrial and ethnic mix which comprised a variety of ethnic groups. Grade 10 and 12 students were chosen since these grades represented critical levels for career and educational choices. We experienced acute difficulties in gaining final access to the students because of the fear of administrators that we were treading on very sensitive grounds dealing specifically with racism in the schools.

The individuals upon which the data was based were randomly selected from the total sample of over 1 400 students of both sexes. The final sample consisted of 200 males and 200 females. Since distribution was insufficient to include all categories of ethnicity, the groups were subsequently condensed and redefined on the basis of equal group representation by sex and grade. The final groups therefore constituted 20 males and 20 females allocated by grade to the following categories of ethnic grouping: English-Canadian, European, Italian, Oriental, Jamaican and Portuguese.

Administration of the Questionnaires

Upon approval by the Public and Separate School Board, the instrument was administered to students in the schools during the academic term of 1986. Protocol for administration was greatly aided by the cooperation of each school principal, by guidance counsellors and by home room teachers in the schools.

Analysis of the Data

Questionnaires were examined for completeness. They were then coded and hand-sorted to establish ethnic group identification and the table of random numbers was used to determine inclusion in the final sample. Biographical and socio-economic data were recorded for each case selected. A proportion of questionnaires was randomly selected for follow-up telephone interviews. The interviewer registered the perception of students and solicited information on any problems encountered in completing the questionnaire. The data was scrutinized for errors and inconsistencies.

Research Findings

The results encapsulate the two basic aspects of the study, namely, to identify: the educational and vocational goals of ethnic minority group students in comparison with their mainstream cohorts; and the guidance services provided to meet the special needs of the students in relation to their ethnic group membership.

Educational and Vocational Aspirations

All groups indicate a high expectation of completing high school, but there are major differences in what they expect to do thereafter. The majority of English-Canadian and Oriental respondents intend to go to university while many fewer Portuguese and Jamaicans expect to do so. Conversely, more than twice as many Italian, Portuguese and Jamaican respondents propose to go to work directly from high school than do English-Canadian, European and Oriental respondents.

Corresponding to these educational differences are occupational choices: many Oriental and English-Canadian respondents intend to have careers as professionals, while few among the Italian and Portuguese do so. And conversely, many Italian and Portuguese are selecting skilled and unskilled labor, while few of the others do so. We thus observe a strong split among the ethnic groups, one that appears to be related more to cultural values than to racial distinctions: English-Canadians, Europeans and Orientals have much in common in their educational and occupational aspirations, as do the Italian, Portuguese and Jamaicans among themselves; but these two sets are clearly different one from the other.

One of the most important findings is that Oriental students "look like" English-Canadian and European students in our data, while Italian and Portuguese students "look like" Jamaicans. Thus, we have been forced to move away from the rather simplistic categorization and use of the term "minority" in order not to violate the findings.

There are strong similarities across all groups with respect to naming those who influenced their educational and occupational aspirations, with parents overwhelmingly being identified. We can thus conclude that educational and work values, that are probably widely shared in the ethnic group, are being transmitted within the family. It is also likely that this high level of parental influence is indicative of minimal intergenerational disagreement between parents and offspring. Both these observations suggest a good deal of perpetuation of these ethnic-linked educational and work values across generations into the future. Combined with the earlier results on group differences in educational goals, they may lead to a possible return of the "vertical mosaic" in Canadian society, but with different ethnic groups occupying the higher and lower strata. This possible re-emergence of the link between ethnicity and status is a cause for concern.

While there are few differences across ethnic groups in rating which factor affects one's ability to obtain a job, there were significant differences in the perception of barriers to reaching one's occupational goals: color and race were seen to be relatively greater impediments by Portuguese and Jamaicans (but only race was so judged by Orientals) than by other groups. However, seen in the context of the other barriers (such as the high cross-group agreement about lack of education and training) these racial factors are judged to be relatively less important. We may conclude that such racial factors appear to be viewed as **relatively** more serious by these three groups, but not so serious in the overall scaling of barriers to attaining one's occupational goals.

Finally, there is considerable cross-group agreement about the values that are important in one's life now, and at age 30: staying in school, being honest, happy, rich and healthy, are all subscribed to uniformly. Slight variations from this general pattern (for example, higher ranking of family and religious values among the Portuguese) do not seriously detract from what is a very high level of consensus about what makes for the "good life" in Canada.

Guidance Services

Several critical conclusions emerge from the data relating to the delivery of guidance services for ethnic group students. The essential inference to be drawn is that counsellors are not meeting the special educational and vocational needs of some of the multicultural students they serve. More specifically, the students expressed concerns about the lack of guidance services available to them. It is clear that guidance services meet the needs of the status quo through delivery methods which appear to be seen by some of the ethnic minority group students to be traditional and insufficient for their particular needs. When viewed from the comparative perspectives of board of education directives and school practice, there seems to be a gap between policies established by the school boards and their implementation in the guidance and counselling taking place in the schools.

Implications and Recommendations

The data clearly indicates differences in the perception of certain ethnic minority group students when compared with those of their dominant majority group counterpart. Ethnic minority group students are aware that structural barriers in Canadian society will inhibit their attainment of occupational goals. In other words, Jamaican, Italian and Portuguese groups are more conscious of structural barriers than are those of Canadian Anglo-Saxon and Oriental backgrounds. Consequently, it is not surprising to find that the shift in the vertical mosaic consists of a sharing of the top echelons among individuals of WASP and Oriental backgrounds while the Southern European and Caribbean students see themselves as suffering from the endemic racism that exists in schools and in the society at large. The data therefore leads us to recommend the following:

At the School Board level, administrators should:

- undertake a review of current policies and practices regarding the counselling, assessment, and placement of minority students to determine fairness in relation to Ministry of Education guidelines;

- conduct a survey of student populations to ascertain the demographic composition of ethnic group students in programs;

- determine if there is a disproportionately high number of ethnic group students in vocational, special education, or basic level classes. And if so, refine and develop policies and procedures to ensure equitable proportions;

- implement, in collaboration with institutions of higher learning, in-service courses in anti-racist education, assessment, and intercultural counselling;

- encourage and expect superintendents, principals, resource teachers and guidance counsellors, to assume leadership roles in implementing fair multicultural practices within the schools.

At the school level, principals should:

- assume a leadership role locally regarding the implementation of fair anti-racist practices in the counselling, assessment and placement of ethnic minority group students;

- implement school level policy for communicating with parents, especially where ethnic and intercultural issues are involved;

- to the extent that a principal is responsible for hiring, appoint staff who are knowledgeable and skilled in the area of anti-racist education and representative of the community in the areas of language, ethnicity and culture.

Given the existence of the present demography (the multiethnic student mix in the schools), the goals of intervention into such a system must necessarily be fourfold: to understand culture as a concept; to value cultural differences; to accept the rights of others to be different; and to design procedures for the harmony of all cultures within the school system. To this end, teachers, administrators, and counsellors in particular, need specific pre-service and in-service professional education in multicultural methods and programs.

Interventive training should include:

- knowledge of Canada's multicultural policies;

- knowledge of individual school board policies;

- awareness of cultural encapsulation;

- leadership in battling encapsulation and ethnocentric attitudes;

- expression of staff problems and issues;

- emphasis on success and solutions;

- awareness of cultural similarities and differences;

- use of human resources in the community;

- acknowledgment of variables in relation to ethnicity (age, socio-economic class, religion and so on);

- acknowledgment of within-group differences;

- awareness of contemporary culture portraits of multiethnic and multicultural students rather than timeworn stereotyped notions of the culture of the student;

- cultural awareness across the curriculum;

- adoption of race-relations codes of behaviors for students and staff;

- solicitation of qualitative and quantitative evaluation of programs implemented in the schools.

The Need for Intercultural Counsellor Training

The preceding recommendations for intervention are aimed primarily at administrators, for it is at this level that change must first be initiated. Guidance delivery services will not be improved without a dedicated approach to anti-racist methods at the level of the administration. As counsellors and teachers come to realize the serious intent of policy makers, they in turn will be more prepared to shift attitudes and seek out ways of developing better methods of meeting the needs of a multicultural school population.

Guidance personnel should become cognizant of the fact that ethnic group students in the study perceive that their special needs are not being served. Why do the students hold such views? Is it because counsellors, as a whole, have defined their role in the traditional format, namely, to spread their efforts equally across the entire school population without making special provisions for intercultural and inter-ethnic student groups? There appears to exist few theoretical models for multicultural counselling in the present school systems and a dearth of specific in-service or pre-service training programs in the area of multicultural counselling for counsellors and school psychologists in the faculties of education.

It might be the case that constraints such as lack of educational support systems, and apparent apathy on the part of school boards and community leaders, have led the counsellors to the conclusion that multicultural counselling methods geared to serve specific ethnic groups are unnecessary or are regarded as low in priority. Yet, intercultural counselling has been highlighted in a recent thrust in the counselling literature (for example, Sue, Bernier, Duncan, Feinberg, Pedersen, Smith & Vasquez-Nuttal, 1982; Ibrahim, 1985; Chodzinski, 1985; Lloyd, 1987; Pedersen, 1988; Lewis, 1989; Samuda, Kong, Cummins, Lewis & Pascual-Leone, 1989).

Counsellors are urged to:

* become aware of personal biases, racisms, bigotries, prejudices and stereotypical attitudes.

* develop sensitivity to the unique needs and pressures of being an ethnic group adolescent.

* use appropriate simple language (an interpreter if needed); meet students in culturally accepted places; express interest in and/or ignorance of the culture; demonstrate unconditional positive regard.

* be aware that lack of social acceptability often leads to low self-concept.

* develop means to quickly integrate new ethnic group students with peers.

* learn about different cultures; participate in minority activities; learn key phrases in the other language.

* learn about the specific historical environmental and physical context in which the student operates.

* be aware of tension from family and peer pressure to conform.

* help the student achieve social acceptability and a realistic self-concept.

* consider the student's attitudes and aspirations in the cultural context (personal and community values).

* reduce reactive office procedures; concentrate rather on student interactions and listen to "gossip" in an effort to catch problems that might not surface through conventional channels. In short, adopt a proactive stance to the counselling of minority students.

- use peer group counsellors, volunteers, and community leaders of similar backgrounds as "partners" in counselling.

In addition to those precepts listed above, counsellors should seek to steer clear of certain negative attitudes and characteristics. For example, they should avoid: preaching mainstream cultural values; underestimating the existence of personal biases and prejudices; assuming that students can be treated alike; assuming that students know the English language well enough to perform on culturally biased tests; losing sight of the individual in the context of the culture; overestimating cultural differences to the detriment of similarities; ignoring the effects of racial discrimination on personality development, self-esteem, realization of self, and choice of vocation; assuming that a simple interaction with a culturally different environment will give others a positive attitude; assuming that goodwill will replace a student's pain of past prejudices, reduce class distinction or lessen the suspicions of minority clients.

This study has demonstrated the need for counsellor in-service training. Counsellors must come to understand and acknowledge the impact of systemic, structural and institutional racism on the educational and career aspirations of visible ethnic group students and particularly on the realization of their vocational goals. Specifically, counsellors need to be provided with special multicultural counselling techniques that take into account the racist social barriers that face those visible ethnic group students who are striving for their piece of the pie in Canadian society.

Finally, in general terms, we need a comprehensive approach to the delivery of guidance services specifically geared for ethnic minority group students, defined by Sue & Sue (1990) as the "culturally different," in order to foster a fairer degree of educational equity within the educational systems and within the workplace. It is simply not good enough to "treat them all alike." It might be well to reiterate the need for School Boards to give priority to the establishment of better counselling methods as part of an anti-racist policy. But, it is even more essential being implemented at the school level. In particular, those responsible for the administration of guidance services should seek ways and means of providing appropriate in-service education.

Concomitantly, faculties of education should be prepared to organize such in-service programs. This would require a shift on the part of most faculties especially in terms of their hiring practices and the priorities of their counsellor training programs. As Canada's demography increasingly reflects cultural diversity, such a wide scale policy of restructuring becomes not only desirable but imperative.

It is true that Porter's "vertical mosaic" may no longer hold true for certain ethnic groups who have used education to overcome their disadvantages and to establish themselves at the higher echelons of the social and economic structure of Canadian society (Boyd et al., 1985). But it is also true, as Samuel (1987) has so clearly demonstrated, that racial discrimination against visible ethnic minorities, in particular, is still a major factor in the Canadian labor market. In our quest for a fair and equitable system of social justice, the programs of guidance and counselling in the schools are of central significance. Counsellors are more powerful than they realize. They can function either as gatekeepers or as facilitators to the educational and occupational opportunities that exist in the world of work; but they need both the proper attitudes and the proper intercultural training if their work in the schools is to help in fostering a harmonious multicultural and multiracial Canadian society.

References

Anisef, P. (1975). "Consequences of ethnicity for education plans among grade 12 students." In A. Wolfgang (ed.), *Education of Immigrant Students*. Toronto: OISE Press.

Berry, J., Kalin, R. & Taylor, D.M. (1977). *Multiculturalism and Ethnic Attitudes in Canada*. Ottawa: Ministry of Supply and Services.

Boyd, M., Goyder, J., Jones, A., McRoberts, H., Pineo, P. & Porter, J. (1985). *Ascription and Achievement: Studies of Mobility and Status Attainment in Canada*. Ottawa: Carleton University Press.

Breton, R. (1978). "The structure of relationships between ethnic collectivities." In L. Dreiger (ed.), *The Canadian Ethnic Mosaic: A Quest for Identity*. Toronto: McClelland & Stewart.

Breton, H. & Rosenborough, H. (1968). "Ethnic differences in status." In R.B. Bishen et al. (eds.), *Canadian Society*, (3rd Ed.). Toronto: Macmillan.

Chozinski, R. (1985). "The role of the school counsellor in multicultural education." In R. Samuda & S. Kong (eds.), *Multicultural Education: Programs and Methods*. Vancouver: ISSP.

Clifton, R.A. (1982). "Ethnic differences in the academic achievement process in Canada." *Social Science Research*, 11:67-87.

Clifton, R.A. (1984). *Ethnicity, Teachers' Expectations and Students' Performances*. Unpublished paper, University of Manitoba.

Darroch, S. (1979). "Another look at ethnicity, stratification and social mobility in Canada." *Canadian Journal of Sociology*, 4:1-25.

Ibrahim, F.A. (1985). "Effective cross-cultural counselling and psychotherapy." *The Counseling Psychologist*, 13(4):625-638

Lewis, J.E. (1989). "Inferences in cross-cultural counselling." *Orientation*, 3:49-53.

Li, P.S. (1978). "The stratification of ethnic immigrants: The case of Toronto." *Canadian Review of Sociology and Anthropology*, 15(1):31-40.

Lloyd, A.P. (1987). "Multicultural counselling, does it belong in a counsellor education program?" *Counsellor Education and Supervision*, 26:164-183.

Ornstein, M. (1981). "The occupational mobility of men in Ontario." *Canadian Review of Sociology and Anthropology*, 18:183-215.

Pedersen, P. (1988). *A Handbook for Developing Multicultural Awareness*. Alexandra, VA.: American Association for Counselling and Development.

Pineo, P.C. (1977). "The social standing of ethnic and racial groupings." *Canadian Review of Sociology and Anthropology*, 14:147-157.

Pineo, P.C. & Porter, J. (1985). "Ethnic origin and occupational attainment." In M. Boyd (ed.), *Ascription and Achievement in Canada*. Ottawa: Carleton University Press.

Samuda, R., Kong, S., Cummins, J., Lewis, J. & Pascual-Leone, J. (1989). *Assessment and Placement of Minority Students*. Toronto/Vancouver: Hogrefe & ISSP.

Samuel, T.J. (1987). *Immigration, Visible Minorities and the Labour Force in Canada: Vision 2,000*. Paper presented at the conference on Canada 2000, Race Relations and Public Policy, October 30 - November 1, 1987. Ottawa: Carleton University.

Sue, D.W. & Sue, D. (1990). *Counseling the Culturally Different: Theory and Practice*, (2nd Edition). Toronto: Wiley & Sons.

Sue, D.W., Bernier, J.E., Duncan, A., Feinberg, L., Pedersen, P., Smith, C.J. & Vasquez-Nuttal, G. (1982). "Cross-cultural counselling competencies." *The Counselling Psychologist*, 19(2):45-52.

Section III

Educational Transformation for Empowerment

A Curriculum for Empowerment, Action and Change

*James A. Banks

When students are empowered, they have the ability to influence their personal, social, political and economic worlds. Students need specific knowledge, skills and attitudes in order to have the ability to influence the worlds in which they live. They need knowledge of their social, political and economic worlds, the skills to influence their environments, and humane values that will motivate them to participate in social change to help create a more just society and world.

This chapter describes the nature of knowledge and the dominant canons, paradigms and perspectives that are institutionalized within the school and university curriculum. I contend that the knowledge that is institutionalized within the schools and the larger society neither enables students to become reflective and critical citizens nor helps them to participate effectively in their society in ways that will make it more democratic and just. I propose and describe a curriculum designed to help students to understand knowledge as a social construction and to acquire the knowledge, skills and values needed to participate in civic action and social change.

The Nature of School Knowledge

Students are usually taught school knowledge as a set of facts and concepts to be memorized and later recalled. They are rarely encouraged to examine the assumptions, values, and the nature of the knowledge they are required to memorize or to examine the ways in which knowledge is constructed. Knowledge in the school curriculum is usually viewed as objective, neutral and immune from critical analysis. Popular writers such as Hirsch (1987) and Ravitch & Finn (1987) have contributed to the school conception of knowledge as a body of facts not to be questioned, critically analyzed and reconstructed. Hirsch (1987) writes as if knowledge is neutral and static. His book contains

*This chapter is reprinted with permission from: Christine E. Sleeter, Editor, *Empowerment Through Multicultural Education*. Albany: State University of New York Press, 1991, pp. 125-141, ff. 311-313.

a list of important facts that students should master in order to become "culturally literate." Ravitch & Finn (1987) identify and lament the factual knowledge that United States high school students do not know. Neither Hirsch nor Ravitch & Finn discuss the limitations of factual knowledge or point out that knowledge is dynamic, changing, and constructed within a social context rather than neutral and static.

I agree with Hirsch and Ravitch & Finn that all United States citizens need to master a common core of shared knowledge. However, the important question is: *Who will participate in the formulation of that knowledge and whose interests will it serve?* We need a broad level of participation in the identification, construction and formulation of the knowledge that we expect all of our citizens to master. Such knowledge should reflect cultural democracy and serve the interests of all of the people within our pluralistic nation and world. It should contribute to public virtue and the public good. The knowledge institutionalized within our schools and colleges and within the popular culture should reflect the interests, experiences and goals of all the nation's citizens and should empower all people to participate effectively in a democratic society.

Knowledge and Empowerment

To empower students to participate effectively in their civic community, we must change the ways in which they acquire, view and evaluate knowledge. We must engage students in a process of attaining knowledge in which they are required to critically analyze conflicting paradigms and explanations and the values and assumptions of different knowledge systems, forms and categories. Students must also be given opportunities to construct knowledge themselves so that they can develop a sophisticated appreciation of the nature and limitations of knowledge and understand the extent to which knowledge is a social construction that reflects the social, political and cultural context in which it is formulated.

Participating in processes in which they formulate and construct various knowledge forms will also enable students to understand how various groups within a society often formulate, shape and disseminate knowledge that supports their interests and legitimizes their power. Groups without power and influence often challenge the dominant paradigms, knowledge systems and perspectives that are institutionalized within society. Knowledge and paradigms consistent with the interests, goals and assumptions of dominant groups are institutionalized within the schools and universities as well as within the popular culture. A latent function of such knowledge is to legitimize the dominant political, economic and cultural arrangements within society.

The Attempt to Reformulate the Canon

The ethnic studies and women studies movements, which emerged from the civil rights movement of the 1960s and 1970s, have as a major goal a reformulation of the canon that is used to select and evaluate knowledge for inclusion into the school and university curriculum (Banks, 1989). The demand for a reformulation of the curriculum canon has evoked a concerted and angry reaction from established mainstream scholars. They have described the push by ethnic and feminist scholars for a reformulation of the canon as an attempt to politicize the curriculum and to promote "special interests." Two national organizations have been formed by established mainstream scholars to resist the efforts by ethnic and feminist scholars to reformulate the canon and transform the school and university curriculum so that it will more accurately reflect the experiences, visions and goals of women and people of color. They are the Madison Center and the National Association of Scholars (Heller, 1989). The mainstream scholars who have labelled the curricular goals of women and people of color "special interests" view their own interests as universal and in the public good and any claims that challenge their interests as "special interests." Dominant groups within a society not only view their own interests as identical to the public interest but are usually able to get other groups, including structurally excluded groups, to internalize this belief. The school and university curriculum help students to acquire the belief that the interests, goals and values of dominant groups are identical to those of the civic community.

School Knowledge and the Dominant Canon

To develop a sense of the need for social change, a commitment to social participation, and the skills to participate effectively in social action that eventuates in change, the knowledge that students acquire must have certain characteristics. It must describe events, concepts and situations from the perspectives of the diverse cultural and racial groups within a society, including those who are politically and culturally dominant as well as those who are structurally excluded from full societal participation. Much of school knowledge as well as knowledge in the popular culture presents events and situations from the perspectives of the victors rather than the vanquished and from the perspectives of those who control the social, economic and political situations in society rather than from the points of view of those who are victimized and marginalized.

School and societal knowledge that present issues, events and concepts primarily from the perspectives of dominant groups tends to justify the status quo, rationalize racial and gender inequality, and to make students content with the status quo. An important latent function of such knowledge is to convince students that the current social, political and economic institutions are just and that substantial change within society is neither justified nor required.

The ways in which the current social, economic and political structures are justified in the school and university curricula are usually subtle rather than blatant. These justifications are consequently more effective because they are infrequently suspected, recognized, questioned or criticized. These dominant perspectives emanate from the canon that is used to define, select and evaluate knowledge in the school and university curriculum in the United States and in other Western nations. This canon is European-centric and male-dominated. It is rarely explicitly defined or discussed. It is taken for granted, unquestioned and internalized by writers, researchers, teachers, professors and students.

The Western-centric and male-centric canon that dominates the school and university curriculum often marginalizes the experiences of people of color, developing nations and cultures, and the perspectives and histories of women. It results in the Americas being called the "New World," in the notion that Columbus "discovered" America, in the Anglo immigrants to the West being called "settlers" rather than "immigrants," and in the description of the Anglo immigrants' rush to the West as the "Westward Movement." Calling the Americas "The New World" subtly denies the nearly 40 000 years that Native Americans have lived in this land. The implication is that history did not begin in the Americas until the Europeans arrived. From the perspectives of the Lakota Sioux the Anglo settlers in the West were invaders and conquerors. The "Westward Movement" is a highly Euro-centric concept. The Lakota Sioux did not consider their homeland the West but the centre of the universe. And, of course, it was the Anglos who were moving West and not the Sioux. From the perspective of the Lakota Sioux it was not a Westward Movement but the Great Invasion.

Concepts such as "The New World," "The Westward Movement," "hostile Indians," and "lazy welfare mothers" not only justify the status quo and current social and economic realities, they also fail to help students understand why there is a need to substantially change current social, political and economic realities or help them to develop a commitment to social change and political action. These Anglo-centric and Euro-centric notions also fail to help students of color and female students to develop a sense of empowerment and efficacy over their lives and their destinies. Both the research by Coleman (1966) and the research on locus of control (Lefcourt, 1976) indicate that people need a sense of control over their destiny in order to become empowered to achieve or to act. Many students of color and female students are victimized and marginalized by the knowledge that results from the Euro-centric canon because they are made to believe that problems such as racism and sexism either do not exist in any substantial way or that such problems result from their own actions or shortcomings. In his book, *The Closing of the American Mind*, Bloom (1987) states that African American students are not well integrated into the structure of predominantly white university campuses because of their own resistance to social integration. This is a classic example of "blaming the victim" (Ryan, 1971) and contradicts the research findings of Fleming (1985). Fleming attributes the structural exclusion of African American students on predominantly white campuses to an inhospitable environment that fails to meet the needs of African American students.

The Dominant Canon and the Popular Culture

The popular culture frequently reinforces and extends the dominant canon and paradigms taught in the school and university curriculum. An example is the popular film, *Mississippi Burning*. This film presents several dominant-group perspectives on the civil rights movement of the 1960s that are notable. In actual history, African Americans were the real heroes of the civil rights movement. They were the primary architects of the movement, lead the first demonstrations and sit-ins, and showed tremendous efficacy in the movement. The FBI (Federal Bureau of Investigation), under the leadership of J. Edgar Hoover, was at best a reluctant protector of civil rights and played a major role spying on and undercutting the civil rights movement and civil rights leaders. Martin Luther King was a frequent victim of Hoover's tactics and undercover agents (Garrow, 1986). Despite these realities, *Mississippi Burning* presents African Americans as shadowy figures who were primarily victims and two FBI agents as the real heroes and defenders of black rights in the civil rights movement. The depiction of the civil rights movement in *Mississippi Burning* is a travesty on history but was a popular film that was believable and credible to many Americans because it is consistent with the canon that is institutionalized and taught within the school and university curriculum.

A Transformative Curriculum for Empowerment

In the above section of this chapter, I described the nature and goals of the dominant Euro-centric curriculum in the nation's schools and colleges. This curriculum reinforces the status quo, makes students passive and content, and encourages them to acquiescently accept the dominant ideologies, political and economic arrangements, and the prevailing myths and paradigms used to rationalize and justify the current social and political structure.

A transformative curriculum designed to empower students, especially those from victimized and marginalized groups, must help students to develop the knowledge and skills needed to critically examine the current political and economic structure and the myths and ideologies used to justify it. Such a curriculum must teach students critical thinking skills, the ways in which knowledge is constructed, the basic assumptions and values that undergird knowledge systems, and how to construct knowledge themselves.

A transformative curriculum cannot be constructed merely by adding content about ethnic groups and women to the existing Euro-centric curriculum or by integrating or infusing ethnic content or content about women into the mainstream curriculum. When the curriculum is revised using either an additive or an infusion approach, the basic assumptions, perspectives, paradigms and values of the dominant curriculum remain unchallenged and substantially unchanged, despite the addition of ethnic content or content about women. In such a revised curriculum, the experiences of women and people of color are viewed from the perspectives and values of mainstream males with power. When the meeting of the Lakota Sioux and the Anglos from the East is conceptualized as "The Westward Movement," adding content about the Lakota and about women neither changes nor challenges the basic assumptions of the curriculum or the canon used to select content for inclusion into it. The Lakota and women heroes selected for study are selected using the Western-centric, male-dominated paradigm. When the dominant paradigm and canon is used to select ethnic and women heroes for inclusion into the curriculum, the heroes selected for study are those who are valued by dominant groups and not necessarily those considered heroes by victimized and non-mainstream groups. Ethnic heroes selected for study and veneration are usually those who helped whites to conquer or oppress powerless people rather than those who challenged the existing social, economic and political order. Consequently, Sacajawea and Booker T. Washington are more likely to be selected for inclusion into the mainstream curriculum than are Geronimo and Nat Turner.

Critical Thinking and Multiple Voices

A curriculum designed to empower students must be transformative in nature and help students to develop the knowledge, skills and values needed to become social critics who can make reflective decisions and implement their decisions in effective personal, social, political and economic action. In other words, reflective decision-making and personal and civic action must be the primary goals of a transformative and empowering curriculum.

The transformative curriculum must help students to reconceptualize and rethink the experience of humans in both the United States and the world, to view the human experience from the perspectives of a range of cultural, ethnic and social-class groups, and to construct their own versions of the past, present and future. In the transformative curriculum multiple voices are heard and legitimized: the voices of textbook, literary and historical writers, the voices of teachers, and the voices of other students. Students can construct their own versions of the past, present and future after listening to and reflecting on the multiple and diverse voices in the transformative classroom. Literacy in the transformative curriculum is reconceptualized to include diverse voices and perspectives and is not limited to the form of literacy promoted by Hirsch (1987), that is, to the mastering of a list of facts constructed by authorities. Writes Starrs (1988), "In the new definition literacy should be seen as a struggle for voice. As such the presence of different voices is an opportunity and a challenge. All students will deal with the fact that their voices differ from one another's, from their teachers', from their authors'. All learners will somehow cope with the issue of translating their many voices, and in the process they will join in creating culture — not simply receiving it."

The transformative curriculum teaches students to think and reflect critically on the materials they read and the voices they hear. Baldwin (1985:326), in a classic essay, "A Talk to Teachers," states that the main purpose of education is to teach students to think: "The purpose of education . . . is to create in a person the ability to look at the world for himself, to make his own decisions, to say to himself this is black or this is white, to decide for himself whether there is a God in heaven or not. To ask questions of the universe, and then to live with those questions, is the way he achieves his identity." Although Baldwin believed that thinking was the real purpose of education, he also believed that no society was serious about teaching its citizens to think. He writes further: "But no society is really anxious to have that kind of person around. What society really, ideally, wants is a citizenry which will simply obey the rules of society. If a society succeeds in this, that society is about to perish" (1985:326).

The transformative curriculum can teach students to think by encouraging them, when they are reading or listening to resources, to consider the author's purposes for writing or speaking, his/her basic assumptions, and how the author's perspective or point of view compares with that of other authors and resources. Students can develop the skills to critically analyze historical and contemporary resources by being given two accounts of the same event or situation that present different perspectives and points of view.

A Lesson with Different Voices

In a lesson I developed for a junior high school United States history textbook (Banks with Sebesta, 1982) entitled, "Christopher Columbus and the Arawak Indians," the students are presented with an excerpt from Columbus' diary that describes his arrival in an Arawak community in the Caribbean in 1492. These are among the things that Columbus writes about the Arawaks:

> They took all and gave all, such as they had, with good will, but it seemed to me that they were a people very lacking in everything. They all go naked

as their mothers bore them, and the women also, although I saw only one very young girl . . . They should be good servants and quick to learn, since I see that they very soon say all that is said to them, and I believe that they would easily be made Christians, for it appeared to me that they had no religious beliefs. Our Lord willing, at the time of my departure, I will bring back six of them to Your Highnesses, that they may learn to talk. I saw no beast of any kind in this island, except parrots (January, 1930).

The students are then encouraged to view Columbus's voice from the perspective of the Arawaks. The Arawaks had an aural culture and consequently left no written documents. However, archaeologist Fred Olsen studied Arawak artifacts and used what he learned from them to construct a day in the life of the Arawaks, which he describes in his book, *On the Trail of the Arawaks* (Olsen, 1974). The students are asked to read an excerpt from Olsen's account of a day in the life of the Arawaks and to respond to these questions:

Columbus wrote in his diary that he thought the Arawaks had no religious beliefs. You read about Arawak life in the report by Fred Olsen. Do you think Columbus was correct? Why?

Accounts written by people who took part in or witnessed (saw) an historical event are called primary sources. Can historians believe everything they read in a primary source? Explain (Banks with Sebesta, 1982:43).

Key Concepts and Issues

In addition to helping students view events and situations from diverse ethnic, gender and social-class perspectives, a transformative curriculum should also be organized around key concepts and social issues. The conceptual-issue oriented curriculum facilitates the teaching of decision-making and social action skills in several important ways. First, a conceptual curriculum helps students to understand the ways in which knowledge is constructed, enables them to formulate concepts themselves, and to understand the ways in which the concepts formulated reflect the values, purposes and assumptions of the conceptualizers. In an inquiry-oriented conceptual curriculum, students are not passive consumers of previously constructed knowledge, but are encouraged to formulate new ways to organize, conceptualize and think about data and information.

The conceptual approach also allows the teacher to rethink the ways that topics, periods and literary movements are structured and labelled. Periodization in history, literature and art tend to reflect a Euro-centric bias, such as the Middle Ages, the Renaissance and the Westward Movement. When content is organized around key interdisciplinary concepts such as culture, communication and values, the teacher can structure lessons and units that facilitate the inclusion of content from diverse cultures as well as content that will help students to develop the knowledge, values, commitments and skills needed to participate in effective personal, economic and civic action.

In the United States junior high school textbook cited earlier (Banks with Sebesta, 1982), I used a key concept, **revolution,** to organize a unit rather than focus the unit exclusively on the revolution in the English colonies in 1776. By organizing the unit around the concept of revolution rather than a particular revolution, the students were able to examine three American revolutions, to study each in depth, and to derive generalizations about revolutions in general. They were also able to identify ways in which these three revolutions were alike and different. They also used the definition and generalizations they derived about revolutions from this unit to determine whether events such as the civil rights movement of the 1960s and 1970s and the women rights movement of the 1970s could accurately be called "revolutions." The three American revolutions they studied were:

(1) The Pueblo Revolt of 1680, in which Popé led a resistance against the conquering Spaniards; (2) The Revolution in the British Colonies, 1776; and (3) The Mexican Revolution of 1810, whose aim was to acquire Mexico's independence from Spain.

The Moral Component of Action

After students have mastered interdisciplinary knowledge related to a concept or issue such as racism or sexism, they should participate in value or moral inquiry exercises. The goal of such exercises should be to help students to develop a set of consistent, clarified values that can guide purposeful and reflective personal or civic action related to the issue examined. This goal can best be attained by teaching students a method or process for deriving their values within a democratic classroom atmosphere. In this kind of democratic classroom, students must be free to express their value choices, determine how those choices conflict, examine alternative values, consider the consequences of different value choices, make value choices, and defend their moral choices within the context of human dignity and other American creed values. Students must be given an opportunity to reflectively derive their own values in order to develop a commitment to human dignity, equality, and to other democratic values. They must be encouraged to reflect upon value choices within a democratic atmosphere in order to internalize them (Banks with Clegg, 1990).

I have developed a value inquiry model that teachers can use to help students identify and clarify their values and to make reflective moral choices. It consists of these steps (Banks with Clegg, 1990:445):

1. defining and recognizing value problems.

2. describing value-relevant behavior.

3. naming values exemplified by the behavior.

4. determining conflicting values in behavior described.

5. hypothesizing about the possible consequence of the values analyzed.

6. naming alternative values to those described by behavior observed.

7. hypothesizing about the possible consequences of values analyzed.

8. declaring value preferences; choosing.

9. stating reasons, sources, and possible consequences of value choice: justifying, hypothesizing, predicting.

I will illustrate how Mr. Carson, a junior high school social studies teacher, used this model while teaching a unit on the civil rights movement. Mr. Carson wanted his students to acquire an understanding of the historical development of the civil rights movement, to analyze and clarify their values related to integration and segregation, as well as to conceptualize and perhaps take some kinds of actions related to racism and desegregation in their personal life, the school or the local community. Mr. Carson is a social studies teacher in a predominantly white suburban school district near a city in the Northwest that has a population of about 500 000. The metropolitan area in which Mr. Carson's school is located has a population of about one million.

The Long Shadow of Little Rock

Mr. Carson used the Banks value inquiry model to help his students analyze the value issues revealed in Chapter 8 of *The Long Shadow of Little Rock* by Daisy Bates (1987). In this excellently written and moving chapter, Mrs. Bates describes the moral dilemma she faced when serving as head of the National Association for the Advancement of Colored People (NAACP) in Little Rock when Central High School was desegregated by nine African American high school students. The desegregation of Central High school began during the 1957-58 school year.

Mrs. Bates was the leading supporter and organizer for the nine students. Her husband, L.C. Bates, was a journalist. They owned a newspaper, *The States Press*. In Chapter 8 of *The Long Shadow of Little Rock*, Mrs. Bates describes how a middle-aged white woman came to her home at three in the afternoon and told her to call a press conference and announce that she was withdrawing her support for the nine students and advising them to withdraw from Central High School and return to the Negro schools. The woman said she represented a group of "Southern Christian women." Mrs. Bates asked the woman what would happen if she didn't do what she told her to do. She looked at Mrs. Bates straight in the eye and said, "You'll be destroyed — you, your newspaper, your reputation . . . Everything."

During her long, anguished night, Mrs. Bates wondered whether she had the right to destroy 16 years of her husband's work — the newspaper. Yet she felt that she could not abandon a cause to which she and many other African Americans were deeply committed. By morning, Mrs. Bates had made her difficult and painful decision. She called her visitor and said, "No." Later, she told her husband, L.C., what she had done. He said, "Daisy, you did the right thing." Mrs. Bates' visitor kept her promise. *The State Press* was closed because advertising from it was withdrawn by all of the major stores and businesses in Little Rock. The Bates family suffered financial and personal turmoil because of the closing of *The State Press* and because of threats and attempts on Mrs. Bates' life.

Using the Banks Value inquiry model, these are some of the questions Mr. Carson asked his students:

Defining and Recognizing Value Problems

1. What value problem did Mrs. Bates face after she was visited by the woman?

Naming Values Exemplified by Behavior Described

2. What did the visitor value or think was important? What did Mrs. Bates value? What did Mr. Bates value?

Hypothesizing about the Sources of Values Analyzed

3. How do you think Mrs. Bates' visitor developed the values she had? How do you think Mr. and Mrs. Bates developed the values they showed in this selection?

Declaring Value Preferences: Choosing

4. Try to put yourself in Mrs. Daisy Bates' place on October 29, 1959. What decision would you have made?

Stating Reasons, Sources, and Possible Consequences of Value Choice

5. Why should Mrs. Bates have made the decision you stated above? What were the possible consequences of her saying "no" and saying "yes" to her visitor? Give as many reasons as you can about why Mrs. Bates should have made the decision you stated above.

Keeping in mind that Mrs. Bates knew that if she said yes to her visitor she would probably have been able to keep her property but that the nine students would have probably had to return to black schools and that segregation would have been maintained in Little Rock. On the other hand, by saying no, she risked losing all of her property and her husband's property, including his newspaper. Also, consider the fact that she did not involve him in making her decision.

Decision-Making and Citizen Action

After Mr. Carson's students had derived knowledge about the civil rights movement of the 1950s and 1960s, and clarified their values regarding these issues, he asked them to list all of the possible actions they could take to increase desegregation in their personal lives as well as in the life of the school and the community. Mr. Carson was careful to explain to the students that action should be broadly conceptualized. He defined action in a way that might include a personal commitment to do something, such as making an effort to have more friends from different racial and ethnic groups, making a commitment to see the videotape, *Roots*, and discussing it with a friend, as well as reading a play or book that will help you to better understand another racial or ethnic group, such as *A Raisin in the Sun* by Lorraine Hansberry or *Beloved* by Toni Morrison. Among the possible actions that the students listed that they could take were these:

1. Make a personal commitment to stop telling racist jokes.

2. Make a commitment to challenge our own racial and ethnic stereotypes either before or after we verbalize them.

3. Compile an annotated list of books about ethnic groups that we will ask the librarian to order for our school library.

4. Ask the principal to order sets of photographs that show African Americans and other people of color who have jobs that represent a variety of careers. Asking the principal to encourage our teachers to display these photographs on their classroom walls.

5. Observe television programs to determine the extent to which people of color, such as African Americans and Asian Americans, are represented in such jobs as news anchors and hosts of programs. Writing to local and national television stations to express our concern if we discover that people of color are not represented in powerful and visible roles in news or other kinds of television programs.

6. Contact a school in the inner city to determine if there are joint activities and projects in which we and they might participate.

7. Ask the principal or the board of education in our school district to require our teachers to attend in-service staff development workshops that will help them learn ways in which to integrate content about ethnic and racial groups into our courses.

8. Share some of the facts that we have learned in this unit with our parents and discuss these facts with them, for example that by the year 2000 one out of three Americans will be a person of color.

9. Make a personal commitment to have a friend from another racial, ethnic or religious group by the end of the year.

10. Make a personal commitment to read at least one book a year that deals with a racial, cultural or ethnic group other than my own.

11. Do nothing, take no actions.

The Decision Making Process

After the students had made a list of possible actions they could take regarding the issues studied in the unit (including no actions), Mr. Carson asked them to consider the possible consequences of each of the actions identified, such as:

• **If I take no actions,**

Then I will be doing nothing to improve race relations in my personal life, in my school, my community or nation.

But I will not risk trying to do something that could fail. I will also be indicating to others, by my behavior, that I am not concerned about improving race relations in my personal life, my family, school or community.

• **If I make a personal commitment to tell no more racist jokes,**

Then I will be improving my personal behavior that relates to other racial, ethnic and cultural groups. I will also demonstrate to others that I am concerned about improving race relations in my personal life.

But I will be doing little directly to improve the behaviors of other people in my family, school and community.

After the students had worked in groups of five to identify and state the possible consequences of various courses of actions, Mr. Carson asked them to continue working in their groups and to select one or two personal or group actions they would like to take related to the problems they had studied in the unit. Mr. Carson also asked the students to be prepared to defend and/or explain the course of action or actions they chose, tell whether it was feasible for them to carry out the action or actions, and to provide a timeline for its initiation and completion (if possible). These are among the actions the students chose:

Kathy and Susan decided to read the play, *A Raisin in the Sun* by Lorraine Hansberry, to try to get a better understanding of the experiences of African Americans in the United States.

Clay, Pete, Tessie, Rosie and Maria, decided that they would prepare a list of books on ethnic cultures and ask the school librarian to order them for the school library. They planned to ask Mr. Carson to help them find resources for the preparation of the annotated list of books.

Roselyn decided that she wanted to improve her understanding of ethnic cultures by reading. She decided to read these books during the year: *Let the Circle be Unbroken* by Mildred D. Taylor, *A Jar of Dreams* by Yoshiko Uchida, and *America Is in the Heart* by Carlos Bulosan.

Aralean, Juan, James, Angela and Patricia decided they wanted to develop a proposal that would require teachers in the district to attend multicultural education workshops. They will develop their plan with Mr. Carson and present it to the principal and then to the Board of Education for possible adoption.

The Role of the Teacher in an Empowerment and Transformative Curriculum

An effective transformative and empowerment curriculum must be implemented by teachers who have the knowledge, skills and attitudes needed to help students to understand the ways in which knowledge is constructed and used to support power group relationships in society. Teachers are human beings who bring their cultural perspectives, values, hopes and dreams to the classroom. They also bring their prejudices, stereotypes and misconceptions to the classroom. The teacher's values and perspectives mediate and interact with what they teach and influence the way that messages are communicated and perceived by their students. A teacher who believes that Christopher Columbus discovered America, and one who believes that Columbus came to America when it was peopled by groups with rich and diverse cultures will send different messages to their students when the European exploration of America is studied.

Because the teacher mediates the messages and symbols communicated to the students through the curriculum, it is important for teachers to come to grips with their own personal and cultural values and identities in order for them to help students from diverse racial, ethnic and cultural groups to develop clarified cultural identities and to relate positively to each other. I am hypothesizing that self-clarification is a prerequisite to dealing effectively with and relating positively to outside ethnic and cultural groups. An Anglo-American teacher who is confused about his or her cultural identity and who has a non-reflective conception of the ways that Anglo-American culture relates to other groups in the United States, will have a very difficult time relating positively to outside ethnic groups such as African Americans and Mexican Americans.

Effective teacher education programs should help pre- and in-service teachers to explore and clarify their own ethnic and cultural identities and to develop more positive attitudes toward other racial, ethnic and cultural groups. To do this, such programs must recognize and reflect the complex ethnic and cultural identities and characteristics of the individuals within teacher education programs (Banks, 1988). Teachers should also learn how to facilitate the identity quest among students and help them to become effective and able participants in the common civic culture.

Effective teachers in the transformative curriculum must not only have clarified personal and cultural identifications, they must also be keenly aware of the various paradigms, canons and knowledge systems on which the dominant curriculum is based and those that it eschews. Because teacher-education students attain most of their knowledge without analyzing its assumptions and values or engaging in the process of constructing knowledge themselves, they often leave teacher-education programs with many misconceptions about culturally and racially different groups and with conceptions about their national history and culture that are incomplete, misleading and chauvinistic. Consequently, the knowledge that many teachers bring to the classroom contributes to the mystification rather than to the clarification of social, historical and political realities. This knowledge also perpetuates inequality and oppression rather than contributes to justice, liberation and empowerment.

In order to educate teachers so that they will convey images, perspectives and points of view in the curriculum that will demystify social realities and promote cultural freedom and empowerment, we must radically change the ways in which they acquire knowledge. We must engage them in a process of attaining knowledge in which they are required to analyze the values and assumptions of different paradigms and theories. Teacher education students must also be given the opportunity to construct concepts, generalizations and theories so that they can develop an understanding of the nature and limitations of knowledge and comprehend the extent to which knowledge reflects the social and cultural context in which it is formulated.

Participating in processes in which they formulate and construct knowledge forms will also help teacher-education students to understand how various groups in society who formulate, shape and disseminate knowledge often structure and disseminate knowledge that supports their interests and legitimizes their power. This knowledge often legitimizes dominant institutions and helps to make victimized groups politically passive and content with their deprived status. Teachers must not only understand how the dominant paradigms and canon help keep victimized groups powerless but also must be committed to social change and action if they are to become agents of liberation and empowerment.

References

Baldwin, J. (1985). *The Price of the Ticket: Collected Nonfiction, 1948-1985.* New York: St. Martin's Press.

Banks, J. A. with Sebesta, S.L. (1982). *We Americans: Our History and People.* Volumes I and II. Boston: Allyn & Bacon.

Banks, J. A. (1988). *Multiethnic Education: Theory and Practice,* Second edition. Boston: Allyn & Bacon.

Banks, J. A. with Clegg, A.A. Jr. (1990). *Teaching Strategies for the Social Studies: Inquiry, Valuing and Decision-Making,* Fourth Edition. White Plains, New York: Longman, Inc.

Banks, J. A. (1989). "The battle over the canon: Cultural diversity and curriculum reform." *Allyn & Bacon Educators' Forum,* 1:11-13.

Bates, D. (1987). *The Long Shadow of Little Rock.* Fayetteville: The University of Arkansas Press.

Berger, P. L. & Luckman, T. (1966). *The Social Construction or Reality.* New York: Doubleday.

Bloom, A. (1987). *The Closing of the American Mind.* New York: Simon & Schuster.

Coleman, J. S. et al. (1966). *Equality of Educational Opportunity.* Washington, D.C.: U.S. Government Printing Office.

Fleming, J. (1985). *Blacks in College: A Comparative Study of Students' Success in Black and White Institutions.* San Francisco: Jossey-Bass Publishers.

Garrow, D. J. (1986). *Bearing the Cross: Martin Luther King and the Southern Christian Leadership Conference.* New York: Vintage.

Heller, S. (1989). "Press for campus diversity leading to more closed minds, say critics." *The Chronicle of Higher Education.* November 8, 1989:A13 and A22.

Hirsch, E.D., Jr. (1987). *Cultural Literacy: What Every American Needs to Know.* Boston: Houghton Mifflin.

Jan, C. (1930). *The Voyages of Christopher Columbus.* London: The Argonaut Press.

Lefcourt, H. M. (1976). *Locus of Control: Current Trends in Theory and Research.* New York: John Wiley.

Olsen, F. (1974). *On the Trail of the Arawaks.* Norman, OK: University of Oklahoma Press.

Ravitch, D. & Finn, C. E. Jr. (1987). *What Do Our 17-Year-Olds Know? A Report on the First National Assessment of History and Literature.* New York: Harper & Row.

Ryan, W. (1971). *Blaming the Victim*. New York: Vintage.

Starrs, J. (1988). "Cultural Literacy and Black Education." A paper submitted to James A. Banks as a partial requirement for the course, EDC&I 469, University of Washington.

Strengthening Multicultural and Global Perspectives in the Curriculum

*Christine Bennett

Throughout the 1970s and 1980s educators have made a case for multi-cultural and global education in the United States.[1] These ideas have acquired a new urgency today as we face the 21st century. Despite the growing body of global and multicultural literature and research, however, and despite a new emphasis on global and multicultural perspectives in teacher education, we find little evidence of either in most classrooms today. Current research indicates that novice teachers who do experience multicultural preservice education find few role models and receive little to no encouragement in the development of global or multicultural perspectives in their teaching (Grant & Koskela, 1986). Why is this? Why haven't the ideas of multicultural and global educators been widely translated into classroom instruction?

Several factors are involved. First, many experienced teachers were edu-cated prior to the current concern with global and multicultural teacher education and the National Council for Accreditation of Teacher Education (NCATE) guidelines. Second, precollege and postsecondary teachers are pressured to cover a set curriculum, and the prescribed curriculum at all levels has traditionally been monoethnic. There is a lack of multicultural texts and materials, and a fear of handling controversial issues. In a era where the emphasis is on cultural literacy *à la* Hirsch, (that is, Western culture) and concern about the Scholastic Aptitude Test, multicultural and global education is often perceived as irrelevant or dangerous. A third factor is the traditional separation, even competitiveness between multicultural and global educators, (as well as a range of competing movements in global education, for example, peace studies, environmental concerns, global economics and futurism). Multicultural education has focused on ethnic diversity and cultural pluralism within the United States, including problems of racism, inequities and ethnic

---

*This chapter is based upon Part III and Chapter 7 in Christine Bennett, *Comprehensive Multicultural Education: Theory and Practice,* Second Edition, Needham Heights, Mass: Allyn and Bacon, 1990.

prejudices. Global education on the other hand, has focused on interdependence among nations, and major problems which threaten the future of the planet and the well-being of humanity. A fourth factor consists of several deficits: a lack of conceptual clarity, a lack of agreement on the goals of multicultural and global education, and the lack of a theoretical framework to guide teachers. This is especially problematic in the areas of multicultural and global education where there exist ideological overtones that are not present in less controversial areas of the curriculum; for example, math or reading. Hard-and-fast facts or formulas are not available in either multicultural or global education. Educators disagree not only about what each field is or should be but also whether they should exist at all.

To move beyond these barriers teachers can benefit from a curriculum model that provides guidelines for translating the ideas and theories of global and multicultural education into practice. There are a number of possible ways to conceptualize an approach for integrating multicultural and global perspectives in the curriculum. This chapter proposes a model which attempts to unify global and multicultural education by combining Robert Hanvey's (1975) *Attainable Global Perspective* and the work of global educators such as James M. Becker (1980) and Betty Reardon (1988) with the author's original model of a multicultural curriculum. It is based on the belief that neither multiethnic nor global education alone is sufficient for the 21st century.

Both movements began in the late 1960s and early 1970s. In its early stages multicultural education focused on ethnic studies, or the study of the history and culture of various ethnic groups in the United States, particularly ethnic minorities. From an anthropological perspective, multicultural education was later defined as "the process whereby a person develops competencies in multiple systems of standards for perceiving, evaluating, believing, and doing" (Gibson, 1984:112). This conception of multicultural education freed it from its earlier focus on ethnic diversity within a single nation to include cultures and nations across the globe. Global education on the other hand deals with world trends, developments, issues, change and the interrelatedness of all peoples. Many groups and organizations are associated with global education, including environmentalists, human rights advocates, futurists and advocates of peace studies.

Despite the separate histories, rationales, identities and special interests associated with global education and multicultural education, there is sufficient similarity in their goals and content that makes cooperation possible. Cortez notes that "both reform movements seek to improve intergroup and global understandings and relations, to improve intercultural communication, to reduce stereotyping, and to help students comprehend human diversity without losing sight of the traits that all people share" (Cortez, 1983:569).

Banks (1984) identifies "globalism and global competency" as the sixth and highest stage in his typology of stages of ethnicity.

To show how global education and multicultural education might be combined, the following table identifies key value concepts from each approach, emphasizing the most compatible ideas. Neither the concepts nor the categories are mutually exclusive, for there is a good deal of overlap. The table is intended to illuminate the separate identities of each and how they might become more integrated.

Global Perspectives	Multicultural Perspectives	Possible Integration of Global and Multicultural Perspectives
world-wide pluralism	ethnic pluralism	cultural pluralism (acceptance and appreciation of cultal diversity within and among nations)
human rights	civil rights	respect for human dignity and universal human rights
colonialism and its legacy in colonized nations	racism, prejudice, stereotypes and discrimination	combatting racism, prejudice and discrimination perpetuated globally, nationally and locally
global interdependence	positive intergroup relations	multiple loyalties in a world community
earth as an ecosystem	basic human similarities (typical not a main emphasis)	global dynamics reverence for the earth and its inhabitants
international understanding, national perspectives	sense of ethnic identity, becoming bi- and multi-cultural	cultural consciousness intercultural competence
participatory world citizens	participatory local and national citizens	responsibility to a world community that begins at home
problems of the population/poverty dynamic; the environmental/eco-logical crises; war and nuclear weapons	problems of personal prejudice and discrimination, social injustice and inequalities; ignorance, lack of ethnic/cultural literacy	awareness of the state of the planet and global dynamics multiple historical perspectives cultural consciousness

Margaret Mead expressed the connections between these two fields of education when she wrote: "You can no longer save your family, tribe, or nation. You can only save the whole world." Some global educators, most notably Becker (1980), have stressed the centrality of **basic human similarities,** and others such as Hanvey (1975) and Rhinesmith (1979) have emphasized the importance of cultural perspectives. Typically, however, global educators neglect the importance of culture and alternative world views associated with different peoples and nations. The same is generally true of multiethnic education, an early phase of multicultural education that stressed ethnic literacy over cross-cultural awareness and understanding. Multicultural educators often overlook opportunities for making global connections, for example, the cultural traditions and heritage of the nations-of-origin associated with immigrant groups in the United States. Global educators, for the most part, focus on the nation-state and overlook the importance of ethnicity and culture in international affairs. Furthermore, there is a danger among global educators of focusing on world problems and forgetting about problems at home, particularly issues concerning racism and personal prejudices.

Given these separate histories and identities, both movements provide different dimensions to the educational imperatives for the 21st century. These dimensions are essential, compatible and interactive, and are probably stronger in combination than apart.

The model described in this chapter identifies four democratic values taken from the "Universal Declaration of Human Rights" and Native American traditional philosophy. Out of these values are generated six goals that teachers can use to develop global and multicultural perspectives in their teaching. Basic assumptions that underlie each goal are also identified. The chapter concludes with a discussion of possible criticisms of the model.

An Overview of the Model

The model shown in Figure 1 is based upon four underlying democratic values: (1) acceptance and appreciation of cultural diversity; (2) respect for human dignity and universal human rights; (3) responsibility to the world community; and (4) reverence for the earth.[3] The first three values are based upon the "Universal Declaration of Human Rights" that was adopted by the United Nations' General Assembly in 1948. The declaration is designed to serve "as a common standard of achievement for all peoples and all nations" (Planetary Citizens Registry, 1976:29). It also states that all persons are born free and equal in dignity, and expresses the basic civil, economic, political, and social rights of all humans. The fourth value, reverence for the earth, originates in American Indian traditional philosophy. All these values are reflected in the Human Manifesto.

Figure 1: Global and Multicultural Perspectives in Curriculum

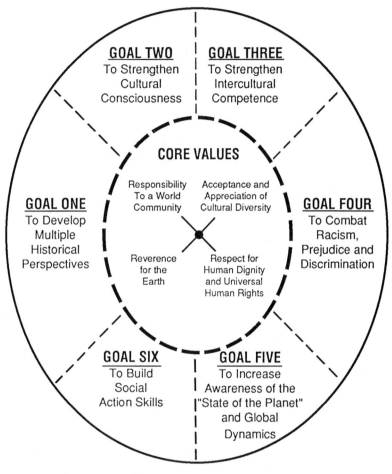

Out of these values six curriculum goals are generated that teachers can use to develop global and multicultural perspectives in their curriculum. Together, the core values and related goals capture the connections between global and multicultural education. These connections spring from the inter-actions among personal, intranational and international events, and the fact that both movements share similar quests for human understanding, commu-nication and equity (Cortez, 1983).

The core values also enable teachers to clarify basic assumptions about teaching and learning that underlie the model. This clarification is essential in protecting, improving, and building the case for global and multicultural perspectives in the curriculum and points the way to needed changes should presently held assumptions be found untrue in the future. The core values can also enable teachers to deal more effectively with controversial issues that are an integral part of global and multicultural education, such as violations of human rights and destruction of the environment.

The Curriculum Model: Goals, Assumptions and Content

1. Understanding Multiple Historical Perspectives

Most of us tend to be ahistorical when it comes to both less developed nations and ethnic minorities within our own society. It is difficult to be otherwise, given the nature of the traditional curriculum which emphasizes the political development of Euro-American civilization. An important goal of a multicultural curriculum, therefore, is the development of multiple historical perspectives in order to correct this Anglo-Western European bias. Past and current world events must be understood from multiple national perspectives, and both minority and non-minority points of views must be considered when interpreting local and national events.

Among the assumptions underlying this goal are the following:

- People must possess a degree of self- and group esteem, as well as personal security, before they can be empathetic in their interrelations with others.

- Awareness of the achievements of one's culture group will enhance one's self- and group esteem.

- Knowledge that corrects misconceptions about certain people (that non-industrialized people, for example, are less civilized than industrialized people) helps destroy the myth of Euro-American superiority.

- People can achieve a psychological balance between cultural pride and identity on the one hand and appreciation of cultures different from their own on the other. (For example, increased group pride does not necessarily increase ethnocentrism.)

Chun-Hoon (1973:139) in *Teaching the Asian-American Experience* expresses the importance of minority perspectives: "The greatest danger to an open society is an education that homogenizes its people into limited and fixed conformity; the greatest danger to a small minority like Asian-Americans is that they will be imprisoned in the images created for them by mass society and that their own personal reality will not be able to transcend the imposed psychological colonization of society-as-a-whole." He asserts further that schools bear a large responsibility for ensuring that minorities are accurately represented. He believes this can happen only when the majority and the minority perspective is used in teaching the experience of minority groups.

But how are multiple historical perspectives developed? Such perspectives are based upon knowledge and understanding of the world views, heritage, and contributions of diverse nations and ethnic groups, including one's own. Subject matter from the fields of history, literature and the arts can be used to provide understanding about people's contemporary culture, world view and differing interpretations of human events. This knowledge builds an awareness of historical and contemporary developments among the world's diverse nations and ethnic groups, awareness of traditional and contemporary attitudes held by the members of the macroculture with respect to these groups, and knowledge about minority perspectives.

Content that builds within each student a sense of ethnic pride and identity is central, as is content about the achievements of people from other nations and cultures. Therefore, teachers could use subject matter that has traditionally been confined to ethnic studies courses such as black history, Mexican American literature, Native American cultures, and white ethnics, as well as world culture courses. Teachers then use this content in ways that would encourage students to get at the underlying values and patterns of socialization of a particular culture rather than focusing only on the more superficial cultural trappings such as, food, holidays, heroes and historical events.

Every classroom offers opportunities for developing historical perspectives. Students can interview family members about their own ethnic roots and experiences. Bulletin boards can display people of the week or points of view on a variety of topics, or who's who in math, music, science and so on. A multicultural calendar provides an excellent way to introduce students to people from many ethnic groups and nations. Indeed Tiedt and Tiedt (1979) offer several suggestions of ways the calendar can be used.

If multiple historical perspectives are to be understood, textbook distortions, stereotypes and serious omissions surrounding ethnic minorities and developing nations must be corrected. Acceptable revisions of the curriculum must be guided by an understanding of their viewpoints, as well as the traditional majority point of view. Consider two phenomena that have traditionally been examined only from the Anglo-European viewpoints: slavery and Manifest Destiny.

Slavery

Slavery and emancipation are classic examples of how textbooks have excluded the black point of view. Slavery is often introduced as an economic necessity and later treated as a problem for whites. The black perspective on slavery would include African cultural origins and histories of the array of

African civilizations (just as England and Europe are discussed prior to colonization among whites). It would also include evidence of black people's strength under conditions of extreme oppression (in many cases the strongest and most intelligent Africans were sold into slavery and survived the middle passage), and of the expressions of black culture that emerged in United States society.

A vivid example of how one's intelligence can be dulled by limited frames of reference is the erroneous assumption often made concerning the social status structure among American slaves: house slaves, drivers, artisans and mulattoes are accorded higher status than field slaves. According to Berry & Blassingame (1982), however, the social structure from the slaves' viewpoint was far more complex, with hierarchies based on the nature of their occupation.

Furthermore, native-born Africans were revered as links to the ancestral home, as were educators. "Old men and women with great stores of riddles, proverbs, and folktales (creators and preservers of culture) played a crucial role in teaching morality and training youths to solve problems and to develop their memories. Literate slaves had even more status than the sources of racial lore because they could read the Bible, tell the bondsmen what was transpiring in the newspapers, and write letters and passes" (Berry & Blassingame, 1982:31). Rebel slaves who resisted floggings, violated racial taboos, or escaped from their masters were held in the highest esteem by the slaves, and were preserved as heroes in slave folktales and songs. "Physical strength, skill in outwitting whites, possession of attractive clothes, and ability to read signs and interpret dreams also contributed to a slave's social standing" (Berry & Blassingame, 1982:31).

Hamilton (1977) has described the lack of black perspectives in the curriculum as part of the reason many black parents give up on traditionally desegregated schools and prefer black community control of schools serving black children and youth. He quotes Killens and Bennett to illustrate how African Americans may view history differently from what is in the textbooks. According to Killens,

> We [black Americans] even have a different historical perspective. Most white Americans, even today, look upon the Reconstruction period as a horrible time of "carpetbagging," and "black politicians," and "black corruption" the absolutely lowest ebb in the Great American Story (Killens, 1965:14-15).

Manifest Destiny and the Native American and Hispanic Perspectives

One of the most blatant examples of Anglo-European bias in the curriculum is the fact that United States history is traditionally taught as an east-to-west phenomenon. The northward flow of peoples and cultures from central Mexico is largely overlooked. Our legacy from the Spanish colonizers who imposed Catholicism, the Spanish language, an economic system of mining and agriculture on the native populations, and who helped create Mestizo and Creole populations is largely ignored. If, on the other hand, history were taught according to a greater-America frame of reference, alternative perspectives to Manifest Destiny could be presented, particularly Chicano and Native American perspectives. Our legacy from the native peoples, which is just beginning to be discovered, would be recognized. People would realize that Native American contributions penetrate all aspects of society, including our form of government, a federation copied after the Iroquois League (*More than Bows and Arrows*, 1978; Hirschfelder, 1986).

What is the native perspective that should become part of the revised curriculum? Forbes (1973) provides excellent guidelines in the following illustrations of what teachers must do to teach the history of Indian people from their viewpoint.

- The unsubstantiated theories of white anthropologists should be treated as such.

- The Bering Straits migration theory should be treated with great skepticism since there is absolutely no evidence (except logic) to support it.

- Indians should be treated as the original Americans and the first 20 000 years of American history must be discussed prior to any discussion of European, African or Asian migrations to the Americas.

- The on-going evolution of Indian groups must be dealt with, from 1492 to the present. That is, one must deal with the internal history of native tribes and not merely with European relations.

- The teacher must deal truthfully with European expansion, native wars of liberation and independence must be dealt with as such and not as acts of aggression carried out against so-called peaceful whites.

- The teacher will want to try to use accurate names of the Indian groups in his or her region.

- Native heroes and resistance leaders of the post-1890 period (such as Carlos Montezuma and Yukioma) must be dealt with — Indian resistance **did not** cease with the "last Indian war."

• American history, from a native perspective, is not merely a material success story (bigger and bigger, more and more, better and better), nor does it consist solely in the reverse (that whites have actually brought about the near-destruction of this land). History is not progressive, but cyclical (adapted from Forbes, 1973:218-219).

Establishing Multiple Historical Perspectives: The Challenge

An accurate representation of multiple historical perspectives is not always possible. Even when one wants a full, unbiased depiction of ethnic minority viewpoints and experiences, for example, lack of available knowledge is a major problem. Political history in the schools has emphasized white males in power positions, and past omissions and inaccuracies make it difficult to establish the experiences and contributions of all groups (Johnson, 1987). Racist and sexist practices of the past make the rediscovery of history difficult. Because copyrights and patents were not available to women and non-whites until relatively recently, many early contributions remain unrecognized. Literature, art, even monuments, are all tainted with bias.

Although oral history and folklore are not free of distortions and are often inaccessible to outsiders, oral literature and oral history along with music and the visual arts remain some of the best means of discovering ethnic minority perspectives. The fact that most slaves were barred from learning to read or write and that many immigrant groups such as the Chinese, Japanese, Mexicans and Eastern European Jews entered initially as illiterate laborers means that few pieces of literature or documents written by these people for themselves are available. Oral history, including songs, folk tales, jokes, proverbs, aphorisms, verbal games and (among African Americans) toasts offer the richest sources for understanding ethnic perspectives. Levine's (1977) exceptionally rich study of black folklore, for example, has led him to paint a picture of slavery that differs dramatically from the view traditionally accepted by popular culture as well as by many scholars.

It should be clear that minority perspectives are not built only from heroes and success stories, or from an emphasis on foods, fads and festivals. Cortez cautions against this in "Teaching the Chicano Experience" with words that can be applied to every ethnic group.

Certainly heroes and success stories comprise part of the Chicano experience. Chicanos can develop greater pride and non-Chicanos can develop greater respect by learning of Chicano lawyers, doctors, educators, athletes, musicians, artists, writers, businessmen, etc., as well as Mexican and Chicano heroes (heroes either to their own culture or to the nation at large). However, the teaching of the Chicano experience often becomes little more than the display of Emiliano Zapata, Pancho Villa, Benito Juarez, and Miguel Hidalgo posters or an extended exercise in "me too-ism" — the list of Mexican Americans who have "made it" according to Anglo standards.

In falling into these educational cliches, the very essence of the Chicano experience is overlooked. For this essence is neither heroes nor "me too" success stories, but rather the masses of Mexican-American people . . . (The) teacher should focus on these Chicanos, their way of life, their activities, their culture, their joys and sufferings, their conflicts, and their adaptation to an often hostile societal environment. Such an examination of the lives of Mexican Americans — not Chicano heroes or "successes" — can provide new dimensions for the understanding of and sensitivity to this important part of our nation's heritage (Cortez, 1973:191).

Obviously, people differ in their awareness of alternative ethnic and national perspectives. Most of us are more aware of some minority perspectives than others, particularly if we have lived a minority experience. Each of us, however, needs to become more informed about ethnic and national perspectives beyond our own — especially when we have grown up in a racist society, with an incomplete, biased curriculum.

2. Developing the Cultural Consciousness

Closely linked to the development of multiple historical perspectives, is the second goal, the development of cultural consciousness. This goal makes the following assumptions:

- An individual must have an understanding of his or her own world view.

- Humans have the capacity to reduce their ethnocentrism.

Cultural consciousness is defined in terms of two dimensions of Hanvey's "attainable global perspective": perspective consciousness and cross-cultural awareness. Perspective consciousness is "The recognition or awareness on the part of the individual that he or she has a view of the world that is not universally shared, that this view of the world has been and continues to be shaped by influences that often escape conscious detection, and that others have views of the world that are profoundly different from one's own" (Hanvey, 1975:4). Most Japanese, for example, do not see themselves as racist. Yet, their deep assumptions about the inferiority of certain races has recently resulted in statements by Japanese officials about the "inferiority" of American blacks and Hispanics, as well as discrimination against Japanese citizens of Korean or Chinese parentage. As another example, Westerners have assumed until very recently that human dominance over nature is both attainable and desirable. Teachers can foster the development of perspective consciousness by helping students examine their assumptions, evaluations, and concepts of time, space, causality and so on.

The second aspect of cultural consciousness, Hanvey's cross-cultural awareness, refers to "an awareness of the diversity of ideas and practices to be found in human societies around the world, of how such ideas and practices compare, and including some limited recognition of how the ideas and ways of one's own society might be viewed from other vantage points" (Hanvey, 1975:8). Cross-cultural awareness, a difficult but attainable goal, is seen by Hanvey as an antidote for the human "practice of naming one's own group 'the people' and by implication relegating all others to not-quite-human status." This human trait of chauvinism "has been documented in nonliterate groups all over the world . . . [and] shows itself in modern populations as well. It is there in the hostile faces of the white parents demonstrating against school busing . . . [it lurks] in the background as Russians and Chinese meet at the negotiating table to work out what is ostensibly a boundary dispute. And it flares into the open during tribal disputes in Kenya" (Hanvey, 1975: 10).

Hanvey (1975:11) identifies four levels of cross-cultural awareness as follows:

Level	Information	Mode	Interpretation
1	awareness of superficial tourism, or very visible cultural	tourism, textbooks, books, National Geographic	unbelievable, i.e., exotic, bizarre
2	awareness of significant and subtle cultural traits that contrast markedly with one's own	culture conflict situations	unbelievable, i.e. frustrating, irrational
3	awareness of significant and subtle cultural traits that contrast markedly with one's own	intellectual analysis	believable cognitively
4	awareness of how another culture feels from the standpoint of the insider	cultural immersion: living the culture	believable because of subjective familiarity

According to Hanvey's scheme, **believability** is achieved only at levels three and four. He argues that believability is a necessary condition "if one group of humans is to accept other members of the biological species as human" (Hanvey, 1975:11). The attainment of these higher levels of cross-cultural awareness are an integral part of the third multicultural curriculum goal, development of intercultural competence.

3. Developing Intercultural Competence

Intercultural competence is the ability to interpret intentional communications (language, signs, gestures), some unconscious cues (such as body language), and customs in cultural styles different from one's own. The emphasis is on empathy and communication. This goal recognizes that communication among persons of different cultural backgrounds can be hindered by culturally conditioned assumptions made about each other's behavior and cognitions. It is also based on the fact that, as Kraemer states, "the effects of cultural conditioning are sometimes so pervasive that people whose experience has been limited to the norms of their own culture simply cannot understand a communication based on a different set of norms . . . [and] cannot understand why a 'self-evident' communication from them cannot be comprehended by others" (Kraemer, 1975:2).

Some of the assumptions underlying this goal are as follows:

- Language is at the heart of culture and cognition.

- People's effectiveness in multicultural communication can be improved by developing their cultural self-awareness (their abilities to recognize cultural differences in their own cognitions).

- There are modes of human communication that can transcend cultural barriers.

- Certain dimensions of the different cultures in one society, such as the Black experience in the United States, are static enough to be identified, defined and taught.

- Persons can achieve a psychological balance between cultural pride and identity on the one hand, and appreciation of cultures very different from their own on the other (that is, increased intercultural contact will not necessarily lead to cultural assimilation).

Although this goal clearly overlaps the goals of developing historical perspectives and cultural consciousness, to teach for intercultural competence means going beyond the study of world views, heritage and contributions associated with a particular people. It means building an understanding of how one is shaped by the values, priorities, language, and norms of one's culture. This knowledge then can grow into the realization that every person's perception of reality is shaped by experience. Once people understand how their own language, experience, and current modes of cognition relate to their own culture, contrasts may be made with the cultural experience and modes of cognition of culturally different others. Ultimately, they are able to move to a level of transpection, what Hanvey refers to as "the capacity to imagine oneself in a role within the context of a foreign culture" (Hanvey, 1975:12).

Gudykunst and Kim define intercultural competence in terms of the **intercultural person**. "The intercultural person represents one who has achieved an advanced level in the process of becoming intercultural and whose cognitive, affective, and behavioral characteristics are not limited but are open to growth beyond the psychological parameters of any one culture . . . The intercultural person possesses an intellectual and emotional commitment to the fundamental unity of all humans and, at the same time, accepts and appreciates the differences that lie between people of different cultures" (Gudykunst & Kim, 1984:230). According to Gudykunst and Kim, intercultural people are individuals who:

- have encountered experiences that challenge their own cultural assumptions (e.g., culture shock, dynamic disequilibrium) and that provide insight into how their view of the world has been shaped by their culture;

- can serve as a facilitator and catalyst for contacts between cultures;

- come to terms with the roots of their own ethnocentrism and achieve an objectivity in viewing other cultures;

- develop a "third world" perspective "which enables them to interpret and evaluate intercultural encounters more accurately and thus to act as a communication link between two cultures; and

- show cultural empathy and can "imaginatively participate in the other's world view" (Gudykunst & Kim, 1984:231).

It is one thing to develop knowledge and awareness of human similarities and another to develop empathy. Knowledge is a necessary but insufficient ingredient. According to Dufty, the goal is informed empathy, or "knowledge plus sensitivity in trying to imagine oneself in another's shoes or bare feet. Empathy varies from trying to understand how other people think and view the world to how other people emote, feel or sense" (Dufty, Sawkins, Pickard, Power & Bowe, 1976:42). As an illustration, consider the following three responses made by students who were asked to imagine themselves as someone from another culture. Responses A and B exemplify **informed empathy** while response C seems totally lacking in empathy, however informed it may be. Negative empathy or nonempathy, as illustrated in response C, shows "a lack of skill in identifying with others, a lack of cultural imagination, or an inability to think in terms other than those of your own culture" (Dufty, Sawkins, Pickard, Power & Bowe, 1976:42).

> **Student A's Response:** The holy man came to ward off the spirits which were giving my daughter headaches.

> **Student B's Response:** When I die I hope my body will be cremated and my ashes thrown into the sacred Godavari River.

> **Student C's Response:** I live in a typical agricultural village in a crude mud hut. I am a New Guinea highlander. Our tribe's religion is animism. My diet is essentially vegetative. The natural vegetation is chopped away with primitive stone axes, the lower story plants are burnt producing nutrients for the soil. After 50 years the ecology of my area returns to its original state.

The goal of intercultural competence is a major objective of curriculum writers connected with UNESCO's efforts toward international understanding through education (Wolsk, 1976; Castell, 1976). Although these educators have limited the scope of intercultural competence to the international scene, many of the accompanying theories and practices are appropriate for education within a domestic multicultural society.

The work of Harry Triandis (1975) and his associates has led to a form of cross-cultural training called **culture assimilator,** a programmed learning approach designed to increase understanding between members of two cultures.

> As the reader of the assimilator goes through the items, he learns to what features in the episodes he should attend, and which aspects he should ignore (discrimination learning). The episodes are selected so that they expose the trainee to situations that emphasize the distinctive features of social situations [that] he must learn to discriminate. The items are also selected to give the trainee contrasting experiences with situations differing sharply on such features. The training, then, emphasizes the distinctive features of events which make the situation in the other culture most different from the situations that the trainee has already learned in his own culture. As he receives more and more training with related items, he can abstract features which such items have in common. We call such invariances "cultural principles." After the trainee goes through a half a dozen items featuring the same principle, he is presented with a summary sheet in which the principle is stated as a conclusion. Thus, if he has not abstracted the principle by that point, it is given to him.

As an example . . . consider some recent work on black/white subcultural differences. Black subjects have a tendency to assume that all white persons are prejudiced against blacks. This has major implications for social perception in interracial encounters. Almost any behavior of the white can be misinterpreted, if the context in which it is seen reflects prejudice (Triandis, 1975:70-71).

Culture assimilators have been developed for a number of nations, such as Israel and Iran, and for black and white cultures within the United States. To date, these assimilators have been developed entirely for industrial work settings. Similar approaches to multicultural education, however, can be developed for school settings.

Although the culture assimilator can alert teachers to potential sources of misunderstanding in verbal and non-verbal communication, it typically does not provide instruction in the host language or host dialect. Language, chorus, drama, and speech teachers have multiple opportunities for building intercultural competence by teaching accurate pronunciation, intonation, syntax, and word meanings associated with different languages and dialects. In classrooms where multiple dialects of English are spoken, for example, teachers can draw from each one to teach the parts of speech and rules of grammar. Similarly, they can build up student vocabulary and analytical thinking skills. Speech teachers can develop understandings of culturally different styles of posturing and other non-verbal cues. Business teachers could include instruction on culturally different expectations concerning punctuality, eye contact and handshaking or bows during job interviews. Physical educators and directors of athletic events can alert students to culturally different rules, notions of fair play, and body moves associated with certain sports.

Language is one of the great barriers to intercultural competence in United States society and to empathy and respect among culturally different people. Writing from a Chicano perspective, Rivera states the following:

Historically, state and local institutions have insisted that to become "good Americans" all minority and immigrant groups have to abandon their native languages and cultures, give up their group identity, and become absorbed as individuals into the dominant group. If any group has resisted . . . it has been regarded as uncivilized, un-American, and potentially subversive. Furthermore, it is difficult for many people to accept the idea that a native-born Mexican American who happens to speak Spanish and who retains many of the values of his native culture might well be a loyal American. As a result, social and educational institutions in the Southwest and California have directed their activities toward the elimination of both the Spanish language and Mexican culture (Rivera, 1971:200).

Ironically, millions of dollars are spent to encourage schoolchildren to learn a foreign language.

A multicultural curriculum offers guidelines for moving beyond these contradictions. When teachers accept the goal of developing competencies in multiple systems of standards for perceiving, evaluating, believing and doing, it becomes obvious that knowledge about multiple dialects and languages is part of becoming educated. A society and a world comprised of linguistically different peoples require the ability to interpret an array of verbal and non-verbal communication modes to at least minimal degrees, and accurate interpretation requires some degree of empathy.

Literature and the arts provide rich sources for developing informed student empathy. Short stories, poems, song lyrics, drama and pieces of visual art often hold messages about universal human experiences and emotions such as love, grief, anger, protest and death. Literature and artistic achievements by one's own people provide sources of identity and pride within the individual, and sources of respect from others. They can help expand students' readiness for empathy. Self-knowledge, self-acceptance and security are necessary before people can understand and accept others with whom they may disagree. Furthermore, literature and the arts provide numerous opportunities for asking students to imagine themselves as someone else. What is a certain character feeling? What is the artist or composer expressing?

4. Combatting Racism, Prejudice and Discrimination

Combatting racism, prejudice and discrimination means lessening negative attitudes and behaviors, which are based upon misconceptions about the inferiority of races and cultures different from one's own. Emphasis is on clearing up myths and stereotypes associated with different races and ethnic groups. Basic human similarities are stressed. The following lists several crucial assumptions that underlie this goal:

- It is worthwhile for educators to focus on the reduction of racial/ethnic prejudice and discrimination even though powerful sectors of the society and the world do not presently value this goal.

- It is appropriate for schools to teach certain humanistic and democratic values, such as the negative effects of racial and ethnic prejudice and discrimination.

- A reduction of racial/ethnic prejudice and discrimination is possible through appropriate educational experiences.

The goal is to develop anti-racist behavior based upon awareness of historical and contemporary evidence of individual, institutional, and cultural racism in the United States and elsewhere in the world. It is directed at developing greater awareness of the existence and impact of racism and ethnic prejudice and discrimination in American society as well as within other nations and across national boundaries. Distinctions between cultural, individual and institutional racism are important. Prejudice and discrimination are studied within the contexts of American and world history, science, literature and the arts. Teaching efforts to reduce racial and cultural prejudice and discrimination are directed at clarifying students' values and at building moral reasoning skills. This, it is hoped, leads to understandings, attitudes, and behaviors that are consistent with basic democratic ideals, such as liberty, justice, and equal opportunity. Global issues related to Western colonialism and violations of human rights are a focus.

Science and health teachers can debunk myths surrounding the concept of race and teach facts about the biological attributes shared by all humans. Scientists estimate that 90 percent of one's genetic makeup is shared with all members of the human species, leaving only six to seven percent related to gender and racial attributes and the remainder to individual variance. Misconceptions about the origins of the races and erroneous beliefs about the superiority of some races must be cleared up. Social studies educators can focus on the power dimension of racism. The fact that racial justice still eludes us must be made clear, and the possibility that our quest for racial justice has been misdirected (and needs to be redirected) must be considered (Young, 1987; Bell, 1987).

Teachers in all content areas can help students develop skills in detecting bias in texts and media. In math and general business classes, students can learn about racist loan shark practices that keep people in poverty while also learning percentages and interest rates. Typing teachers can include news articles that discuss racism in their typing skill assignments. Teachers in the humanities can use selected pieces of literature, art and music to discuss themes related to racism and prejudice.

Positive interracial attitudes can also be fostered without modifying the curriculum extensively if the school population is racially and culturally diverse. Wherever students have a chance to work together to achieve a common goal, chances are excellent for improving mutual respect and appreciation. Sports and team efforts of every kind, musical or dramatic performances, and cooperative class projects are examples of activities many teachers use to develop positive interracial contact experiences. A necessary first step in creating a revised curriculum is to face the facts of a racist past and present. It is essential to recognize the impact of racism on the oppressor as well as on the oppressed.

Most race relations experts have studied racism in terms of the costs of racism to the victims, especially the denial of equal access to educational, economic, and political power. Other deleterious effects include loss of role models and knowledge of the past, physical and mental suffering, and even loss of life. Scholars have begun to recognize that racism victimizes whites as well. Forbes, for example, in his studies of Native American and Chicano peoples, wrote that "Anglo-American young people grow up in a never-never land of mythology as regards non-Whites, and it is crucial for our society's future that damaging myths must be exposed and eliminated" (Forbes, 1969:50).

In a discussion of the effects of racism on white children, Dennis stresses ignorance of other people, development of a double social psychological consciousness, group conformity, and moral confusion and social ambivalence (Dennis, 1981). A dual consciousness develops within white children who are taught to hate and fear others and to conform to racial etiquette on the one hand while being taught Christian love on the other. Because racism deprives whites of getting to know blacks, it fosters "their ignorance of the many-sidedness of the black population" and thus reinforces stereotypes (Dennis, 1981). Given the interdependency of the human race and the great variety of cultures on earth, this ignorance is not only senseless but dangerous.

Among adults, Dennis sees three effects of racism on the white population: irrationality, inhibition of intellectual growth, and negation of democracy. He refers to Silver's assertion that white supremacy contributes to "the basic immaturity of the White population and the inability of Whites' to grow up, to accept the judgements of civilization'" (Dennis, 1981:82). Dennis also reminds us of the words Booker T. Washington spoke in 1911: "It is a grave mistake for the vast majority of Whites to assume that they can remain free and enjoy democracy while they are denying it to Blacks. The antidemocrat not only wants to ensure that Blacks do not enjoy certain rights, he also wants to ensure that no White is free to question or challenge this denial" (Dennis, 1981:82).

As painful as it may be, children and young adults must face facts about the racist past. Under the guidance of knowledgeable and caring teachers, minorities and non-minorities can gain insight into a social context that helps explain current patterns of poverty, protest and apathy. These insights can help convert anger, rage, denial, guilt and paternalism into the commitment and knowledge needed to combat racism and social injustice wherever it occurs. Since these are still prevalent, an emphasis on combatting racism is imperative. This necessity, however, must not blind us to other manifestations of prejudice and discrimination such as those directed at lower socio-economic groups, the gay community, and certain religious groups (for example, the Bahais, Universalists). The fight against racism can be extended into a broader fight for universal human rights and respect for human dignity.

5. Raising Awareness of the State of the Planet and Global Dynamics

An awareness of the state of the planet and global dynamics consists of the second and fourth dimensions of Hanvey's "attainable global perspective." Hanvey defines his second dimension as an "awareness of prevailing world conditions and developments, including emergent conditions and trends, e.g. population growth, migrations, economic conditions, resources and physical environment, political developments, science and technology, law, health, inter-nation and intra-nation conflicts, etc." (Hanvey, 1975:6).

This goal is based on the following assumptions:

- The world can best be understood as a singular, complex global system (Anderson, u.d.:6).

- An individual's private and collective decisions and behaviors influence for better or worse the future of the world system (Anderson, u.d.:6).

- Multiple loyalties are possible, that is humans can be committed to a series of concentric groups such as family, religion, nation and all of humankind (Lasswell, 1968; Allport, 1979).

- Knowledge and understanding of problems facing the global eco-system will enable and motivate students to participate effectively and responsibly in the world community.

Hanvey (1975) stresses examining the media and political thought when attempting further awareness of global conditions and dynamics. What is important is not whether the information from these sources will shed any light on the subject but rather the recognition of the students that these sources lack and distort information and, in some cases, even withhold it. Typically the media focuses on **extraordinary** events, for example, an outbreak in influenza or a rapid decline on the stock exchange rather than on the long-standing poverty of hundreds of millions or endemic malaria. There are significant limits and distortions in what we can learn from the news media. Political ideology is another source of distortion since it limits access to information about certain nations, for example, the Soviet Union, Cuba, South Africa, and China during the Cultural Revolution. Political ideology also distorts what we know about the testing of nuclear weapons, and the disposal of nuclear wastes.

Hanvey (1975) points out that the **technical nature** of much of the data about the world is another important deterrent to developing an awareness of the state of the planet. He illustrates his case with an example of the depletion of ozone in the stratosphere. Is this a problem that can be widely understood by the world's populace? Or is it destined to remain "within the private realms of specialists?" Hanvey makes a strong case for the former, provided that educators become involved. "If from the earliest grades on students examined and puzzled over cases where seemingly innocent behaviors — the diet rich in animal protein, the lavish use of fertilizer on the suburban lawn and golf course — are shown to have effects that were both unintended and global in scope, then there could be a receptivity for the kind of information involved in the ozone case" (Hanvey, 1975:7). The notion of global "unintended effects" brings us to dimension four, knowledge of global dynamics, which Hanvey defines as "some modest comprehension of key traits and mechanisms of the world system, with emphasis on theories and concepts that may increase intelligent consciousness of global change" (Hanvey, 1975:13).

Knowing that causes and effects are complex and interactive and that "simple events ramify — unbelievably" is essential to an understanding of the world as a system (Hanvey, 1975). There are often surprise effects. Hanvey illustrates this with descriptions of unanticipated results from adding new species to a pond, farm weapons to the Papago community, and the introduction of bottle feeding technology to developing nations, which led to such surprise effects as infant mortality, poor growth and brain development, and economic loss.

How can this goal be developed in the curriculum? Hanvey (1975) provides teachers with four targets to help students comprehend technological innovation and change:

1. Sensitize students to the global consequences of technological decisions, for example, stratospheric ozone depletion.

2. Help students imagine the unimaginable, for example, abolishing certain technologies such as nuclear energy because of the problem of nuclear wastes.

3. Examine our beliefs about the naturalness and goodness of technological change and the naturalness and goodness of economic growth.

4. Help students understand the dynamics of feedback and the characteristics of exponential growth.

A world system paradigm similar to Hanvey's is central to the work of most, if not all, global educators in the United States. Anderson, for example, identifies four characteristics of the world system paradigm that are essential to the curriculum:

1. Humankind as a biologically, historically, and culturally interlinked species of life.

2. Planet earth as a global ecosystem.

3. The global social order as the basis for human social and ecological organization.

4. Each member of the human species as responsible participatory citizens in the global social order (Anderson, u.d.:6).

6. Developing Social Action Skills

Major problems threaten the future of the planet and the well-being of humanity. The aim of this goal is to give students the knowledge, attitudes and skills that are necessary for active citizen participation. The emphasis is on thinking globally and acting locally and engendering a sense of personal and political efficacy and a participatory attitude, both of which are essential to the development of global responsibility among the citizens of the earth. Underlying this goal are the following assumptions:

• The subjugation and unjust treatment of any cultural group dehumanizes everyone.

• Most people will, at some time in their lives, find themselves in the position of being a political minority.

• All groups in society should have equal opportunity to bring about social and political change.

• Political access and participation for all citizens are valued.

• The more learners can actively participate in decision-making activities and work on self-selected problems beyond the classroom, the more likely they are to increase their feelings of personal and political effectiveness.

• Citizens have a right to know about global crises that threaten human survival, and about actions that can be taken to lessen these problems.

This goal moves us beyond study, reflection and analysis into a state of action. In view of the fact that certain ethnic groups and nations are cut off from their fair share of the world's resources, suffer from poverty and starvation, serve as the world's dumping ground for toxic wastes, and are unable to gain, maintain, and effectively use political power, to ignore this goal would make the other goals meaningless. Consequently, the development of social action skills encompasses Hanvey's fifth dimension. He defines this dimension as "some awareness of the problems of choice confronting individuals, nations, and the human species as consciousness and knowledge of the global system expands" (Hanvey, 1975:22). Decision making skills are an integral part of these social action skills. It assumes that students can learn to identify alternative choices for themselves as well as for public policy-makers and that they can reflect upon the possible consequences of their choices.

There are however, special impediments to social action in the global arena that deserve attention. There is a lack of global government and other appropriate institutions to carry out action plans at a global level. Joyce and Nicholson explain the situation this way:

> Although there are a number of agreed-on domains of international action in such fields as health, postal service, air traffic, weather observation, and international communications, most issues must be negotiated specifically in the absence of general policy. There is no universal language of learning comparable to Latin in the Middle Ages. The problem of creating international institutions, moreover, involves much more difficulty than merely extending existing national institutions to international dimensions. The deficiencies of the international monetary and legal systems point up this fact only too well. Added to this inherent difficulty are the differences in perceived self-interest among nations (Joyce & Nicholson, 1979:101).

Although many educators feel schools should encourage students to be more effective agents of social change, the present curricula is inadequate to meet this end (*Multicultural Teaching*, 1987; Grant & Sleeter, 1985). Political socialization research, however, offers numerous insights into what kind of curricula and instructional strategies may be effective (Hess & Newman 1968; Seashole, 1972; Ehman, 1970; Button, 1974; Muller, 1982). These insights range from simply encouraging class discussion of social issues, to political change case studies, small-group problem solving, and community action research. Seasholes outlines the necessary ingredients for teaching students to be active agents of change.

> Perhaps the greatest contribution educators can make to school-age . . . (youth) who will be tomorrow's adult citizens is to reorient their thinking about the development and use of political strategy. This means spelling out with approval the various techniques of bargaining, forced demands, concession, and occasional retreat that are used by politically successful subgroups in our society. It means being candid on two scores when dealing with heterogeneous groups of students in the classroom — candid about the probable maximum of political potential that a given subgroup could have (just how successful groups can expect to be, given their total resources of numbers, money, effort, education, and so forth) and candid about the kinds of political techniques that are in fact being used currently or may be used in the reasonably near future.
>
> Political activity in this day and age, after all, involves not only voting, contributing money, and writing letters to congressmen. It sometimes involves street demonstrations and civil disobedience. These need talking out in the classroom, too, not in normative terms but in terms of strategies which

sometimes succeed or fail because they tread so close to the border of normatively acceptable political behavior (Seaholes, 1972).

Students also need opportunities to make choices and evaluate their decisions. They need to practice self-expression, decision-making skills and problem resolution. The practice can begin in kindergarten with opportunities to make simple choices, express opinions, set goals, and discuss classroom rules. Participatory learning can be expanded at the high school level to include community or political action projects, simulations and games.

The Interactive Nature of the Goals

The six goals contained in the curriculum model overlap; each one individually represents a necessary but insufficient focus for multicultural education. For example, to increase cultural consciousness without also developing the understanding, skills, and attitudes that cluster around intercultural competence might lead to greater ethnocentrism and polarization. It would be impossible to develop people's intercultural competence (such as empathy) without also developing their senses of personal identity and security, which come with cultural consciousness. Furthermore, these goals should foster an appreciation of both human similarities and ethnic diversity and an awareness of how racism and certain prejudices originate and subjugate. The sixth goal, enabling people to become change agents, goes beyond study and discussion and deals with the skills and behaviors needed to eradicate discriminatory practices as well as to bring about other desired changes.

The cluster of goals in the curriculum model does not require that teachers stress each goal equally. Rather, these six goals should be woven into an overall curriculum design that allows separate subject areas and courses to emphasize those goals that are most compatible with the subject matter boundaries and age groupings of a particular school system. In some school settings, for example, historical perspectives and cultural consciousness might be emphasized in literature and the arts; intercultural competence in language and communications; reduction of racial/ethnic prejudice and discrimination in biology and world and United States history; and social action skills in government, business, or economics.

Furthermore, a careful sequence of learning experiences designed to foster social action skills could begin in kindergarten with simple decision-making activities and culminate in the final year of high school with a community action project. Ideally, teams of teachers within a school, school system, college, or university would collaborate on the sequencing and articulation of multicultural and global perspectives in curriculum objectives, strategies, and materials. With clarification of global and multicultural goals, it becomes possible to build them into the curriculum.

Conclusion

The model proposed in this chapter takes a position that may not be widely accepted. It could be viewed as overly idealistic and based upon unrealistic assumptions about the possibilities for human altruism. Many parents and students, for example, may not be ready for such an approach and may regard global and multicultural education as contrary and alien to their personal needs.

It would be possible to develop an alternative, perhaps more negative, model, one based on fear of human annihilation and concerns about the survival, health, and future of one's grandchildren. People become concerned about multicultural and global issues when the focus is on economic competition in the world arena, unsafe storage of nuclear wastes, the greenhouse effect, and futile military or diplomatic efforts based on ignorance of history and culture. Even the goal of combatting racism, one that has never been a national policy, could be viewed positively by perpetrators of racism once it is realized that economic and political gains in (or cooperation with) developing nations cannot be taken seriously as long as we practice racism at home and abroad.

The fact is, however, that the multicultural movement, and much of the global movement, is idealistic. These approaches are positive. They are based on visions of humans living in greater harmony with each other and with the Earth. They require that we develop citizens who are able to consider alternative viewpoints, are able to examine values and assumptions — one's own as well as those of others — and are willing to learn to think critically. Both require a degree of open-mindedness that may be impossible to develop in people with a highly rigid belief structure. This does not mean that the visions of multicultural and global education should be abandoned. Rather, by developing a model that clearly reflects the idealistic nature of multicultural and global education, it becomes possible to articulate reasons for disagreement. This can lead to a healthy dialogue, even among strong supporters, that can move us beyond theory and rhetoric into practice.

The concept of cultural relativism, or the notion that anything goes, is a frequently voiced concern. Many adults who have school-age children, for example, see multicultural education as a one-way proposition that requires students to accept abhorrent socio-political practices. These objectionable practices may include news making events such as the stifling of political dissenters within ethnic communities, and physical violence such as female infanticide, or genitalia mutilation. A model similar to the one proposed here can deal with the issue of cultural relativism in at least three ways. First, if we accept respect for human dignity and universal human rights as a basic value, then we cannot be neutral about injury to or destruction of human life.

Ultimately the goal is for these practices to end. Second, if we consider multiple historical perspectives we can at least understand why such practices occur. And third, if we develop cultural consciousness and intercultural competence we may be able to understand that we might very well accept and even participate in such behaviors had we been born and raised in that society.

Another important concern is that many nations, ethnic minorities, and the economically disadvantaged people will not participate in multicultural education or global education efforts. We know, for example, that the global movement supported by Western governments is often viewed with suspicion by non-Western peoples who fear it is a continuation of Western racism and imperialism. This is a sobering limitation. If we were to take seriously our own national creed of justice and equality for all and if combatting racism were to become a national policy, this suspicion might be lessened.

If teachers are to develop global and multicultural perspectives in their teaching, they will need to develop new plans for instruction. A curriculum model such as the one proposed here can guide teachers as they select subject matter content; identify instructional goals and objectives for student attitudes, skills, and knowledge; and gather sources of information (media, texts, speakers, and so on). By providing a rationale for global and multicultural education, the model also gives teachers the support they need in facing pressures and questions from colleagues, the community and students.

Notes

1. The 1973 National Council of Social Studies Yearbook, for example, *Teaching Ethnic Studies: Concepts and Strategies*, is a seminal work that contains powerful statements by social scientists and educators such as J. Banks, J. Forbes, C. Cortez, G. Gay, & B. Sizemore. The first edition of Bank's classic test, *Teaching Strategies for Ethnic Studies* was published in 1979. R. Hanvey wrote *An Attainable Global Perspective* in 1975, a classic piece that remains one of the most compelling statements in the area of global education. E. Reischauer's book, *Toward the 21st Century: Education for a Changing World*, was published in 1973, followed up in 1980 by *Schooling for a Global Age*, edited by J. Becker. The annotated bibliographies of Becker's book are evidence of the fervent activities among global educators throughout the 1970s.

2. The original model was developed by the author for presentation at a curriculum institute sponsored by the Association for Supervision and Curriculum Development, Boston, October 17-18, 1975. A later version was included in M.C. Mills. (ed.). (1976). *Multi-Cultural Education*. Charleston, WV:West Virginia Department of Education. The revised model integrates into the older model dimensions from R. Hanvey's, *An Attainable Global Perspective*.

3. In choosing these particular core values and developing the conceptual model of comprehensive multicultural education, I am indebted to global educators such

as Lee Anderson, Charlotte Anderson, James M. Becker, Robert Hanvey, and Betty Reardon. I am also indebted to Anna Ochoa for the guidance she provided in our team-taught seminar on global and multicultural education. See also S. Totten, (ed.). "Teaching about universal human rights," in a special issue of *Social Education,* (September, 1985) and W.M. Kniep, "Defining Global Education by its Content," *Social Education,* October 1986:437-446.

References

Allport, G. (1979). *Nature of Prejudice.* Reading, MA: Addison-Wesley.

Anderson, L. (u.d.) "Some propositions about the nature of global studies." Northwestern University, MS.

Banks, J.A. (1984). *Teaching Strategies for Ethnic Studies,* 3rd ed. Boston: Allyn and Bacon.

Becker, J.M., (ed.). (1980). *Schooling for Global Age.* New York: McGraw Hill.

Bell, D. (1987). *And We Are Not Yet Saved: The Elusive Quest for Racial Justice.* New York: Basic Books.

Bennett Button, C. (1974). "Political education and minority youth." In R.G. Niemi, (ed.). *New Views of Children and Politics.* San Francisco: Jossey-Ball.

Berry, M.F. & Blassingame, J.W. (1982). *Long Memory: The Black Experience in America.* New York: Oxford University Press.

Castell, D. (1976). *Cross-Cultural Models of Teaching: Latin American Example.* Gainesville, Florida: University of Florida Press.

Chun-Hoon, L.K.Y. (1973). "Teaching Asian-American experience." In J.A. Banks, (ed)., *Teaching Ethnic Studies: Concepts and Strategies.* Washington DC: National Council for the Social Studies.

Cortez, C. (1983). "Multiethnic and global education: Partners for the eighties?" *Phi Delta Kappan,* April.

Cortez, C.E. (1973). "Teaching the Chicano Experience." In J.A. Banks, (ed.), *Teaching Ethnic Studies: Concepts and Strategies.*Washington, DC: National Council for the Social Studies.

Dennis, R.M. (1981). "Socialization and racism: The White experience." In B.P. Bowser & R.G. Hunt, (eds), *Impacts of Racism on White Americans.* Beverly Hills, CA: Sage.

Dufty, D., Sawkins, S., Pickard, N., Power, J., & Bowe, A. (1976). *Seeing It Their Way: Ideas, Activities and Resources for Intercultural Studies.* London, England: Reed Education.

Ehman, L.H. (1970). "Political socialization and the high school social studies curriculum," unpublished Ph.D. diss., University of Michigan.

Forbes, J. (1969). *Education of the Culturally Different: A Multi-Cultural Approach.* San Francisco: Far West Laboratory for Educational Research and Development.

Forbes, J.D. (1973). "Teaching Native American values and cultures." In J.A. Banks, (ed.), *Teaching Ethnic Studies: Concepts and Strategies.* Washington, DC: National Council for the Social Studies.

Gibson, M. (1984). "Approaches to multicultural education in the United States: Some concepts and assumptions," *Anthropology and Education Quarterly,* 15:112.

Grant, C.A. & R.A. Koskela. (1986). "Education that is multicultural and the relationship between preserved campus learning and field experiences," *Journal of Educational Research.* 79, (4):204.

Grant, C. & Sleeter, C. (1985). "The literature on multicultural education: Review and analysis," *Educational Review.* 37, (2).

Gudykunst, W.B. & Kim, Y.Y. (1984). *Communicating with Strangers: An Approach to Intercultural Communication.* New York. Addison Wooley.

Hamilton, C.V. (1977). "Race and education: A search for legitimacy." In J. Rotherman, (ed.), *Issues in Race and Ethnic Relations.* Itasca, IL: F.E. Peacock.

Hanvey R. (1975). *An Attainable Global Perspective.* New York: Center for War/Peace Studies

Hess, R.D. & Newman, F.M. (1968). "Political socialization in the schools." *Harvard Education Review,* 38.

Hirschfelder, A. (1986). *Happily May I Walk: American Indians and Alaska Natives Today.* New York: Scribner.

Johnson, D. (1987). "The contribution of the humanities to a global perspective in teacher education." ERIC ED 265 114.

Joyce, B.R.& Nicholson, A.M. (1979). "Imperatives for global education." In J.A. Becker, (ed.), *Schooling for a Global Age,* New York: McGraw-Hill.

Killens, J.O. (1965). *Black Man's Burden.* New York: Trident Press.

Kraemer, A.J. (1975). *A Cultural Self-Awareness Approach to Improving Intercultural Communication Skills,* ERIC ED 079 213, April.

Lasswell, H.D. (1968). "Multiple loyalties in a shrinking world." paper presented at the National Council of the Social Studies conference, Washington DC, November 29.

Levine, L.W. (1977). *Black Culture and Black Consciousness.* Oxford, England: Oxford University Press.

More Than Bows and Arrows. (1978). Seattle, WA: Cinema Associates.

Muller, R. (1982). *New Genesis, Shaping a Global Spirituality.* Garden City, NJ: Doubleday

Multicultural Teaching. (1987). "Education for racial equality under attack." 5,(3) Summer.

Planetary Citizens' Registry. In Dufty, D., Sawkins, S., Pickard, N., Power, J., & Bowe, A. (1976). *Seeing It Their Way: Ideas, Activities and Resources for Intercultural Studies.* London, England: Reed Education.

Rhinesmith, S. (1979). "Americans in the Global Learning Process," *Annals,* March: 442.

Rivera, F. (1971). "The teaching of Chicano history." In E.W. Ludwig & James Santibanez, (eds.), *The Chicanos: Mexican American Voices*. New York: Penguin.

Seasholes, B. (1972). "Political socialization of blacks: Implications for self and society." In J.A. Banks & J.D. Grambs, (eds.), *Black Self-Concept*. New York: McGraw-Hill.

Tiedt, P.L. & Tiedt, I.M. (1979). *Multicultural Teaching: A Handbook of Activities, Information, and Resources*. Boston: Allyn and Bacon.

Triandis, H.C. (1975) "Culture training, cognitive complexity and interpersonal attitudes." In R.W. Brislin, S. Bochner & W.J. Lonner, (eds.), *Cross-Cultural Perspectives on Learning*. New York: John Wiley.

van Oudenhoven, No. (1982). "Act locally, think globally: Some comments on prosocial behavior, information processing and development education." *Development Education Paper No. 24*. New York: UNICEF, Information Division.

Wolsk, D. (1976). *An experience centered curriculum: Exercises in personal and social reality*. United Nations Education, Scientific and Cultural Organization (Paris), ERIC ED 099 269, 1974.

Young, R.M. (1987). "Racist society, racist science," *Multicultural Teaching*, 5(3):43-50

Research and Multicultural Education:
Barriers, Needs and Boundaries

Carl A. Grant and Susan Millar

It is slowly becoming standard for schools in the United States to explicitly take into account the ascribed characteristics (race, class, gender and disability) of their students and the human diversity in society. The nomenclature for these aspects of education may change — as it has over the last 30 or more years — but the attention focused on student diversity in the schools and classrooms will continue to increase. This attention is a function of: the increasing number of students of color entering schools, many of whom have a primary language other than English; the demands of women who seek to have their history, culture, ideology and pedagogy fully accepted, appreciated and affirmed in every aspect of the policies and practices of the educational system; the accelerated movement of the United States population into a "have" and "have not" society; and the national fear that this country is losing its technological and economic eminence to other countries.

During the late 1980s, education that deals with human diversity is most commonly referred to as "multicultural education." Other terms used synonymously in the past and the present for multicultural education have included, "pluralism" or "pluralistic," "multiethnic," "cross-cultural," "bi-cultural," and "human relations." Recently, multicultural education as an ideology and concept expressed through policies and practices has begun to make some small inroads into almost every aspect of schooling. It has also become more popularly accepted (at least with lip service attention) and thereby received a noticeable increase in status over the last 10 years. However, scholarly research about multicultural education has not kept abreast of attempts to actualize the various ideas that school personnel hold about multicultural education. Teacher education (pre-service and in-service) has perhaps received the most research attention. However, Grant & Secada (1989) were able to locate only

*This chapter appears in *Research Directions for Multicultural Education*, Carl A. Grant, Editor, Falmer Press, 1992.

23 research studies in the pre-service and in-service area of teacher education. There are a variety of reasons why research that takes into account multi-culturalism is proceeding at a snail's pace. This chapter presents some of the more salient reasons, discusses the kinds of research about multicultural education that needs to occur, and concludes by suggesting a set of boundaries on multicultural research.

Barriers to Multicultural Research

There are several reasons why research on multicultural education as well as educational research that takes multiculturalism into account have not kept pace with the discussion and debate.

Faculty Demographics

The demographic characteristics of higher education faculties are not conducive to the development of research on multicultural education. In education, 93 percent of the professors are white, and of this number, 70 percent are male. In addition, the average age for full professors is 53, associate professors, 47, and assistant professors, 42. Given this profile, it is reasonable to assume that the great majority of education faculty have had little exposure to multiculturalism during their formative years of professional development. Examination of the bibliographies of their publications and of the syllabi for their courses (Grant & Koskela, 1986) indicate that their working knowledge of multicultural education is very limited.

This demographic picture is not likely to change quickly. The percentage of persons of color receiving doctorates is half of their representation in the general population. The number of African Americans receiving Ph.D.'s has declined since 1976 (*On Campus*, September 1989:11).

Lack of Clarity

The meaning of multicultural education has been, and very often still is, presented in an unclear manner. Authors usually do not clearly define what they mean by the term (Banks, 1977; Grant & Sleeter, 1985; Sleeter & Grant, 1987). As a result, some educators/authors include under the rubric of multi-cultural education only work related in some way to students of color or to some aspect of human diversity (Grant & Sleeter 1985; Grant, Sleeter & Anderson, 1986). This lack of definition allows critics to either ignore multi-cultural education or view it as an idea without meaning and structure.

Limited Funding

Monies to support multicultural research have been extraordinarily limited. Occasionally, isolated projects with multicultural education in the title receive funding. For example, Zeicher and Grant received $30 000 per year over three years from the Department of Education to prepare pre-service students to effectively teach diverse students in multicultural settings. However, such studies are the exception in educational funding. Also, of the research studies on multicultural pre-service and in-service programs that Grant & Secada (1990) reviewed, only a few were supported with additional institution, state or federal funds. It is important here to point out that although federal monies regularly support The Bureau for Equal Educational Opportunity and Bilingual Centres, the contractual purposes of these bureaus and centres are to provide training and technical assistance to schools and parents. For example, the mission of the Upper Great Lakes Multifunctional Resource Center — one of the 16 regional resource centers funded by the United States Department of Education — is to, "provide training and technical assistance to educators and parents in the education of students who have a limited proficiency in English (LEP)" (Upper Great Lake Multifunctional Resource Center document, 1989). The centres and the bureaus are not budgeted to conduct general research. Furthermore, research on the effectiveness of their training and technical assistance activities is not considered primary to the scope of their mission.

Ethnocentrism and Elitism

Academic ethnocentrism and elitism act to limit multicultural education research. Academic ethnocentrism has been discussed recently in a number of educational publications. For example, in an issue of the *Chronicle of Higher Education* (1988) scholars of color pointed out that, for a variety of reasons, their work frequently is not accepted as solid scholarship. In particular, they note that the standards used to judge work in the social sciences, including education, are not sufficiently independent of the personal interests of the reviewers. In other words, the criteria used for evaluation are a "moving target" rather than a standard understood by all ahead of time. It is significant, these scholars of color argue, that this moving target is an artifact of the perspectives of white males.

Another form of academic ethnocentrism is expressed when reviewers hold that the work of scholars of color is only or mainly for people of color, and therefore not considered relevant for the majority of education scholars. Linda Grant (1988) has argued that patterns of "ghettoization" exist in journal publication. She points out that articles on students of color in schools most often appear in journals that have a smaller specialized readership than mainstream journals. Staples (1984:9) earlier made a similar observation when referring to the general written scholarship of African Americans. He concluded, ". . . few established White journals will publish the works of Black scholars, work that generally challenges the prevailing White view of the racial situation. Most are forced to publish in Black-oriented periodicals" (Staples, 1984:9).

To avoid this ghettoization in journal publication, many scholars of color "play the game," that is, abandon their desires to work from an ethnic perspective and instead work from a mainstream/traditional perspective. This point becomes doubly compounded because of the small number of scholars of color. Presently, even an informal review of conference papers and of published articles and books would point out that almost all of the research being conducted on educational problems and issues, including issues pertaining to people of color, is being conducted by white researchers.

Academic elitism is sometimes experienced by white scholars who have an interest in multicultural research. This occurs when their colleagues — both white and of color — ridicule their interest in this line of research, and suggest it should be left to people of color. As one white scholar told me, some of his white colleagues question why he works in this area and advise him that research on this topic is, "their [people of color] problem." Academic elitism in the form of patriarchy is also present when women (of color and white) who employ feminist ideologies and methodologies experience barriers to their research programs (Harding, 1987; Hartsock, 1987; Raymond, 1985).

At the 1986 American Educational Research Association conference, the Sig for Examining the Application of Gender, Race, and Social Class in Educational Theory and Research was formed in part to ameliorate this academic elitism and ethnocentrism. The Sig is encouraging mainstream researchers to study the interactions between and among the actors in schools in terms of race, class, and gender issues.

Ghettoization

The ghettoization of academic conference participants who are advocates of multicultural education acts to inhibit research in this area. At conferences or meetings, it frequently happens that only a few or no white males participate in or attend sessions that have "multicultural," "gender," or "minority" in the title unless the work is "done on" people of color. In other words, when researchers of color are presenting their research, relatively few white male researchers attend. However, when the session involves a white researcher discussing, for example, "blacks," a good-sized audience of all colors attends. This ghettoization, although not documented, has become so commonplace that presenters and audience participants openly comment on it.

Formal and Informal Socialization

Formal and informal socialization about research methodology and academic expectations rarely entails multicultural education. It is well known that this kind of socialization often takes place in advanced level seminars. These seminars provide force not only for learning about research methodology and procedures. Popkewitz (1984:3) argues that,

> [A]s people are trained to participate in a research community, the learning involves more than the content or the field. Learning the exemplars of a field of inquiry is also to learn how to see, think about and act towards the world. An individual is taught the appropriate expectations, demands, and consistent attitudes and emotions that are involved in doing science.

Courses at either the undergraduate or graduate level (let alone at the advanced seminar level) in multicultural education are not often available at colleges or universities.[1] The absence of seminars and other forums for analysis and debate about multicultural education undercuts conceptual development in this area and discourages young scholars from becoming involved in this field.

Lack of Leadership

Lack of leadership by scholars of color is another reason multicultural education research has not flourished. It could be argued, based upon civil rights history, that until scholars of color assume prominent leadership positions in determining research directions, educational programs for students of color, and **all** female students, will be flawed and progress will be slow.

There are, no doubt, additional reasons why multicultural education research has not flourished. These, as well as the reasons discussed above, act as resistance, or barriers to change (Zaltman & Duncan, 1977) and are probably impeding the development of research on multicultural education at your institution. An understanding of these resistances will, according to Rubin (1974), give you valuable insight into the nature of the university, "who it is," and what it considers valuable research.

What Multicultural Research Needs to Take Place

Multicultural research must be carried out on all areas of schooling, including school routines and interactions, teaching and learning practices, and the effects of educational policy and practices. A few illustrations of prominent research themes will help to make this clear.

Research on Teaching

The *Third Edition of the Handbook of Research on Teaching* (1986) has identified five major areas presently receiving research attention: Part I: Theory and Method of Research on Teaching; Part II: Research on Teaching and Teachers; Part III: The Social and Instructional Context of Teaching; Part IV: Adapting Teaching to Differences Among Learners; and Part V: Research on the Teaching of Subjects and Grade Levels. These five parts are divided into 35 chapters, each of which includes a bibliography listing the research studies reviewed. It seems logical, given the great student diversity in the nation's schools and the civic mission of schooling, that a careful study of teaching must take into account multiculturalism. For example, in Part II, Chapter Eleven, "Students' Thought Processes," Wittrock, the Handbook editor, explains that, ". . . research on students' thought processes examines how teaching and teachers influence what students think, believe, feel, say, or do that affects their achievement" (1986:297). He further explains how teachers influence student achievement: ". . . the distinctive characteristic of the research on students' thought processes is the idea that teaching affects achievement through students' processes. That is, teaching influences student thinking. Student thinking mediates learning and achievement" (1986:297). In reviewing the research in this area, his discussion includes: teacher expectations, student behavior, student self-concept, students' perception of schools, teachers, and teachers' behavior. It would be reasonable to conclude that research that takes into account multiculturalism is vital to these areas of study. For example, the educational literature is replete with accounts of students of color self-concepts being detrimentally affected by school policies and practices (Beane & Lipka, 1987; Kvaraceus, et al., 1965; Rosenfeld, 1971). In fact, the issue that school segregation led to low self-esteem among blacks was a major argument offered by the social scientists who testified in Brown v. Board of Education. The literature is also replete with reports of how teachers' behavior has negatively affected low income students, students of color and female students (Goulder, 1978; Grant & Sleeter, 1986). Research that includes multiculturalism would make certain that students' ascribed characteristics (race, class and gender) are analyzed within the context of the above mentioned research areas, or it would address this omission if this was the case. Yet, such research studies were not included in this piece.

It can be concluded that the *Handbook* would be of greater benefit to educators if multiculturalism had been included in more of the chapters.

Teacher-Student Interaction

Very closely related to teachers and teaching is the research on "interactions" between teachers and students. For example, differences in interactions between teachers and students attributable to race/ethnicity and gender have been observed to account for differences in student performance (Brophy & Good, 1974; Fennema & Peterson, 1986; Reyes, 1981). Also, research on expectancy theory and social group theory argues that teachers' behavior toward students is influenced by their expectations of the students' ability. Research that takes into account multiculturalism is important to this area because of recent demographic projections. Demographic projections suggest that interactions between and among these actors will need careful study. In 1984, 29 percent of the total student enrolment in schools was non-white. In the country's 20 largest school districts, students of color constituted between 60 percent and 70 percent (Center for Education Statistics, CES, 1987a:64). It is projected that by the year 2000, students of color will comprise between 30 percent and 40 percent of the total school enrolment. In contrast to the increasingly diverse student population, the teaching force in this country is becoming increasingly white and female (CES, 1987b:60, 175, 183, 195). This contrast is compounded by socio-economic class differences that frequently separate teachers and students. One in every four students is poor (Kennedy, Jund & Orland, 1986:71) and one in every five students lives in a single-parent home (CES, 1987b:21). The importance of this area is further compounded by a legacy of judicial, legislative and social inequities experienced by students of color, female students and poor students in their interactions with school officials.

Research Funding

All research thrusts of the Department of Education and of funding foundations such as Ford or Carnegie need to include multicultural education as an integral part of their research efforts on schooling. The Department of Education's current agenda for research on elementary and secondary schooling is fairly comprehensive, including both policy and practice initiatives. The research agenda is also fairly deep in that it includes research in the following areas: governance and finance, evaluation, student testing, writing, reading, effective secondary schools, elementary and middle school, art, teacher evaluation and educational technology. Research development centres are handsomely funded. The Center for School Leadership and the Centre on Student Testing, Evaluation and Standards each receive $1 000 000 for each of five years. Other centres may receive even more money annually. For example, the Center for the Study of Learning receives $1 300 000 for each of five years (The National Institute of Education, 1985).

Sometimes the focus of these research efforts is on students of color or, as the Government puts it, "Schooling of Disadvantaged Students" (See for example, FY 1989 Application for Educational Research and Development

Centers Program, U.S. Office of Education, 1988). This, however, is not the same as a focus on multicultural education. For example, the bibliography (1988:48-58) of the application package described above does not include publications on multicultural education. This omission could influence the way these research centres will operate in regards to multiculturalism.

Boundaries of Multicultural Research

Schooling can be compared to a ladder, with the first rung pre-school and the final rung undergraduate/graduate or professional school. The breadth of schooling encompasses technical training through the arts and sciences. Both the length and breadth of schooling needs to include curriculum and instruction that has multiculturalism comprehensively integrated throughout. Important to the success of this integration is research that examines this integration. In other words, it is important to actually know — not guess about — the attitudes and behaviors of the members of the educational community. Even at our institutions of higher education, it is becoming commonplace to hear or read about physical and verbal race and gender violence occurring on the campuses. According to an article in *Education Week* (September 1989:30) that discussed a report from the National Institute Against Prejudice and Violence, "174 universities reported incidents of violence against ethnic groups during the school years 1986-87 and 1987-88." This unrest is further exacerbated by the debate to include or not to include non-Western studies in the traditional college core curriculum.

This debate has increased tensions between and among faculty members, students, and university officials. For example, Stephen H. Balch, President of The National Association of Scholars, argues that "ethnic and women studies are synonymous with lower standards. By and large, the emphasis is not scholarly. These courses are severely corrupting, they incorporate wrong values" (*On Campus*, 1989:10). Rhetoric of this nature and actions that prevent people of color and women from seeing their history and culture in the core curriculum increase the intensity of the debate over "whose" ideology and culture will be included in the core college curriculum. It fuels the growing tension on the campus. The boundaries of multicultural research therefore have to include all of schooling, from pre-school through professional school, and from the learning of the alphabet to appreciating and comparing the differences and similarities of the poetry of Gwendolyn Brooks to the poetry of Carl Sandburg.

Research on Policy

Research has only recently become formally associated with the formulation and evaluation of policy. It was in the 1960s that the relationship between the social sciences and public policy moved from the periphery to the main-stream. During the 1960s, research on equity issues, especially desegregation, influenced educational policy decisions. The Coleman report (1966) stands out as research that significantly influenced public policy. The Westinghouse study which reported that Head Start programs did not positively improve academic achievement can be cited as another piece of research that greatly impacted schooling for poor people and students of color. Other research studies during the decades of the 1960s and the 1970s dealt with equity issues such as class. Wise's (1967) examination of poor and wealthy schools caused some policy analysts to suggest different funding policies — policies that took into consideration the wealth of a school district. Wise argued that,

> Differences in per-pupil expenditure could not be based on the accident of location, as is now the practice in most states. Undoubtedly, this conclusion will not meet with the favor of wealthier communities. But if we are to heed the equal protection clause of the Constitution, it seems that the state cannot deny to some what it grants to others (1967:214).

Research on Hispanic students in particular led to language policy as written in the Bilingual Act. Research on gender disparities in school program-ming and the lack of equal opportunities for female students led to such policies as Title IX of the Education Amendments of 1972, while research on disabled students led to policies that demand that these students be placed in less restricted environments, as stated in the 1975 Public Law 94-142 (the Educa-tion for all Handicapped).

Research since the 1960s has had a significant impact on policy related to race, class, gender, language and disability. Some of this policy has had a positive impact on race, class, gender, language and disability practices in schools, especially as it relates to equal opportunity as expressed through "equal access." For example, Title IX and PL 94-142 opened doors in schools to students who had been previously denied access. However, some other research has had the opposite impact, for example, the Coleman report and the Westinghouse study. Both of these research reports led to unwritten policy that guided the day-to-day schooling practices affecting students based on their race and class. After the Coleman report was released and discussed, it was not uncommon for school people to argue that poor children of color could not learn because they were from homes that did not foster learning, and that school could make very little difference in their future lives. Similarly, discus-sions of the putatively negligible impact of Head Start programs on the achievement of poor minority students influenced unwritten day-to-day policy. White & Buka (1987:70) point out that, "the findings of the Westinghouse study were widely discussed and almost all the discussion centred on the measure of intellectual function."

Rather than critique these policies, the purpose here is to point out that policy based upon "equity" research impacts the schooling of **all** students, and therefore needs to include multiculturalism. It is important to point out that most of the research that was and is considered "equity" research erroneously assumes that the concept of "equity" is synonymous with the concept of "equal opportunity." "Equal opportunity," meaning having equal access is not synonymous with "equity," which means having a fair and just opportunity. Grant (1989) and Secada (1989) have raised questions regarding this interpretation. Secada asserts, "Equity attempts to look at the justice of a given state of affairs, a justice that goes beyond acting in agreed-upon ways and seeks to look at the justice of the arrangements leading up to and resulting from those actions" (1989:81). Secada further clarifies this difference when he argues:

> The fundamental difference between equity and equality is that equity is a qualitative property while equality is quantitative. Yet one of the most powerful constructs at the disposal of equity is equality, and the recognition that group inequalities may be unjust. The two terms, however, are — or at least should be — different. Work in educational equity needs to discriminate when its concerns coincide with those of equality and when they do not (1989:81).

Additionally, it should be noted that "access" into a classroom doesn't necessarily include with it an analysis of race, class, gender and disability interactions that take into account curriculum, staffing, instruction and other schooling factors that are critical to equitable education. Multicultural research would take this neglected dimension into account. Furthermore, research that reports no significant increase in student achievement (such as that reported in the Westinghouse study), has not considered other important non-cognitive outcomes such as improved home-school relationships and increased student self-esteem. In other words, the social and emotional impacts of the program on the students and their significant others were not adequately assessed and reported. Bronfenbrenner made this point when he took issue back in 1976 with the testing procedures in early childhood studies. He argued:

> Information available across the board is limited to the cognitive area only and consists of IQ scores on the Stanford-Binet (with a few exceptions as noted) and, once the children have entered school, measures of academic achievement on standardized tests . . . The restriction of available data to measures of this type sets limitations to the conclusions that can be drawn (U.S. Children's Bureau: Vol. 2, 1976:2).

Finally, Mitchell (1985) describes four basic themes of recent educational policy research: equity, pattern of school governance, teaching and learning, and the economics of education. We already have discussed two of these themes — equity, and teaching and learning. An example related to a very popular aspect of school governance — school base management — is also instructive with regard to the matter of the boundaries of multicultural research. School base management is currently being promoted and adopted by many school districts because it is considered to be a way to give teachers, parents and local school officials a greater role in running their school. Research in this area must seek to determine if parents are involved on the community councils, and if so, which parents. Are they mainly middle-class parents? Are meetings scheduled in a manner that ensures that parents of color and "second language" parents can attend as easily as other groups? Are they organized so that all parents can understand what is taking place? In other words, are language translators available and is the English free of jargon? Does the community council have significant decision-making responsibilities, and if so, is the decision-making understood in terms of multiculturalism? Research that is multicultural must be a part of all of these areas of educational research on policy.

Conclusion

It has been argued here that there are numerous barriers to multicultural research, including an unclear definition, lack of money, academic ethnocentrism, and academic ghettoization. It was further pointed out that multicultural research must be included in all areas of research on education and schools and it should not be bound to any particular area of the curriculum or instructional process. It has also been argued that educational research would better serve its clients, especially students of color, poor students, and all female students, if multiculturalism was an integrated part of the research paradigm, design and method. In summary, it is argued that barriers and boundaries should not obstruct the important need for scholars to conduct research in multicultural education.

Additionally, various educational research practices which act as barriers to people pursuing access to multicultural research have been challenged. It was pointed out that serious and extensive educational research is only a few decades old and this research received a great impetus from conditions in schools as identified by the civil rights movement and the War on Poverty. Therefore, advocates of multicultural research should realize that they have a close kinship to the equal opportunity and equity movement and should not be intimidated and stopped by the barriers. In fact, they have an obligation to demand to be included as part of this research cadre in positions of leadership.

Notes

1. It is unfortunate that when such courses are presented, they frequently promote what Sleeter & Grant (1987) describe as "education for the culturally and exceptionally different." By this they mean that the courses present an assimilationist ideology and hold traditional educational aims.

References

Banks, J.A. (1977). "The implications of multicultural education for teacher education." In F.H. Klassen & D.M. Gollnick (eds.), *Pluralism and the American Teacher*. Washington, DC: American Association of Colleges for Teacher Education.

Beane, J.A. & Lipka, R.P. (1987). *When the Kids Come First: Enhancing Self Esteem.* Columbus, OH.: National Middle School Association.

Blum, D.E. (1988). "To get ahead in research, some minority scholars choose to 'Play the game'." *The Chronicle of Higher Education,* June 22:A17.

Bronfenbrenner, U. (1979). *The Ecology of Human Development: Experiments by Nature and by Design.* Cambridge, MA: Harvard University Press.

Caldwell, J. (1989). "The need for 'anti-racism' education." *Education Week,* September 20:32.

Center for Education Statistics. (1987a). *The Condition of Education.* Washington, DC: U.S. Government Printing Office.

Center for Education Statistics. (1987b). *Digest of Education Statistics.* Washington, DC: U.S. Government Printing Office.

Gouldner, H. (1978). *Teachers' Pets, Troublemakers, and Nobodies: Black Children in Elementary School.* Westport, CT: Greenwood Press.

Grant, C. (1989). "Equity, equality, and classroom life." In W.G. Secada (ed.), *Equity in Education.* London: Falmer Press.

Grant, C. & Koskela, R. (1986). "Education that is multicultural and the relationship between pre-service campus learning and field experiences." *The Journal of Educational Research,* 79(4):197-203.

Grant, C. & Secada, W.G. (1990). "Preparing teachers for diversity." In W.R. Houston (ed.), *Handbook of Research on Teacher Education.* New York: Macmillan Publishing Co.

Grant, C. & Sleeter, C. (1985). "The literature on multicultural education: Review and analysis." *Educational Review,* 37(2):97-118.

Grant, C. & Sleeter, C. (1986). *After the School Bell Rings.* Philadelphia: Falmer.

Grant, C., Sleeter, C. & Anderson, J. (1986). "The literature on multicultural education: Review and analysis." *Review of Educational Research,* 56:195-211.

Grant, C., Sleeter, C. & Anderson, J. (1986). "The literature on multicultural education: Review and analysis." *Educational Studies,* 12:47-71.

Grant, L. (1988). "Introduction: Regenerating and refocusing research on minorities and education." *The Elementary School Journal*, 88(5):441-448.

Harding, S. (1987). "Introduction: Is there a feminist method?" In S. Harding (ed.), *Feminism and Methodology*. Bloomington and Indianapolis: Indiana University Press.

Hartsock, N. (1987). "The feminist standpoint: Developing the groundwork for a specifically feminist historical materialism." In S. Harding (ed.), *Feminism and Methodology*. Bloomington and Indianapolis: Indiana University Press.

Kennedy, M.M., Jund, R.K. & Orland, M.E. (1986). *Poverty, Achievement, and the Distribution of Compensatory Education Services*, (An interim report from the National Assessment of Chapter I). Washington, DC: U.S. Government Printing Office.

Kvaraceus, W.C., Gibson, J.S., Patterson, F., Seasholes, B. & Grambs, J.D. (1965). *Negro Self-Concept: Implications for School and Citizenship*, The report of a conference sponsored by the Lincoln Filene Center for Citizenship and Public Affairs. New York: McGraw-Hill.

McKenna, B. (1989). "College faculty: An endangered species?" *On Campus*. Washington, DC: American Federation of Teachers.

Midwest Bilingual Education Multifunctional Resource Center. (1986). *Annual Report: 1985-1986*, (Contract no. 300850188). Rosslyn, VA: InterAmerica Research Associates.

Parkay, F. (1983). *White Teacher, Black School*. New York: Praeger.

Popkewitz, T.S. (1984). *Paradigm and Ideology in Educational Research*. London: The Falmer Press.

Raymond, J. (1985). "Women's studies: A knowledge of one's own." In M. Culley & C. Pontage (eds.), *Gendered Subjects: The Dynamics of Feminist Teaching*. Boston: Routledge & Kegan Paul.

Rosenfeld, G. (1971). *Shut Those Thick Lips!: A Study of Slum School Failure*. New York: Holt, Rinehart & Winston.

Russell, W.J. (1989). *Educational Researcher*, 18(6):30.

Rubin, I., et al. (1974). "Initiating planned change in health care system." *JABS*, 10(1):108.

Secada, W.G. (1989). "Equity in education versus equality of education: Toward an alternative conception." In W.G. Secada (ed.), *Equity in Education*. London: Falmer Press.

Sleeter, C. & Grant, C. (1987). "An analysis of multicultural education in the United States." *Harvard Educational Review*, 57:421-444.

Staples, R. (1984). "Racial ideology and intellectual racism: Blacks in academia." *The Black Scholar*, 15, 2.

White, H.S. & Buka, S.L. (1987). "Early education: Programs, traditions, and policies." In E.Z. Rothkopp (ed.), *Review of Research in Education*. Washington, DC: American Education Research Association.

Wittrock, M.C. (ed.) (1986). *Third Edition of the Handbook of Research on Teaching.* New York: Macmillan.

Wise, A.E. (1967). *Rich Schools, Poor Schools: The Promise of Equal Education Opportunity.* Chicago: The University of Chicago Press.

Zaltman, G. & Duncan, R. (1977). *Strategies for Planned Change.* New York: John Wiley.

Multiculturalism and Multicultural Education in Canada: Human Rights and Human Rights Education

Keith A. McLeod

It is now two decades since the policy of multiculturalism was announced in the Canadian House of Commons on October 7, 1971. In that time there has continued to be considerable debate regarding the policy; in the same period multiculturalism has been increasingly implemented, broadened and defined. Have the policy and the implementation been a success? The answer will depend in part on what specific actions, changes, analysis, developments, events, or programs we look at and what criteria we use to measure the "success." In this chapter I shall briefly examine the development of the policy itself, and I will analyze how multiculturalism has had an impact upon education and schooling. Multiculturalism within the context of Canada is an aspect of human rights, and multicultural education can be seen as an aspect of human rights education. The political, social, cultural, and economic issues which multiculturalism addresses within the context of politics, schooling, health, or welfare have to do with many of the same aspects of human dignity, fairness and responsibilities that we traditionally associate with human rights. Multiculturalism, as will become increasingly clear, is also the recognition that the Canadian society is pluralistic ethnically, racially and culturally.

In the context of an analysis of human rights and human rights education, it is my contention that multicultural education has been instrumental in developing awareness, sensitivity, and the implementation of human rights and human rights education regarding ethnicity, race, religion, national origin, citizenship, and such associated rights as equality before the law. Multicultural policy in Canada, or awareness and acceptance of pluralism; has grown in Canada hand in hand with the concern for human rights, and human rights legislation (McLeod, 1985). Multiculturalism must be seen within the context

---

*This chapter is being published simultaneously in a book edited by Hugh Starkey, *The Challenge of Human Rights Education*, London: Cassell, 1991.

216/ Educational Transformation for Empowerment

of human rights and it will be recognized that in turn multiculturalism is part of human rights in a pluralistic society. Human rights is also associated with the concept of multiculturalism in two other ways. Firstly, human rights, in part, places limits upon cultural pluralism. I shall cite the instance of sexual equality. Within Canada human rights legislation specifies that men and women are to be equal not only in law but in economic and social treatment. The cultural background of many ethno-cultural groups in Canada was not based upon the equality of the sexes; however, within the context of overall Canadian culture, all must now accommodate to this provision of human rights. It becomes a limitation on **my** right to exercise **my** cultural heritage. Secondly, while Canadian society is historically based upon the idea of individual rights, multiculturalism implies that there are group or collective rights. These are still somewhat vague and ill-defined perhaps, but they are there nevertheless. Undoubtedly, the Canadian courts and social and cultural practice will increasingly define the parameters. Let me suggest, immediately, that there is no suggestion that individual rights and responsibilities will cease to be primary, rather, it is a matter that they are tempered and interpreted within a broader context, a pluralist context. In a very real sense though, as I have stated earlier, multiculturalism is also supportive of individual personal rights.

Sociologists and anthropologists have analyzed pluralistic societies and derived three broad umbrella concepts or theories of social and cultural relationships: dominant conformity, melting pot and cultural pluralism. These have been succinctly summarized by an American scholar (Newman, 1973).[1] Dominant conformity is seen as $A + B + C + D + \_\_ = A$, where A is the ethnic group with the greatest power. The melting pot is seen as $A + B + C + D + \_ = X$ or a new culture. Cultural pluralism is seen as $A + B + C + D + \_\_ = A^1 + B^1 + C^1 + D^1 + \_\_$; the superscript has been added to indicate that in the process of immigrating, migrating, or associating with other cultures, the original cultures change. One, of course, could make the same claim with reference to dominant conformity; the dominant group is bound to change by the sheer effort or process of assimilating or attempting to assimilate the subordinate.

A great deal has been written on each of the above concepts, and in this brief chapter I have no intention even to summarize the analyses and debates. I just wish to acknowledge the concepts and the literature and to provide the most essential background. One interesting phenomenon of the application of the three concepts is that within the context of political and cultural debate people seem to think the adoption or prevalence of one precludes aspects of the other two theories, processes, or concepts being present. In cultural practice I would suggest that aspects of all three theories are often present in a pluralistic society. For example at the same time that some persons are emulating those whom they see as superordinate or with whom they simply associate, others are collectively evolving new cultural practices or norms, and still others are respecting similarities and differences. The foregoing does not diminish the role or importance of overall national cultural trends or policy, it merely recognizes social and cultural reality. There are many other aspects of the adoption and implementation of multicultural national policy that are impossible for me to deal with here, such as what in fact constitutes a culturally pluralistic society. Is it a matter of percentages? Of awareness and sensitivity? Of what relationships exist among ethnicity, race, or religion? Another aspect of multiculturalism is the question: When do groups of people cease to be "minorities" within the context of a culture and when does the reality of cultural pluralism begin? I can only suggest that the answers to these questions are not wholly quantitative but somewhat qualitative.[2]

Before going on to discuss multicultural education, and particularly for the benefit of international readers, I should outline more definitively the Canadian concept of multiculturalism. This is, perhaps, especially important in that since the term was coined it has come to be used in many other countries and in other contexts (Bullivant, 1981).

When Canada's multicultural policy was announced in 1971, the Prime Minister outlined three main aspects: firstly, that there was no official culture in Canada; secondly, that there must be creative exchanges or relationships among the various cultural groups; and thirdly, that all immigrants to Canada should have access to learning one of Canada's two official languages. From the beginning multicultural policy was to be seen within the context of official bilingualism, the two **link** languages. It was also to be seen within the context of the actual ethnic and racial diversity, and within the context of the fact that immigrants must be given opportunities to adjust. The concept of multiculturalism has developed. At first the emphasis was on life-style: on opportunities to demonstrate cultural affinities. One result was that there was criticism that too much emphasis was being placed on "song and dance" and "life-style." Nevertheless, in this early period, and despite the criticisms, this kind of symbolic multiculturalism was very important in smoothing the way, and introducing Canadians in general to a positive view of pluralism. In the second phase, the implementation and development of multiculturalism featured greater attention to cultures as a "way of life." Much more attention was given to language retention and to other aspects of cultural retention and development including the increasing presence of the various cultures in mainstream institutions. There was also beginning to be an increasing number of questions as to whether all persons were being given equal opportunity. In the third phase, in the 1980s, multicultural policy has emphasized not only equality of opportunity but attention to equality of outcome and equality of success. There has been increasing attention to access and participation, and to structural barriers. Much of this has been summed up by the concerns for "equity."[3]

It must be noted that international events have also influenced multi-culturalism in Canada. Concern about race relations in the United States have spilled across the border and there have been increasing demands in the late 1980s that multiculturalism must emphasize race relations. To some this has meant the twinning of the terms, "multiculturalism and race relations" even though race relations were a part of the multicultural policy from the beginning. A much more critical criticism has come from left- wing political sources; there has been an increasingly strident demand that anti-racism is what matters and that multicultural education is outdated and must be replaced by "anti-racist education." Another explanation of the origin of this trend to singularly emphasize racism may be the experience and writings of the British. In Britain, human relations issues seem to have focused upon color and racism: those who are not "white" are "black." The terms racism and anti-racist are used there frequently probably because of the lack of belief in Britain that it is culturally pluralistic, and partly because of the lack of response in Britain to multi-culturalism compared to charges of racism and the demand for anti-racist programs (Gundara, Jones & Kimberley, 1968; Skutnabb-Kangas & Cummins, 1988). However, in Canada general support for the policy and implementation of multiculturalism continues and the principle is now incorporated into a written portion of the Canadian Constitution (1982), and the policy has been made statutory (1988). The 1982 additions to the Canadian Constitution also featured a Canadian Charter of Rights and Freedoms; in a very real sense this Charter has given support to the concept of social, economic, racial and cultural equity.

The changes within Canadian society, and culture, and related policy in the past and present generations have resulted in a new basis or set of assumptions for Canadian culture and society. These have been or are being constitutionally enshrined in the provisions for Aboriginal Rights, the Official Languages Act, Multiculturalism, Human Rights, and Citizenship. Each of these supports pluralism in one way or another.[4]

The Canadian Multicultural Act of July 1988 included an updated outline of the policy:

It is hereby declared to be the policy of the Government of Canada to:

a) recognize and promote the understanding that multiculturalism reflects the cultural and racial diversity of Canadian society and acknowledges the freedom of all members of Canadian society to preserve, enhance and share their cultural heritage;

b) recognize and promote the understanding that multiculturalism is a fundamental characteristic of the Canadian heritage and identity and that it provides an invaluable resource in the shaping of Canada's future;

c) promote the full and equitable participation of individuals and communities of all origins in the continuing evolution and shaping of all aspects of Canadian society and assist them in the elimination of any barrier to such participation;

d) recognize the existence of communities whose members share a common origin and their historic contribution to Canadian society, and enhance their development;

e) ensure that all individuals receive equal treatment and equal protection under law, while respecting and valuing their diversity;

f) encourage and assist the social, cultural, economic and political institutions of Canada to be both respectful and inclusive of Canada's multicultural character;

g) promote the understanding and creativity that arise from the interaction between individuals and communities of different origins;

h) foster the recognition and appreciation of the diverse cultures of Canadian society and promote the reflection and the evolving expressions of those cultures;

i) preserve and enhance the use of languages other than English and French, while strengthening the status and use of the official languages of Canada; and

j) advance multiculturalism throughout Canada in harmony with the national commitment to the official languages of Canada (Canada, Canadian Multiculturalism Act, 1988).

It will quickly be recognized that the policy is a commitment by Canadians not only to rights but to freedoms and responsibilities. The policy, in the generic sense, has been increasingly implemented by the federal government as well as the 10 provinces since 1971. The federal statute of 1988 referred to above is but another step not only in policy development but in implementation, for the same Act declares that all federal institutions shall not only ensure equal opportunity in employment and advancement but shall promote policies, programs and practices that will enhance awareness and response to diversity, pluralism, or "multicultural reality."

In order to explore multiculturalism within the context of education and schooling I shall have to turn specifically to the provincial level within the Canadian federal system as constitutionally the provinces have sole jurisdiction over education. Culture on the other hand is an area of open jurisdiction as neither the central government nor the provinces have any written or exclusive constitutional jurisdiction in the area. In order to be able to be specific I shall usually use the most populated and diverse province of Canada, Ontario, as my major example. However, before looking at the specifics of Ontario let me look at the general approaches to multicultural education that have been characteristic of Canada.

In a previous analysis of the state of multicultural education I adopted a typology in order to characterize the general approaches to multicultural education (McLeod, 1981). Three categories emerged from the analysis.

1. **Ethnic Specific Approach.** By this I mean those who approach or plan for multicultural education on the basis of specific ethno-cultural perspectives. This approach tends to focus upon cultural retention or the cultural perpetuation or development aspect of the multicultural policy. It is also clear recognition that in order to have cultural sharing there must be something there to share. Examples of this perspective range from language programs, Black Heritage programs, and ethno-cultural programs and events to the more entertaining folk events.

2. **Problem Oriented Approach.** This includes those persons and groups whose fundamental orientation to multiculturalism is responding to problems. Immigrants or immigrant integration is seen as a problem which evokes the responses of reception centres, interpreter programs, and immigrant services. Similarly, racism may be seen as a critical issue which leads some to focus upon anti-racism as an aspect of multiculturalism. For others inter-group relations may be seen as the paramount issue so intercultural or inter-group programs are developed.

3. **Cultural/ Intercultural Approach.** This is a more general approach to multicultural education: it is where multiculturalism is an ethic underlying education or the total school program. It includes concern for cultural and linguistic continuity and development, issues related to ethnic and race relations, cultural sharing, immigrant integration, Aboriginal Rights, bilingualism, and human rights. It is a more comprehensive commitment socially and culturally; it is an approach which is based upon the definition of multiculturalism which includes or incorporates culture in the general sense as well as in the ethno-cultural sense; it includes attention to ethnic, racial, linguistic and religious diversity or pluralism.

The culture/intercultural approach includes issues related to the education of children from different ethnic, racial and cultural backgrounds and it also includes teaching for and about the cultures of all students; it addresses ethnic and race relations, human identity, self-esteem and cultural development, as well as issues associated with power and empowerment such as minority and human rights concerns and structural or systemic discrimination. It is directly related to global education. The goal is to not only remove discrimination but to foster education that is equitable in terms of the learning and success of all students.

Although these are the characterizations or the typology that I have used frequently, other characterizations have been used in the Canadian context.[5] For example, some have referred to the museum approach — seeing ethnic cultures as some kind of historical remnant; the song and dance approach, emphasizing what are regarded as superficial or symbolic cultural features; the anti-racist approach, focusing upon racism often interpreted as structural inequities; the values approach, the view that attitudes and values are the foundations for behavior, action and discrimination; the cross-cultural communication approach, where discrimination and inequities are viewed as due to lack of communication and understanding; the training approach which tends to view discrimination, especially racism, as a pathology which has to be treated; the intercultural approach, which suggests that group relations is the crucial issue; the linguistic approach, where culture and language are regarded as inseparable, and where cultural survival depends upon language maintenance. There is also a human rights approach that supports broader multicultural perspectives but also incorporates human rights objectives; the multicultural/human rights approach is only starting to gain a foothold. As will readily be observed many of these characterizations or approaches could be included within the three more general approaches I suggested. The point must also be made that many of these so called approaches are associated with some group of supporters who wish to rationalize or legitimize their position or maintain their territory (Mallea, 1989).The essential issue however, that we must focus upon, is whether the underlying assumptions, aims, and objectives of an approach or group, or a program, are consistent with valid definitions of multiculturalism — and to what extent. For example, an English as a Second Language program for immigrants that is predicated upon substituting English for the original language would be regarded as inconsistent with multiculturalism. If the program was additive, or aimed at adding a language, it would be predicated upon multiculturalism. In a society such as that in Canada which receives many immigrants, the distinction is very important.

Ontario: Policy, Practice, Education

In a sense Ontario typifies many of the issues and approaches that have been outlined in the previous section. Ontario was the first political jurisdiction in Canada to initiate legislation to protect persons from discrimination. In the early 1940s legislation was put into place to protect "minorities" from discrimination in contracts, housing and work. This "minority" legislation soon evolved into "human rights" legislation; a Human Rights Commission was established to enforce the legislation when it was pulled together to form the Ontario Human Rights Code (McLeod, 1985; Purcell, 1985).

Following the 1971 federal policy, the Ontario provincial government announced a provincial multicultural policy. Some activity was promoted in education; for example, the aims and objectives of elementary schooling were revised to reflect a multicultural perspective. The first course in Cross-Cultural Education was offered by a Faculty of Education, as part of a pre-service teacher education program in 1972. Curriculum support documents for teachers began to be initiated by the Ontario Ministry of Education, and a Heritage Languages Program to sustain and support mother tongue retention was initiated in 1977. Attempts were also made to improve the quality and availability of English as a Second Language courses for immigrants. It might be added parenthetically that many of these changes were taking place at the same time as the vast increase was made in the availability of French language education for both Francophones and non-Francophones in Ontario. Steps were also being taken to deal with racism and to provide cultural support to students from the black community. This was especially true after the government adopted a Race Relations Policy in 1983; the policy complemented the multicultural policy.[6]

In 1985 a new government came to power. It reaffirmed the Race Relations Policy and went on to outline a multicultural strategy. In the field of education, the Liberal government called together a Committee to organize a provincial conference on multicultural education that was held in March 1986. This Conference was stimulated in part by the work of the Ontario Human Rights Commission which had slowly but surely been working on developing a generic multicultural education policy which local education authorities, Boards of Education, could adopt. School board trustees, teachers, teacher educators, Ministry of Education personnel and community representatives met and examined and analyzed multicultural education issues. At the end of the Conference the Minister of Education committed himself to provincial action. What the action would be was left open.

By September of 1987 a follow-up report, *The Development of a Policy on Race and Ethnocultural Equity*, had been developed by the Provincial Advisory Committee on Race Relations (Ontario, Ministry of Education, 1987). The Committee had been presumably appointed to address race relations at a very critical time in Ontario's history. Large numbers of "visible minorities" had entered Canada since the revision in the immigration policy of 1966; a significant number of people from the Caribbean, Africa and Asia had moved to Ontario, particularly Toronto. For example, whereas "visible minorities" constitute about seven percent of the Canadian population, in Toronto at present they are about 15 percent of the population.

"Anti-racist" proponents were prominent and vocal on the Committee and the result was that the Report for Ontario education became anti-racist in approach. As one commentator stated, the Report misleads the readers into faulting multiculturalism because some people had not sufficiently practiced and implemented it. Multiculturalism, the Report states, was too culturally oriented, and too fragmented; it paid insufficient attention to values, and ignored color differences or race. When one looks at the above charges, and reflects upon the growing policies and programs it is clear that the selected information was misleading and the charges were inaccurate; some have stated that the analysis in the Report was somewhat superficial, inaccurate, and biased. In order to compare these complaints with the actual texts I shall quote five paragraphs for the reader:

> However, multicultural education, as interpreted and practised over the last decade, has demonstrable limitations. Changes have often been fragmented in content and lacked clarity, continuity and coordination. Initiatives have often relied upon untested assumptions about culture and the process of cultural transmission.

> Content often focuses on such material and exotic dimensions of culture as food, dress, and holidays, instead of linking these to the values and belief systems which undergird cultural diversity.

> Important factors shaping cultural identity, such as racial, linguistic, religious, regional, socio-economic, and gender differences have often been ignored. Not least among these problems has been the expectation that teachers from the dominant culture could easily teach about highly complex cultures.

> Too often well-intentioned educators have sought to ignore colour differences. "Pretending to be colourblind in the face of the hardships encountered by young Asian, Native and Black youngsters, and professing not to perceive any differences in treatment, is still tantamount to side-stepping the problem." [Thornhill:3]. Gradually, questions have been raised about the merits of this multicultural approach. Many believe that multicultural initiatives have not adequately addressed racial discrimination and inequities which are systemic within the policies and practices of educational institutions.

> Parents, community spokespersons, volunteers, and professionals have repeatedly asserted the fundamental problems limiting the education of [sic] achievement of many racial and ethnocultural students result from discrimination by race rather that diversity of culture. As one parent stated in the

foreword to a school board policy on race relations: "The issues facing the colour of my skin are more pressing than those facing my culture" (Ontario, Ministry of Education, 1987:37).

From the perspective of a commentator there are a few ironies in the quotation above. Esmerelda Thornhill, referred to in the text, was one of the persons from the Quebec black community who was frequently called upon for assistance. Multicultural education, as those who had been involved in its formulation and implementation know, had from the beginning addressed race relations and racism. However, having established that multicultural educators were simple minded and misguided, the Report's authors go on to point out what true multicultural education is: it is anti-racist education.

> School boards can play a central role in eliminating racism in society, if anti-racist educational policies are developed and implemented. Such policies for schools should be developed in concert with efforts to bring other areas of Ontario society closer to equity.
>
> The goal of anti-racist education is to change institutional policies and practices which are discriminatory, and individual behaviours and attitudes that reinforce racism. Its premise is that cultural diversity is "not" the cause of the denial of equal educational opportunity to students from certain racial and ethnocultural groups.
>
> Anti-racist education does not negate the value of multicultural education. Rather, it is education that is truly multicultural, in a truly equitable multiracial society. It acknowledges the existence of racism and forthrightly seeks its eradication within schools and in society at large (Ontario, Ministry of Education, 1987:39).[7]

Some ramifications of the denigrating of multiculturalism and singularly emphasizing anti-racist education have already appeared. Some have isolated racial issues from general multicultural policy and support; others have suggested that racial issues are something for the visible minorities to deal with. The net effect could be seriously diminished or fractured support for pluralism if these divisions continue and become more general. The Ontario Ministry of Education has however apparently rejected anti-racist education as the unifying rubric and moved on to talking about multicultural education in terms of "race and ethnocultural equity education." (See endnote 7.)

Despite these unfortunate aspects to the Report, multicultural education has continued to develop: it has continued to address cultural and linguistic issues as well as racial issues. People are addressing questions having to do not only with symbols, and attitudes and values, but concerns associated with structures and institutions, including structural issues related to economics, access and participation. This continuity will become increasingly evident as we examine more specific areas of education and schooling, namely administration, teachers, curricula, teaching strategies, students, and parents and communities. By examining each of these in turn we shall have a deeper sense of the meaning of multicultural education and of its implementation. One interesting phenomenon is that although the Ontario government has adopted both multicultural and race relations policies, the Ontario Ministry of Education has not adopted an overtly stated multicultural education policy despite its current efforts to encourage the some 125 local Boards of Education in the province to adopt policies.

Administration

Of the 125 Boards of Education in the province there are now over 40 Boards with explicit multicultural education policies. A recent report for the Ministry of Education also indicates that some 25 other Boards are currently contemplating or developing policies (Mock & Masemann, 1991). The policies tend to cover much the same aspects despite the variety of nomenclature: they are variously called multicultural, race relations, ethnic relations, policies or other combinations thereof. They usually include: an explicit statement of support for multiculturalism and multicultural education; a statement on the importance of leadership by the trustees and school administrators; a commitment to revising and revamping the curricula so that pluralism is reflected in the programs and the resources used; a statement committing the school jurisdiction to using fair and appropriate means of assessment and of placement of students in various programs and streams; a commitment to providing for staff development and to fair and just personnel policies and practices; there is almost inevitably a section on developing positive school-community relations; and there is usually some kind of statement or commitment to counter discrimination, racism, or racial and ethnocultural harassment. The recent report for the Ontario Ministry of Education indicates that the Boards which adopt policies that concentrate on anti-racist education are also the Boards that are less likely to plan for ameliorative programs. It would seem that the less strident the vocabulary the more positive the approach. The most committed boards do not leave the implementation of the policy to chance but rather include implementation guidelines and a commitment to providing the human and financial resources needed to fulfil the policy.

There is a little doubt that where one or more of the School Board trustees (in Ontario they are elected) take up the cause of pluralism the chances of commitment and action increase. There is also no doubt that where the chief executive officer of the Board, the Director, takes up the cause the results are positive. Another aspect that has increased the chances of a good policy is where the community has been directly involved in developing the policy. Community involvement is often done through initial hearings with follow-up meetings to develop awareness and commitment; eventually a final draft of the policy is submitted to the public for comment and suggested changes. Polices are often officially adopted at Board meetings which the public has been encouraged to attend.

As part of the administrative support, Ontario Boards in their policies or as part of the implementation process have often appointed a person within their bureaucracy with the responsibility to oversee implementation and development. These Multicultural or Ethnic and Race Relations consultants or workers have extensive responsibilities; they assist principals and teachers in dealing with discriminatory incidents; provide for staff development; work with communities and community representatives; advise on currricula and resources; assist with personnel policies and practices; and promote special programs including those that encourage student leadership in multicultural education. Sometimes the Boards also establish school-community relations offices. The staff in these are usually responsible for outreach into ethnic and cultural communities that are cut-off or remote from the school and teachers.

At the school level much has depended upon the school principals (head teachers). Where they have taken up the cause of multicultural education the relationship between the school and community has improved, teachers have received assistance, students have received support, and parents have been better informed and more involved. Principals encourage multicultural implementation in a variety of ways: through finding the means to send multilingual information to parents; to reallocating personnel and resources for staff development, and through involving parents and the community in the school. The ultimate aim is to improve students' performance and success by working with parents and the community.

In conclusion, it is fair to say that collectively the trustees and the administrators are responsible for the commitment, the direction and implementation of policy, and the appropriation of human and financial resources that will not only negate ethnic and racial discrimination but which will enhance cultural identity and development and positive human and group relations. The willingness not only to admit that racial and ethnic bias or discrimination existed but to exert influence and allocate resources to support cultural pluralism and positive human relations has been a major step forward. It is a step which some jurisdictions both provincial and local have yet to make. There is little doubt that much remains to be done. Some educational authorities have been slow in committing themselves to extensive implementation of multicultural education.

Curriculum

Curriculum change in Ontario, as elsewhere in Canada, has had its origins in community influence, professional ethics and concerns, and development elsewhere, such as in the United States. Curriculum change has varied in nature and focus: in some instances it has been linguistic and cultural in emphasis, in other instances it has been ethnic specific, anti-discriminatory, anti-racist, human rights, or human relations oriented.

Early attempts at curricula change in the elementary school (grades 1-8) tended to be based upon the general concern that the curricula should reflect the children's cultures so that they can identify with the school, the content, and the attitudes and values. The obverse side of the coin was that educators became increasingly concerned that there was a cultural gap between the community and parents and the school, that the school was reflecting and reproducing knowledge that was alien to the child and the family's culture. Children were being educated away from their language and culture (Toronto Board of Education, 1976; Breton, Reitz & Vallentine, 1980). In the mid-70s, as a result of a consultation process, multicultural objectives were incorporated into the elementary school provincial guidelines which provide guidance and a sense of direction to teachers. Ontario elementary school education is based upon a progressive, child-centred philosophy of education. Elementary teachers were often more adaptable and ready to adjust the content to the children's backgrounds. Teachers organized units and learning experiences where cultural, ethnic, racial, and religious diversity were a fundamental underpinning or assumption. Teachers increasingly consulted with community representatives and invited people of diverse origins into their classrooms. A broader range of cultural knowledge was legitimized in the schools and classrooms. Gradually there emerged a set of criteria that have become increasingly characteristic of multicultural curriculum development. These include, that:

1. multiculturalism must be integrated into the total school program and in all aspects of school;

2. there must be a balance of similarities and differences so that ethnic relations are not exacerbated by an overemphasis on differences; some differences could even be seen in the context of similarities; however, students must be taught skills and attitudes in terms of coping or working with differences. At the appropriate cognitive and moral reasoning levels students must also be helped to learn how to cope with prejudice and discrimination;

3. the resources which students use must be unbiased or sensitive and that where materials with a bias are used, the bias, the stereotypes,

or the discrimination (by commission or omission) must be dealt with and the students' are to be taught how to recognize and deal with it personally and collectively;

4. special days, occasions, programs, and activities are important but that in order for them to have more lasting effect that they must be integrated in some way into the regular program;

5. within the curriculum content that the levels of intellectual and of moral reasoning of the students be taken into account;

6. the teaching of content must be accompanied by teaching appropriate skills (which together constituted the cognitive domain), and that there must also be appropriate attention to teaching for the affective domain (attitudes and values);

7. in teaching for the affective domain or even the cognitive domain it is not simply a matter of "teaching about" human relations, human rights, or human and group identity and self-esteem but of using teaching methods and strategies that are more appropriate, that focus upon relating the cognitive and the affective, that make issues more personal, that build upon the positive, and that provide for critical thinking.

Beyond the above kinds of criteria, teachers have also developed increased understanding that the community context, the teaching methods, and peer relationships are very crucial to successful multicultural education.[8]

Associated with the changes in curricula have been changes in the role of languages in education. Ontario in 1977 adopted a Heritage Languages Program whereby on community request mother-tongue or heritage languages could be taught for two and one-half hours a week on week-ends or after school hours, or during the day where the school day was lengthened by half an hour. Thus the students from several classrooms in a school could be brought together to be taught, for example, the Greek, Chinese, Portuguese, or the Italian language. The program proved to be a significant immediate success. Within two years some 50 000 students were studying some 50 languages. By the late 1980s there were some 100 000 students studying some 80 languages. Again the change has resulted in a positive reinforcement of the childrens' cultures and improved their sense of identity and security. As of 1989 the government legislated that School Boards must respond to community requests.[9]

What will happen to the Heritage Languages Program in the future is an open question. It may remain a "community request" based program. Another possibility is that it could become the basis of a languages program for all children in the elementary schools. In any case there is evidence that the program has improved opportunities and access to education, and assisted students by making school more culturally appropriate or relevant to the children.

At the secondary level in all provinces there has been much less success in adjusting the curricula. The areas that have received the greatest attention are history and social science. Courses in Canadian society and history now usually incorporate the multicultural heritage. In addition, the courses in literature now sometimes include books on a broader range of cultural topics. In Ontario for a few years, an optional grade 10 history course that focused upon "Canada's Multicultural Heritage" was promoted by the Ministry of Education; however, this course has now been integrated into the general Canadian history courses.

As I indicated earlier, the Ministry of Education in Ontario in 1975 revised the elementary school curriculum guide by including multicultural objectives. In 1977 the Ministry also published the document *Multiculturalism In Action, Curriculum Ideas For Teachers*. In that same year the Minister of Education established a committee to develop guidelines that would assist authors and publishers to avoid bias and discriminatory references and omissions in learning materials. *Race, Religion and Culture in Ontario School Materials*, was subsequently published after many revisions in 1980. Another curriculum support document, *Black Studies: A Resource Guide for Teachers, Intermediate Division*, was published in 1983 to assist teachers to be aware of cultural content that could be used in assisting students to recognize the participation and the diverse roles and contributions of people from the Canadian and international black communities. The Ontario Ministry has added a new document in 1989: *Changing Perspectives —A Resource Guide for Race and Ethnocultural Equity*, Junior Kindergarten, Grade XII/OACs.

Thus the curriculum pattern in Ontario is one of support documents for teachers, adjustment of curricular objectives and content, and the specific inclusion of ethnocultural and race relations objectives. The elementary schools in Ontario and elsewhere in Canada now better reflect the multicultural reality. Resources and materials are chosen with greater care so that racial diversity and many cultures are portrayed. A serious deficiency exists in secondary education despite efforts to change. Secondary education in Canada is traditional and content oriented, and there has been considerable resistance to changing the cultural content.

Teachers and Teaching Strategies

There are two key aspects to the roles and functions of teachers that must be examined: the teacher as exemplary person, and the teacher as methodologist or strategist. The concept of the teacher as exemplary person means that one should first and foremost bring to teaching an "open mind." It is unlikely that any person will have grown up without some bias, cultural preferences, or even prejudicial attitudes and values. These may be religious, cultural, racial, or ethnic or they may be related to other areas covered by human rights. The most important intellectual endeavour is for the teachers to recognize their own bias and prejudices. Recognition is the first and most fundamental step in being able to come to terms with oneself and with people from other cultural, racial, or religious backgrounds (Morrison, 1980).

Teachers who are secure about themselves, and their own identity are less likely to diminish others; teachers who are reflective are less likely to reinforce structural inequities and institutionalized discrimination. The reflective teacher (which is increasingly becoming a catch phrase for teachers who continually analyze their assumptions and practices) should further enhance multicultural education. In Canadian and Ontario education the aware and sensitive teacher is expected to set standards of behavior and be exemplary in how they treat children of diverse backgrounds. This exemplary conduct is crucial to the educative process, to teaching attitudes and values, or what is referred to in pedagogy as the affective domain.

Another aspect of the role of teachers, associated with their ethical and professional standards, is the code of ethics of their professional organizations which in greater or less detail eschew discriminatory practices and support human rights. One of the most detailed ethical statements on anti-discrimination is in Saskatchewan; one of the shortest is that of the Ontario Teachers' Federation which simply states, in section VI regarding discrimination, that "a society in which all people may participate equally with equal access to opportunity is a basic tenet." It continues:

It is the policy of the Ontario Teachers' Federation:

a) that discrimination against any person be opposed with vigour.

b) that teachers, because of their influential position in the development of attitudes, pursue a leadership role in the opposition of discrimination.

c) that teachers avoid discrimination in their work places by acting to eliminate all forms of discrimination that may appear in areas such as:

i) the delegation of responsibilities in the school,

ii) school programs,

iii) curricula,

iv) the use of instructional materials,

v) the use of language, and any other areas in their work place which reinforce or perpetuate any form of discrimination (Ontario Teachers' Federation, 1984).

The teacher as methodologist or strategist, research increasingly indicates, is a crucial aspect of teaching. In short it is not just a matter of what you teach but how it is taught, or more aptly how it is learned. Research on techniques and strategies in Canada and the United States has indicated that it is possible to teach for the affective domain. The research has indicated that simply teaching "content" will not necessarily result in the appropriate human rights attitudes. Ingrained prejudices, community circumstances, or family bias may prevent or inhibit positive attitudes to human relations or human rights in the student. Teachers in classrooms also have to take into account the research which indicates that children start learning attitudes and values toward groups as early as age three and that attitudes and values are difficult to change. There is often a resistance to change — the values are emotionally held (Allport, 1954). However, research on contact theory, principle testing, classical conditioning and identification theory in relation to teaching and learning also indicates that when the following criteria are characteristic to the learning situation the possibilities of learning or developing positive attitudes and values are enhanced. Many of these criteria, as will be quickly recognized, are also characteristic of what is generally referred to as "good pedagogy." In any event, in extrapolating from the research the following appear to be some of the significant characteristics of the learning situations (for example, environment, methods, strategies, students, context) that are conducive to attitudinal change or the development of positive human relations:[10]

1. **Experiential.** The more real the situation and the more actively involved the students are the greater the possibility of change.

2. **Enjoyable or satisfying.** The research indicates that situations that are enjoyable are more likely to have a positive result on attitudes. Although there may be apprehension and even some discomfort at first, if the end result is satisfying the change may be made and be "permanent" or longlasting .

3. **Personal.** The more involved personally the persons or students are, the more they are in the position where they personally relate or identify with the victim, case, or situation and the greater the likelihood of positive change.

4. **Common goal.** When students or persons who are of different ethnic, racial, and/or cultural backgrounds work together towards a common goal, the chances of positive relations are enhanced.

5. **Equal status.** The chances are further enhanced when the persons of different backgrounds are of equal status. This equal status may be in terms of social class, or power, or position. It may simply be that they are all students in the same grade or of about the same age.

6. **Continuous and on-going.** Many projects and educational activities in the area of human and group relations tend to be of short duration or episodic. Classical conditioning or even behavior psychology tells us that the more continuous or on-going the motivation, value and attitude clarification, or the critical thinking process the greater is the possibility of change. Most teachers understand the relationship between this factor and teaching when they relate this idea to their use of positive reinforcement.

7. **Exemplary educators.** Teachers, other school personnel, and parents, and community educators will enhance positive attitudinal development and positive human and group relations through their own overt behavior and activity.

8. **Community support.** As suggested in the previous point the greater the community support, the greater the chance of effect; the more pervasive the support the greater the chance of impact.

9. **Across the curriculum and school program.** Again the more frequent the opportunities are and the more consistent the learning environment is in terms of positive human and group relations the greater the likelihood of success. It is not a matter of dogmatic expostulations but of exemplary patterns of behavior and positive encouragement, and positive ethics, in all subjects and in all parts of the educational program.

10. **Setting limits.** Nevertheless chances of enhancing positive attitudes are also improved where it is quite clear that discriminatory behavior is unacceptable. Ethnic and racial, as well as other forms of discrimination must meet with immediate disapproval.

11. **Levels of reasoning.** It is important in the context of teaching for values and attitudes that the level of moral reasoning and of critical thinking and reasoning of the students be taken into account; it enables the teacher to use appropriate materials and reflective techniques.

The above concepts are based upon the cultural/intercultural educative model, that is where the underlying assumption is that we can educate people regarding human rights and behavior. There has been an increasing tendency among "trainers" to use a therapeutic model or to approach ethnic and race relations and attitudes and values as a pathology that needs treatment. The educative model is philosophically appropriate to public education and to child and human development. The educative model addresses not only the individual but encourages institutional and structural change. The human thought and action become part of peoples' social, economic, and political life or part of their commitment to rights and freedoms. The educational system changes. At the same time educators and society must be aware that in the socialization and cultural reproduction processes in any society there is failure, there sometimes is lack of achievement; there are those who do not learn or who for a variety of reasons do not achieve what society has deemed good.

The International Declaration of Human Rights, the Canadian Charter of Rights and Freedoms, Human Rights Codes, and our concepts of social justice and human dignity all sanction tolerance and positive human and group relations. It is a matter of cultural and social reality that ethnic and race relations must be provided for — that children, that all people must be provided with opportunities, experiences, and examples by which they can learn. The Canadian teacher, by example and by appropriate methods is being increasingly asked to participate in the process. The community has mandated multiculturalism and human rights.

Students

There are several ways in which students have been involved in the development and implementation of multiculturalism and human rights education in Canada. In particular I shall outline examples of student initiatives, peer relationships and support systems, student exchanges, peer counselling, and multicultural/ multiracial leadership camps.

It was initiatives from students in secondary schools that led to some of the first cultural and identity support systems for the students. Students, to counteract the lack of cultural support, awareness, and sensitivity in schools began to organize school clubs — Italo-Canadian Student Clubs or the Black or Caribbean Student groups. In some instances this frightened both teachers and administrators, especially those who were already suffering discomfort because of their lack of knowledge and understanding of the students and their culture. In some instances teachers' conscious or unconscious deprecation of students and their community's culture resulted in severe hostility. Students responded. Pedagogical reflection upon the needs and the requests of the students, however, led some schools and teachers to support the organizational efforts of students; they encouraged them to express their culture not only through club activities but in the wider school setting. The only stipulation was that the clubs were to be open to any student.

The clubs and student participation provided cultural and identity support to the minority students. Students were able to come together and discuss mutual problems and issues. In a very real sense these associations or group-ings provided some of the first examples of the legitimation of the cultural knowledge the students had acquired at home or in the community. Teachers not fearful of expanding their horizons and the subject content began to relate the culture and activities to their classrooms. In some instances schools began to "celebrate" the diversity through ethno-cultural activities and even commu-nity programs. Although some of these activities come under the scrutiny of critics for their "superficiality," (they were criticized for making human relations and multiculturalism a song and dance affair) the activities provided an initial basis for intercultural and interracial contact and understanding. In a very real sense the schools and teachers and community were recognizing the diversity or pluralism. In many schools these clubs or associations still exist and help provide a basic level of support and understanding.

These clubs and support systems have also operated within communities, and within ethno-cultural organizations and structures for a long time. For example, among the "older" immigrant groups in Canada there have been Ukrainian, Scottish, Jewish, Irish, German, and Chinese youth groups. Some groups' youth have also worked within mainstream community organizations; for example, there are Boy Scouts groups within the Polish-Canadian commu-nity structure. There have also been numerous music, literary and arts groups within ethno-cultural community groups. Such groups and activities have provided major assistance in human and group relations and intercultural understanding. As such they have played a fundamental role in avoiding inter-group misunderstanding and conflict. The obverse side is that such groups are a classic example not only of people exercising their rights and freedoms but of mutual self-help and responsibility.[11]

Peer support has been recognized as a means of mutual aid. Peer relation-ships among students have sometimes been given sanction within the class-room especially in relation to immigrant students. Teachers have often opted for "buddy systems" by which students become responsible to introduce and to assist a newly arrived student. In some instance the students may have mutual linguistic capabilities, in other instances they may not. Such informal systems, especially when legitimated by the teacher, provide a basic system for contact and they smooth the process for both the immigrant student and the receiving students.

However, teachers have gone beyond "buddy systems" in utilizing peer teaching. Teachers have had students from various cultural backgrounds not only teach them but the class. It may be a few words of a language, it may be cultural patterns and knowledge. Teachers have also been cautioned not to place too much burden on students to be the "experts" on their ethnic group. In some instances a student's own knowledge may be fragmentary and undeveloped. Nevertheless, such teaching opportunities may help immigrant students to integrate well into the school and larger community. Opportunities to demonstrate knowledge of their group may be very crucial in assisting students to maintain their sense of self-esteem and self-worth.

At the secondary school level, Students' Councils have been encouraged to help set standards of behavior, promote participation, and to reflect the student body in their activities and program. This encourages democratic participation and mutual respect of human rights. In some instances the student body has given support to inter-school programs and exchanges not only with students in other Canadian communities but in other countries. Such support broadens students' cultural and racial perspectives. In the case of international exchanges there has been some success not only in developing broader perspectives but in developing perspectives on global living. There have, however, also been some misguided efforts. Students competing on a national basis at international gatherings have in some instances produced friction and some hostility instead. Why organizers of student athletic and cultural exchanges continue to stress national teams and international competition is difficult to understand in the light of the research on human relations.

There have also been some problems among students when teams from schools with a particular racial mix meet school teams with a different ethnic and racial mix. The physical education teachers or instructors have at times not prepared their students and sometimes the first reaction to frustration in competition is an ethnic or racial slur. The same has happened internationally even in professional sport.

There have been extensive student exchange programs in Canada that have been based upon exchange between students in French and English Canada. These have helped to develop understanding and they have promoted the mutual learning of the two official languages. Most recently there has been one trial student exchange based upon multicultural criteria. Students were selected on the basis of their intercultural and cultural interests. The two groups were both very diverse ethnically, racially and culturally. The program for the students included developing awarenesss, sensitivity, mutual respect and support. The focus was on co-operation and co-operative activities.

Another feature of Canadian educational development has been the multi-cultural/multiracial leadership camps. These leadership camps that some of the large urban boards have developed have attempted to promote: peer leadership, multi-ethnic and multi-racial understanding and co-operation, intercultural skills and co-operation, as well as self-identity and self-esteem. The camps are held outside of the formal school setting at a centre or a "camp." They usually last from one to three days. The students are encouraged to discuss human rights and group relations in their community and in the school environment. They are given opportunities to develop skills in dealing with kinds of discriminatory behavior; leadership skills are taught and students are given an opportunity to develop understanding of their families and communities. In some instances, such issues as interreligious, intercultural and interracial dating, family perceptions, parental reactions, and community values and attitudes are examined. As with other issues the students have an opportunity to develop skills, knowledge, attitudes and values (Burke, 1982).

An old phenomenon and a new form of human relations education is "peer counselling," or peer mediation/conflict resolution techniques. Students have been assisting one another for generations; however, students are now being offered assistance in learning how to assist and care about others: how to understand, and how to help and what it is like to be "the one with the problem." Helping skills for most people are learned behavior. Students are given opportunities to not only develop self-understanding but on how to assist others to understand themselves, their parents or family. They are helped to learn how to cope with other peers, and to work more effectively in school. Some studies indicate peer counselling can be particularly effective during adolescence. Students do turn to one another for assistance often more readily than they turn to parents or teachers.

To conclude this discussion on students I would like to emphasize that increasing importance is being placed upon student involvement and student based or centred activities to complement the work of teachers and administrators. I shall refer to several sections from a Board of Education multicultural policy statement in order to highlight the importance that is placed upon student participation. The Board "condemns and does not tolerate any expression of racial or cultural bias by its trustees, staff, or students"; the board "reaffirms its commitment to develop and promote racial harmony among its students, staff, and the community, and to provide education that is antiracist and multicultural"; the Board "will continue to develop curricular and co-curricular programs that provide opportunities for students to acquire positive attitudes toward racial, cultural, and religious diversity"; the Board "will attempt to ensure that schools in their day-to-day operations, and co-curricular activities identify and eliminate those policies and practices which, while not intentionally discriminatory, have a discriminatory effect"; the Board recognizes that "in order to ensure equal access and opportunity for achievement of their full potential, students from racial and cultural minority groups may require special considerations with respect to (a) reception, (b) assessment, (c) placement, (d) programming, (e) monitoring, (f) meaningful communication with parents/guardians." The focus of policy is very clearly student oriented and designed to enhance achievement.

• Moreover, among the guiding principles set out in the multicultural policy of this Board, the first reads that they "will strive to maintain a student-centred approach which places the development of student potential as the first priority." The Board also commits itself: to support multicultural clubs when requested by students and/or staff; to provide opportunities for students in all schools to participate in multicultural leadership camps; and to further strengthen the leadership programs. The Board also states clearly that discriminatory behavior by students will not be tolerated (Board of Education for the City of Scarborough, 1988).

The Community

In one sense it is fitting, in the final analysis, to address the role of the community in some specifics. As I have alluded to earlier, community action in Canada has been the basis for the development of human rights legislation and multicultural policy. In a very real sense, the community has been the first and foremost underpinning of human rights and human relations. It was community political action which brought about anti-discriminatory legislation; it has also been community based political action which has brought about the recognition of pluralism. In the democratic sense of community responsibility, policy must be set by the community. Legislation is the manifestation of the commitment. The international community has brought about the various Universal Declarations on Human Rights and in Canada human rights and the recognition of pluralism have been codified in human rights and multicultural legislation and constitutional provisions.

At the local community level in education, Boards of Education adopt or support multicultural education policy. In the province of Ontario as I have indicated out of some 125 School Boards some one third have policies and another third are in the process of developing policies. However, when we analyze community participation in multicultural education in Canada the extent of the participation ranges well beyond policy. The roles of the community, can be seen in the context of (1) initiation (policy and commitment but also program initiation), (2) support, (3) implementation, (4) administration, and (5) evaluation.

1. **Initiation** not only includes the initial development of multicultural policy but activities and programs for cultural retention and development, and human rights and human relations. It was the various ethno-cultural groups who for many years before multicultural policy resisted unicultural nationalism and developed programs for human rights and cultural retention: language classes, cultural programs, libraries, literacy societies, writing clubs and educational societies. They also encouraged human rights and human relations

as did other community groups such as Womens' Institutes, labor unions, the Canadian Red Cross and religious groups. Many ethnic groups initiated their own programs and activities.[12]

2. The community has also been the basis of **support**. Again even before the adoption by the governments of policies and program, the same community groups referred to above were also allocating some of their financial resources, as well as their volunteer time, to human rights and human relations. This willingness to fund human rights and human relations has now also become a feature of the government sector — all the provincial governments as well as the federal government fund Human Rights Commissions which not only arbitrate and mediate but often also educate. Similarly multicultural/ human rights education within the mainstream public schools is now supported and funded. It is also true that some mainstream institutions, including some in the field of education have only progressed as far as the community has pushed and provided the support.

3. In the **implementation** aspect of human rights and human relations education the community has also played a crucial role. Within a multicultural society it is not only important to be able to exercise cultural retention and development but to be ready and able to mix and to share cultures within mainstream institutions.

There are other aspects to implementation and the community. Community representatives become resource persons in the school, explaining and demonstrating their culture to students so that they develop an understanding of other cultures. In addition community centres, such as Sikh Temples and Italo-Canadian cultural centres and even family homes have accepted persons who wish to learn. Members of the community have also continued to participate on school committees. There have been some notable instances of where, when the community base has been absent, that implementation of human rights and human relations education has failed or faltered. The willingness and readiness of communities to ensure that there is not just policy but implementation has been enhanced where there has been involvement in the planning.

4. The **administrative** aspect of the community in multiculturalism involves two issues: the involvement of the communities in overseeing the carrying out of programs, and the involvement of increasingly broad representation in the educational control. At the national level in Canada the umbrella organization of ethnocultural groups, the Canadian Ethnocultural Council has taken an administrative role in overseeing multicultural development. At the level of the provinces, in some instances provincial governments and departments have sought community participation in administering programs. Local Boards of Education have sometimes maintained a community consultation

process to advise them on administration. In another area, Boards have also used formal Community Liaison Departments to develop links with groups with whom they have had tenuous relations.

Increasingly there also has been a trend to examine who the administrators are. Do they reflect or represent the community? Are groups participating in control? Why are school trustees, school board personnel and even principals still coming from too few groups or from only some cultural backgrounds? Questions such as these relating to fair administrative access and promotion are being answered through community scrutiny of hiring and promotion practices.

5. The community, or the communities are in the final analysis the ultimate **evaluators** of multicultural education. The continued evidence of discriminatory practices or ethnic and racial discrimination, some people have stated is evidence we have not sufficiently implemented multicultural education. However, that view must be tempered by caution. Various values have been legitimated for centuries even by laws and through religious codes yet the values are still being violated. There is agreement that there is still much to be done in responding to the requests of the community and the communities for language education, anti-discriminatory education, fairness and equity, openness and access. One aspect of democratic participation is continual on-going assessment and evaluation by the community (Canada, House of Commons, 1984).[13]

Conclusion

Multicultural education in Canada is an aspect of human rights education. The issues involved are much the same in multicultural education as they are in other aspects of human rights and education, for example, for the disabled or handicapped, or for women. As with all these groups and the issues involved, human rights education must be for all, not just a group that is at a disadvantage. Multicultural education in Canada has been a response to and in turn has helped to create a more humane and human rights conscious society where there is a desire for equity and fairness for all, where there is not only consciousness of equality of opportunity but of equality of outcomes. It is recognition that where there are differences there is pluralism and where there is pluralism we must educate for it (Fisher & Echols, 1989).[14]

Notes

1. See also the work of Milton Gordon, Michael Banton, Pierre van den Berghe, and Philip Mason on pluralism and human relations.

2. I would refer readers to the writings of several Canadians: Jonathan Young, Howard Palmer, Vandra Masemann, Dean Wood, John Mallea, Enid Lee, and to reports such as the Report of the Special Committee on Visible Minorities in Canadian Society. (1984). *Equality Now!* Canada, House of Commons; and *Multiculturalism: Building the Canadian Mosaic,* June 1987, Report of the Standing Committee on Multiculturalism, Canda, House of Commons.

3. See for example Saskatchewan Human Rights Commission, (1985), *Education Equity. A Report on Indian/Native Education in Saskatchewan;* Canada, Multiculturalism Canada, (1985), *Education: Cultural and Linguistic Pluralism in Canada;* Canadian Public Health Association, (1989), *Ethnicity and Aging;* Children's Aid Society of Metropolitan Toronto, (1982), *Task Force on Multicultural Programs,* (final report).

4. See the writings of Jonathan Young, Vandra Masemann, Enid Lee, John Mallea and Dean Wood; an interesting study by Paul Anisef, (1986), Models and *Methodologies Appropriate to the Study of Outcomes of Schooling in Ontario's Multicultural Society,* also helps clarify approaches and perspectives.

5. The inter-relationships of these foundations of modern Canadian society have really not been explored. In Keith A. McLeod, (ed.), (1989), *Canada and Citizenship Education,* published by the Canadian Education Association, some aspects of a modern concept of citizenship education in a multicultural-bilingual context is explored. In D. Ray & V.D'Oyley, (eds.), (1983), *Human Rights in Canadian Education,* Dubuque, Iowa, Kendall/ Hunt, some writers explore human rights issues related to education with particular reference to access and participation.

6. See for example J. Cummins, (ed.), (1981), *Heritage Language Education, Issues and Directions,* Ottawa: Minister of Supply and Services; *TESL TALK,* 10(3), Summer, 1979; McLeod, (ed.), (1984), *Multicultural Early Childhood Education,* Toronto: OISE Press; and various issues of *MC, Multiculturalism/Multiculturalisme,* a Canadian journal printed by the University of Toronto Press.

7. On the concept of anti-racist education one educator commented that it is not a positive human relations approach, and not good pedagogy. It was seen as a negative approach on both counts. The most recent educational document, dated June 1989, from the Ontario Ministry of Education regarding multicultural education seems to make "equity" the central focus. The document entitled *Changing Perspectives: A Resource Guide for Race and Ethnocultural Equity,* Junior Kindergarten, Grade 12/OACs obviously does not feature anti-racism in the title and in the body of the document suggests that it is part of "race and ethnocultural equity education." It all leads one to wonder if some people confuse changing rhetoric with changing actuality.

8. Curriculum studies in Canada have been done, for example, by Jack Kehoe, Frank Echols, Ahmed Ijaz, Walter Werner, Richard L. Butt, and Keith A. McLeod. One of the most noted American writers is James Banks; for Britain see the book by James Lynch. The Canadian Human Rights Foundation is currently testing some elementary school materials.

9. On the subject of heritage language education see the writings of Jim Cummins, Marcel Danesi, Rebecca Ullmann, the research of Sonia Morris, the historical research of Keith A. McLeod, and the report *Cultural and Linguistic Diversity in Canada*, by Vandra Masemann & Jim Cummins, (1985), Ottawa: Multiculturalism Canada.

10. See Allport and in the Canadian context this analysis is based upon the works of Jack Kehoe, Ahmed Ijaz, Walter Werner, Richard Butt and Frank Echols; the work on co-operative learning techniques has also been taken into account. Internationally, the works of James Banks, Shlomo Sharan and Lawrence Kohlberg are important. Increasing attention is being given in Ontario and Canadian schools to co-operative learning. I would also refer readers to a revisionist analysis by Francis Aboud, (1988), *Children and Prejudice.*

11. See the reports and manuals done for the Boy Scouts of Canada.

12. The community United Nations Associations in Canada as well as the League of Human Rights of B'nai B'rith have also been very active.

13. There are several cities that have municipal committees working in the area of ethnic and race relations; there are also many volunteer organizations including the Canadian Council for Multicultural and Intercultural Education.

14. The most recent province to ask school boards to develop policies is New Brunswick; in this instance a direct association is being made — Boards are being asked to develop multicultural and human rights policies. See the *Canadian Education Association Newsletter*, January 1990.

References

Aboud, Frances. (1988). *Children and Prejudice.* Oxford & New York: Basil Blackwell Ltd.

Allport, Gordon. (1954). *The Nature of Prejudice.* New York: Doubleday.

Anisef, Paul. (1986). *Models and Methodologies Appropriate To The Study of Outcomes of Schooling in Ontario's Multicultural Society.* Ontario: Ontario Ministry of Education.

Board of Education for the City of Scarborough. (1988). *Race Relations, Ethnic Relations, and Multicultural Policy.*

Breton, R., Reitz J.G. & Vallentine, V., (eds.). (1980). *Cultural Boundaries and the Cohesion of Canada.* Montreal: The Institute for Research on Public Policy.

Bullivant, Brian. (1981). *The Pluralist Dilemma in Education: Six Case Studies.* London: George Allen & Unwin.

Burke, Mavis E. (1982). "The Ontario multicultural, multiracial student leadership program." *MC, Multiculturalism, Multiculturalisme*, 1(1).

Canada, House of Commons. (1984). *Equality Now!* The Report of the Special Committee on Visible Minorities in Canadian Society.

Canada, House of Commons. (1987). *Multiculturalism: Building The Canadian Mosaic*, Report of the Standing Committee on Multiculturalism.

Canada. (1988). *Canadian Multiculturalism Act*. The Multiculturalism Policy of Canada.

Fisher, Donald & Echols, Frank, (1989). *Evaluation Report On The Vancouver School Boards Race Relations Policy*. Vancouver: School Board of the City of Vancouver.

Gundara, J., Jones C., & Kimberley K., (eds.). (1986). *Racism, Diversity, and Education*. London: Hodder and Stoughton.

Mallea, J.R. (1989). *Schooling In A Plural Canada*. London: Multilingual Matters.

McLeod, Keith A. (1981). "Multiculturalism and multicultural education: Policy and practice." In *Canadian Society for the Study of Education, Eighth Yearbook*.

McLeod, Keith A. (1985). "Multiculturalism and Ontario." In Bicentennial Conference Proceeding, *Two Hundred Years: Learning To Live Together*. Toronto: Government of Ontario.

Mock, Karen & Masemann, Vandra. (1991). "Report." Ontario Ministry of Education. The Report was completed in 1989 — it was edited for publication.

Morrison, T.R. (1980). "Transcending culture: Cultural selection and multicultural education." In K.A. McLeod, (ed.), (1980). *Intercultural Education and Community Development*. Toronto: University of Toronto.

Newman, Willliam M. (1973). *American Pluraism, A Study of Minority Groups and Social Theory*. New York: Harper & Row.

Ontario Teachers' Federation. (1984). *We the Teachers of Ontario*. Toronto: Ontario Teachers' Federation.

Ontario, Ministry of Education. (1987). *The Development of a Policy On Race and Ethnocultural Equity*, Report of the Provincial Advisory Committee on Race Relations.

Purcell, Cannon. (1985). "The Development of Human Rights and Race Relations in Ontario." In Bicentennial Conference Proceedings, *Two Hundred Years: Learning to Live Together*. Toronto: Government of Ontario.

Saskatchewan Human Rights Commission. (1985). *Education Equity: A Report on Indian/Native Education in Saskatchewan*. Saskatchewan.

Skutnabb-Kangas, T. & Cummins, J. (eds.). (1988). *Minority Education*. Clevedon: Multilingual Matters.

Toronto Board of Education. (1976). *We Are All Immigrants To This Place*. Toronto: Toronto Board of Education.

Enhancing Cross-Cultural Understanding in Multicultural and Multiracial Educational Settings: A Perceptual Framework

Carole Pigler Christensen

Professionals working in educational settings throughout North America are faced with the need to enhance their understanding of increasingly diverse student populations. From elementary schools to universities, teachers, consellors, social workers and administrators are interacting with populations that may differ from themselves in cultural, ethnic and racial background. In the United States, it is estimated that by the year 2000, one-third of the population will be non-white. In Canada, where only the British and the French are officially recognized as the "founding peoples," 37 percent of the population is of neither British nor French origin, and approximately 6 percent of the population is non-white (Statistics Canada, 1986).

These demographic trends suggest that in future years, personnel in educational institutions will continue to interact with populations from many cultural, ethnic, and racial backgrounds. Currently, all personnel in urban schools in North America are likely to be engaged in cross-cultural interactions, defined as interactions in which the persons involved come from different cultural backgrounds. Moreover, educational settings typically have a multicultural and multiracial student body, and may have educators and other personnel from diverse cultural and racial backgrounds. However, the literature suggests that when educational personnel work with people who differ from themselves in ethnicity, culture, or race, mutually satisfying relationships, educational experiences, and outcomes, may not be achieved (Arab, 1983; Banks, 1981; The Protestant School Board of Greater Montreal, 1988).

Apparently, those involved in pluralistic educational settings in Canada and in the United States perceive somewhat similar educational dilemmas and concerns, despite differences in the specifics of their histories, current circumstances and responses (Findlater, 1987; Samuda & Kong, 1986). For example, both countries have the following in common: (1) students who are exposed to the rhetoric of democracy and equal opportunity; (2) a history of colonialism and racist ideology (white superiority), which was espoused by the British, the

French, and other Europeans to justify enslavement and colonization of non-white peoples; (3) student populations which, at all educational levels, are apparently becoming multicultural and multiracial at a faster rate than teachers and other personnel; (4) educators and other personnel who do not generally receive the necessary training to deal competently and effectively with a multicultural and multiracial population; (5) parents of immigrants and minorities who are becoming increasingly vocal in demanding sensitive, quality education for their children.

Recent studies have documented the many concerns of personnel in educational settings, as student bodies become more pluralistic (Canadian Association of Schools of Social Work, 1991; Roe, 1982). Most of these concerns centre on how to create a learning environment responsive to the needs of students from different backgrounds, and with varied learning styles and expectations (Parsonson, 1986; Pedersen, 1984). In schools, colleges, and universities in Canada and in the United States, students are increasingly being drawn from aboriginal and immigrant populations. Also present are minority groups of long-standing including those of European, black, and Asian ancestry, many of whom have lived in North America for generations, if not centuries (Atkinson, Morten & Sue, 1983). Not unlike the United States, inner city schools in Halifax, Montreal, Toronto, Calgary and Vancouver may have student bodies in which 25 to 80 percent come from backgrounds other than white, British or French; many speak neither English nor French. Nonetheless, teachers and other personnel continue to be drawn mainly from the two dominant cultures (that is, French in Quebec, British elsewhere), or of other European origins.

Despite professing a melting pot philosophy, the pluralistic nature of the classroom has long been recognized in the United States (Herr, 1979). Particularly since the black civil rights movement of the 1960s, the need to prepare educators and guidance consellors to work in multicultural and multiracial settings has been widely discussed (Atkinson, Morten, & Sue, 1983; Sedlacek & Brooks, 1976). When Headstart programs were in full swing in the United States, Canadian educators generally continued to perceive Canada as, basically, a British and French society (Werner, Corners, Aoki & Dahlie, 1977). Only after the official pronouncement of an official multiculturalism policy did various Canadian school boards and administrators begin to adopt policies to respond to ethnic, cultural, and racial diversity (Kehoe, 1984). In provinces other than Quebec, responses generally took the form of heritage language programs, and increased emphasis on bilingual education.

In recent years, parents and students from minority backgrounds have become more vocal than ever before in expressing concerns about the learning environment and opportunities offered to them (James, 1990; The Black

Community Workshop on Education, 1978). Mainly, these relate to: whether teachers are sufficiently knowledgeable about culturally-based roles, expectations and learning styles which may affect student-teacher relationships and student progress (Buchignani, 1980); whether teachers hold stereotypical, or biased views and expectations of different groups (Singh, 1986); whether historical and current contributions to the country by groups other than British and French are recognized (The Protestant School Board of Greater Montreal, 1988); and the extent to which all such factors may influence the learning environment of the classroom, and the educational setting as a whole (Wolfgang, 1983).

Several years ago, I presented a multi-dimensional model for cross-cultural counselling based on perceptual, or phenomenological, theory (Christensen, 1985). The model is reported to be helpful in training teachers, counsellors, social workers and other professionals to gain a deeper understanding of the complex factors affecting students and professionals in helping relationships, which may lead to more beneficial and satisfying outcomes. (Evaluations of training workshops presented to: Scarborough Board of Education, 1990 Conference on Race and Ethnocultural Equity and Programs; Dalhousie University, Continuing Education Program, Maritime School of Social Work (1990); SIETAR International Congress Training Workshop, Banff, 1991; The Protestant School Board of Greater Montreal, Staff Development, 1991).

This chapter applies the perceptual model to the educational setting. More specifically, the purpose of this chapter is to provide a framework for understanding why, and how, the perceptions of the parties interacting in pluralistic educational settings may differ; and to offer suggestions for using perception as a tool to enhance understanding that may lead to planned change.

Basic Concepts of Perceptual Theory

The perceptual field was first described by Lewin (1951) as a fundamental element in the psychological treatment of the individual. Indeed, Rogers (1951) referred to the perceptual field as the private map by which a person lives. For some time now, an understanding of perceptual theory has been recognized as an aid to helping professionals (Coombs, Avila & Purkey, 1972), but it is only recently that it has been applied to cross-cultural encounters (Christensen, 1985). It is one of the few theories that is sufficiently comprehensive to address individual, ethnocultural, and sociopolitical factors such as those affecting everyone involved in multicultural and multiracial schools and universities. Often, efforts to examine the situations and circumstances arising in such educational settings centre around either students' or educators' concerns (Mock, 1986; Pedersen, 1984). This generally excludes economic and sociopolitical factors which have direct effects on administrative and policy decisions that ultimately affect students. The multidimensional frame-work presented here is applicable to students and educational personnel alike, and allows for an analysis of the behavior which may originate from within, or from outside of the individual.

The perceptual field is graphically illustrated in Figure 1, which indicates that its various components, represented by four concentric circles, have permeable boundaries, penetrated by information from the other aspects of the system. The basic premises of the perceptual framework are briefly outlined below.

Figure 1
The perceptual field as experienced by each participant in the cross-cultural encounter.

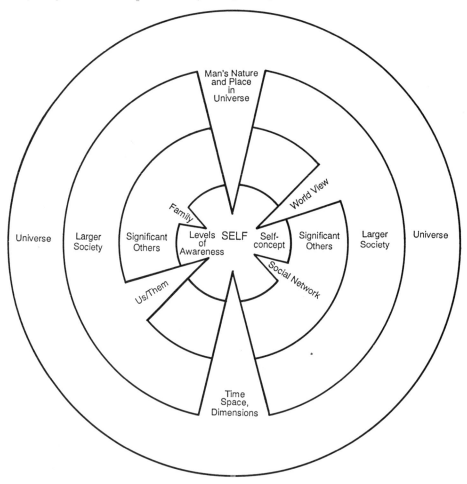

The perceptual field is defined as including everything experienced as the individual's reality at a given moment, from the self to the entire universe (Rogers, 1951). It is characterized by: stability, flexibility, fluidity, and direction or need satisfaction. The self, which strives toward self-actualization, is perceived as being at the centre of the perceptual field. Events at the centre are the most influential, while those near the periphery usually exert less influence. At any given moment, perceptions are occurring at varying levels of a person's awareness, from vague and undifferentiated perceptions to those toward which behavior is directed. The notion of the unconscious, as totally distinct from conscious awareness, is rejected by phenomenological theorists, however. A change in any one aspect of the perceptual field affects all other aspects of the system because it operates as a unified system where all aspects are interrelated.

Through interaction with significant others, a concept of self ("me" or "I") develops which, due to its tendency toward differentiation (an aspect of self-actualization), is experienced as being at the centre of the perceptual field. This includes the concept of self as, for example, good, bad; fat, thin; beautiful, unattractive; smart, stupid.

Although what a person perceives about him/herself may, or may not, reflect reality, it determines all else perceived; the individual is selective — to maintain congruity and in the interests of "economy."

Culture and Perception

From a perceptual viewpoint, culture must be understood as more than artifacts, traditions, and "old world" values. It consists too of the life-styles and behavior patterns that groups develop in response to the economic, social, and political forces that they face in a given society. Thus, immigrant cultures change over time, depending on their perceived degree of acceptance, rejection or oppression.

The culture(s) to which an individual is exposed determines the perimeters of the perceptual field in terms of what is learned about self and others as part of the particular social context. Values, taboos, moral precepts, and beliefs about various ethnic, cultural, and racial groups become part of our perceptions and determine how we behave toward those that we learn to consider similar to, or unlike, ourselves. Thus, from the perceptual viewpoint, learning is the discovery of personal meaning, stemming from the kinds of differentiations an individual makes as she/he is socialized during the developmental process.

Communication is both what is said, or intended, and what is comprehended. For communication to be experienced as meaningful or satisfactory, some common experience to which the parties involved can relate must be discovered. When the meanings attached to communication overlap, people experience that they understand and are understood (Kohut, 1959).

Based upon the above discussion, the following underlying assumptions form the basis for the framework presented below:

a) A most significant and fundamental aspect of the self is one's ethnic, cultural, and racial identity.

b) At any given moment, perceptions of significant others, the larger society and the universe are present simultaneously, although at varying levels of awareness.

c) People from the same, or similar, cultural backgrounds are more likely to have similarities in their perceptual fields than those from dissimilar backgrounds.

d) In the North American context, ethnic, racial, and cultural background are believed by many to be significantly related to fundamental human qualities such as moral codes, intelligence and innate capacities. Such beliefs are supported by popular jokes and stereotypes, the media, and in the historical and current literature, including literature in the field of education. Actual or assumed ethnic, cultural, and/or racial background, therefore, play an important role in determining how students fare in educational systems, which in turn affects the life chances of the individual.

It should be noted that the above assumptions apply equally to students and personnel in educational settings.

Application of the Perceptual Framework to Educational Settings

The two outer concentric circles of Figure 1 are helpful in examining and understanding the organizational response of administrators and other decision-makers in educational settings to multicultural and multiracial issues. In addition, the assumptions which underlie policy decisions become more apparent when examined in the light of perceptual theory.

The fourth, or outermost concentric circle represents the universe dimension of the perceptual field. Those in a given society are exposed to certain philosophical assumptions about humankind's fundamental nature and place in the universe. Formal education is a major method of ensuring that the world view of the dominant group in a given society is passed on to future generations. For example, North Americans are generally taught that "man is the master of his fate" (since the women's movement, one assumes women to be included in a generic understanding of the term, although in practice this remains debatable); and that humans are the highest life form, meant (by God, according to Judeo-Christian beliefs) to rule over all creatures on the land and in the sea.

The third, or "larger society" concentric circle, represents perceptions of society and the world view, including perceptions about which ethnic cultural, or racial groups are perceived as "us" or "them." Although seldom analyzed in this regard, educational theories have underlying assumptions about how learning takes place, and about the factors that spell success or failure in educational settings which are closely related to the world view of those holding decision-making power at all levels (that is, from teachers to board members). Most commonly used North American-based theories assume that factors originating within the individual, such as innate intelligence, motivation and cognitive ability determine the student's success or failure in the educational setting. Even social class status, although generally conceded to be a factor external to the individual, is perceived to be within the individual's ability to alter through hard work and determination. Similarly, a world view of humans as a competitive species normalizes competition in the educational system. This is in sharp contrast to the perceptions of those coming from any of the following backgrounds: (1) those which emphasize sharing and the collective good over that of the individual; (2) where one's social class is determined by birth; (3) North American minorities who find themselves relegated to lower-class status generation after generation (for example, aboriginal peoples; blacks), whether or not the individual works hard and desires upward mobility. Such individuals may perceive factors external to the individual (economic and sociopolitical) as having most weight. Theories allowing an analysis of such factors might give equal weight to factors external and internal to the individual.

The two innermost concentric circles help to provide an understanding of student-teacher relationships and peer relations, in educational settings. The second concentric circle represents the individual's perceptions of significant others, such as family members, educators and the social network. As indicated above, students, teachers and other personnel in educational settings will have learned about norms and rules governing social interaction from their significant others. Johnson (1990) has noted that interaction rules learned from significant others may have negative and unintended effects on communication processes when those involved are unaware of the rules of interaction in their respective social networks.

In Canada and in the United States, students and educational personnel alike are exposed to numerous myths and stereotypes about different ethnic, cultural, and racial groups which may form the basis of positive and negative perceptions and attitudes, determining levels of interaction between groups. This is especially likely when opportunities for intimate and personal contact with various groups are absent, such as in neighborhoods that are segregated ethnically or racially (Laferriere, 1978).

It is often overlooked that the perceptual field, for increasing numbers of students, has bicultural elements (Sue, 1983). Their social networks challenge them daily to negotiate languages with different cognitive dimensions, and norms and values which may be incompatible and even contradictory. For example, a dilemma may be experienced in both Canada and the United States by students who are immigrants, and by members of non-white (or "visible") minorities of long-standing, when educators and others from the dominant culture suggest that immigrants are welcomed, and that all members of society have equal opportunity. In fact, these groups often perceive rejection, discrimination or oppression at some level of awareness, as identifiable members of society, especially if they do not have characteristics associated with high status in these countries (for example, white skin and European features, Judeo-Christian religious beliefs, extensive formal education, or command of the language of the dominant cultural group) (Banks, 1983; Kallen, 1982).

A recent study by Burrell & Christensen (1987) indicated that the same school setting may be perceived differently by students of different ethnic, cultural, and racial backgrounds. For example, a higher percentage of white students (51 percent) than students from non-white minorities (36 percent) considered the urban Canadian high school to either be free or "most of the time" free from racial discrimination. Students also reported differences in their perceptions concerning whether parents, teachers, counsellors, or the school principal was the most helpful in terms of career information and problemsolving. Black students' perceptions differed from those of other non-whites on several variables.

A national survey conducted in the United States confirmed a similar pattern. Blacks were distinguished from other groups in perceiving that they had experienced barriers to their personal opportunity, with college-educated blacks perceiving less equality of opportunity for their group, the poor and women than less-educated blacks (Kluegel & Smith, 1986:73). Clearly, there is a need for research documenting how students, as well as educators and other personnel, perceive various aspects of educational settings.

The innermost concentric circle represents the "self." An examination of this component of the perceptual field offers insight into many of the concerns of students and personnel in educational settings. Ethnic, cultural, and racial identity are important components of self, whether positively or negatively perceived. As depicted in Figure 1, the cultural environment and its events are continuously penetrating the self boundary. In multicultural and multiracial educational settings, a number of events, seldom discussed in teacher training, may be impinging upon students. The various concerns and life experiences that face immigrant students have been discussed by Toomer (1983), who suggests that all who come in contact with immigrant students should be familiar with the stages in the immigrant adaptation process. Immigrants' perceptions of themselves and others vary as this process proceeds. During stage one, immigrant students may be euphoric about having arrived in the new host culture and perceive themselves as being welcomed. Stage two may involve daily life situations being experienced as a series of crises, resulting in longing for home and perceptions of rejection by those in the host culture. People begin to have a deeper understanding of the host culture during stage three and they may, therefore, begin to perceive themselves as belonging. By stage four, immigrants are able to view their new home as offering both positive and negative alternatives and opportunities.

The sense of grief and estrangement may be exacerbated when those who were part of the majority in their country of origin experience minority status upon immigration. If, by virtue of personal characteristics (for example, accent, skin color, or other features) immigrants find themselves arbitrarily perceived as part of an ethnic category (such as, Asian), expected to fit stereotypes and roles assigned by the dominant culture in the host country, self perceptions will change. Identity diffusion and self-disparagement may result, as immigrants to North America come to realize that minority status is determined mainly by race and national origin (Creese, 1984; Toomer, 1983:239). Even Canada's multiculturalism policy, suggesting pride in one's heritage and mother tongue has but limited positive effect for aboriginal peoples and indigenous minorities such as blacks and Acadians. These groups still find little in history books and the media to foster positive images and recognize contributions (Mannette, 1984). Popular images continue to present, to minority and majority groups alike, limiting or uncomplimentary career choices (for example, blacks limited to sports, entertainment, criminality, violence; the Chinese limited to technological occupations, business and gang warfare). If models among significant others in a wide variety of careers are few, or not publicly acknowledged, perceptions of life-chances are likely to be negatively affected (James, 1990; Stikes, 1978). Similarly, features which characterize the life-style of self and significant others, such as the extended family, may be viewed as an anomaly and devalued in the wider society.

Suggestions for Using the Perceptual Framework in Educational Settings

The perceptual framework can be applied in three major areas in order to enhance understanding in multicultural and multiracial educational settings: in the training of educators, counsellors, social workers and other personnel; to empower students by enhancing their understanding of the dynamics of ethnicity, culture, and race in educational settings; and as a tool to foster policy and organizational change. Table 1 indicates how the areas in question relate to different levels of awareness and various aspects of the perceptual field.

Table 1

Level of Perceptual Analysis	Elements of Perceptual Field of Students and Educational Personnel	Perceptual Goals for the Educational Setting	Policy/Organizational Implications
Self	Self-concept and value given to various attributes (e.g., age, sex, race, ethnicity, socioeconomic status) perceived as positive or negative.	Educational goals, processes, and daily events occurring in educational setting perceived as positive and meaningful.	Programs that promote a positive self-concept should be instituted for minority students. Academic and personal supports should be provided.
	Perception of cultural, racial, ethnic, and class differences between self and others in educational setting.	Perception of mutual trust, openness, sincerity, acceptance, respect.	Personnel from varied backgrounds should be valued and made welcome.
	Educational events perceived as satisfying and relevant.	Perception of agreement and comfort with educational goals, role expectations, teaching methods, learning styles, written and verbal/non-verbal expression.	The existence of institutional racism must be acknowledged, and measures to combat it must be developed.
	Culturally determined cognitions, educational philosophy, expectations learning styles, accommodated, understood, valued.	Perception of positive learning environment free of discrimination based on ethnicity, culture, race.	Educational policies should include measures to assess the climate of the school.
	Perception of various cultural influences, at varying levels of awareness, during educational processes and events.	Experience of mutual understanding, empathy, genuineness, rapport.	Opportunities for positive interaction should be created and fostered.
Significant Others	Extended or nuclear family organization; physical environment and emotional atmosphere of home. Climate created by educational personnel, peer group.	Understanding of impact of North-American education and its processes for students and their families in the context of pluralism; recognition of inherent strengths to be found in all cultures.	More teachers from varied ethnic/cultural/racial backgrounds should be hired through equal access and recruitment programs.

Level of Perceptual Analysis	Elements of Perceptual Field of Students and Educational Personnel	Perceptual Goals for the Educational Setting	Policy/Organizational Implications
	Cultural group identified with; and who is considered "us," who "them."	Educators and other personnel are sufficiently knowledgeable about students' cultural backgrounds (e.g., norms; values; life-styles; child-rearing practices; religion; meaning of educational success/failure in various cultural groups).	All students should have opportunities to interact with significant others, as educational personnel at all levels.
	Cultural groups represented among intimate friends and associates.	Recognition of bicultural aspects of students'/personnel's perceptual fields, when relevant.	Decision-makers must be drawn from backgrounds representative of our society.
	Neighborhood as multicultural or homogeneous; socio-economic levels represented.	Personnel's knowledge of daily life as it exists in neighborhoods where various ethnic/cultural/racial groups are located.	Opportunities for continuing education must be made available to allow multicultural learning opportunities.
	Educational environment and culture which it represents; degree of acceptance experienced.	Realistic appraisal of students' abilities and levels of achievement; assignments perceived to be graded impartially and fairly.	Ongoing opportunities should be available for staff training and self-awareness development.
	Societal and cultural factors relating to educational attainments and role models found in various groups; degree of employment/underemployment; job-related stress/satisfaction; job network.	Ability to recognize, and find ways to deal with, individual, cultural, and institutional racism, prejudice and discrimination.	Organizational structures must be in place to ensure that discrimination based on backgrounds is not condoned.
Larger Society	View of one's place in society and in the world (e.g., oppressed, free) as determined by experience with significant others in minority and dominant cultures; impact in educational setting.	Understanding of how students'/personnel's world views were formulated; recognition of societal factors which influence world view presented in educational institution.	The effects on students and personnel of past and present societal events must be recognized and integrated in a useful manner. Policies must reflect and acknowledge multiple world views, as opposed to a monocultural view.

Level of Perceptual Analysis	Elements of Perceptual Field of Students and Educational Personnel	Perceptual Goals for the Educational Setting	Policy/Organizational Implications
	National, political, ideological, and educational viewpoints; and loyalties.	Non-judgmental understanding and appreciation regarding response to societal and educational systems and events, despite differences in viewpoints.	The true history of all peoples on Canadian shores, their struggles and contributions, must be incorporated in historical and literary accounts.
	Future, present, or past orientation and effects in educational setting.	Sensitive but realistic appraisal of meaning of time/space orientation and its consequences, including preference for action-oriented/reflective cognition and learning modalities.	Administrators must assume responsibility for ensuring that personnel help to create an environment where a variety of orientations and learning modalities are accepted.
Universe	Man in relation to nature; the nature of man; spiritual values. Impact in educational setting.	Perception of personnel's understanding and appreciation of students' world views and life experiences, including "folk-ways" and beliefs.	That humankind's place in the universe is open to an infinite number of interpretations must be acknowledged.
	View of man's place in the universe (i.e., man in relation to oral and written knowledge, time, space, and the cosmos).	Recognition of role of culture in determining frames of reference.	Variations in world views should be legitimized in policies and practices.
	Fundamental meaning of learning in relation to creation, life, death.	Ability to distinquish between individual and cultural attributes. Pluralism is valued.	Policies and structures should be reviewed regularly to ensure commitment to valuing diversity.

Using Perception for Training Purposes

Popular belief suggests that efforts to increase multicultural and multiracial understanding should be concentrated on the young, but administrators, teachers and other personnel are clearly those who have the power and control to bring about change in educational systems. Therefore, effective training programs for these groups are particularly important (Christensen, 1984; Ghosh, 1990).

Currently, there are a number of popular approaches to training educators, counsellors, school social workers, and others working in Canadian multicultural and multiracial educational settings. Although more research is needed to determine which approaches are most helpful, under what specific conditions, and with which population groups, some of these approaches have been identified as less useful than others (Stenhouse, 1975).

For example, most people now realize that education alone does not change attitudes and behavior (Wein & Buckley, 1976). Similarly, "multicultural" training programs which emphasize equality and the heritage or contributions of various groups have failed to bring about needed results. Educational personnel remain concerned by the number of children from certain backgrounds who continue to perceive that they are devalued by teachers and peers; "streamed" into non-academic or high-tech programs; or unable to complete high school or to enter post-secondary educational systems (Fernando, 1984). The more recent anti-racist approaches attempt to expose and eliminate racism in educational settings at the individual, cultural, and institutional levels, and to analyze its negative consequences for majority and minority populations. However, these approaches pose the dilemma of requiring those who benefit from racism in terms of privilege, prestige and power, to work actively against it.

Unlike any of the above methods, the perceptual framework allows those involved in training programs to locate the origins of their viewpoints and attitudes, in order to plan activities for change. Trainees can examine how their perceptions, at various levels of awareness, affect current cross-cultural or interracial interactions. Therefore, the framework offers trainees personal and experiential opportunities to examine and change behavior *vis-à-vis* those from various backgrounds, rather than providing only an intellectual approach.

The use of the perceptual framework also provides opportunities to: heighten awareness of perceptions of the individual's racial identity as part of the self-concept (in addition to the perhaps more comfortable perceptions pertaining to cultural and ethnic identity); discover how perceptions and attitudes about ethnicity, culture and race were influenced by significant others during socialization processes, including formal and informal education; and enhance understanding of how perceptions related to world views of decision-makers are ingrained in formal and informal policy decisions and organizational structures in education systems.

Empowering Students by Enhancing their Understanding of the Dynamics of Ethnicity, Culture and Race in Educational Settings

Students enrolled in multicultural and multiracial educational systems fall broadly into five major categories: (1) majority group Canadians; (2) immigrants of European background other than British or French; (3) foreign students on temporary visas; (4) aboriginal Canadians; and (5) those classified as "visible" minorities, generally perceived as immigrants whether they are recent arrivals or have Canadian ancestry. Students in each of these categories may perceive themselves to be in very different situations, each of which generate unique educational experiences. It appears that these experiences are similar across Canada, and indeed throughout North America. This suggests that certain dynamics may operate independently of the individual student, or the particular time and place where particular events occur. The common factor affecting these students may be related to similarities in perceptions of certain ethnic, cultural, and racial categories in the North American context, which are likely to result in similarities in the dynamics generated in multicultural and multiracial educational settings.

1, Students from majority group backgrounds are likely to perceive congruence in what they are taught at home and in educational settings. Therefore, unless prompted to do so, these students may not question cultural biases ingrained in aspects of their educational experience. The perceptual framework can help these students to become aware of perceptions of those considered "different," whether peers or persons in positions of authority; and help them to discover the origins of their cognitive and emotional content.

2. Students from European cultures other than British or French often find that they are able to escape negative consequences of immigrant status if they are willing to assume the cultural traits of the dominant cultural group. Once accents are lost, white skin allows these students to be perceived, visually, as part of the majority group. Furthermore, the European cultures are generally viewed more favorably than non-European cultures, as witnessed by history texts, celebrated authors and media coverage. Should they be recent immigrants, the perceptual framework can help these students to understand the dynamics of dual identity and intergenerational conflicts with significant others.

3. Foreign visa students soon become aware that the perceptions North Americans have of them are heavily influenced by the media. These may be more or less realistic depending on the quality of media reports, the political situation in their region at a given time, and the climate and extent of the relationship existing between Canada and their country of origin. Since these students generally come with a specific goal in mind, (that is, to obtain a degree and return to their country of origin), they are often able to place the dynamics perceived in educational settings in a perspective different from that of students who are permanent immigrants.

4. Aboriginal students are in the peculiar situation of being perceived negatively in their home country, where they have generally been portrayed in a disparaging manner. This has fostered distorted perceptions of the historical and current realities of the lives of aboriginal peoples. As the colonized people, common perceptions of "Indians" and "Eskimos" as less than human, heathen,

violent, drunk, unable and unwilling, remain. The circumstances under which aboriginal peoples are educated (often in a second language and away from their home environment) and the content of that education, may produce what is perceived as an alien and hostile environment.

5. Visible minorities are perceived as immigrants by majority group Canadians no matter what their factual history indicates. People who are proud of their origins may find it difficult to be perceived in distorted ways by peers and educators. Whether immigrants or Canadian-born, visible groups are arbitrarily placed in an ethnic category perceived by the dominant cultures (for example, "orientals" in the West, and "allophones" used in Quebec to categorize all non-British and non-French groups). Blacks in Canada tend to be perceived as having a common culture and ethnic background, no matter from where they originate. This perception is encouraged by heritage weeks celebrated in schools which often include a module on "Black culture," "Greek culture," "Italian culture," and so on. Culturally, blacks in Canada, unlike whites, seem expected to define themselves first by color, rather than by cultural background or national origin. Educational programs seldom take into account that the bond perceived by most black people stems, in great measure, from the experience of slavery, colonialism and racism experienced in predominantly white societies worldwide.

A major problem in textbooks and research produced in the United States, but also used to educate teachers and other professionals in Canada, is the emphasis placed on color, or "race," as a variable in educational settings. Studies carried out in educational settings often discuss results in terms of "blacks" and "whites," suggesting that whites are perceived as a monolithic, homogeneous, group, representing the "norm." For **this** purpose, race overrides culture and ethnicity for whites in the United States. The controversy about intelligence tests is a prime example of this problem (Samuda, 1986). In addition, in educators' textbooks, black Americans are often associated with poverty, disadvantage, behavior problems, lack of motivation and poor educational performance. Since little factual information has been gathered and made available about the situation of blacks in Canada (who are themselves multicultural) reliance on United States-based information is problematic.

An understanding of the above dynamics surrounding ethnicity, culture and race in educational settings would empower students. An accurate perception of individual and institutional factors that serve to limit opportunity and create an unwelcoming climate would free them to use their energies appropriately and productively and to promote change.

Planning for Policy and Organizational Change

It is generally acknowledged that, for change to occur, policies and organizational structures must support it. Application of the perceptual framework to organizational structures has the advantage of allowing decision-makers to formulate policies with awareness of their personal views and their origins (self level). Using the framework also clarifies whose opinions are considered important in decisionmaking (significant others), and provides opportunities to analyze the role of factors found in the wider society that may impinge upon various constituencies involved with the educational institution. The middle and left-hand columns of Table 1 suggest how goals and policies may be linked.

A major problem in Canada is the lack of documentation on the numbers of persons from various backgrounds that are present in educational institutions at all levels. Although the lack of statistics indicating racial and ethnic origins has been seen as promoting fair play in a "color-blind" society, administrators are increasingly recognizing the need to have this information in order to assess needs and procure funding necessary for innovative programs. Administrators must take the lead in making the hiring of underrepresented population groups and staff training an expectation to allow the quality of education for all students to be enhanced. In particular, teachers, who become significant persons in the life of the student, must be expected to learn to work with students of varied backgrounds in a manner that fosters mutual respect based on their knowledge and effectiveness in working with all students.

As indicated above, there are several categories of students in our institutions that have special needs, whether for support services, personal or career counselling, English or French language courses, or reaching out to encourage family involvement.

It is now widely acknowledged that multiculturalism policies cannot be substituted for policies that deal directly with racism as a factor in Canadian educational institutions.

Decision-makers should be drawn from all levels and constituencies of the institution, including lay persons who have a stake in maintaining the quality of the institution. Boards should have more than a token representation of minority populations, since these groups have a particular role to play in bringing the reality of their group's situation to the attention of educational personnel.

Conclusion

Canadian educational settings are no longer a place where people go strictly to learn academic subjects. Schools are becoming social laboratories where experiments in multicultural and multiracial interactions are occurring on a daily basis, whether planned or not. Universities must establish required teacher training programs that prepare them for the realities of the pluralistic classroom. We must move beyond promoting tolerance to valuing diversity. The perceptual framework is offered as a tool to help us achieve this goal.

References

Arab, S. (1983). *International Students: Policy and Practices.* Ottawa: Canadian Federation of Students.

Atkinson, D.R., Morten, G. & Sue, D.W. (eds.) (1983). *Counseling American Minorities,* 2nd Edition. Dubuque, Iowa: Wm. C. Brown Co.

Banks, J.A. (1981). *Multiethnic Education: Theory and Practice.* Boston: Allyn & Bacon.

Banks, J.A. (1983). "Ethnicity and curriculum reform." In R.J. Samuda & S.L. Wood, (eds.), *Perspectives in Immigrant and Minority Education.* New York: University Press of America.

Buchignani, N. (1980). "Culture or identity? Addressing ethnicity in Canadian education." *McGill Journal of Education,* 15, 79-93.

Burrell, L.F. & Christensen, C.P. (1987). "Minority students' perceptions of high school: Implications for Canadian school personnel." *Journal of Multicultural Counseling and Development,* 15:3-15.

Canadian Association of Schools of Social Work. (1991). *Social Work Education at the Crossroads: The Challenge of Diversity,* Report of the Task Force on Multicultural and Multiracial Issues in Social Work Education. Ottawa: Canadian Association of Schools of Social Work.

Christensen, C.P. (1984). "Effects of cross-cultural training on counselor response." *Counselor Education and Supervision,* 23:311-320.

Christensen, C.P. (1985). "A perceptual approach to cross-cultural counselling." *Canadian Counsellor,* 19:63-81.

Christensen, C.P. (1986). "Immigrant Minorities in Canada." In J. Turner & F. Turner, (eds.), *Canadian Social Welfare.* Toronto: Collier MacMillan Ltd.

Creese, G. (1984). "Immigration policies and the creation of an ethnically segmented working class in British Columbia." *Alternate Routes, A Critical Review.* Special Issue on Class and Ethnicity, 1-34.

Coombs, A.W., Avila, D.L. & Purkey, W.W. (1972). *Helping Relationships: Basic Concepts for the Helping Professions.* Boston: Allyn & Bacon, Inc.

Fernando, S. (1984). "Streaming, a critique of community organizing around the issue." *"The Fourth R?" Racism and Education. Currents, Readings in Race Relations,* 2:32-34.

Findlater, S. (1987). *Rapport-synthese des politiques et des orientations concernant le multiculturalisme l'education antiraciste dans les dix provinces du Canada.* Quebec: Commission des droits de la personne du Quebec.

Ghosh, R. (1990). "Multicultural and international development education." *McGill Journal of Education*. Special Publication, 25th Anniversary Issue.

Herr, E.L. (1979). *Guidance and Counseling in the Schools, Perspectives on the Past, Present, and Future*. Falls Church, Va.: American Personnel and Guidance Association.

James, C.E. (1990). *Making It. Black Youth, Racism, and Career Aspirations in a Big City*. Oakville, Ontario: Mosaic Press.

Johnson, S. (1990). "Toward clarifying culture, race, and ethnicity in the context of multicultural counselling." *Journal of Multicultural Counseling and Development*, 18:41-50.

Kallen, E. (1982). *Ethnicity and Human Rights in Canada*. Toronto: Gage Publishing Ltd.

Kehoe, J.W. (1984). *A Handbook for Enhancing the Multicultural Climate of the School*. British Columbia: University of British Columbia, Faculty of Education, Western Education Development Group.

Kluegel, J.R. & Smith, E.R. (eds.). (1986). *Beliefs about Inequality: Americans' View of What Is and What Ought To Be*.

Kohut, H. (1959). "Introspection, empathy and psychoanalysis." *Journal of the American Psychoanalytic Association*, 7:459-483.

Laferriere, M. (1978). "The education of black students in Montreal schools: An emerging Anglophone problem, a non-existent Francophone preoccupation." In M.L. Kovacs (ed.). *Ethnic Canadians: Culture and Education*. Regina: Canadian Plans Research Centre.

Lewin, K. (1951). *Field Theory in Social Science: Selected Theoretical Papers*. Edited by D. Cartwright, New York: Harper & Row.

Mannette, J.A., (1984). "Stark remnants of "Blackpast": Thinking on gender, race and class in 1780's Nova Scotia." *Alternate Routes, A Critical Review*. Special Issue on Class and Ethnicity, 7:103-133.

Mock, K. (1986). "Integrating multiculturalism in early childhood education from theory to practice." In R.J. Samuda & S.L. Kong (eds.), *Multicultural Education Programmes and Methods*. Toronto: Intercultural Social Sciences Publication, Inc.

Parsonson, K. (1986). "Review of the effects of learning styles on achievement." In R.J. Samuda & S.L. Kong (eds.), *Multicultural Education Programmes and Methods*. Toronto: Intercultural Social Sciences Publication, Inc.

Pedersen, P. (1984). "Cultural assumptions of education and non-western alternatives." In D.S. Sanders & P. Pedersen, *Education for International Social Welfare*. Hawaii: School of Social Work, University of Hawaii.

Roe, P. (1982). *Multiculturalism, Racism and the Classroom*, Report, Canadian Education Association. Toronto: Canadian Education Association.

Rogers, C.R. (1951). *Client-Centered Therapy*. Boston: Houghton Mifflin.

Samuda, R.J. (1986). "The role of psychometry in multicultural education: Implications and consequences." In R.J. Samuda & S.L. Kong (eds.). *Multicultural*

Education Programmes and Methods. Toronto: Intercultural Social Sciences Publication, Inc.

Samuda, R.J. & Kong, S.L. (eds.). (1986). *Multicultural Education Programs and Methods*. Toronto: Intercultural Social Sciences Publication, Inc.

Sedlacek, W.E. & Brooks, G.C. (1976). *Racism in American Education: A Model for Change*. Chicago: Nelson-Hall.

Singh, A. (1986). "Effects of teacher perception on achievement." In R.J. Samuda & S.L. Kong (eds.), *Multicultural Education Programmes and Methods*. Toronto: Intercultural Social Sciences Publication, Inc.

Statistics Canada. (1986). *Census of Canada*. Ottawa: Ministry of Supply and Services Canada.

Stenhouse, L. (1975). "Problems of research in teaching about race relations." In G. Verma & C. Bagley (eds.), *Race and Education Across Cultures*. London: Heinemann.

Stikes, C.S. (1978). "Black student development problems — implications for teaching." *Journal of Non-White Concerns*, 6:191-199.

Sue, D.W. (1983). "Ethnic identity: The impact of two cultures on the psychological development of Asians in America." In D.R. Atkinson, G. Morten & D.W. Sue (eds.), *Counseling American Minorities*, (2nd Edition). Dubuque, Iowa: Wm. C. Brown Company Publishers.

The Black Community Workshop on Education. (1978). *Final Report of the Aspirations and Expectations of the Quebec Black Community With Regard to Education*. Quebec: Commission des droits de la personne du Quebec.

The Protestant School Board of Greater Montreal. (1988). *Multicultural-Multiracial Approach to Education in the Schools of the Protestant School Board of Greater Montreal*, Report of the Task Force on Multicultural/Multiracial Education. Montreal: The Protestant School Board of Greater Montreal.

Toomer, J.W. (1983). "Counseling the ethnic minority immigrant: A second look." In R.J. Samuda & S.L. Woods, (eds.), *Perspectives in Immigrant and Minority Education*. New York: University Press of America.

Werner, W., Connors, B., Aoki, T. & Dahlie, J. (1977). *Whose Culture, Whose Heritage? Ethnicity within Canadian Social Studies Curricula*. Vancouver: The University of British Columbia, Faculty of Education.

Wein, F.C., Buckely, P.C. & Desmond, K.E. (1976). *Opinions from the Centre: The Position of Minorities in a Canadian University*. Halifax: Institute of Public Affairs, Dalhousie University.

Wolfgang, A. (1983). "Intercultural counseling: The state of the art." In Samuda, R.J., Berry, J. & Laferriere, M. (eds.), *Multicultural Education of Canada*. Toronto: Allyn & Bacon.

Section IV

Alternative Models

The First Nations House of Learning:
A Case of Successful Transformation

Verna J. Kirkness

The First Nations[1] in Canada like other emerging nations of the world recognize education as the panacea for a better life. Prior to the arrival of the European to this country, the First People were providing their own form of education. In this traditional education, the community was the classroom, its members were the teachers, and each adult was responsible to ensure that each child learned all he or she needed to know to live a good life. The teachings were based on the peoples culture and addressed, not only cognitive development, but spiritual, emotional and physical growth of the child. Through these teachings each individual was helped to develop his/her potential as a contributing member of the society (Kirkness, 1981:449).

From the 17th Century to the present day, the education of First Nations people has been largely designed and directed by missionaries and federal and provincial public servants. The failure of this educational process has been well documented (Archibald, 1986; Barman, Herbert & McCaskill, 1987; Brown, 1988; Chrisjohn & Lanigan, 1986; Emerson, 1987; Hamilton, 1986; Henry & Pepper, 1988; Kirkness, 1987).

Despite the years of disappointment and frustration with this imposed system of education, Canada's First Nations continue to believe that education is necessary in order to function in a meaningful and equal way in today's society. In 1972 the First Nations articulated a policy in education which included a statement of philosophy, principles, goals and directions. The policy known as "The Indian Control of Indian Education" stated:

> Our aim is to make education relevant to the philosophy and needs of Indian people. We want education to give our children a strong sense of identity with confidence in their personal worth and ability. We believe in education;
>
> • as a preparation for total living
>
> • as a means of free choice of where to live and work
>
> • as a means of enabling us to participate in our own social, economic, political and educational advancement (N.I.B., 1973:3).

The policy further states:

> Native teachers and counsellors who have an intimate understanding of Indian traditions, psychology, way of life and language, are best able to create the learning environment suited to the habits and interests of the Indian child (N.I.B., 1973:18).

In reference to the training of Indians as teachers, the policy states:

> It is evident that the Federal Government must take the initiative in providing opportunities for Indian people to train as teachers and counsellors. Efforts in this direction require experimental approaches and flexible structures to accommodate the Native person who has talent and interest, but lacks minimum academic qualifications. Provincial involvement is also needed in this venture to introduce special teacher and counsellor training programs which will allow Native people to advance their academic standing at the same time as they are receiving professional training. Because of the importance to the Indian community, these training programs must be developed in collaboration with the Indian people and their representatives in the national and provincial organizations. The national and provincial organizations have a major role to play in evolving and implementing the training programs and in encouraging Native young people to enter the education field (N.I.B., 1973:18).

It was in response to this statement that a number of programs in teacher education were established in Canada.

The purpose of this chapter is to show how the Native Indian Teacher Education Program (NITEP) was used as a model for subsequent programs established at the University of British Columbia aimed at expanding the range and depth of program and course offerings related to the needs identified by First Nations in British Columbia. Six factors will be considered as forming the key elements of five programs established at the University.

The Native Indian Teacher Education Program (NITEP)

In 1974 when NITEP was established at the University of British Columbia (UBC), there were only 26 Native Indian teachers in the province of British Columbia in a teaching force of some 23 000. If the proportion of Native Indian teachers had been equal to the percentage of Indian people in the general population, there would have been about 1 300 Native Indian teachers in the province (University of British Columbia, 1974). Moreover, among Native Indian students generally, there was a massive dropout rate, low levels of achievement, and problems of adjustment to those in the mainstream of Canadian life. It was hoped that an increase in the number of Native Indian teachers would help to overcome some of these difficulties since there would be greater involvement in local curriculum development as well as a keener understanding by teachers of the situation of their students. Furthermore, at this time, there was a growing desire by Native Indian people to attain greater control of the education of their children, and the federal government (Department of Indian Affairs) was being forced to change its policies to take account of this desire. It was obvious, however, that an alternative to the existing teacher training program in British Columbia had to be devised if the training of the native teachers were to be successful.

NITEP was initiated by a group of Native Indian educators in the 1960s. It took the group at least five years to convince the University and government agencies of the need to provide an alternative approach to teacher education for Native Indians. This group, along with faculty members who became involved in the early planning stages, became the NITEP Advisory Committee within the Faculty of Education. The Committee subsequently included student representatives (McEachern & Kirkness, 1987:134).

The overall objective of NITEP, stated in the original proposal, was to, "increase the number of Native Indian teachers certified to teach in British Columbia schools (both federal and provincial) by developing an alternative program which is more appropriate to the educational background, heritage, needs and desires of people of Indian ancestry in this province" (UBC, 1974:1).

NITEP began as a four-year program leading to a Bachelor of Education degree and professional teacher certification in British Columbia. Students could leave the program with the minimum teacher certification after completing three years of study, but were encouraged to continue through to the degree. Students were admitted to the program through regular university admission or the mature student admission category of the university (Kirkness & More, 1981). The majority of NITEP students were/are admitted under the latter category which defines a mature student as a resident of the province of British Columbia who lacks formal university entrance requirements and has been out of school for some time. Applicants are admitted on the basis of their secondary school record, their related experience, attitude and demonstrated interest. The courses required for graduation are generally the same courses taken by students in the regular UBC Bachelor of Education program.

Courses Unique to NITEP

The Indian Studies courses are the only courses in NITEP which are unique to the Program. These courses are designed to reflect the cultural milieu of the NITEP students. The majority of the students received their education in schools that gave little or no recognition to the history, culture and contributions of Native North Americans. It is, therefore, necessary for a program to address this omission. It relates directly to the "Indian Control of Indian Education" policy statement quoted earlier, that to know oneself and one's potential, it is necessary to know one's history and one's culture. The question of identity becomes fundamental.

The first course, Introduction to Indian Studies (EDUC 140) is designed to develop and enhance student awareness of such topics as traditional Indian cultures, economic and community development, Indian government, the constitution, land claims, Indian rights, Indian organizations, assimilation, integration and cultural conflict. These are presented with a chronological perspective utilizing resource people and materials to present further information and various viewpoints. The second course, A Native Cultural Study (EDUC 141) focuses on the study of a Native Indian cultural group with an emphasis on traditional values and practices related to education. The third course, Issues in Indian Education (EDUC 240) is designed to develop students' knowledge of the historical trend of Indian education and an awareness of issues confronting Indian education today. The topics include philosophies, policies, objectives, resources, achievement, identity and evaluation. A critical analysis approach is used, as well as teaching how to construct a meaningful, relevant program for the education of Native Indian children. Students may also elect to take two additional Indian studies courses in year three or four. One is Teaching Native Languages in Elementary Schools (EDUC 342). The course emphasizes strategies, materials and programs for teaching Native Indian languages as first and second languages. The other course is Native Curriculum Study (EDCI 396) which concentrates on the rationale and objectives of developing and evaluating Native Indian curricula.

The specific objectives related to Indian Studies are important because NITEP graduates are in a unique position to provide leadership in explaining and analyzing Indian issues. Their understanding is regularly required in the classroom, in the school, in the Indian community and in the general community. Most important is the need to pass their understanding and analytical skills on to their Native Indian students.

Upon successful completion of the Indian Studies program, NITEP graduates should be able to understand and assist their Indian students more effectively; to help fellow teachers who are non-Indians to understand the Indian students better; to assist in course development related to Native Indians; to better understand their own cultural group within the larger context of Indian cultures; to assist their students in developing their Indian identity; and to help their students develop a base from which to build more effective bridges to other cultures.

Field Centre Concept

One of the distinguishing features of NITEP is in the location of the first two years of study. Students attend classes for the first two years at a field centre. Since the inception of the program in 1974 it has been located in 10 different communities for varying lengths of time. At present there are four full-time centres. The purpose of locating the first two years of study away from campus is to permit the students to complete their studies much closer to home, allowing them to maintain a closer contact with their own people. Providing field-based programs also enables students to embark on university studies without the added burden of coping with the wider urban and university milieu. In addition, a group cohesiveness develops which is supportive and continues when the students transfer to the main campus. Peer support and peer counselling are great strengths in the program.

Student Services

An extremely important component of NITEP is the support service provided to assist students to overcome academic and social gaps which may exist at entry to the program. This support is more effectively provided at a field centre where the students are together. The service continues throughout the program and includes counselling, tutoring, advice and friendship. The key person in directing and monitoring the program at each centre is the Coordinator. Coordinators are master teachers who administer the centres, conduct student seminars, organize student teaching placements, coordinate itinerant instructors, counsel and tutor students. If necessary, they arrange for specific expertise in counselling and tutoring.

Third and fourth year NITEP students attend regular classes but continue to maintain a closeness to one another by having a NITEP Centre on campus. This Centre houses the central administration for NITEP and has a comfortable lounge where students can visit, study and hold social get-togethers. A library of resources pertaining to Native Indians is adjacent to the lounge and is a valuable resource for students. An on-site coordinator and a counsellor are available to the on-campus students at the centre.

The Question of Legitimacy

Alternative programs, particularly those designed for minorities, constantly face the question of legitimacy. NITEP is no exception to this questioning. While it is structured differently from the regular program, the requirement for a standard teaching certificate and a Bachelor of Education degree is the same for NITEP students as it is for any other student in a B.Ed. program. To date, there are 144 graduates with B.Ed. degrees; several have returned to do a fifth year specialization or graduate work; seven have attained M.Ed. degrees; one went on to law school, graduated and was called to the bar in 1985. Most NITEP graduates are teaching while others are working with their people in fields related to education. The teaching records of the graduates are generally of high quality. They are employed throughout the province in Band, federal, provincial and urban schools. Several have gone out of the province or to Washington State (McEachern & Kirkness, 1987:139)

Several external evaluations have been conducted on NITEP. The most recent evaluation was completed in 1988 as the four-year B.Ed. program was being phased out and replaced by a five-year program. The purpose of the evaluation by Rudolf Dreikurs Institute was four-fold:

- to determine if the objectives and guidelines as stated in the original 1974 proposal are being met.

- to determine if an alternative program such as NITEP is necessary.

- to determine ways in which NITEP differs from regular programs.

- to determine if NITEP is effective (Pepper, 1988:i)

The evaluation found that:

The objectives and guidelines as stated in the original 1974 proposal are being met. The primary objective was **to increase the number of Native Indian teachers certified to teach in B.C.** 539 Native persons have entered the program, 96 have graduated, and 19 others hold Standard Teaching Certificates. Many who left early work as para-professionals in the education field.

It remains necessary to have an alternative teacher education program for Indian people. 86 percent of the respondents felt that NITEP was necessary, 72 percent of the NITEP student population preferred NITEP over the regular education program, and 86 percent believed that Native Studies is a necessary component of the program.

NITEP does differ from regular teacher education programs in a variety of ways, and in ways which are appropriate to the educational background, heritage, needs, and desires of people of Indian ancestry. The first two years are held at an off-campus field centre closer to home; there is an Advisory Committee composed for the most part of Native educators; there is a much larger practical component of student teaching at a much earlier scheduling than in the regular program; the sequence of courses differ in order to accommodate the earlier practicum work; Native Studies courses replace general social science courses; there is a greater degree of support services available; candidates can enter as mature students, class sizes are smaller and more personalized; students have been able to receive a Standard Teaching Certificate after completing three years of work; and there are Block classes (five-hour classes one or two days a month rather than three one-hour classes per week).

NITEP is an effective program. Responses to the questions pertaining to the differences, functions, services, standards, and courses within the program were very positive and supportive of NITEP. The cultural framework provided by the Native Studies courses combined with the required courses from the Faculty of Education should provide NITEP graduates with greater skills and sensitivity for working with Native students than regular graduates would have, and should equip NITEP graduates with skills to teach in Band schools, public or private schools. NITEP graduates have a solid foundation for teaching wherever they choose to teach (Pepper, 1988:ii-iii).

In 1980, a NITEP Think-In Workshop was introduced to enable representatives of all component groups to come together to review the program and to set short and long term goals together. This not only had an evaluative dimension but provided for students, staff, faculty, advisory committee members, sponsor teachers, school districts and colleges to be involved in shaping the direction of NITEP. The guiding questions used are: Where are we now? How did we get to where we are? Where are we going? How will we get there? How will we know when we are there?[2] The NITEP Think-In has continued to be conducted during alternative years.

The significance of having Native Indian staff for NITEP, while not initially stated, became a goal in 1980. In 1989 the NITEP staff was almost entirely Native Indian as indicated by an asterix in the organizational chart below, with

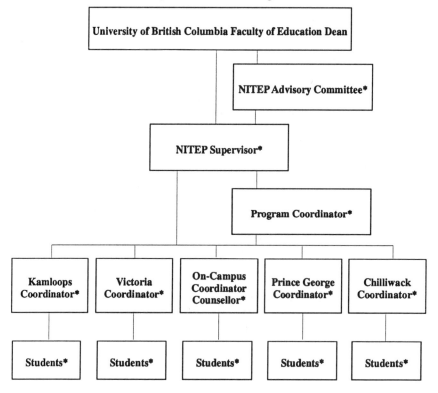

all field centre coordinators, the on-campus program coordinator and the counsellor being NITEP graduates.

In summary, NITEP has had considerable success both in terms of the model and the graduates. While the five-year program has created changes to the program, the key factors upon which subsequent programs were based remain intact. These are: the Advisory Committee, Indian Studies courses, Field Centre concept, Support Service, Evaluation and First Nations staff.

Application to Subsequent Programs at the University of British Columbia

The Native Law Program

The interest in Native Law began as early as 1973 because of a number of prominent Law Faculty members who were involved in the Indian question. These faculty members included Professors Lysyk, Berger, Jackson, Sanders and Thompson. In 1984, a Native Indian Law graduate was appointed as Director of the Native Law Program. It is his responsibility to promote law as a field of study among Native people and to ensure that the academic and personal needs of the students are met. As well, he is instrumental in organizing special speakers, courses and programs. An Advisory Committee was formed with membership from the Law Faculty appointed by the Dean. The committee has monitored the program and conducted internal evaluations of a formative nature.

Several courses are offered which relate to Native law. These courses are open to all law students and are not a requirement for Native law students, however, most elect to take the courses. Native Peoples and the Law (LAW 367) examines the history and present status of the legal relationships between Canada's Native peoples and the state, including the concept of aboriginal title to land and resources; the legal effect of treaties; Native hunting, fishing and trapping rights; the role of the Indian Act and the nature of the legal regime governing the administration of Indian reserve land; the negotiation and settlement of Native claims; alternate forms of confederation and the constitutional entrenchment of the distinctive legal and political rights of Native people. Topics in Native Self-Government (LAW 455) examines frameworks that may be applied to control Bands through by-law enactments, membership rules, and negotiated self-government agreements in questions of jurisdiction, drafting and enforcement of such instruments. Native Claims Seminar (LAW 456) addresses the legal context for the negotiation and settlement of Native claims. Topics in Comparative Law (LAW 478) deal with indigenous peoples and the law in the international arena.

To date, the Native Law Program has graduated 51 lawyers with an additional six expected to graduate this year. While several graduates have been from out-of-province the majority are from British Columbia.

Ts''kel Administration Program (M.Ed.)

The Ts''kel[3] Administration Program (M.Ed.) began in 1984 in response to a need for advanced educational leadership training for Native Indian people. By that time NITEP had been in operation for a decade and had 50 graduates with B.Ed. degrees. Several had already moved into leadership positions; others aspired to do so (Downey, 1987:9) The NITEP Advisory provided the guidance and support for the development of the Ts''kel Program. To reflect the Committee's expanded role, it became known as the Native Indian Education Advisory Committee.

The Ts''kel program provides an opportunity for interested and qualified First Nations people to develop expertise needed for First Nations Schools and other related institutions. Specifically, students in Ts''kel are:

- involved in the regular programs offered by the respective departments.

- provided with a seminar in which they can develop their own unique interpretations and applications of educational research related to First Nations education.

- provided with a course which has a particular reference to administering a First Nations Band School.

- provided with opportunities for a field experience in either a First Nations or public education setting.

- able to interact with all students and faculty in the respective departments and both contribute to and benefit from the wide variety of backgrounds and interests which this provides.

As in NITEP and the Native Law Program, Ts''kel has courses designed to meet the particular interest of the Native Indian graduate students. Relating Educational Concepts and Approaches to First Nations Education (EADM 508) is a seminar intended to give First Nations students an opportunity to develop their own unique interpretations and applications of related educational research. An examination of the historical and current developments in First Nations education forms the basis of inquiry. Administering a Band School (EADM 561) is a simulated decision-making lab course. It is designed to improve the decision-making and communication skills of the school administrator. The extensive set of simulation materials are drawn from actual

Band Schools' administrative, educational, social and political problems. Field experience (EADM 598) is a practicum where a student spends time working with a school principal as an assistant, to experience the role of a principal in a real situation. Teacher supervision, discipline, communication with parents are among the interests of the students. Field experience locations are determined by the students' previous experience. A student who has taught in a Band School will be directed to a field experience in a public school and vice versa.

A support function is provided by the program head, a First Nations person who initiated the program. Further support is provided by the staff of NITEP and the First Nations House of Learning.

During the first two years of the Ts''kel Administration Program, formative evaluations were conducted. In the final year of the three-year experiment (1987), a summative evaluation was conducted by external examiners. Their concluding remarks were as follows:

> When Ts''kel was introduced three years ago, it was difficult to imagine that even the most optimistic of its founding professionals could have envisioned its accomplishments to date. The story of Ts''kel must surely be one of the true success stories of Canadian Native education in recent years. Beyond the comments gleaned from the evaluation interviews was perhaps a more important, and certainly very powerful, intangible. Perhaps it is attitude; perhaps it is pride; perhaps it is simply that indefinable affect that people project when they know that their mission is of undeniable importance. The dedication of the people of Ts''kel, the expertise they bring to the program, and their willingness continuously to examine Ts''kel with a view constantly to improving the program have resulted in the successes experienced to date. That solid foundation, together with the quality of people remaining with the program, has an optimism for a continuation of the success of Ts''kel. Very simply, Ts''kel has been most successful and has the ingredients necessary for a continuation of that success (Downey, 1987:105-106).

To date, 15 students have attained their M.Ed. degrees and are in responsible jobs, 25 are at various phases of their programs; three have discontinued. A total of 43 candidates, three of whom are in doctoral studies,[4] have enrolled in Ts''kel. While the majority of students are from British Columbia, others are enrolled from as far east as New Brunswick, south to Guatemala, and north to the Yukon and the Northwest Territories.

First Nations House of Learning

The First Nations House of Learning proudly opened its doors in September 1987. The mandate of the House of Learning is to make the University's vast resources more accessible to the Province's First People and to improve the University's ability to meet the needs of First Nations. It is dedicated to quality preparation in all fields of post-secondary study with quality of education being determined by its relevance to the philosophy and values of First Nations.

The objectives of the First Nations House of Learning can be summarized as follows:

- to facilitate the participation of First Nations people in a wide range of study areas by providing information on post-secondary opportunities and support services;

- to expand the range and depth of program and course offerings within the faculties, schools and institutes at the University related to needs identified by First Nations people and communities in British Columbia;

- to identify and promote research that would extend the frontiers of knowledge for the benefit of First Nations (for example, legal studies of land claims and self-government, resource management, delivery of social services);

- to increase the First Nations leadership on campus;

- to establish a physical facility (longhouse) on campus to enhance access and support services for First Nations students;

- and a longer range plan to include the possibility of founding an international component for the advancement of indigenous people around the world.

The First Nations House of Learning is responsible directly to the President's Office, and is guided by a President's Advisory Committee. This committee includes representatives of the First Nations community and University faculty and students. Members have been appointed by the Vice-President (Academic) and Provost for a three-year term. Students are chosen by their peers as representatives for one-year terms. The First Nations House of Learning's five member staff is made up entirely of First Nations people.

The House of Learning is continuously seeking direction from the First Nations community in determining priorities and approaches. This is being achieved through consultation meetings and workshops held throughout the province. After a series of 10 workshops conducted in 1988, the professional needs identified by communities most often were as follows:

1. **Education:** Teachers at all levels, Teachers Aides, Principals, Directors, Counsellors, Special Education, Speech-Language Pathology, Teaching English as a Second Language, Physical Education, Recreation Directors, Curriculum Developers, Cultural Specialists,

First Nations Language Teachers, Fine Arts, Day Care, Early Childhood Educators.

2. **Health Care:** Counsellors (Family, Drug and Alcohol, Sexual Abuse), Physical Therapists, Doctors, Dentists, Nurses, Nutritionists, General Practitioners, Social Workers, X-Ray Technicians, Speech Pathology, Pharmacists, Psychologists, Psychiatrists and Indian Medicine.

3. **Natural Resource Sciences:** Fisheries, Forestry, Silviculture, Conservation, Marine Biologists, Agriculture, Aquaculture, Mining, Environmentalists and General Sciences.

4. **Commerce and Business Administration:** Administrators, Managers, Business Planners, Bookkeeping, Marketing, Accounting, Band Planners, Auditors and Economic Developers.

5. **First Nations Languages:** First Nations Language Teachers, Linguists, Curriculum Developers, Researchers and Translators (FNHL, 1988: 4).

In summary, the First Nations House of Learning is determined to ensure that the same opportunities available in education through the Native Indian Teacher Education Program and the Native Law Program for First Nations are extended to other faculties, departments and schools at the University.

The First Nations House of Learning is now addressing how these expressed needs can be fulfilled. Discussions are underway with the appropriate departments. Action is expected to take the form of making available promotional materials related to the respective areas, creating or adapting courses to reflect First Nations issues, conducting research and/or establishing support programs within various faculties.

First Nations Health Care Professions Program

This was established under the auspices of the First Nations House of Learning in 1988 in response to identified health needs. The program is designed to encourage First Nations people to enter the field of medicine or any of the health science professions. Specific goals and objectives of the Health Care Professions Program are:

- to increase accessibility and provide support service to First Nations students in Health Care studies;

- to consult with First Nations communities to identify those health care issues which should be addressed;

- to collaborate with the Faculty of Medicine and other Health Science Faculties and Schools in developing courses and seminars relevant to First Nations' health care needs;

- to liaise with First Nations communities in the development of community-based program initiatives or research activities pertinent to local health care;

- to encourage interest in health science careers at the high school level through a summer science program.

The program is guided by an Advisory Committee made up of First Nations community people with a particular interest in medicine and the health sciences, and members of the University faculty. A First Nations person coordinates the program and provides a support function, namely, academic, personal and financial counselling, tutorial assistance and mentoring.

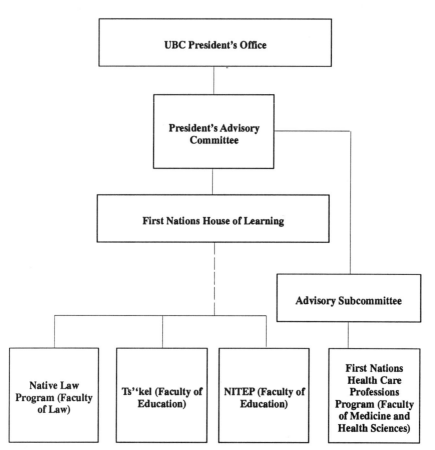

The First Nations House of Learning has a function which can relate to the whole university. While this is the case, the Native Indian Teacher Education Program, Ts''kel, the Native Law Program are autonomous programs established before the creation of the First Nations House of Learning, but which now share a collaborative relationship. The House of Learning is an important mechanism which brings a sense of cohesiveness to the separate programs and facilitates the sharing of ideas and resources.

A First Nations House of Learning longhouse-style building is in the planning stages with an anticipated completion date of November, 1992. This facility will serve to enhance access and create a more efficient support service to First Nations students. The future relationship of the First Nations House of Learning to existing First Nations programs and those yet to be created is under review.

In summary, the Native Law Program, the Ts''kel Program, the First Nations House of Learning and the Health Care Professions Program have had considerable success in terms of using NITEP as a model for programmatic change and improvements in the delivery of university education. All of the programs are growing in terms of student numbers and quality. The success can be attributed to: (1) the involvement of First Nations people, be they Advisory Committee members, staff or workshop participants; (2) the development of courses related to First Nations interests and issues; (3) the home away from home" support function; and (4) the on-going assessment of programs.

This chapter suggests that if the case of the NITEP model works for other programs established at the University of British Columbia, then the model must be transportable to other post-secondary institutions which are seriously committed to providing access to First Nations students. Indications are that prior to 1974, there were very few First Nations students at this University. Today, we estimate that 250 students are enrolled with at least 40 of these in graduate programs. While this represents an increase of nearly 150 percent from 1974, the University has a great challenge to increase its numbers of First Nations students significantly. According to the 1986 Census, people of First Nations origin comprise 4.5 percent of the population in British Columbia. If First Nations students were represented in the same proportion, there should be 1 500 First Nations students in the University of British Columbia — 6 times the present number.

Optimism prevails here that tremendous strides will be made within the next decade. With the exception of NITEP, the other programs are relatively recent developments and therefore, their impact is only at the beginning stages. The First Nations House of Learning should be the catalyst in the move to greatly increase opportunities for First Nations people at this University.

Key Factors for Success

Several key factors have made NITEP a success, a success that has been shared by subsequent programs, and which ought to be considered for application to other post-secondary institutions. These are:

1. **Advisory Committee**

   Such a committee is needed to guide the overall direction and progress of the program. It is essential that this committee be made up predominantly of the group which the program is designed to serve. This provides the valuable link required to the communities. In addition, representatives of the University and government are needed to act as liaison within and outside the university. The committee should have clearly delineated responsibility and its advice seriously considered and respected.

2. **Relevant Studies**

   Constant attention must be made to develop and adapt courses that relate to interests and concerns of the group being served. It is imperative that institutions of higher learning build on and enhance the knowledge and skills of the target group by making the subject matter relevant to the cultures of the communities in which they are likely to work.

3. **Staff**

   The role model effect is very important in these programs. The leadership function becomes evident. As well, staff familiar with the culture and practices of the group being served are best able to provide the bridge between students' lives in their communities and in the university.

4. **Support Function**

   Often students in the programs are the first generation to access the university. Negative high school and residential school experiences may place students at a disadvantage. The support required is sensitivity to the students' needs, be they counselling which may be personal, academic or financial; it may be tutoring and/or being a friend or surrogate family member.

5. **Field Centres**

   The Field Centre concept is based on providing students initial entry to university studies closer to their home communities and in smaller institutional settings. It enables field centre coordinators, who administer the centres to work closely with a small number of students (average 15) in terms of counselling, tutoring and preparation for the larger institution. An important function of the field centre is the development of group cohesion among the students which is supportive and continues when they move to the main campus.

6. **Evaluation**

   In any endeavor, it is necessary to establish long-term evaluation procedures to determine whether the goals and objectives are being met. Programs should have both internal and external evaluations, as well as by way of Think-In Workshops. A willingness to continue to improve programs is critical to success.

Conclusion

This case study reviewed the programmatic and delivery factors perceived to contribute to education of First Nations at the University of British Columbia. Other developments not mentioned in detail are: (1) the crucial institutional support and interest of the University in responding to the needs of First Nations; (2) the NITEP change from a four-year to a five-year B.Ed. program; (3) the expansion of NITEP field centres to accommodate students preparing to enter faculties other than Education; and (4) the expansion of the Ts''kel Program to include Social and Educational Studies, and Curriculum and Instruction as well as promoting the extension of studies to the doctoral level. These can be the subject of future reports.

Notes

1. The term First Nations is the most recent generic designation of Canada's original people. In this paper, terms such as Indian, Native, Native Indian, all refer to the same peoples.

2. Questions were designed by Clive Linklater, Ojibwa Consultant and Trainer.

3. Ts''kel is a Halkomelem word meaning Golden Eagle.

4. Ts''kel was expanded in 1989 to include other departments, and doctoral students.

References

Archibald, J. (1986). "Locally developed Native studies curriculum: An historical and philosophical rationale." *Mokakit Indian Education Research Association - Selected Papers*. Vancouver: University of British Columbia Press.

Barman, J., Herbert, Y. & McCaskill, D. (1987). *Indian Education in Canada: Vol. 1: The Legacy, Vol. 2: The Challenge*. Vancouver: University of British Columbia Press.

Brown, G. (1988). "Cross-cultural self-concept: The best of both worlds." *Mokakit Indian Education Research Association - Selected Papers*. Vancouver: University of British Columbia Press.

Chrisjohn, R. & Lanigan, C. (1986). "Research on Indian intelligence testing: Review and prospects." *Mokakit Indian Education Research Association - Selected Papers* Vancouver: University of British Columbia Press.

Downey, L.W. (1987). "The Story of Ts''kel." First Nations House of Learning, University of British Columbia.

Emerson, L. (1987). "Tradition, change and survival: Cognitive learning process, culture and education." *Canadian Journal of Native Education*, 14(3).

First Nations House of Learning. (1988). "Community Consultation Report for 1988," FNHL, University of British Columbia.

Hamilton, W.D. (1986). "Historical sketch of Indian education in the Maritimes." *Canadian Journal of Native Education*, 13(1).

Henry, H. & Pepper, F. (1988). "Cognitive, social and cultural effects on Indian learning style: Classroom implications." *Mokakit Indian Education Research Association - Selected Papers*. Vancouver: University of British Columbia Press.

Indian and Northern Affairs Canada, (1989).

Kirkness, V.J. (1987). "Indian education: Past, present and future." *AURORA: The Professional Journal of the Northwest Territories Teachers*, 5(1).

Kirkness, V.J. (1981). "The education of Canadian Indian children." *Child Welfare: Child Welfare League of America*, Inc., LX, 7.

Kirkness, V. & More, A. (1981). "The structure of the Native Indian teacher education program and Indianness." Paper presented at the AERA Conference, Los Angeles, California.

McEachern, W. & Kirkness, V. (1987). "Teacher education for Aboriginal groups: One model and suggested application." *Journal of Education for Teaching*, 13(2).

National Indian Brotherhood, (1973). Indian Control of Indian Education, Assembly of First Nations, Ottawa.

Pepper, F. C. (1988). "Summative evaluation findings of NITEP, UBC."

A Proposal for a NITEP Program, (1974). University of British Columbia.

Education in a Pluralistic Society: Proposal for an Enrichment of Teacher Education

Fernand Ouellet

During the last 10 years or so, there have been more and more insistent demands that the Quebec education system give serious consideration to the question of pluralism. It is around the catchword of "intercultural education" that pedagogical initiatives have tried to take into account the growing pluralism of the school population, specially in the Montreal area. With the decline of the birth rate and the promulgation of Bill 101 making French compulsory in school for the children of immigrants, the question of integration of immigrants to Quebec society has become a major political issue in Quebec, and intercultural education is now one of the priorities of the Quebec government.

But the relevance of the question of pluralism for education in Quebec does not depend only on the sociological reality of cultural pluralism in the Montreal area. Its main source is the general evolution of Quebec society which in a few decades has gone from the ideological monolithism of a traditional rural society to the scattered pluralism of a post-industrial society. This passage from a society characterized by what at the beginning of the 60s, Jean Lesage called "la possession tranquille de la vérité" — "quiet possession of truth"[1] to a society where many systems of global conviction co-exist in the same social space has been experienced by many people as "un effondrement du ciel québécois" — "a collapse of Quebec sky."

In this situation, the school and the teachers had to face new educational challenges. Already in 1968, Fernand Dumont had put forward a promising approach to face these challenges. A synthetic summary of this proposal has been published in the *Rapport du comité d'étude sur la formation et le perfectionnement des enseignants* de la Commission d'étude sur les universités:[2]

> The first part of this suggestion deals with the student who should become "a critique and an heir." A pluralist society is already full of "critics." But real critics are scarcer. To be a critic means to be able to discern temporary fads from true seeds of the future, penetrate through the scrubs of heterogeneous information to find essential data, explore a variety of opinions before

taking an option, not to renounce one's freedom when adopting an ideology, accept results only after having examined the procedures leading to them.

On the other hand, in order that the student becomes an heir, one does not have to transmit to him the organized heritage of ancient times, but to communicate the art of critically recuperating the values of the past and to give him back "the sense of genesis."

The second part of the proposal deals with the school. In a society where a culture which would have simply to be translated to the students by the educators does not exist any more, the school must put the stress on creativity. It must become a "laboratory of culture." Such a mutation would transform the school in a primordial factor of cultural and social development, an essential means of reintegration of a fragmented surrounding culture.

The third part of this suggestion deals with the role of the teacher "integrator and initiator of a culture in gestation." This implies that the teacher has a vast and complex role; he tries to make possible the experiences of the student critic and heir. That supposes also that the teacher has himself been initiated into the problems of contemporary culture, to the main directions of its past evolution, to the processes through which it redefines itself (1979:15).

This proposal has not lost its relevance after 20 years, if we include among the "values of the past," which the student should learn to recuperate in a critical way, the totality of the values shared by the inhabitants of the Quebec territory and not only those of the French Catholic majority.

To define the role of the teacher as an "integrator and an initiator of culture in gestation" is to propose a challenge of a peculiar actuality in the present context where the dynamics of interethnic relations has become an important preoccupation for all those who are concerned for the future of Quebec as a distinct society in Canada and North America. The question I would like to explore briefly here is the following: how can those responsible for the formation and further training of teachers prepare them to face that challenge not only in those laboratories of culture which are in all evidence the multi-ethnic schools but also in those schools where ethnic plurality is not part of the early experience of students? More specifically, what are the main sectors where it would be possible to enrich the training of teachers so that they be better prepared to face the challenges of pluralism?

I will present here only general orientations in the light of a definition of intercultural education in which I try to define the main components of the basic training essential to make the teacher aware of the complexity of problems raised by pluralism in education:

The concept of intercultural education refers to any systematic pedagogical effort to develop among members of majority and minority groups:

a) a better understanding of the situation of culture in modern societies;

b) a better capacity to communicate with persons belonging to other cultures;

c) attitudes more adapted to the context of cultural and group diversity in a given society, through a better understanding of psychosocial mechanisms and socio-political factors likely to generate heterophoby and racism;

d) and a better capacity to participate in social interaction, creative of identities and of common humanity (Ouellet, 1991).

In the light of this definition, it is possible to identify five main fields of knowledge whose systematic exploration would enrich the content of teachers' training:

• the fate of culture in the modern world;

• risks of conflict in pluralistic societies, racism and anti-racism;

• intercultural communication and its pedagogical implications;

• intercultural education and equality of chances in education;

• intercultural education and global education.

It is around these five themes that I have analyzed systematically some recent publications dealing with intercultural education in my recent book (Ouellet, 1991). In the first four chapters, I have tried to identify and summarize some publications which could be used to strengthen the scientific content of teachers' training for intercultural education and to go beyond what Todorov (1986:7) calls the "la banalisation paralysante des bons sentiments" — "the paralysing banality of good sentiments." The last chapter raises the problem of intercultural education in mono-ethnic schools and suggests a close collaboration of the promoters of intercultural education and the educators involved in development education or global education.

I will present here a brief summary of each of these chapters and conclude with some reflections on an in-service teachers training formula providing the teachers with the opportunity to combine these theoretical analysis with opportunities of exploring a cultural tradition different from their own and of experimentating projects of intercultural education.

The conception of intercultural education which will be outlined here is based on five main options:

1. Option for an education where the critical exploration of the main issues related to life in a pluralistic society is an integral part of the

    curriculum for **all** students, whether they belong to minority or majority groups.

2. Options for an education where the students from minority groups are not forced to abandon their mother tongue and where bilingualism is perceived as an asset rather than a handicap.

3. Option for an education where the family culture of the child, whether he or she comes from a minority or a majority group, is not the object of denial or devaluation when he or she comes to school.

4. Option for an education where concrete measures are taken to make sure that students from minority groups get an academic success rate comparable to those from majority groups.

5. Option for an education reflecting a model of pluralistic integration which favors interactions between members of all groups so that they may participate actively in the creation of an open and dynamic society.

The Fate of "Ethnic Culture" in the "Cultural Matrix" of Modernity

I have had the luck to know from the inside Quebec *"pure laine"* — "pure wool" ethnic culture in a small village of Lower St. Laurence where I was born at the beginning of the 40s. In that culture there was still, in rural context, at least, a relative homogeneity of the world view. Roman Catholicism occupied a central place and social roles were well defined. However, the social transformations brought by the Second Great War, rapid urbanization in particular, had already begun to change all this. It was not evident that the instructions for the use of life transmitted by tradition would be adequate for the years to come. When I started my *"cours classique,"* in 1952, instead of working on my father's farm, I was not yet aware of the fact that I was beginning an experience of migration in my own country, an experience of integration into a new culture, the "culture of modernity."

It is only later, after long periods of inner struggle that I have understood what had happened. I have found in the writing of my colleague Jean-Jacques Simard, a sociologist at Laval University, very enlightening analysis which have helped me to understand this more or less forced convergence of my Quebec ethnic culture with the culture of modernity. His distinction between "ethnic culture" and "cultural matrix" is particularly useful to make sense what happens to culture in today's society. He defines a "cultural matrix" as a way of producing culture, as a mode of material and symbolic appropriation of the world.[3] According to him, what is generally referred to as the "Western culture" is not a particular ethnic culture but a cultural matrix, the matrix of modernity. In order to make clear what he means, he proposes, as illustration, a tentative typology of the two main cultural matrices which have been superseded by the matrix of modernity:

The matrix of the hunters-gatherers where nomadic bands lived off hunting, fishing and wild plants on immense territories supporting small populations and inhabited by "spirits." He suggests to speak of a "first" or of a "primitive" matrix to refer to this first mode of material and symbolic appropriation of the world.

The matrix of the cities-states whose emergence has been made possible by the surplus generated by the introduction of agriculture. Whereas in nomadic bands, the social relations where egalitarian and the political decisions were taken by consensus, we now observe a specialization by crafts and by functions and social relations have become hierachized. This hierarchy is also visible in the supernatural world inhabited by gods whose functions are also specialized. This second cultural matrix can be referred to as "archaic" to distinguish it from the first.

The validity of certain aspects of the typology could be questioned, but it has the advantage of making clear some basic differences in the mode of production of culture in each of these two matrices of which we can still find traces in the matrix of modernity. And this last matrix possesses itself very specific characteristics. The apparition of market in European merchant cities at the end of the Middle Age marks the apparition of a new mode of social relations which escape completely the control of civil and religious authority. In its emerging capitalist shape, the market is *"du social qui fonctionne tout seul"* by cybernetic retroaction. According to Simard,[4] it is essentially by its cybernetic character that the new cultural matrix is different from the precedent.

After the economic realms, the political has begun to function in this manner with the apparition of democracy: then, progressively, all the spheres of social life have been invaded by this "virus." Fashion as a mechanism of auto-regulation of individual choices and preferences, science as a mode of production of knowledge through a constant auto-critique based on the judgment of the peers are two important manifestations of this matrix of modernity. Simard suggests that even the way individuals construct their identity in what Christopher Lasch (1979) calls the "culture of narcissism" can be understood in the framework of this process of cybernetization of social life. We live in the "era of emptiness" (Lipovesky, 1983). There are no more transcendent values in relation to which an individual could orient their life as if they were directed by a gyroscope. Today, it is as if they were equipped with a radar transmitting data to a control centre which constantly readjusts the individual trajectory in response to changes in the environment.

Simard is referring here not to particular cultures, to ethnic cultures, but to a specific mode of fabrication of culture, to a cultural matrix which transcends all cultures and carries them in its movement. Because it functions through auto-critique and continuous destruction and reconstruction of the particular cultures, the new matrix produces profound modifications in the connection of individuals with their particular culture, their "endemic culture" to use the term he has coined to distinguish anthropological culture from the matrix of modernity which constitutes a new "epidemic" culture. Because they live in a world in constant transformation, individuals cannot any more find completely in tradition, in the heritage provided by endemic culture, the "direction for the use of life." Endemic culture is like a dictionary where pages are missing. Simard uses the image of *"culture ébréchée"* — "notched culture" to allude to the situation of particular cultures in the matrix of modernity. There is now a sphere of indetermination in the life of individuals. The meaning of the world is not given anymore but must be constructed in "projects" by individuals and groups. Whereas in the two preceding matrixes, men lived in a world marked by the "wisdom of certitude" where tradition was an undisputed reference to define the meaning of life and to find solution to the various problems of existence, we live now in a world marked by the "wisdom of incertitude" and by reflexivity. Endemic and epidemic cultures appear then as two horizons, whose limits are always fleeing, in relation to which individuals and groups have to situate themselves and to define their identity. According to Simard, and I fully agree with him on this, it is impossible to escape this inner tension between endemic and epidemic culture. At various degrees, this situation appears to me to be the same for all peoples of the planet. Everywhere, it is possible to find traces of a nostalgia of *"culture pleine"* — "plump culture." This nostalgia is itself a manifestation of the tension generated by this forced convergence of ethnic cultures and of the culture of modernity.

This analysis provides a general framework for a critical treatment of two problems which inevitably arise when one tries to give a specific content to intercultural education: the problem of conflicting ideologies and the problem of relativism.

The debates on the opportunity of introducing an intercultural perspective in education reflect a great diversity of ideological options underlying the position of those who support or reject the introduction by the State of specific measures to take into account the cultural diversity in education. This diversity can be reduced to four main options:

- **The mono-cultural option**: the State has the responsibility to socialize all citizens to the "national culture" in which members of all ethnic groups must melt, abandoning their ethnic specificity.

- **The multicultural option**: the State has the responsibility of helping all ethnic groups to preserve their language and their cultural heritage.

- **The intercultural option**: The State must take measures to enhance harmonious relations between the various ethnic groups by increasing the opportunities of exchange and collaboration between members of these groups.

- **The transcultural option**: The State must encourage the members of the various ethnic groups to go beyond the borders of their group and to face with creativity and dynamism the new challenges raised by the acceleration of change in world economy.

These four options rarely appear in a pure shape. Generally, we are in the presence of a mix of two or three options with an accentuation on one of them. In the light of the preceding discussion, I believe that the transcultural option is the one which should be stressed. In the context of the modern cultural matrix, intercultural education should not consist in the development of new programs or of a new "specialty" in the educational system, itself an instrument of the propagation of the cybernetic matrix; it should rather help the student to participate in the elaboration of the cultural field which will be theirs in this matrix. This cultural field will necessarily be located at the intersection of the two horizons referred to earlier, that of endemic culture and that of epidemic culture. This cultural field is not given but to be constructed in projects, individual and collective, through which everyone will be able to participate with others in the creation of a meaningful world.

The general framework alluded to here makes it possible for educators to accept one of the main contributions of anthropology, the recognition of the relativity of all cultures, without sinking into the quicksand of a cultural relativism which encloses people in their cultures and prohibits any judgment on foreign cultural manifestations.

It is often postulated that the characteristics which Simard attributes to the matrix of modernity belong intrinsically to "Western culture." According to him, this mistake blocks completely the possibility to understand what is really happening on the planet today. It leads to the accusation that Western or "White" culture is responsible for all the evils which affect other cultures around the world today. This is to forget, as Simard (1988:45-55) has shown at length, that Western cultures have been the first victims of all these evils because they have been the first vectors of the matrix of modernity.

Does the distinction established by Simard between particular cultures and cultural matrix make it possible to formulate non-ethnocentric judgments on foreign cultural manifestations? This is still a controversial issue, but Simard (1988a) claims with eloquence that such judgment are not only possible but inescapable in the matrix of modernity:[5]

> Let us suppose that history had, by unforeseeable and unnecessary mutation, given rise to a cultural matrix whose specific field be the planet of Men. That it had constituted the whole world as a network of cultural interaction. That this matrix had invented a concept to define its members, "the human species," leaving behind only animals and rocks and beyond only "**extraterrestrials.**" Then, it would have had to appropriate all the different manners of belonging to its cultural field and to invent for this the word **culture** with a way of **explaining** how no one belonging to the human species can be excluded as "**earth monkey**" or "**louse egg**"* and it would have called this way of seeing: anthropological. At the same time and of necessity it would have imposed upon all men and women (since its specific field includes all of them), the **normative** right and duty of participating in the formulation of what distinguishes **all humanity** from the rest of the cosmos, and of defining all that must be considered desirable, good, human — because, of course, it believes that only the animals called **homo sapiens** (according to its own categories), are able to define themselves and to make clear their reasons for living and the meaning of their world. In that this cultural matrix is not different from those which came before; it claims to embrace the whole universe except that its imaginary universe reduces all animals capable of symbolism, that is capable of giving reasons why life is worth living, to one single category.

> In other words, **epistemological** relativism, the only means of explaining differences between humans once it has been admitted that they all belong to the same species, calls up the **moral** duty of defining **normatively** the horizon of common humanity. Each human being can (and must) then make a moral judgement on any particular cultural feature, at whatever place or time it might have appeared. During my lifetime, I must **understand**, but I cannot **accept** that money, power and science provide reasons for living sufficient for me or that I can teach to my children. I will also understand that circumcisions practiced on girls might have a meaning but I will maintain that it no **longer** has any meaning (1988a:98-99).

---

*"Most of the peoples we call primite designate themselves with a name which means the true, the good, the excellent or simply the men; and they apply to others qualificatives which deny them the human condition, like ground monkey or louse egg" (C. Levi-Strauss quoted in Bouchard, 1987:20).

In this perspective, when general Namphy claimed that in the name of respect for Haitian culture Duvalierism must be re-established in Haiti, it was not necessary to be born in that country to have the right and even the duty to reject this call for cultural community.

Camilleri (1988:565-592) brings very important precisions on the way the teachers must face this difficult problem of relativism. According to him the perspective of cultural anthropology contributes to the elimination of a major obstacle to intercultural education: the natural tendency of students to establish a hierarchy among the various cultural manifestations. However, in its pedagogical applications, the relativist perspective of a "romantic" version of cultures makes the teacher hesitant and anxious concerning what he can teach to students whose culture is defined as radically different from his own.

Camilleri sees there is an abusive application of the principle of cultural relativism, an application which does not take into account the fact that this principle establishes a point of view which permits one to be go beyond cultural differences and to **formulate judgments on them**, but in another way and according to other criteria than those which were used before. An option for cultural relativism is an option for the **values which establish the conditions for the co-existence of divergent cultural values**:[6]

> So it appears that relativism entails the relativization of all values **except of those on which it is based** and that it does not lead to the suppression of all normativity but to the establishment of a new, more dialectical, normative field: the insaturation of the minimum of norms necessary for the advent and the coexistence of the greatest possible diversity of norms (1988a:20).

In this view, there exists a superior standpoint from which individuals can formulate judgments on cultural manifestations whether in their own culture or in a foreign culture. And "when these individuals or a group accept the foundation values of this standpoint, they recognize values whose non-respect makes **impossible this relativism itself which gives legitimacy to their culture**" (1988a:20):[7]

> In other words, relativism can be rejected: it does not claim to be imperative as one of the evidences classical rationalism was so fond of. But if we reject it, we put ourselves in the position of going back to the ancient state of affairs: war, at least potential war of cultural systems each of which considers itself as the best hierarchizations imposed by the strongest group and a return of heteronomy (1988a:20).

Through his insistence on the foundation values of cultural relativism and on the consequences of the rejection of those values, Camilleri contributes to the diminution of the malaise which could grasp the relativist teacher for whom this respect of other cultures is incompatible with the fact of formulating judgment on some of their manifestations. By bringing back, as he does, culture in the realm of profane things, and by insisting on the fact that anthropological culture is only one element of the construction of identity by individuals and groups, he opens the way to a pedagogy capable not only of taking into account the cultural parameter but also of focusing "deliberately on diversity of cultures" so that then may become, "through their relations suitably regulated, a mean for a certain type of formation of man considered advantageous" (1988:565).

It is from this definition of intercultural pedagogy that Camilleri makes very specific suggestions on the way teachers should deal with culture in the classroom. His suggestions can be summarized in seven statements:

- insist on the similarities between cultures and on the constant evolution of cultures through borrowings and exchanges;

- illustrate the relativity of differences through a description of the situation where they have appeared with the help of a functionalist approach;

- show that cultures do not belong to the realm of the sacred and that they can be analyzed rationally;

- try to identify the "cultural formula" of individual rather than define their *"culture d'origine"* — "heritage culture";

- analyze the relations between the groups which produce culture rather the relations between cultures;

- distinguish anthropological culture from "promotional" culture. In the matrix of modernity, scientific knowledge is one of the important manifestations of this promotional culture. Cultural relativism does not apply to this corpus of knowledge which is not exclusively "western" but which has distinguished itself in the Western world by its extreme systematization formalization and extension; and

- fight against all that limits access to that knowledge and create in relation to it inequalities which cannot be reduced to diversity.

These statements like Simard's analysis suggests that it is not possible to consider school as an instrument for the promotion of the values of a particular ethnic culture, whether it be the culture of the majority or of the minorities. Of course, schools cannot help reflect the endemic culture of its social milieu, but in so far as it defines itself as "public," its intrinsic mission is not the promotion of particular cultures but to prepare the future citizens to live in a world where particular cultures do not provide completely the directions for the use of life. Then, in the context of the matrix of modernity, "good education" must help students to go beyond the borders of their particular culture to build with others a meaningful world. Today, good education must be transcultural.

The previous analysis provides orientations for an approach of culture which would not be alienating for individuals and collectivities. In the light of these analyses, any conception of intercultural education which makes conspicuous particular groups of students and eventually marginalizes them because of cultural characteristics, must be rejected as inadequate. One of the main tasks of intercultural education is to legitimize in the eyes of all citizens the presence of members of diverse cultures in a pluralist society. (See Banks in this volume). It is difficult to see how it could accomplish this task if it did not rely on a critical conception of culture like the one which has been sketched here. If the school is to be able to approach the treatment of cultural differences without either exaggerating the place of culture in the life of individuals or underestimating it, a critical analysis of the fate of culture in the modern world must be an important component of teachers' training. To use the lapidary formulation of Camilleri (1988:24). "In general, spreading everywhere scientific teaching on socio-cultural systems should be considered as a serious undertaking."

In the light of these theoretical considerations, it is now possible to outline a conception of intercultural education which goes beyond that which is held by many of the promoters of this relatively new educative movement. Many authors (Dasen, 1989; Cohen-Emerique, 1989; McAll, 1989) insist on the necessity for any person who wants to get training in this field to develop a greater capacity of decentration in relation to his or her own cultural schemes as well as the attitudes and skills necessary to enter with empathy inside the world of representations of members of other cultures. This is, I believe, an important task upon which I have myself insisted in previous articles (Ouellet, 1984 ; 1985). But a training which would be limited to the accomplishment of this task would be incomplete and would run the risk of generating among educators the feeling of hesitation and perplexity which has well been described by Kleinfield (1975) and Camilleri (1988). Then, it is very important that any training program for intercultural education should include a component of critical reflection on culture and cultural relativism along the perspective which has been outlined by Simard and Camilleri.

Finally, it is important to insist on the fact that, in the theoretical perspective which has been alluded to here, the primary aim of intercultural education is the development not so much of an "understanding of other cultures" as an understanding of the dynamics of cultures in today's societies. Whether this understanding supposes or not the exploration of at least one cultural tradition different from one's own is an open question. I, for one, believe that such an exploration constitutes a privileged means to create the distantiation and decentration without which a true specific approach of culture is impossible. This exploration must, however, go beyond culturalism and give sufficient importance to the socio-politic dynamics with which the cultural variables constantly interact.

Risks of Conflict in Pluralistic Societies.
Racism and Anti-Racism

Training for intercultural education does not rely on a solid basis if it takes its inspiration in an idealized conception of culture or in a culturalism which attributes to culture an exaggerated importance in view of its effective influence in the life of individuals. It is also with a good measure of realism that a second field of knowledge — whose relevance for intercultural education is evident — should be approached: the field of intergroups, interethnic and interracial conflicts. The educators must be trained to use in a critical way the numerous scientific and non-scientific writings on those topics. It is possible to identify three main types of factors likely to generate intergroup conflicts:

- Factors relating to economic and politic competition for "scarce resources" and the favors of the State;

- Factors which, in the light of recent researches on social categorization and categorial differentiation, appear related to the very dynamics of intergroup encounters; and

- Symbolic factors relating to the dynamics of identity construction.

I will limit myself here, because of lack of space, to illustrate the third type of factor through a striking analysis by Bernard Lorreyte of the rise of xenophobia toward immigrants from Maghreb in France. According to him, this phenomena is related for an important part to the disarray of classes socially disqualified having to face rapid changes in French society. The immigrants are "ambiguous minors" which return to members of those disqualified classes the image of their situation for exclusion. And, it is to try to take some distance, in the imaginary realm at least, from this intolerable situation that those who belong to these social classes need to stress their differences from the immigrants. The tendency to attribute an exaggerated importance to cultural difference originates from there.

According to Lorreyte, the main root of xeonophobia does not lie in specific features of the culture of immigrants, but, in the process of identity construction itself. In order to fight against this kind of xenophobia which is not limited to France, it is not enough to "open oneself to the other" and to try to know his culture. Instead, Lorreyte puts forward a pedagogy of "deconstruction" where the accent is no more on the culture of immigrants but on an analysis of French society.

This analysis of the symbolic factors related to the dynamics of identity construction should be an important component of teacher training in a pluralistic society. Combined with a study of the first two factors which have been identified here, it would provide a general framework for an interpretation of ever new forms of hetherophobia and of racism which arise in our societies. Moreover, racist and anti-racist ideologies should be the object of an extensive study in teachers' training programs.

Cummins (1988:138) identified four main areas where teachers can contribute to the reduction of institutional racism[8] which has a very negative impact on the education of minority students:

- The incorporation of minority languages and cultures into the school program;

- The participation of parents from minority groups in the education of their children;

- The elaboration of a pedagogy which favors an active participation of children;

- The application of a policy of evaluation which locates the minority children's problems in the school structures rather than in the children.

A teacher's training program for intercultural education should provide a serious initiation to researchers and successful experiences in each of these four areas. Moreover, in this struggle against institutional racism, it is important that some educational interventions provide all students, including those of majority groups, with the opportunity of a critical analysis of various forms of institutional racism. The manual developed in Ontario by Simon and others (1988) for "decoding discrimination" through the analysis of films constitutes a very interesting example of what can be done in this area.

Intercultural Communication and its Pedagogical Applications

Intercultural communication constitutes a third field where there exists an important scientific and pedagogic literature. This literature, whose major part is American, has an essentially practical orientation. It tries to answer to the needs of Americans who must work or do business abroad. These researchers insist on the importance of identifying differences in cultural schemes, traditional behavior, cultural postulates, values, cognitive models and communication styles. If one is not conscious of these differences, they could block communication conceived as the transmission of a message by a source to a receptor.

In the light of recent research which develops a conception of communication as a common realization by two or more partners (Ghiglione, 1986), one can question the relevance of all this literature for teachers' training in intercultural education. Moreover, many authors in this school of research tend to attribute a central place to cultural factors in the analysis of communications problems between persons of different cultures. I do not deny that these factors might be important in certain situations, but it seems dangerous, in the light of what we have said in the previous sections, to make of them the main issue in intercultural relations. This literature on intercultural communication cannot then be used without a serious critical examination. This critique is all the more necessary since the practical applications of these works generally take the shape of brief sessions where there is never enough time to explore seriously the more complex questions which have been alluded to here and which, according to me, constitutes the core of a teachers' training program in intercultural education.

Francoise Henry Lorcerie (1983) suggests an approach which appears much more relevant for teachers' training. In light of the research by Watzlawick and his collaborators, Lorcerie presents a conception of communication which implies a mobilization of the identity of the partners and not only on the transmission of a message. In all relations with others, everyone puts forward a self-definition to which the other can react by three types of comportments: confirmation, rejection or denial. According to her, in France, school culture is dominated by an attitude of denial of the child's family culture, combined in the case of immigrant children with a denial of their immigrant culture. According to her, a genuine intercultural education is not possible unless this denial is replaced by a confirmation of the family culture of the student. This supposes a pedagogical revolution where a pedagogy of denial is replaced by a *"pédagogie différenciée"* — "pedagogy of differentiation." An intercultural pedagogy which does not rely on such a pedagogy of differentiation is according to Henry-Lorcerie an aberration which must be denounced.

One of the difficulties encountered by those who train teachers for intercultural education is to find a middle path between the denial of cultural differences and their celebration which can lead either to their sacralization or to their folkloric banalization. This path appears to me to consist of the "recognition of differences," cultural and others, which the students who come to the public school bring with them and in the mobilization of all these students on an educative project where all these differences are transcended without being denied. If this is taken into account, the abundant literature on intercultural communication can bring a useful contribution to a pedagogy of differentiation where cultural differences are recognized and brought to contribute in the pedagogical relation. The pedagogy of complex instruction presented by Cohen in this volume constitutes a fascinating example of this type of pedagogy.

Intercultural Education and Equality of Chances in Education

The ultimate test of the validity of any initiative in intercultural education is doubtless its contribution to the promotion of equality of opportunities in education. Two main types of obstacles to equality of chances in education for students belonging to minority cultural groups are:

- The negative evaluation by the school system of the tongues of minority students and the denial of their cultures;

- The marginalization of those students through educational interventions focusing on their cultural "differences."

According to many critics of intercultural education (Shutnabb-Kansgas & Cummins, 1988) one of the main shortcomings of this liberal progressive educational movement lies in its ambiguity and its lack of serious concern for the mother tongues of minority students. According to these radical critics, intercultural education cannot contribute to promoting equality of chances for minority students unless it challenges "linguicism," that ideology which "is used to legitimate, effectuate and reproduce an unequal division of power and resources (both material and non-material) between groups which are defined on the basis of language" (Shutnabb-Kangas, 1988:13).

According to this school of research, bilingualism should replace monolingualism as the norm of educative policy in pluralinguist democratic countries. The pedagogy of "complex instruction" developed by Cohen (1989) provides a very flexible formula to face the complex practical problems which would be raised if this revolution in educational policy were to be implemented in schools.

A second area where many initiatives in intercultural education have been rightly criticized is that by focusing too much on cultural differences it has often led to a greater marginalization of minority students. In her devastating critique of the first French experiments in intercultural education, Henry-Lorcerie (1971) has shown the "perverse effects" of these initiatives which had no real impact on the immigrant culture of the students and which often lead to an accentuation of the characteristic of "stranger" to immigrant students. And, she rightly judges very severely these initiatives which had very little chance of promoting equality of opportunity for these students.

An American black scholar (Steele, 1989) reaches similar conclusions after trying to explain the recent manifestations of racism in many American colleges and universities. He finds these phenomena all the more surprising because until very recently, universities and colleges had been oases of liberalism in a society where racial discrimination was omnipresent. According to him this situation is not without relations to the "generous" measures taken by universities and colleges to respond to the specific problems of black people:

> A pattern of demand and concession develops in which each side uses the other to escape itself. Black studies departments, black deans of student affairs, black counseling programs, Afro houses, black theme houses, black homecoming dances and graduation ceremonies — black students and white administrators have slowly engineered a machinery of separatism that, in the name of sacred difference, redraws the ugly lines of segregation (1989:55).

These initiatives take place in what Steele calls a "politics of difference" which the Black Power movement has largely contributed to establish by making "blackness itself an object of celebration and allegiance" (1989:52). These politics of difference create a climate unsuitable for the mobilization required for an accession of American blacks to a genuine equality of chance, and create a climate which makes inevitable racial tensions on the campuses:

> This elevation of difference undermines the communal impulse by making each group foreign and inaccessible to others. When difference is celebrated rather than remarked, people must think in terms of difference, they must find meaning difference, and this meaning comes from an endless process of contrasting one's group with other groups. Blacks use whites to define themselves as different, women use men, Hispanics use whites and blacks, and on it goes. And in the process each group mythologizes and mystifies its difference, puts it beyond the full comprehension of outsiders. Difference becomes an inaccessible preciousness toward which outsiders are expected to be simply and uncomprehendingly reverential. But beware: In this world, even the insulated world of the college campus, preciousness is a balloon asking for a needle. At Smith College, graffiti appears: "Niggers, Spics, and Chinks quit complaining or get out" (1989:53).

According to Steele, there is only one way out of this dead end — put an end to the politics of difference and dismantle the separatist machinery which flows from it:

> I think universities should emphasize **commonality** as a higher value than "diversity" and "pluralism"- buzzwords for the **politics of difference**. Difference that does not rest on a clearly delineated foundation of commonality not only is inaccessible to those who are not part of the ethnic or racial group but is **antagonistic to them**. Difference can enrich only **the common ground** (1989:55).

This suggestion converges with the previous analysis on the fate of culture in the modern world and on the risks of conflicts in intergroup relations. It provides a vivid illustration of the dangers which had been identified there. These are very real dangers and a training for intercultural education which does not take them seriously would be irresponsible.

Intercultural Education and Global Education

The link of global education with our definition of intercultural education is not as clear as in the case of the four previous themes. Indeed, most initiatives referred to an intercultural education almost exclusively as the "problems" of immigrants seen from a "national" perspective. The educators who want to initiate their students into international issues are considered to do "peace education," "development education" or "international education." The concept of "global education" is also used to refer to this educative field which appears clearly distinct from the field of intercultural education.

This distinction between the two fields is no doubt relevant at the level of curriculum organization or of pedagogical practice. However, when we deal with the theoretical questions relevant for teachers' training, this cutting out appears much less useful. Most of the themes discussed here would be relevant for the educator concerned with the promotion of international education. Conversely, the insistence of those who promote intercultural education on the economic and political dimensions of relations between nations (Ouellet, 1988:377-402) could certainly enrich the content of intercultural education and reduce its idealistic and utopian character. There could be it seems a natural complementarity of many elements which could include in a training program preparing educators to work efficiently and creatively in these two fields. This complementarity is very well illustrated in the model developed by Bennett in this volume.

A close articulation of training programs in intercultural and international education would have another advantage: it would provide a lever for initiatives of intercultural education in culturally homogeneous schools where cultural diversity is not an element of the immediate educative environment. Global education could be a good starting point for educators working in this type of school if they wish to start a reflection on the evolution of their society which receives more and more immigrants coming from "developing" countries.

Global education should also be a priority in multi-ethnic schools. A reflection on the conditions of life and the development problems in developing countries and on the interdependence of poor and rich countries would help all students understand the demographic and social transformations of their society in the larger context of world economy and of the political relations between nations.

It must be recognized however that intercultural and global education constitute two distinct educational fields and that enrichment of one would not lead to the fulfilment of the objectives of the other. We are rather in the presence of two related and complementary fields which would benefit from concentration both in teachers' training and in initiatives aiming at an enrichment of school programs and the realization of special projects.

Conclusion

According to Bikhu Parekh (1986), in modern pluralistic societies an education which would not be intercultural would simply not be a "good education." I agree with this affirmation if intercultural education is defined in a way which takes into account the five themes which have been briefly examined here. A systematic exploration of these themes would contribute toward a more specific content on the notion of intercultural education and would help educators to find their way between the various conflicting ideologies which clash on many points in relation with each of these themes.

However, training for intercultural education does not need only solid theoretical basis. In education, it is not enough to learn to manipulate abstract concepts. Conceptual analysis must be grounded in an experience. It seems to me that one of the most efficient means to help educators in their acquisition of a formation which will help them to be "integrators and initiators of culture in gestation" in the pluralistic society of today and tomorrow is to invite them to explore systematically a cultural tradition different from their own and to have regular contacts with members of this cultural tradition both in their own society and in the country of origin. If this experience is supported by a serious effort to understand the multiple facets of that culture and to analyze the specific modalities of its articulations with the cultural matrix of modernity, it will very likely help the teachers to approach with sensibility and nuance the difficult task of forming *"des héritiers critiques"* — "critical heirs" able to work together, whatever their ethnic origins, to the construction of a human and dynamic society.

Lastly, theory and experience could be combined in the realization of projects to enrich the content of school programs and to improve the quality of life in the school. If schools and colleges are to be "laboratories of culture" where experimentation of various formula for program enrichment and of positive interactions between students belonging to different ethnic groups are seriously undertaken, it will be important to create networks of teachers and scholars of various disciplines working together to improve practice in the light of theory and to stimulate theory out of the problems raised by practice.

It is this complex interaction of theory, experience and experimentation which appears to me as the most promising formula in order that the proposal brought forward twenty years ago by Fernand Dumont might take shape in an action program through which the educative institution will be able to face, in a dynamic and creative way, one of the most important challenges which our society will have to face during the next decade: the challenge of pluralism.

Notes

1. Translations from French by Fernand Ouellet.

2. *Le premier volet de cette suggestion concerne l'élève dont il faut faire "un critique et un héritier." Une société pluraliste est déjà remplie de "critiqueux," constate Dumont. Mais les critiques sont plus rares. Etre critique signifie pouvoir discerner entre les modes temporaires et les vraies prémisses de l'avenir, écarter les broussailles des informations hétéroclites pour retrouver les données essentielles, faire dialoguer les opinions avant de prendre partie, ne pas renoncer à sa liberté quand on épouse une idéologie, n'admettre des résultats qu'après avoir examiné les démarches qui y ont conduit.*

   Quand à faire de l'élève un héritier, cela ne consiste pas à lui transmettre l'héritage organisé des temps anciens, mais à lui communiquer l'art de récupérer d'une façon critique les valeurs du passé et à lui "redonner le sens des genèses."

   Le deuxième volet de la conception proposée concerne l'école. Dans une société ou n'existe plus une culture que le milieu scolaire n'aurait qu'à traduire pour les enfants, l'école doit se faire créatrice. Elle doit devenir "laboratoire de culture." Une telle mutation ferait de l'école un facteur primordial de développement social et culturel, un moyen essentiel de réintégration de la culture ambiante morcelée.

   Le troisième volet de cette suggestion concerne le rôle du maître "intégrateur et initiateur de culture en gestation." Cela implique que l'enseignant a un rôle vaste et complexe: il tente de rendre possible les expériences d'apprentissage de l'élève critique et héritier. Cela suppose aussi que l'enseignant soit lui-même *initié aux problèmes que pose la culture actuelle, aux lignes de force de son évolution passée, aux processus par lesquel elle se redéfinit (1979:15).*

3. *"J'entends par matrice de civilisation un mode génral de production de la société par elle-même, conjuguant dialectiquement dans une structure d'ensemble un mode d'appropriation instrumentale et un mode d'appropriation symbolique du monde, par l'intermédiaire de rapports sociaux déterminés de coopération et de communication." (Simard, 1988: 51).*

   "I define a matrix of civilization as a general mode of autoproduction of society, combining dialectically in a global structure a mode of instrumental appropriation and a mode of symbolic appropriation of the world, through social relations marked by cooperation and communication" (Simard, 1988:51).

4. Conference given at the University of Sherbrooke in August 1988.

5. *Supposons que l'histoire ait, par mutation imprévisible et non seulement nécessaire, donné naissance à une matrice culturelle dont l'aire spécifique soit la planète des Hommes. Qu'elle ait constitué le monte entier en tant que circuit d'interaction culturelle. Que cette matrice ait inventé un concept pour définir ses membres, "l'espèce humaine," n'excluant, derrière elle, que les animaux, les arbres et les roches et, au-dela d'elle, que les extra-terrestres. Alors, elle aurait dû s'approprier toutes les manières différentes d'appartenir à son aire culturelle, et inventer pour cela le mot* **culture** *avec une manière d'***expliquer** *comment personne de l'espèce humaine ne peut en être exclue au titre de "singe de terre" ou d'oeuf de pou"; et elle eût imposé à tous les homme (puisque son aire spécifique les englobe tous et toutes), le droit et le devoir* **normatifs** *de participer à la formulation de ce qui distingue* **toute l'humanité** *du reste du cosmos, et de définir tout ce qu'elle doit considéror comme souhaitable, bon, humain —car bien sûr, elle s'imagine que seuls les animaux appelés* **homo sapiens** *(selon ses propres catégories), sont aptes à définir eux-mêmes, à expliciter leurs raisons de vivre et le sens de leur monde. En cela, cette matrice culturelle fait comme toutes celles qui l'ont précédée: elle prétend embrasser l'univers, sauf que son univers imaginaire réduit tous les animaux capable de symbolisation, c'est-à-dire aptes à fournir des raisons pour lesquelles la vie mérite d'être vécue, à une seule et même catégorie.*

En d'autres termes, le relativisme *épistémologique, seul moyen d'expliquer les différences entre les humaines une fois admis que tous et toutes appartiennent à la même espèce, appelle le devoir* **moral** *de définir* **normativement** *l'horizon de la commune humanité. Toute être humain peut (ou doit), dès lors, porter un jugement moral sur n'importe quel trait culturel particulier, n'importe où, n'importe quand, de quelques moeurs que ce soit (1988a:98-99).*

6. *Ainsi, il apparait que le relativisme entraîne la relativisation de toutes les valeurs sauf de celles qui le* **fondent** *et qu'il n'aboutit pas à la suppression de toute normativité mais à l'établissement d'un nouveau champ normatif, de type dialectique: instauration du minimum de normes nécessaires pour permettre l'avènement et la coexistence de la plus grande diversité possible des normes...(1988a:20).*

7. *En d'autres termes, on peut refuser le relativisme: il ne prétend pas s'imposer comme une de ces évidences affectionnées par le rationalisme classique. Mais si on le rejette, on se met en position de retourner a l'ancien etat de choses: la guerre, au moins potentielle des systèmes culturels dont chacun se considere comme meilleur, les hiérarchisations tour à tour imposées par le groupe le plus fort et le retour du régime de l'hétéronomie (1988a:20).*

8. Cummins (1988:131) defines institutional racism as "ideologies and structures which are systematically used to legitimize the unequal division of power and resources (both material and non-material) between groups which are defined on the basis of race."

References

Bouchard, S. (1987). "La nowendature du mépris." *Recherches Amérindiennes au Québec,* XVI(4):17-26.

Camilleri, C. (1988). "Pertinence d'une approche scientifique de la culture pour une formation par l'éducation interculturelle." Dans F. Ouellet, (ed.) *Pluralisme et école. Jalons pour une approche critiquterculturelle des éducateurs.* Québec: Institute québécois de recherce sur la culture.

Camilleri, C. (1988a). "La culture d'hier a demain." *Anthropologie et société,* 12(1):13-27.

Cohen-Emerique, M. (1989). "Le modèle individualiste de sujet, écran à la compréhension de personnes issues de sociétés non occidentales." *Communication présentée au troisième congrès de l'ARIC,* Sherbrooke, août 1989.

Commission d'étude sur les Universités, (1979). "Rapport du comité d'étude sur la formation et le perfectionnement des enseignants." Québec, Gouvernement du Québec.

Cummins, J. (1988). "From multicultural to anti-racist education: An analysis of programmes and policies in Ontario." Dans T. Shutnabb-Kangas et J. Cummins.

Dasen, P. (1989). "La contribution de la psychologie interculturelle à la formation des enseignants pour une éducation interculturelle." *Communication présentée au troisième congrès de l'ARIC,* Sherbrooke, août 1989.

Dumont, F. (1971). "Le rôle du maître: aujourd'hui et demain." *Action pédagogique,* 17, avril 1971:49-61.

Ghiglione, R. (1986). *L'homme communiquant.* Paris: Armand Collin.

Henry-Lorcerie, F. (1971). "Enfants d'immigrés et école francaise. A propos du mot d'ordre de pédagogie interculturelle." *Les Maghrébins en France: émigrés ou immigrés,* Paris, éd. CNRS, 1971:223-270.

Kleinfield, J. (1975). "Positive stereotyping: the cultural relativist in the classroom." *Human Organization,* Washington, 34(3).

Lorreyte, B. (1989). "Française et immigrés des miroirs ambigus." Dans C. Camilleri et M. Cohen-Emerique, (éd.) *Choc des cultures. Concepts et enjeux pratiques de l'interculturel.* Paris: L'Harmattan.

McAll, C. (1989). "Capitalisme et culture." *Communication présenté au troisième congrès de l'ARIC,* Sherbrooke.

Ouellet, F. (1984). "Education, compréhension et communication interculturelles: essai de clarification des concepts." *Education permanente,* Sept. 1984:142-165.

Ouellet, F. (1985). "Vers un virage interculturel en éducation." *Revue internationale d'action communautaire,* 14/15, août 1985:123-129.

Ouellet, F. (éd.) (1988). *Pluralisme et école. Jalons pour une approche critique de la formation interculturelle des éducateurs.* Québec: Institut québécois de recherche sur la culture.

Ouellet, F. (1991). *L'éducation interculturelle. Essai sur le contenu de la formation des maîtres.* Collection "Espaces interculturels," Paris: Harmattan.

Parekh, B. (1986). "The concept of multicultural education." In Modgil et al (eds.), *Multicultural Education: The Interminable Debate*. London: The Falmer Press.

Simard, J.J. (1988). "La révolution pluraliste. Une mutation des rapports de l'homme au monde." Dans Ouellet, (éd), *Pluralisme et école. Jalons pour une approche critique de la formation interculturelle des éducateurs*. Québec: Institut québécois de recherche sur la culture.

Simard, J.J. "L'anthropologie et son casse-tête." *Anthropologie et société*, 12:(1988a) 77-102.

Simon, R.I., et al. (1988). *Decoding Discrimination. A Student-Based Approach to Anti-racist Education Using Film*. London, Ont.: Althouse Press.

Steele, S. (1989), "The recoloring of campus life. Student racism academic pluralism and the end of a dream." *Harper's Magazine*, February 1989:47-55.

Todorov, T. (1986). "Le croisement des cultures." *Communications*, 43, Paris: Seuil.

Waltzlawick, P. et al. (1972). *Une logigue de la communication*. Paris: Seuil.

Teaching in the Heterogeneous Classroom

Elizabeth G. Cohen

Cultural differences are only one type of heterogeneity in the multicultural classroom. Multicultural classrooms often include students who have limited proficiency in the language of instruction. These children from a language minority background frequently come to school without the standard repertoire that makes for success in school. Thus the multicultural classroom is also a classroom with a wide range of academic achievement.

The problems that the teacher faces are not just those of cultural difference. Rather, the problem is that some cultural groups have a lower status than others in the society at large. In places such as California, there are large numbers of culturally different children who also come from economically oppressed groups in the society. In addition, we have large numbers of linguistically and culturally different immigrants who enter the classroom to take up positions of very low social status among their peers. They are not socially accepted. They face overt prejudice from their classmates (Olsen, 1988), and may be forced to cling together with the only other children who speak their language.

The teachers of such classrooms face many technical difficulties for which teacher training leaves them unprepared. In the first place, they face the problem of level of instruction. If they use traditional methods of instruction and pitch that instruction at a high level, many of the students, even if they understood the language of the presentation, would be lost. If they pitch the instruction at a low level, the material is inadequate for those functioning at grade level and above. Furthermore, unless there is some way for all children to receive the content expected for their grade level, those who are working well below grade level will only fall further behind.

If the teacher tries to meet these different needs by dividing the students into three ability groups for instruction in critically important subjects, the net result will be further retardation of those in the low ability groups. In a review of 217 studies, Persell (1977) found that there is a slight trend toward improving the achievement of high ability groups, but that is offset by substantial losses in the average and low groups. Hallinan (1984) states that the research she summarized led to the same conclusion: namely, that tracking and ability grouping depress growth in academic achievement for students in low groups.

In the second place, the educator faces the problem of language. If he or she is fortunate, and only has one language group that is limited in the language of instruction, and if they are fully bilingual, then there are a set of reasonable strategies available in teacher training programs that prepare teachers for this situation. However, in states such as California, we have multilingual classrooms where it is not uncommon that the students speak four or five different languages, none of which is known by the teacher. Schools often respond by segregating such children into special classes for the purpose of teaching them English. Grouping students by language ability is the most common approach used by districts in order to meet the needs of limited English proficient students. However, these educational practices fail to recognize some basic tenets of second language acquisition that linguistic research has demonstrated. If limited English proficient students are placed in classrooms where they are a significant numerical majority, the opportunities for meaningful language exposure are nonexistent. If the students who do not speak the language of instruction or those who have only a limited proficiency are mainstreamed, the teacher faces the significant problem of insuring access to instruction for these students. Handing over such children to an adult aide who speaks their language represents a common solution, but one that consigns these students to instruction by a relatively unprepared and often undereducated instructor.

In the third place, the teacher is concerned with how the students from different groups relate to each other. In a conventional classroom where the teacher uses direct instruction, there is very little opportunity for students from different groups to get to know each other. Language barriers may make new relationships most improbable. The result is often self-segregation of the various language and cultural groups. If the teacher uses traditional, competitive methods of evaluation and tasks that are standardized for all students, there will be a high level of agreement between students on the ranking of their classmates in an academic status order (Rosenholtz & Wilson, 1980). Members of minority groups from low income families and newcomers are especially likely to be found at the very bottom of this status order.

Research by the Program for Complex Instruction at Stanford University School of Education offers an alternative to traditional instruction that is capable of dealing with this triple challenge of academic, cultural, and linguistic heterogeneity. Students can be taught to use each other as linguistic and academic resources. Learning activities that can use a wide range of skills and abilities enable each student to make an important contribution. With students talking and working together, using various languages, and with materials in different languages, language learning occurs without isolating non-English speaking students.

This type of instruction enables the teacher of heterogeneous classes to teach at a high level. Children who arrive at school without a middle-class repertoire frequently fail to benefit from conventional curriculum and instruction. Instead of segregating these children in remedial classes or low-ability groups, this approach permits access to advanced instruction that involves higher-order thinking skills.

Modification of Current Practice

Since 1978, the Program for Complex Instruction, under the author's direction, has developed, implemented and evaluated an innovative instructional approach. Instruction is complex when a variety of grouping patterns and materials are in simultaneous use in the classroom. Complex instruction is particularly suitable for classrooms with language-minority students and for other settings that feature students with a wide range of academic skills. The curriculum materials presently used were developed by Edward De Avila and are called *Finding Out/ Descubrimiento* (FO/D).[1] These materials use concepts of math and science for the purpose of developing thinking skills in children. They consist of activity cards and worksheets prepared in English, Spanish and pictographs.

From its inception, the goal of the program has been the educational development of children whose socioeconomic and language backgrounds do not prepare them for success in conventional school programs. In contrast to the commonly used methods of compensatory education, FO/D exposes the students in Grades 2-5 to concepts of mathematics, physics and chemistry in the context of highly demanding tasks. The curriculum materials consist of intrinsically interesting manipulatives which permit the children to understand highly abstract concepts by experimenting, hypothesizing, measuring, solving problems, talking, manipulating and working together. Activities have been created and/or adapted so that they do not presume middle-class, Anglo experiences. Activity cards contain instructions for students to engage in such activities as experimenting with electricity, measuring in litres, or plotting coordinates. For each activity there is a worksheet which requires the child to describe what happened, to make estimates and computations, or to form inferences about why things happened the way they did.

Children are assigned to heterogeneous small groups at learning centres. Each learning centre has a different activity card and worksheet. The use of individual worksheets in addition to responsibilities for the group represents a blend of individual accountability and collective responsibility for learning. Students take responsibility for their own and for others' learning through the assignment of roles to each group member. For example, one person is a facilitator whose job is to see that everyone gets the help he or she needs. The roles are rotated over time.

Students are trained to use each other as resources, asking questions, explaining, offering assistance, and helping others without doing things for them. Behavior is governed by a new set of norms such as "You have the right to ask anyone else in your group for help" and "You have the duty to assist anyone who asks for help." In this way, students gain access to the instructional activities that represent opportunities for learning. Because of the peer inter-action, they understand the nature of the tasks at the learning centres; they receive assistance in filling out their worksheets.

Because the tasks are so varied and challenging, children who do not have basic skills find that they can make intellectual contributions while accepting help from classmates with better academic skills in reading the activity card and in writing on the worksheets. For example, children who are lacking in basic skills may make accurate estimates, keen observations, or clever predictions.

As a result of such engaging tasks in which the basic skills of reading, writing and computation are integrated with higher order thinking skills, students make broad gains in achievement. Of particular interest is the finding reported by De Avila (1981) that learning in the program seems to take place across a broad front. That is, students improve in linguistic proficiency at the same time that they improve academically and cognitively. Moreover, the improvement that was found took place regardless of whether the child was LEP (Limited English Proficient) or FES (Fluent English Speaker). There were statistically significant gains on the California Test of Basic Skills (CTBS) for both. What this means is that both types of children can learn in the same atmosphere, and that learning for one group need not be at the expense of the other.

Achievement Data for 1982-83 and 1983-84

Teachers administered pre- and post-tests in the fall and spring of 1982-83 and 1983-84 in classrooms in which the curriculum was implemented. The tests used were from the CTBS. Statistical tests were used to ascertain whether or not the differences between pre- and post-test means for each class could have occurred by chance. There were statistically significant gains in every subscale of the Reading, Language Arts and Math Battery. In 1983-84, when the CTBS Science test was administered for the first time, there was also a statistically significant gain for that test. Scores for the overall batteries show that the sample was operating at near or better than grade level despite the fact that the average pre-test scores for some of the scales were far below grade level. The gain was particularly large for the Computation scale. In 1982-83, the average gains per classroom for the total Math Battery were as high as 20 units of Normal Curve Equivalents. Clearly, these students greatly improved their position relative to national norms. (For a more detailed description of the results of data analyses for 1982-83, see Cohen & De Avila, 1983).

Achievement Data for 1984-85

Data for this year were analyzed with a special focus on low-achieving children. Results for the group of students who scored below the 25th national percentile on the Total Reading Subscale of the CTBS in the fall are of particular interest because so many language minority children in these classrooms obtain very low scores on this scale. For all grade levels (2nd through 6th) there were statistically significant differences between the pre- and post-test scores of these children on the Computation as well as the Math Concepts and Application subscales. Achievement gains were particularly impressive for the second graders in the sample. On the average, these children started out in the 29th and 17th percentile (well below grade level) on the subscales measuring computation and math concepts and application, respectively. By spring, the students, on the average, were performing at grade level; the average scale scores were at the 64th percentile in computation and at the 45th percentile in concepts and application.

Currently this approach is being used in over 200 California classrooms. In collaboration with the California State University system, it is being disseminated throughout the state. Gradually, other curricular materials are being adapted to the basic instructional approach.

Concern for the Low-Status Child

There is considerable evidence that ethnicity, language accent, and visible ethnic appearance (Rosenholtz & Cohen, 1985) act as status characteristics. Research on status characteristics has demonstrated the power of differences in race, ethnicity, and perceived academic ability to activate differential expectations for competence (Berger, Rosenholtz & Zelditch, 1980). On a wide variety of intellectually important tasks, those who rank low in the status order are expected to be less competent than those who rank high. Once these general expectations become salient in a social situation, a status-organizing process takes place whereby high-status individuals are expected to be more competent on the specific task at hand. The initial differences in status become the basis for a self-fulfilling prophecy whereby those who are expected to be more competent become more active and influential in group interaction and are thus likely to be perceived as having made a more important contribution to the group task.

The most powerful status characteristics studied in classroom situations are perceived reading and academic ability. When language-minority children from lower social class backgrounds have difficulty with the English curriculum and are placed in the lowest ability groups and tracks, they can quickly become low-status students on an academic status characteristic as well. Likewise, members of any racial or cultural group that comes to school without preparation at home or in special pre-schools are very likely to acquire low academic status in a short time. In learning environments, where there is socioeconomic and academic heterogeneity, those who are in the low-ability groups are expected to do poorly at a wide range of academic/ intellectual tasks (Cohen, 1988).

The educators we have worked with frequently say that language-minority children or lower class black children have difficulty thinking abstractly and need to learn the fundamentals before they are ready for more advanced, abstract concepts. Their beliefs are not based on research; they are not even based on experience, because these children are rarely given the chance to try more advanced and abstract curricular materials. These beliefs, however, are consistent with educators' preconceptions about the intellectual competence of minority children from poor families. Such beliefs are also consistent with the operation of status organizing processes in which general expectations for incompetence are activated by characteristics such as race, ethnicity, accented speech, or lack of English proficiency.

Even the popular recommendation of co-operative learning for heterogeneous classrooms does not remove the problems connected with status differences between students. In classrooms with many language-minority students that encouraged children to work together, Cohen (1984) found that children who were more popular and who were seen as better in math and science talked more about their work, and as a result, learned more. This unequal pattern of interaction is a status problem resulting from differences in expectations for competence held by peers. The lowest status students in multilingual classrooms are often newcomers who do not speak much English, as well as children who test as "limited" in both English and Spanish (Neves, 1983).

The Program for Complex Instruction has had a special concern with low-status children who have few friends and are seen by classmates as lacking ability in academic subjects. (Teachers learn how to improve expectations for intellectual competence of low-status children while also increasing their social acceptance by classmates.) Program research has documented three important outcomes for low-status children. (1) There is increased social acceptance of these children during the course of the school year. (2) Although the low-status children tend to start out with very low scores on achievement tests in the fall of the school year, they gain just as much as the high-status children, according to tests in the spring. (3) There are more classmates who choose them as "good in math and science" in the spring than in the fall (Cohen, Lotan & Catanzarite, 1988). Such children in conventional classrooms may not understand the assignments, but may be unwilling to ask for help. In these classrooms, co-operative training gives them access to interaction with their peers and thus to learning.

An Alternative Model

Complex instruction is grounded in sociological and psychological theory and research. Using these theories, researchers have conducted detailed studies of classroom processes, and have linked these processes to measures of achievement. Thus they have been able to develop clear evidence for how the model works, why it is successful, and under what conditions it will continue to be successful. This extensive theory and research permits generalization beyond the particular curricular materials used, to an alternative model of instruction that allows for instruction that is intellectually demanding in academically heterogeneous, multicultural classrooms.

What do theory and research have to say about what can be done in classrooms containing students with limited English proficiency as well as English-speaking students, classrooms with a wide range of academic skills? What are the major features that permit accelerated instruction in linguistically and academically diverse classrooms?

Changed Classroom Organization

If the curriculum is to include higher-order thinking skills, there must be more than one opportunity to grasp difficult concepts. If students are divided into small heterogeneous groups, each group can engage in an activity illustrating underlying concepts in different ways. The repeated experience of fundamental concepts in different contexts, using different media, will lead to the formation of a learning set so that a general and transferable understanding develops (DeAvila, 1985).

When multiple groups and materials are in simultaneous operation, we say that the instruction is "complex." Complex instruction can be combined with direct instruction for whole classes or for small groups in which teachers work with particular language lessons they feel are indicated for particular confusions that students exhibit.

The differentiation of the curriculum into small groups or learning centres assists the learning process in several ways: the more learning centres in operation, the more the students have an opportunity for talking and working together and thus more opportunities for active learning. In addition, the more learning centres in operation, the less likely are teachers to attempt direct instruction (Cohen, Lotan & Leechor, 1989). Direct instruction has been found to be counterproductive for those periods of class time devoted to discovery and active learning processes. For example, the correlation between an index of direct instruction and the average gains for a class in 1984-85 in math concepts and applications was -.75 ($P \leq .01$); the correlation between the same index and the average gains in computation was -.58($p \leq .05$)(Cohen, Lotan & Leechor, 1989). The use of direct instruction was significantly, negatively related to the percentage of students talking and working together. And finally, talking and working together has been repeatedly found to relate to achievement gains on CTBS both at the classroom and the individual level.

At the classroom level, the average gain scores in national percentiles in 1982-83 were 15.48 for Math Concepts and Applications and 26.62 for Computation. For the school year 1984-85, the average gain in scale scores was 46.82 for Concepts and Applications and 74.39 for Computation. In two analyses of the average gain scores for each classroom, the larger the percentage of students talking and working together the greater were the average gains in both of the standardized achievement test scales for math.

For example, the zero-order correlation between the percentage of students talking and working together with the average gains in math concepts and application for the sample of classrooms in 1982-83 was .72($P \leq .01$)(Cohen, Lotan & Leechor, 1989).

At the individual level, Leechor (1987) found that students who were reading English below grade level benefited even more from interaction in heterogeneous groups than students who were closer to grade level in reading skills. Leechor argued that interaction with peers reduced uncertainty for students who were perhaps unable to read the activity cards and worksheets unassisted. In other words, we have learned that a key to achievement in heterogeneous settings is **the students' use of each other as resources for learning**.

Classroom Management

From the students' point of view, solving problems in connection with challenging instructional tasks is highly uncertain. According to sociologists, once the technology becomes uncertain in this way, supervision must shift from routine, bureaucratic supervision to delegation of authority and lateral communication between the workers (students) must increase. If this does not happen, there will be a loss of organizational effectiveness (Perrow, 1967). These general principles from organizational sociology have proven very useful for classrooms with the kind of instructional approach we have described. The teacher can delegate authority to groups and to individuals through their role assignments. Students literally "mind each other's business," keeping each other on task, enforcing safety procedures, making sure that work is completed and reducing uncertainty for each other through procuring help when it is needed.

The assignment of roles in small groups such as that of the facilitator has a highly favorable effect on the percentage of students talking and working together (Zack, 1988). The facilitator role represents a delegation of authority from the teacher who, in more conventional classrooms, spends much of his or her time helping students complete their tasks. In this case, a student is given the authority to see that people receive necessary help and that everyone understands what they are doing. Even if the facilitator does not have requisite academic skills, he or she can and does act as a catalyst encouraging group members to share the skills and insights they have achieved with each other. This delegation of authority to the group allows the teachers to increase the amount of teaching behavior in the classroom dramatically without having to do it all themselves.

Teachers are assured that student behavior is under control in still another way. When students internalize norms for co-operative behavior such as "You have the duty to assist anyone who asks for help," they are more willing to help each other and to demand that others conform to this rule. If students learn exactly how to behave during complex instruction, there are few discipline problems and the number of students who are disengaged is minimal (Cohen & DeAvila, 1983). These new norms must, however, be explicitly taught to students in a series of skill-building exercises (Cohen, 1986).

Helping teachers learn to delegate authority is not an easy task. They must be assured that they are not losing control of the classroom. Furthermore, they require assistance with an alternative role, substituting for the familiar tasks of instructing and facilitating students' completion of their assignments. Unless teachers learn to avoid use of this traditional role while small groups are in operation, they will inadvertently cut down on the amount of communication between the students, and will thus "short-circuit" the learning process (Cohen, Lotan & Leechor, 1989). Lotan (1985) found that the teacher's grasp of the underlying theory concerning delegation of authority is related to their ability to implement the management system we have just described. Teachers do not learn about delegation of authority solely through lectures in workshops. They also need specific feedback on how well they are doing through videotapes and through systematic observation and problem-solving sessions based on data collected during classroom observation.

Multiple Ability Curricula

Curriculum materials should consist of challenging and uncertain, but intrinsically interesting tasks utilizing real objects. Science curricula such as

Science Curriculum Improvement Study (SCIS) or Elementary Science Study (ESS) developed in the 60s include many excellent tasks that can be adapted to this approach (Rowe, 1978). Tasks should be open-ended so that precocious students can carry them further, while less mature students can complete the tasks on a simpler level. For example, the level of inference the child makes on a worksheet as to why an experiment worked could differ greatly. Or, one child can carry out multiple experiments with a set of materials while another will only be able to complete one task.

Instructions should be in as many languages as the students require; and the inclusion of pictographic representations is additionally helpful. Reading and writing should be integrated in a meaningful context, they become means to the end of accomplishing a fascinating task. Systematic observation of a sample of target children using FO/D has shown that the number of observations which included reading instructions or writing on worksheets was a significant predictor of post-test scores on CTBS Reading Scales (Beta Coefficient of .188, F = 8.59; p≤001). In this analysis, the Reading post-test score was regressed on the frequency of reading or writing, the Reading pre-test score, the number of learning centres in use and the average rate at which the children were observed talking and working together (Cohen & Intili, 1981).

Multilingual groups should include a bilingual student to act as a bridge. The use of real objects facilitates communication among students who do not share the same language. Names of real objects should be included on the instructional materials so that they become the subject of discussion among peers. In this arrangement, students can speak in their own language, but they also hear English-speaking students discuss concrete objects as they are touched and manipulated. Students will attempt to communicate across the language barrier. This is the ideal situation for second language acquisition. Neves found that the more frequently initially monolingual Spanish speakers were heard interacting in Spanish, the higher were their gains in English proficiency over the school year r = .243 (p≤05) (Neves, 1983:66). This seemingly counter-intuitive result can be explained by the mixture of English and Spanish-speakers in the same groups. Receptive language is greatly increased when everyone is talking about the same thing even if the conversation proceeds in several languages. Reading and writing are only two of the abilities required in this type of curricular approach. Visual and spatial reasoning, interpersonal intelligence and a variety of other real-world intellectual abilities should be required.

Multiple Ability curricula are not confined either to young children or to science and math as a subject matter. In a recent study, Bower (1990) created a multiple ability unit for American History suitable for the secondary school heterogeneous class. Bower took the content from the required textbook and transformed it into small group tasks such as role play, interpretation of political cartoons of the period and the preparation of political cartoons and multi-media presentations. These tasks followed the presentation of a lecture using slides and discussion by the teacher. Students were also assigned the textbook chapter to read. This approach was compared to an alternative approach that utilized small group discussion and answering of questions concerning primary source documents. The tasks were challenging but purely verbal in nature. The treatments were identical in using training for co-operative behavior, small group tasks, and the assignment of roles to each student. The treatments were different in the nature of the curriculum and in the use of a treatment for status problems in conjunction with the Multiple Ability curriculum. Analysis of results clearly shows that the multiple ability approach to curriculum construction yields statistically significant improvement in scores in a content-referenced test of the social studies content in comparison to the purely linguistic approach.

If the group tasks require multiple abilities and do not make reading and writing the only prerequisite for success, then those who are weak in reading and writing may request assistance from those who are stronger in academic skills. In return, those who are strong in conventional academic skills receive assistance from others in tasks requiring alternative kinds of abilities. It should be noted that this exchange process **does not take place** unless status problems are explicitly treated.

Status Treatments

Teachers must be trained in the use of several status treatments designed to prevent the domination by high-status students in the groups. The first of these treatments is called the Multiple Ability Treatment which originated in laboratory and experimental classroom research (Tammivarra, 1982). The task of the teacher is to convince the students that many different abilities and skills, in addition to reading and writing, are required by the assigned tasks. Teachers must explicitly state: "No one person is going to be good at all these abilities and everyone will be good on at least one."

The second status treatment is called Assigning of Competence to Low-Status Students. This treatment takes advantage of the power of the teacher to make public evaluations of students that are very likely to be believed by any student within earshot. The teacher carefully observes low-status students as they work in small groups on multiple ability tasks. When they see these students demonstrate competence at one of the intellectual abilities required by the tasks; they publicly and specifically give a favorable evaluation to the student, explaining exactly what he or she did well and why this is an important ability in the adult world. This is a difficult skill for teachers to master. It requires that they **notice** the good things that problematic students do, something that busy teachers often miss. Secondly, it requires giving a specific and public type of feedback, very different from most praise given by teachers. Thirdly, it requires a fundamental understanding of status processes in the classroom so that the process of status generalization can be recognized and treated (Benton, forthcoming).

Recent research has demonstrated the effectiveness of these two treatments in modifying the process of status generalization in heterogeneous elementary school classrooms. In classrooms where teachers use these treatments more frequently, low-status students interact just as frequently as high-status students (Cohen, 1988).

In secondary school classrooms, the status problems are even more severe because academic skills may range from fourth grade level to that of a college student. In Bower's study, the Multiple Ability treatment was included with the Multiple Ability Curriculum. Although, the status problems in some of the classrooms receiving this treatment were less severe than in those classrooms receiving the alternative treatment, status problems remained severe in other classrooms receiving the Multiple Ability treatment. In all probability, teachers will need to use both treatments in order to modify status problems consistently in middle school and secondary school classrooms.

Organizational Support for Teachers

Particularly in the first year of implementation, more sophisticated and complex instruction requires more organizational support for teachers than they usually receive. Teachers who receive specific feedback on the basis of systematically observed classroom performance are better able to implement the most difficult features of their new role (Ellis, 1987). In schools where principals assist teachers with the preparation and storage of materials for complex instruction, teachers implement more units (Ellis, 1987). In addition, the principal's skill and ability in coordinating personnel and meeting times for teaching teams, and implementation of observation and feedback, is a strong predictor of quality of classroom implementation (Parchment, 1989).

In an ongoing analysis of the first year of implementation of complex instruction, Cohen & Lotan (1990) find that the two most powerful predictors of quality implementation are **organizational expectations** that the teacher will follow through with the new instructional methods and **receiving highly specific feedback** based on clear criteria and on an adequate sample of classroom observations. Beyond the first year of implementation, collegial observation and feedback continue to be correlated with quality of implementation. Lotan (1989) found that the use of highly specific and structured feedback based on classroom observations that teachers made of each other was highly correlated with a measure of quality of implementation.

It is not accidental that working together is a solution to dealing with uncertainty for **both students and teachers.** Sociologists who have studied organization have found that uncertainty in the work of the organization demands interdependent work arrangements among the staff. Unless teachers become more interdependent than they are in the typical school, we may expect complex instruction such as co-operation learning to deteriorate over time. Not only do teachers need each other for collegial feedback, but for planning, for problem solving, and for curriculum development.

Conclusion

In summary, there are available technical solutions to the teaching problems faced by teachers of multicultural classrooms. These solutions in no way conflict with the more common recommendations of broadening the curriculum to include representation of various student cultures, teaching students to view the world from multiple perspectives, and designing classroom experiences that will reduce stereotyping and increase social acceptance.

Recommendations for curricular change made by multicultural specialists can easily be adapted to the multiple ability curriculum. Learning about different cultures and taking the perspective of others comprise curricular activities that cry out for multi-media and active learning requiring a variety of intellectual abilities. For example, the curricular materials developed by the Global Education project at Stanford contain some excellent multiple ability activities for groups that are designed to foster multiculturalism. The recommendation of co-operative learning in order to decrease prejudice is already part and parcel of the model we have described. Co-operative learning will produce increased friendliness and social acceptance that is so important in the multicultural classroom (Slavin, 1983). Thus, the strategies that have achieved broad consensus in the multicultural field can easily be incorporated in complex instruction as described in this chapter.

The most important implication of the research reviewed in this chapter is that teachers of multicultural classrooms need much more assistance. They face severe technical problems for which their training is inadequate. Unless they get the technical assistance they require to utilize more sophisticated methods of instruction, the achievement of lower status, culturally different children is unlikely to improve. Nor will the use of techniques such as co-operative learning, by themselves, change expectations of intellectual incompetence for such children held by their classmates and often by themselves.

Teachers need extensive retraining in methods of classroom organization and management so that they can expand their teaching repertoire to include complex instruction such as that involved in co-operative learning. They will need considerable help with the development of curricular materials that are multiple ability and that permit students to use each other as resources. They must be sensitized to problems of status differences and given some strategies for treatment of status problems. Finally, these changes and strategies cannot be carried out in the traditional context of an isolated classroom teacher. Principals and teachers must work together to support these more sophisticated forms of classroom instruction.

What is at stake here is the attempt to undo the effects of inequality in society at large as it affects the day-to-day life of the classroom. Social scientists have documented the ways in which classrooms tend to reproduce the inequalities of the larger society. Undoing these effects is an ambitious undertaking. Nonetheless, the application of sociological theory and research to the problem of increasing equity in heterogeneous classroom leaves me very hopeful that these goals are within our reach.

Notes

1. The *Finding Out/Descubrimiento* curriculum is published by Santilana Publishing Company, 257 Union Street, Northvale, New Jersey 07646-2293.

References

Benton, J. (forthcoming). "Treating status problems in the classroom: Training teachers to assign competence to students exhibiting low-status behavior in the classroom." Dissertation in progress, Stanford University.

Berger, J., Rosenholtz, S.J. & Zelditch, M. Jr. (1980). "Status organizing processes." *Annual Review of Sociology*, 6:479-508.

Bower, A. (1990). "The effect of a multiple ability treatment on status and learning in the cooperative social studies classroom." Unpublished doctoral dissertation, Stanford, California: Stanford University.

Cohen, E.G. (1984). "Talking and working together: Status interaction and learning." In P. Peterson, L. Wilkinson & M. Hallinan (eds.), *The Social Context of Instruction: Group Organization and Group Processes*. New York: Academic Press.

Cohen E.G. (1986). *Designing Groupwork: Strategies for Heterogeneous Classrooms*. New York: Teachers College Press.

Cohen, E.G. (1988). "Producing equal status behavior in cooperative learning." Paper presented at the International Association for the Study of Cooperation in Education. Shefayim, Israel.

Cohen, E.G. & De Avila, E. (1983). *Learning to Think in Math and Science: Improving Local Education for Minority Children.* A Final Report to the Johnson Foundation. Stanford, California: Stanford University, Program for Complex Instruction.

Cohen, E.G., Intili, J.A. & De Avila, E. (1981). *Interdependence and Management in Bilingual Classrooms.* Final Report to NIE, Stanford, California: Stanford University.

Cohen, E.G., Lotan, R.A. & Catanzarite, L. (1988). "Can expectations for competence be altered in the classroom?" In M. Webster, Jr. & M. Foschi (eds.), *Status Generalization: New Theory and Research.* Stanford, California: Stanford University Press.

Cohen, E.G., Lotan, R.A., & Leechor, C. (1989). "Can classrooms learn?" *Sociology of Education,* 62:75-94.

Cohen, E.G. & Lotan, R.A. (1990). "Beyond the workshop: Conditions for first year implementation." Paper presented at meeting of International Association for the Study of Cooperation in Education, Baltimore, Maryland.

De Avila, E. (1981). *Multicultural Improvement of Cognitive Abilities: Final Report to State of California, Department of Education.* Stanford, California: Stanford University, School of Education.

De Avila, E. (1985). "Motivation, intelligence and access: A theoretical framework for the education of language minority kids." *Issues in English Language Development,* National Clearinghouse for Bilingual Education: 21-31.

Hallinan, M.T. (1984). "Summary and implications." In P.L. Peterson, L.C. Wilkinson & Hallinan, M. (eds.), *The Social Context of Instruction: Group Organization and Group Processes.* San Diego: Academic Press.

Ellis, N. (1987). "Collaborative interaction and logistical support for teacher change." Unpublished doctoral dissertation, Stanford, California: Stanford University.

Leechor, C. (1987). "How high and low achieving students differentially benefit from working together in cooperative small groups." Unpublished doctoral dissertation, Stanford, California: Stanford University.

Lotan, R.A. (1985). "Understanding the theories: Training teachers for implementation of complex instructional technology." Unpublished doctoral dissertation, Stanford, California: Stanford University.

Lotan, R. (1989). "Collegial feedback: Necessary conditions for program continuation." Paper presented at the annual meeting of the Sociology of Education Association, Asilomar, California.

Neves, A. (1983). "The effect of various input on the second language acquisition of Mexican American children in nine elementary school classrooms." Unpublished doctoral dissertation, Stanford University.

Olsen, L. (1988). *Immigrant Students and the California Public Schools: Crossing the Schoolhouse Border,* San Francisco, California: California Tomorrow.

Parchment, C. (1989). "The role of the principal in implementation of a complex instructional program." Unpublished doctoral dissertation, Stanford University.

Perrow, C. (1967). "A framework for the comparative analysis of organizations." *American Sociological Review*, 32:194-208.

Persell, C. (1977). *Education and Inequality: The Roots and Results of Stratification in America's Schools*. New York: The Free Press.

Rosenholtz, S.J. & Cohen, E.G. (1985). "Activating ethnic status." In J. Berger & M. Zelditch, Jr. (eds.), *Status Rewards and Influence*. San Francisco, California: Jossey Bass.

Rosenholtz, S.J. & Wilson, B. (1980). "The effects of classroom structure on shared perceptions of ability." *American Educational Research Journal*, 17:175-182.

Rowe, M.B. (1978). *Teaching Science as Continuous Inquiry: A Basic*. 2nd edition, New York: McGraw Hill.

Slavin, R.E. (1983). *Cooperative Learning*. New York: Longman.

Tammivaara, J.S. (1982). "The effects of task structure on beliefs about competence and participation in small groups." *Sociology of Education*, 5(5):212-222.

Zack, M. (1988). "Delegation of authority and the use of the student facilitator role." Paper presented at meeting of the International Association for the Study of Cooperation in Education, Kibbutz Shefayimm, Israel.

Printed in Canada